Accelerating Digital Transformation

Jan Bosch • Jan Carlson • Helena Holmström Olsson • Kristian Sandahl • Miroslaw Staron
Editors

Accelerating Digital Transformation

10 Years of Software Center

Springer

Editors
Jan Bosch (ID)
Department of Computer Science
and Engineering
Chalmers University of Technology
Gothenburg, Sweden

Jan Carlson
Division of Computer Science and Networks
Mälardalen University
Västerås, Sweden

Helena Holmström Olsson
Department of Computer Science
Malmö University
Malmö, Sweden

Kristian Sandahl
Department of Computer and Information
Science (IDA)
Linköping University
Linköping, Sweden

Miroslaw Staron
Department of Computer Science
and Engineering
Chalmers University of Technology
Gothenburg, Sweden

ISBN 978-3-031-10875-4   ISBN 978-3-031-10873-0   (eBook)
https://doi.org/10.1007/978-3-031-10873-0

This Springer imprint is published by the registered company Springer Nature Switzerland AG
The registered company address is: Gewerbestrasse 11, 6330 Cham, Switzerland

Foreword

Effective collaboration between industry and academia is hard. This is the case because of a mismatch in incentives between researchers and industry practitioners that is quite significant and causes natural tension points. Industry practitioners, in the end, want to turn the fruits of the collaboration into benefits for the business. Researchers are interested in high-profile publications. Industry often seeks to achieve these benefits as fast as possible whereas researchers often work on a time line that is much more relaxed. Industry wants access to experts in the field whereas researchers often use collaboration as an education and training context for PhD students and early career staff.

For collaboration between multiple companies and universities to be successful, a carefully designed set of mechanisms needs to be put in place to ensure that the incentives for companies and researchers are as aligned as possible. Over the last decade, Software Center has evolved a set of mechanisms that allow the collaboration between the member companies and the universities to not only survive but positively thrive. These mechanisms include the sprint model where all activities have a 6-month sprint heartbeat, a mechanism where it is the companies, rather than the researchers, that prioritize and fund the research projects, an active and engaged steering committee, and several types of recurring events that allow for frequent dissemination of results as well as constructive engagement around topics of interest.

Also, Software Center has been able to predict and proactively address topics that have become important for the member companies before the need at the companies was there. At the start, the center predominantly focused on software engineering challenges, and over the last 10 years, data and artificial intelligence as well business models and product management challenges have also been addressed.

It is the partners in the center that fund the center with the companies providing cash and the universities in-kind funding. This allows the decision processes as well as the collaboration between researchers and companies to be free from the distractions that publicly funded projects typically bring to a collaboration. Software Center has a broad and mature experience with collaborations between companies and universities. These collaborations have long been a mainstay of research and development – from creating the knowledge foundations for the next generation of solutions, to serving as an extended "workbench" to solve short-term, incremental problems. This provides a flow of newly minted talent and allows for investigation of long-term research challenges.

This book that you are holding and for which I have the pleasure to provide the foreword captures some of the most impactful and relevant research work conducted over the last decade. However, it can truly not be viewed as a fair representation as hundreds of research articles have been published by Software Center researchers. For a full overview, I refer the reader to the Software Center website.

Over the last decade, I have had the honor to act as the chair for the Software Center steering committee. Software Center has become an essential innovation and research partner and to my understanding, the involved partners have significantly benefited from the collaborations. It has been a joy to contribute to building up such an effective collaboration between 17 companies and 5 universities, together with all the others involved in Software Center. And although the last decade was great, I expect even more from the next decade of Software Center!

Chair Software Center Steering Committee   Anders Cáspar
Stockholm, April 2022

Preface

William Gibson, the famous science fiction writer, once stated that the future is already here; it just is not evenly distributed. This basically sums up the state of digitalization and digital transformation in society in one sentence. There are companies that were born digital and that have incorporated digital technologies at the very core of their business, infusing business models, ways of working, and culture with fast iterations, data-driven decision making, and machine learning models.

Most companies, however, were born in a different age, and their initial differentiation was enabled by mechanical engineering, manufacturing, or other physical capabilities. Over the years of their existence, these companies have had to adopt new technologies, mindsets, ways of working, and organizational approaches in response to the latest insights and innovations in order to stay competitive and to drive growth. For instance, many mechanical companies have adopted digital design tools and advanced simulation approaches to analyze the properties of physical designs before the first instance of the design is created. This allows for a much more systematic and structured exploration of the design space, resulting in better outcomes.

Although the majority of companies were not born digital, all of these companies have spent their entire existence focusing on incorporating and embracing new technologies and innovations. This raises the question as to why digital transformation would be different from the continuous flow of change that has existed for decades, if not centuries. Our research shows that the main reason is the scope and magnitude of the change caused by digital transformation. It literally affects everything the company is concerned with, and it represents such a significant paradigm shift that it causes stress and tension in any organization that goes through the transformation as many of the beliefs held by the employees are fundamentally broken and need to be replaced.

Although it is hard to structure a multifaceted transformation such as a digital transformation, using the BAPO model [465] we can discuss several aspects:

- **Business**: One of the key changes during a digital transformation is the change in business model. Traditional business models rooted in "atoms" tend to be transactional in nature. This means that the user buys a product, uses it for a period of time, and then replaces the product with a new instance of the product. Digital companies tend to have continuous business models, such as subscription- or usage-based models, that automatically cause the company and the user to have a continuous relationship as well. This continuous relationship then opens up for continuous improvements to the offering which is initially a delighter but soon becomes an expectation. Once it is an expectation, companies that do not offer continuous improvements are at a distinct disadvantage.

- **Architecture**: The continuous business model, especially the ability to continuously improve the offering to the customer, has significant implications on the architecture and technology used in the product. Traditionally, many products were built with deep integration between different subsystems to optimize for bill of materials. The result was a highly interconnected design that exhibits high coupling between the various parts, which complicates updating of individual components and subsystems. This does not only affect upgradability but also other quality attributes such as testability, as it is virtually impossible to test individual components and subsystems independently. This then requires all testing to take place at the system level, which is complex, expensive, and resource consuming.

- **Process**: Although many companies have adopted agile practices at the team level, it is interesting to observe that beyond the team level, many companies still live in a waterfall world where various activities are performed sequentially rather than in parallel. As these activities are performed occasionally and not very frequently, there is little pressure to automate, and consequently significant manual effort is expended on what basically are repetitive tasks. Digital transformation and the associated continuous improvement models require much higher degrees of automation as tasks that were performed once or twice per year are now conducted every few weeks.

- **Organization**: The changes to the business model, architecture, and technology as well as the process and ways of working also has significant impact on the way companies organize themselves. Rather than functional units organized in a hierarchical organization, digitalization requires cross-functional teams operating in a highly autonomous fashion, guided by quantitative output metrics that they are asked to accomplish, rather than by first and second level line managers that tell people what to do.

The impact of digital transformations as described above only starts to scratch the surface of the required changes in organizations, but it provides an illustration of the breadth and depth of the required changes due to digitalization. Everything has to change and basically at the same time as a continuous business model and a static, immutable product do not go well together. Similarly, agile practices and yearly releases do not mix either, and organizations drop agile ways of working when there is no need to push functionality out to customers. The careful sequencing and building of capabilities as well as the transitioning from the traditional to new ways of working are challenging and many companies struggle with this.

Accelerating Digital Transformation

One of the key questions that many organizations ask themselves is how their digital transformation could be accelerated. Many organizations face competitive pressures not only from their peers in industry, but also from new entrants who are digitally born and embrace all the advantages that this offers. Although the incumbents have the customer base and the new entrants have to overcome this inertia, the threat of being disrupted by pure digital players is real in many industries. The best way to meet the threat is to undo the main advantage that new entrants have and to operate in the same way toward customers as the new entrants.

Although this may seem like a change on the interface between your organization and the customer, the effect is of course much more involved than just that. The interface with the customer includes the business model as well as the way the organization services its customers. As we discussed in the previous section, the main shift in business model typically is to move from a transactional to a continuous model so that the customer experiences a continuously improving offering. Especially for embedded systems, the business model may involve a change in ownership of the physical product itself. Instead of the customer owning the product, the customer has the access and use but is in fact not the owner of the product. These changes go far beyond the interface between the company and its customers.

It is clear that change is needed, and it needs to occur rapidly in order to protect the competitive position of the organization. Our experience is that all companies change, but the pace of change tends to be relatively slow. Organizations are inherently built to resist change, and accelerating the pace of change requires typically external forces.

The history of Software Center starts with the above realization by key R&D leaders at four large software development organizations in Gothenburg, Sweden, i.e., Ericsson, Saab Surveillance, Volvo Car Corporation, and AB Volvo. These leaders requested from the president of Chalmers University of Technology at that time that the university start a center, in part funded by these companies, to help them collaborate in building software development expertise in their respective organizations. Software Center started in 2011 with the four aforementioned companies, with Gothenburg University and Chalmers University of Technology as founding members. Over the last decade, the center has grown to 17 companies and 5 universities, and the scope of research has evolved and expanded dramatically.

Initially, the primary focus of the companies was the adoption of agile software development practices, but over the years, the research has expanded to include work on software architecture, metrics, customer data, business ecosystems, artificial intelligence, business models, digitalization, etc. As you will read in the remainder of the book, there is a multitude of topics addressed in the center—all in response to the digital transformation that the companies are increasingly involved in and pursuing.

The companies use Software Center not only for the research that inspires specific changes and improvements at the company. The other primary mechanism is that companies work on exchanging knowledge between each other, without the involvement of the researchers at the universities. Over the years, we have developed a variety of mechanisms to support the knowledge exchange, research, and adoption for the center members, including our reporting workshop that runs twice per year, our YouTube channel, industrial PhD candidates, weekly brownbag seminars, a monthly newsletter, and our website to mention a few.

This Book

This book aims to celebrate the 10-year anniversary of Software Center by presenting some of the most impactful and relevant publications that the participants in the center have contributed over the last decade.

The book is organized into the five themes that research in Software Center is woven around, i.e., Continuous Delivery, Continuous Architecture, Metrics, Customer Data and Ecosystem-Driven Development, and, finally, AI Engineering.

The focus of the Continuous Delivery theme is to help companies to continuously build high-quality products with the right degree of automation. The researchers of the theme work with improving large-scale utilization of CI/CD (Continuous Integration/Continuous Delivery) in areas such as optimizing automated testing and improving the quality of the test cases and the test environment. Work is also done in finding the role of different manual testing activities and formal verification in CI/CD. Most companies already have a CI/CD tool chain in place that performs its individual functions well, but to get an overview of the process, for instance to assess the confidence about the product quality, is not trivial. One approach investigated in the theme is to use visualization techniques as a means for fulfilling the information needs. The Continuous Architecture theme addresses challenges that arise when balancing the need for architectural quality and more agile ways of working with shorter development cycles. We have, for example, investigated how architectural technical debt can be identified, managed, and prioritized and how companies can keep development artifacts consistent as the system evolves, such as code and models at different levels of abstraction. The research has also addressed how to extend agile principles from pure software to fit the development of mechatronic products, including more incremental processes for safety and security assurance.

The Metrics theme studies and provides insight to understand, monitor, and improve software processes, products, and organizations. It addresses challenges related to finding the right metrics for the right organization (e.g., quantifying productivity during organizational transformations), right product (e.g., finding the optimal feature set for a release), and process (e.g., finding the right metrics to monitor the evolution, or decay, of software architectures). The researchers in the metrics theme utilize the newest methods from machine learning, artificial intelligence, and mining software repositories to optimize test selection, identify cyber-security risks, support agile transformations, and support automotive software development.

The fourth theme, Customer Data and Ecosystem-Driven Development, helps companies make sense of the vast amounts of data that are continuously collected from products in the field. The projects in the theme study how to effectively make use of this data, how it provides the basis for new digital offerings, and how it allows for fundamentally new ways-of-working and of delivering value to customers. The research in the theme studies how companies evolve from traditional toward digital companies and provides companies with methods, techniques, and tools that support the journey that they take when moving beyond agile ways-of-working toward continuous practices involving, e.g., agile requirements engineering, A/B testing and feature experimentation, and continuous validation of customer value.

Finally, the fifth theme, AI Engineering, addresses the challenge that many companies struggle with in terms of deploying machine- and deep-learning models in industrial contexts with production quality. This requires solutions in a variety of dimensions, ranging from monitoring and logging to building dependable data pipelines and from federated learning architectures to heterogeneous hardware.

Each theme has its own part in the book, and each part has an introduction chapter and then a carefully selected reprint of the most important papers from that theme. For the AI Engineering theme, only one chapter was included as the theme was formed quite recently.

As editors, we would like to thank all the partner companies and researchers that, over the last decade, have contributed to building up this collaboration and the amazing results. We are grateful for the last 10 years and yet want to also look forward to what Software Center has to offer going forward.

To you as a reader, we hope you enjoy and appreciate the content and that you are able to use it to your advantage!

Contents

Part V AI Engineering

Part I
Continuous Delivery

Introduction to the Continuous Delivery Theme

Kristian Sandahl (Theme Leader 2015–)

Even though there were many forerunners, the most widespread reference to Continuous Integration as a method was put forward by Grady Booch in 1990 [44] (page 209). In the 1995 book *Microsoft Secrets*, Cusumano and Selby interviewed 38 Microsoft employees to document how the world's leading software provider was managing its own software development [80]. One of the key practices found was the Daily Build concept. In the popular literature, this was described as everyone needed to check in their code and build the product at the end of the workday. In tight connection to the build, some smoke tests were run to ensure that the individual contributions could be integrated. If the build was broken, the person who broke it had to fix his/her code before going home. There was also modern folklore mentioning that the breaker of the build had to wear a funny hat for the remainder of the day.

The elegant marketing of daily build raised an enormous interest from industry; everyone wanted to try. I worked at Ericsson at the time and saw how daily builds were enthusiastically adopted in the teams and resources were spent to create effective test environments, some of them with SMS notifications of the outcome (which was hot those days). Many master thesis projects were initiated to make pilot studies.

The interest was amplified in the year 2000 with Beck's book on extreme programming, which further emphasized the use of automated testing and frequent updates and releases [32]. The large uptake of agile methods was started in combination with ideas about feature-oriented programming, which increased the independence and customer focus of the teams. This development put large requirements on the tool chain for compilation, build, test, and test feed-back, which was evolved into the CI/CD (Continuous Integration/Continuous Delivery) flow as we know it today. The more the teams are relieved from a one-to-one connection to individual system components, the more complicated the CI/CD flow becomes, and with that came research challenges that are the focus of research in Theme 1.

In this collection, we will start with the most-cited paper, "Climbing the Stairway to Heaven – A Multiple-Case Study Exploring Barriers in the Transition from Agile Development towards Continuous Deployment of Software" by H. H. Olsson, H. Alahyari, and J. Bosch. The chapter describes the state of continuous practices of four

J. Bosch et al. (eds.), *Accelerating Digital Transformation*, https://doi.org/10.1007/978-3-031-10873-0_1

3

different companies that lead to formulating the "Stairway to Heaven" model. The model shows a typical evolution path for a company from traditional development to a state where every piece of software is continually deployed at the customer installation of the system and data from everyday use is fed back to guide the R&D organization. Barriers against climbing the stairway are identified from the case companies.

From this article, the CIViT model was created to guide companies about where in their organizations to focus short-term as well as long-term efforts to be successful in automating the CI/CD flow [338].

The second chapter in this collection, "Modeling Continuous Integration Practice Differences in Industry Software Development," by D. Ståhl and J. Bosch, is a systematic literature review of the practical implementation of CI in industry. By analyzing 46 publications, the authors formulated 22 cluster statements that can be thought of as variation points in implementing CI in practice. This contribution is an academic achievement but also a practical guide of decisions to take for the implementer of CI – a typical example of successful research that we are proud of in Software Center.

Recent research in Software Center Theme 1 helps stakeholders to find the information they need from the complex CI/CD process by utilizing data, for instance, from implementations of the Eiffel protocol [106, 423]. These implementations are centered around a unified event bus, where the different tools in the tool chain of a CI/CD pipeline produce and listen for events, thereby creating traceability between events in real time. So far, various types of visualization techniques have been the most prominent approach.

In spring 2017, Software Center companies SAAB Aeronautics, Axis Communication, Grundfos, and Ericsson identified automated testing as a critical bottleneck and joined forces to create a research agenda that was turned into the first company-initiated project proposal complemented with working packages from four universities. This has led to several research contributions, such as diversity-base testing, combinatorial testing, detection and avoidance of flaky tests, cognitive aspects of testing, scheduling of parallel test execution, and static analysis to improve test code quality.

In this collection, this line of research is represented by a recent chapter that got very high appreciation from the publisher: "Efficient and Effective Exploratory Testing of Large-Scale Software Systems" by T. Mårtensson, D. Ståhl, A. Martini, and J. Bosch. The authors make the point that the high degree of automation in CI/CD needs to be complemented with human testing, drawing on the human testers' curiosity and their knowledge of the end users' true needs. The chapter presents and validates the ExET model, which is an empirically founded model used to guide practitioners into the deployment of exploratory testing fulfilling nine key factors found in successful testing processes. On the method pages, the chapter also describes cross-company workshops, which is one of the most common ways of working in the Software Center to gather data and exchange experience between companies.

The future is the only thing we do not know anything about, but we have probably not seen the end of data-driven validation, where the software components are deployed to end-customers and are subject to real usage behavior from which data can be fed back to the development and test. The deployment environment is built with a fallback to earlier releases if the new components fail. This is an alternative to build a testing environment that mimics real usage, which in many cases can be difficult and expensive and can slow down the time to market.

Another ongoing, but not finished, trend is to transfer CI/CD to systems engineering where hardware and environmental components are simulated. A parallel, continuous development of models, simulators, and software might give opportunities for increased collaboration between disciplines and to harvest the benefits from agile methods outside the software world.

For the testing part, many researchers are working on how to test AI/ML software as this type of component is becoming more integrated in industrial software. We would like to welcome well-accepted, industrially validated methods suitable for iterative development and CI/CD.

As the reader realizes, the CI/CD processes consume much computational resources and thus electrical energy that in turn has an environmental impact – in the worst case, through more emission of CO_2. The contribution of information and communication technologies (ICTs) to a low carbon economy is still unclear [417]. This alone would motivate a more purposeful and exact utilization of computational resources in CI/CD and automated testing, not to mention the positive contributions in time and quality.

Chapter 1
Climbing the Stairway to Heaven

Helena Holmström Olsson, Hiva Alahyari, and Jan Bosch

Abstract Agile software development is well-known for its focus on close customer collaboration and customer feedback. In emphasizing flexibility, efficiency and speed, agile practices have led to a paradigm shift in how software is developed. However, while agile practices have succeeded in involving the customer in the development cycle, there is an urgent need to learn from customer usage of software also after delivering and deployment of the software product. The concept of continuous deployment, i.e. the ability to deliver software functionality frequently to customers and subsequently, the ability to continuously learn from real-time customer usage of software, has become attractive to companies realizing the potential in having even shorter feedback loops. However, the transition towards continuous deployment involves a number of barriers. This paper presents a multiple-case study in which we explore barriers associated with the transition towards continuous deployment. Based on interviews at four different software development companies we present key barriers in this transition as well as actions that need to be taken to address these.

1.1 Introduction

Today, software development is conducted in increasingly turbulent business environments. Typically, fast-changing and unpredictable markets, complex and changing customer requirements, pressures of shorter time-to-market, and rapidly advancing information technologies are characteristics found in most software development projects. To address this situation, agile practices advocating flexibility, efficiency and speed are seen as increasingly attractive by software development companies [102]. In emphasizing the use of iterations and development of small features,

---

Reprinted with permission from IEEE. Originally published in 38th Euromicro Conference on Software Engineering and Advanced Applications, 2012 DOI: https://doi.org/10.1109/SEAA.2012.54

agile practices have increased the ability for software development companies to accommodate fast changing customer requirements and fluctuating market needs [102, 480].

However, while many software development companies have indeed succeeded in adopting agile practices in parts of their organization, there are few examples of companies that have succeeded in implementing agile practices to such an extent that software functionality can be continuously deployed at customer sites so that customer feedback and customer usage data can be efficiently utilized throughout development, delivery and deployment of software [404]. In order to advance the concept of agile development and move towards continuous deployment of software there are several steps that need to be taken.

In this paper, we present a multiple-case study in which we explore four companies within the IT industry moving towards continuous deployment of software. While the ability to continuously deploy new functionality at the customer site creates new business opportunities and indeed extends the concept of agile development, it also presents challenges related to current customer collaboration models. As a result of our study, we identify barriers in moving towards continuous deployment of software – as well as actions that need to be taken to overcome these.

1.2 From Agile Development to Continuous Deployment of Software

Companies evolve their software development practices over time. Typically, there is a pattern that most companies follow as their evolution path. We refer to this evolution as the "stairway to heaven" and it is presented in Fig. 1.1.

The phases of the "stairway to heaven" are discussed in more detail in the remainder of this section. As a summary, however, we see that companies evolving from traditional waterfall development (step A in Fig. 1.1) start by experimenting with one or a few agile teams. Once these teams are successful and there is positive momentum, agile practices are adopted by the R&D organization (step B in Fig. 1.1). At this point, product management and system integration and verification are still using traditional work practices. As the R&D organization starts to show the benefits of working agile, system integration and verification becomes involved and the company can adopt continuous integration where system test takes place continuously and where there is always a shippable product (step C in Fig. 1.1). Once continuous integration is up and running internally, lead customers often express an interest to receive software functionality earlier than through the normal release cycle. What they want is to be able to deploy software functionality continuously (step D in Fig. 1.1). The final step is where the software development company not only releases software continuously, but also collects data from its installed base and uses this data to drive an experiment system where new ideas are tested in segments of the installed base and the data collected from these customers is used to steer the direction of R&D efforts [45].

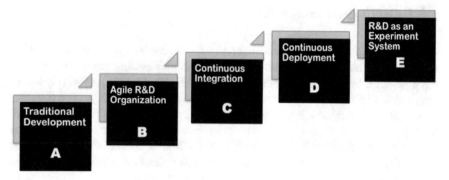

Fig. 1.1 "The stairway to heaven", i.e. the typical evolution path for companies moving towards continuous deployment of software

1.2.1 Traditional Development

In our discussion, we refer to traditional development as an approach to software development characterized by slow development cycles, e.g. yearly, waterfall-style interaction between product management, product development, system test and the customer and, finally, customer feedback processes that are not necessarily well integrated with the product development process [415]. Usually, project teams are large and competences are divided into disciplines such as system architecture, design and test. Development is sequential with a rigorous planning phase in the very beginning of each project. Typically, delivery to the customer takes place in the very end of the project and it is not until then that customers can provide feedback on the software functionality they have received.

1.2.2 Agile R&D Organization

The next step in the evolution is where product development, i.e. the R&D organization, has adopted agile practices, but where product management and system verification still work according to the traditional development model. Although some of the benefits with agile practices are reaped, there is not necessarily short feedback loops with the customer. As defined by Highsmith and Cockburn [181], a team should not be considered agile if the feedback loop with customers and management is six months or more.

1.2.3 Continuous Integration

A company employing continuous integration has succeeded in establishing practices that allow for frequent integration of work, daily builds and fast commit of changes, e.g. automated builds and automated test. Humble and Farley [196] define continuous integration as a software development practice where members of a team integrate their work frequently, leading to multiple integrations per day. The idea of automating test cases, builds, compilation, code coverage etc. allows teams to test and integrate their code on a daily basis which minimizes the time it takes from having an idea to actually implement the idea in software. At this point, both product development and system validation are working according to agile practices.

1.2.4 Continuous Deployment

At this stage, software functionality is deployed continuously, or at least more frequently, at customer site. This allows for continuous customer feedback, the ability to learn from customer usage data, i.e. real usage data, and to eliminate any work that doesn't produce value for the customer. At this point, R&D, product management as well as the customers are all involved in a rapid, agile cycle of product development.

1.2.5 R&D as an 'Experiment System'

The final step on the "stairway to heaven" is where the entire R&D system responds and acts based on instant customer feedback and where actual deployment of software functionality is seen as a way of experimenting and testing what the customer needs. At this step, deployment of software is seen more as a starting point for further 'tuning' of functionality rather than delivery of the final product.

1.2.6 Summary

In this section, we presented the typical evolution path for companies adopting agile practices. It is important to realize, however, that there are different levels at which adoption of agile practices can take place. First, and as can be seen in our study, agile practices are adopted at a team level. As will show, we found that teams are often significantly ahead of the organization as a whole, in particular up to the stage of continuous integration. Second, agile practices are adopted at an organizational level where they evolve into an institutionalized approach to software development. In our paper, we focus on the organizational level in order to identify barriers that need to be addressed by the organization to further accelerate. Finally, there is an ecosystem perspective on the adoption of agile practices. Many companies, and as can be seen in our study, interact closely with suppliers. Although an organization may operate at a high level in the presented model, achieving the same level of agility with suppliers requires a significant effort.

In Table 1.1, we focus on the organizational level. We summarize the involvement of each function in the organization, as well as the customer's role. The 'approach' column refers to the different steps in the "stairway to heaven" (Fig. 1.1).'T' stands for traditional, 'A' for agile and 'SC' for short cycle. The table illustrates the transition towards continuous deployment and a situation, if looking at the final step (E), in which all functions involved enjoy short feedback cycles and hence, the opportunity to experiment with an aim to continuously learn and improve.

Table 1.1 Summary of each step in the "stairway to heaven" (A-E) and how each organizational function (PM, R&D, Validation and Customer) work at this particular step

Approach	PM	R&D	Validation	Customer
A	T	T	T	T
B	T	A	T	T
C	T	SC	SC	T
D	A	SC	SC	A
E	SC	SC	SC	SC

1.3 Research Approach

1.3.1 Research Sites

This paper reports on a multiple-case study involving four software development companies. All four companies are moving towards continuous deployment of software. In representing different stages in this process, we find these companies of particular interest for understanding the barriers that need to be addressed when moving towards continuous deployment of software. Below, the characteristics of each company are presented as well as their current mode of development, i.e. at what step in the model (Fig. 1.1) we place them.

Company A is involved in developing systems for military defense and civil security. The systems focus on surveillance, threat detection, force protection and avionics systems. Often, the system solutions are developed through the use of microwave and antenna technology. Internally, the company is organized in different departments with systems engineering (SE) and quality assurance (QA) being the two departments included in this study. In relation to the model presented in Fig. 1.1, this company is best described as a company doing traditional development but moving towards an agile R&D organization. Already, there are a few pro-active agile teams that work as inspiration for the rest of the organization and the attitude towards agile practices and continuous deployment of software is positive.

Company B is an equipment manufacturer developing, manufacturing and selling a variety of products within the embedded systems domain. The products contain software running on micro-controllers that are connected via computer networks. The company structure is highly distributed with globally distributed development teams. Also, much of the development is done by suppliers. In relation to the model presented in Fig. 1.1, this company can be described as a company that is close to continuous integration. While parts of the organization are still to a large extent traditional and plan-driven, there are a number of pro-active teams that operate in a highly agile manner and continuous integration is already in place in between these teams.

Company C is a manufacturer and supplier of transport solutions for commercial use. The development organization involves coordination of a large number of teams distributed both nationally and internationally. Similar to company B, the development organization is largely dependent on supplier organizations. In relation to the model presented in Fig. 1.1, this company can be described as a company with parts of its R&D organization being traditional and parts of it being highly agile. In similar with company B, this company has continuous integration in place for some of the teams and the experience from these is used to pro-actively coach other parts of the organization in its transition towards continuous deployment.

Company D is a provider of telecommunication systems and equipment, communications networks and multimedia solutions for mobile and fixed network operators. They offer end-to-end solutions for mobile communication and they develop telecommunication infrastructure components for a global market. The organization is highly distributed with globally distributed development and customer teams. In relation to the model presented in Fig. 1.1, this company can be described as a company with established practices for continuous integration and with existing attempts to continuous deployment in place. During our study we could see that this company is very close to continuous deployment of software, making their experiences valuable for other companies trying to address the barriers that are present when moving towards continuous deployment of software.

1.3.2 Research Method

This study builds on a 6 months (July 2011–December 2011) multiple-case study and adopts an interpretive research approach [472]. It emphasizes software development as enacted by people with different values, different expectations and different strategies, as a result of their different frames of interpretation [470]. These frames act as filters enabling people to perceive some things but ignore others [317]. In particular, case study research is considered appropriate to investigate real-life contexts, such as for example software development, where control over the context is not possible [491] and where there is an interest in accessing people's interpretations and expectations in order to create a rich understanding of a particular context [472]. In our study, a multiple-case design is used to ensure that "the events and processes in one well-described setting are not wholly idiosyncratic" [325]. In our study, the four case companies all represent different contexts with different prerequisites. However, they all share the same vision i.e. to enable customer feedback and customer usage data to feed into frequent delivery of software functionality and hence, move closer towards continuous deployment of software. In this way, they all represent interesting examples that well reflect our attempt to better understand the barriers that software development companies face when moving towards continuous deployment.

1.4 Data Collection and Analysis

The main data collection method used in this study is semi-structured interviews with open-ended questions [384]. When doing interviews, there is the delicate task in balancing between passivity and over-direction of interviews [472]. In our study, we chose to have an interview protocol organized in four pre-defined themes, but allow for openness and flexibility within these themes. The themes were (1) current way of working, (2) current customer interaction mechanisms/models, (3) strengths/weaknesses in current way of working, and finally a theme related to (4) an imagined future of continuous deployment and the barriers to get there. In total, 18 interviews were conducted. In company A and B we conducted five interviews in each company, involving software and function developers, software architects, system engineers, configuration managers and project leaders. In company C and D we conducted four interviews in each company, involving software developers, component/system integrators, project/release managers, product line maintenance and a product owner. All 18 interviews were conducted in English and each in-terview lasted for about one hour. During the interviews, we were two researchers sharing the responsibility, i.e. one of us asked the questions and one took notes. In this way, we had the opportunity to discuss the data after each interview and to compare our different insights. In addition to the notes, all interviews were recorded in order for the research team to have a full description of what was said [472]. Each interview was transcribed and the transcriptions were shared among the three researchers to allow for further elaboration on the empirical material. In addition to the interviews, documentation review and field notes were complementary data col-lection methods, including software development documents, project management documents, and corporate websites and brochures. Also, e-mail correspondence was used as a follow-up to all interviews in order to clarify any misunderstandings in the transcription of interviews.

1.5 Validity and Generalizability of Results

As noted by [228], qualitative researchers rarely have the benefit of previously planned comparisons, sampling strategies, or statistical manipulations that control for possible threats. Instead, qualitative researchers must try to rule out validity threats after the research has begun by using evidence collected during the research itself to make alternative hypotheses or interpretations implausible. One important aspect of validity is construct validity [384], which reflects to what extent the operational measures that are studied represent what the researchers have in mind, and what is reflected in the interview questions. To address this aspect, we started each interview with an introduction in which we shared our understanding of 'continuous deployment' with the interviewee. In this way, the researchers and the interviewee had a shared understanding of the concept already before the interview. With respect to external validity, i.e. to what extent it is possible to generalize the findings, our contribution is related to (1) the drawing of specific implications and (2) the contribution of rich insight [472]. Based on our interviews, we present findings and implications in a particular domain of action. While these implications should be regarded as tendencies rather than predictions [472], they might indeed prove useful for other similar organizations and contexts. In relation to rich insight, our study brings together four empirical contexts that allow for a broad understanding of the concept of 'continuous deployment'. Our study aims at capturing the typical evolution path for software companies moving towards continuous deployment, and the findings we present should be regarded as insights valuable for other companies interested in this evolution.

1.6 Case Study Findings

In this section we present the interview findings from each company that was involved in our study. In particular, we present the barriers that each company experiences when climbing from one step to the next in the "stairway to heaven" (see Fig. 1.1).

1.6.1 Company A

As mentioned earlier in this paper, company A is characterized as a company doing traditional development but with a strong interest in agile practices. In our interviews, we learnt that company A has teams that are agile in nature and that these are used as inspiration for the larger organization. In our study, company A represents a company starting its journey way towards more agile practices and there are still many steps to take. While the attitude among the interviewees is positive, and there is anticipation on the benefits that agile practices will bring, there are a number of barriers that need to be addressed. One of the major barriers is the lack of a base product on which improvements can be continually done. This is reflected in the following quote by one of the software developers: *"I think we could deliver better products if we had a better way of working with our products...we do not continually work with improving the products. We only work with the products when we have a customer and a customer project"*.

Another barrier is the current way of working which is sometimes insufficient when it comes to process. This is expressed by one of the configuration managers: *"Sometimes we lack a proper process on how to deploy the builds to our internal systems...we do not really have a process on how to collaborate and exchange information in between teams"*. The common opinion is also that there is a need for automating the process to a larger extent than is done today. In addition to difficulties associated with the current way of working, old tools make work unnecessarily difficult and while people agree on that writing commands sometimes has its advantages, a nice graphical interface would make work easier and more efficient. The barrier with having old tools is described by one of the software developers: *"It is the software, the tools, the installation engine...it is 15 years or so...we don't have any fancy tools"*. Finally, the business model is seen as a barrier itself as it gives a conservative impression with expectations set up front rather than being flexible and responsive towards emerging needs.

To summarize, company A experiences several barriers when moving from traditional development (step A in Fig. 1.1) towards agile development (step B in Fig. 1.1). These barriers are (1) the lack of a base product prohibiting continual improvement, (2) an insufficient process, (3) old tools, and (4) the current conservative business model.

1.6.2 Company B

Company B has a number of agile teams and the organization is moving towards continuous integration. While our interviewees describe a number of initiatives supporting this move, they agree that there is much to be done in order to enhance flexibility and encourage more frequent delivery. One of the software architects reflects on this when saying: *"If you want to change something it is difficult...you need to go through several steps involving several people and this will have a long lead time"*. According to our interviewees, there are a number of barriers that need to be addressed when transitioning from having agile teams to also have continuous integration in place. First, the company is depending on its many suppliers, a situation that makes development complex. *" Everything gets harder to do when you buy it from a supplier...our process depends on their process...some suppliers are fast and some are slow, but in general they have a negative effect on development speed"* (software developer). Accordingly, one of the project leaders mentions that: *"One thing that could indeed be improved is the communication with suppliers...it is sometimes slow"*. In addition, several of the interviewees mention that fitting different components from different suppliers takes time, so it is not only the development lead time that is long but also the integration of components that is time-consuming.

Another barrier which is mentioned by all interviewees is the fact that the company is still very hardware oriented in character and profile. There is a great deal of experience in hardware but not so much in software. One of the project leaders reflects on this when saying: *"We have experience in hardware, but our experience in software is not so rigorous. To some extent we are still a mechanic company and not a software company but we are slowly changing due to all software that is needed in our mechanical products"*. In similar, one of the software developers touches upon this: *"We are moving away from being a mechanical company to being more of a software company, but we still have many of the systems and processes from the mechanical part. In the mechanical part you do not update hardware each day...therefore, the lead-time that we are used to is slow and our background systems and processes are slow"*. In relation to the traditions and the experience within the company, the current ways of working are sometimes seen as problematic. One barrier that is often mentioned is the dependency between components and the dependency between component interfaces. This makes separation difficult and hence, development teams are highly dependent on each other. Furthermore, the interpretation of the current development process is different at different sites – a situation that makes it even more difficult to separate deliveries in a way that all involved parties agree with.

Another common barrier is the testing activities. For example, one developer emphasizes the need for automatic testing while at the same time realizing that this is difficult in an embedded system involving hardware with slow development cycles. Finally, the broad variety of tools is a major barrier, a view that is shared among all the interviewees: *"I think one of the major weaknesses is that we have too many tools... we change tools all the time and learning a new tool is like learning a new language. If you have too many tools and updates it is like learning a new language with a new dictionary all the time"* (developer). The tool issue also brings problems that might affect the testing activities mentioned above. One of the developers stress this when saying: *"The tools are sometimes not mature enough to fill the purpose they were assigned to...sometimes they introduce so much problems that we have to deal with...you get uncertain with how they work and this means doing much more tests"*.

To summarize, company B experiences several barriers when moving from agile development (step B in Fig. 1.1) towards continuous integration (step C in Fig. 1.1). These barriers are (1) communication and coordination with suppliers, (2) company tradition of being hardware oriented, (3) component dependencies, (4) interpretation of the current process model, (5) testing activities, and (6) the broad variety of tools.

1.6.3 Company C

Several teams at company C work in an agile way and there are a number of teams that have established practices for continuous integration. As an organization, company C is moving towards continuous integration and there are several initiatives supporting this. However, to make this transition there are a number of barriers to address. First, the dependency to suppliers is something that the interviewees find troublesome. *"The projects become complex due to the many suppliers...no development is really going on inside the company but instead we have to coordinate and integrate components from our suppliers"* (system integrator). The complexity is highlighted further by one of the software developers: *"...then of course if you want to come to a situation in which you work in shorter loops, then all suppliers must also embrace this and see that it is good for them to have short loops and to abandon the waterfall projects. But as long as one supplier remains in the old paradigm then...yeah, they are a big part of the challenge"*. Moreover, the interviewees find it difficult to be flexible and work more agile in a world which is predetermined by fixed price models and where the business model can be difficult to adjust. One of the developers reflects on this: *"People try to work agile and to stay flexible but this is very difficult in a world which is predetermined due to economics ruling"*. As it seems, the difficulty is not only to navigate in the network of suppliers but also to adjust to the current business model.

One major barrier at company C is the difficulty in getting an overview of the status of the projects. According to one of the software developers: *"...the projects are in our mailboxes and it is very hard to get a picture of the status of the different projects"*. In general, the feeling is that the daily work could be much more efficient if only people made use of the tools that are available for this. Also, there is the need for a connection in between the different systems so that information doesn't have to be pushed out as is done today. Rather, our interviewees would like to see a situation in which information is transparent and in which it was available for anyone that needs it.

In similar with company B, company C is dependent on hardware and many of its processes are adjusted in accordance with the hardware platforms. According to one of the developers this sometimes causes problems: *"I think a problem is that we are still focused on the hardware part of the product. We build our product [the hardware part] and for this we have some tools...this is a slow process compared to how fast you can change software"*. The interviewees agree that in order to change this they need a better hardware platform then what is available today. One of the developers emphasizes this when saying: *"We need a more stable and commoditized hardware platform in order to move towards a more 'software-way-of-working"*. What seems to be a common opinion is that when functionality of the product is distributed between both hardware and software, the hardware part cannot be ignored or viewed as a computing resource only. At the same time, they agree that the overall process cannot be too heavily tailored to fit the mechanical development process. Finally, all interviewees mention the test process as critical for the ability to move towards continuous deployment. To get more confident in the test suite and to be able to automate tests will be important as well as increasing the number of people that are dedicated to software testing.

To summarize, company C experiences several barriers when moving from agile (step B in Fig. 1.1) towards continuous integration (step C in Fig. 1.1). These barriers are (1) dependency on suppliers, (2) current business model, (3) lack of transparency, (4) hardware oriented mindset and process and, (5) the test process.

1.6.4 Company D

At company D, agile processes have been around for several years and they have become widespread within the company. A large part of the organization is familiar with continuous integration and the company is pushing towards continuous deployment for at least parts of the product and for a segment of its customers. Here, the faster feedback loop to customers is regarded the major benefit. With continuous deployment customers get releases more often and software features can be deployed at customer site on a more frequent basis than today. According to one of the release program managers faster feedback means cheaper development since the R&D organization can then spend time on developing the right things rather than correcting mistakes in functionality that is not necessarily what the customer wants.

However, in order to move further towards continuous deployment of software, there are a number of barriers to address. The interviewees at company D all mention the complexity of the network and the many different configurations that their customers have. A very common challenge is when a customer wants a new feature but has an old version of the product to which this new feature has to be configured. Similarly, an upgrade of any kind is considered stressful by customers, something that is highlighted by the release manager: *"it is more difficult to guarantee minimal network impact if the configuration of the product is complex"*. From the interviews it is clear that customers still regard upgrades and new features as a challenge due to the risk of interfering with legacy. Another barrier is the internal verification loop which needs to be shortened and automated in order to meet up with the requirements that continuous deployment raises. As mentioned by one of the product line maintenance managers, more automated tests are needed in order to increase speed and frequency of delivery. Also, several interviewees highlight the importance of improving the quality on each build and to increase awareness on what effect each build has on the overall software package. In this, the teams would benefit from knowing more about the quality status of the development projects, i.e. the current quality of features, the number of errors etc. If such knowledge could be better established, teams could respond faster and act more pro-actively towards customers.

To summarize, company D experiences several barriers when moving from continuous integration (step C in Fig. 1.1) towards continuous deployment (step D in Fig. 1.1). These barriers are (1) network configuration and upgrade complexity, (2) internal verification loop, and (3) quality status of builds/systems.

1.7 Climbing the Stairway to Heaven

In this section the multiple-case study findings are discussed, leading to an under-standing for key barriers that companies experience when moving towards continuous deployment. We use the model in Fig. 1.1 to identify barriers in between the different steps, i.e. from traditional development to agile, from agile development to contin-uous integration and, finally, from continuous integration to continuous deployment of software. Furthermore, and based on the case study findings, we identify actions that need to be taken to address these barriers and succeed in the transition towards continuous deployment of software.

1.7.1 From Traditional to Agile R&D

As can be seen in our study, there are several barriers that need to be addressed when moving from traditional development to an agile R&D organization. For example, in company A, teams struggle with an insufficient process in which collaboration and information exchange is poorly supported. This situation, in combination with the lack of a product on which improvements can be continually made and a conservative business model, in which requirements are defined upfront, makes it difficult for teams to act agile. Moreover, old tools make development unnecessary complex and the developers express a situation in which the tools restrict rather than release activity.

To address these barriers, there are a number of actions that need to be taken. As can be seen in literature, a first and challenging step is to introduce agile working practices into the organization and to get managerial support for such an initiative [2]. Company A shows on several initiatives that supports agile working practices and the general attitude is positive. Having a few agile teams that work as inspiration for the larger organization is one action that will have a positive effect on other teams. Furthermore, and as can be seen in our study, one of the major barriers is the difficulty in collaboration and information exchange, and as an action to address this barrier company A is organizing its development organization in smaller teams. As can be seen in previous research [263], cross-functional teams are critical to overcome barriers associated with collaboration and communication issues. In com-pany A, cross-functional teams are being introduced and they will be one important step towards an agile R&D organization. Finally, companies strive towards having feature teams rather than component teams to shorten lead time and improve release frequency [263]. Feature teams work with only a small part of the functionality and hence, respond quickly to changing requirements. . In introducing agile working practices and re-organizing the development team organization, company A is ad-dressing several of the barriers associated with the transition from traditional to agile software development.

To summarize, the key focus area in the transition from traditional to agile R&D is the adoption of small and, cross-functional teams.

1.7.2 From Agile R&D to Continuous Integration

In our study, we have two companies moving from an agile R&D organization to continuous integration. In doing so, there are several barriers to address. As can be seen in both company B and C, they struggle with being dependent on suppliers which means that a lot of effort is put on communication and coordination with these. In addition, different interpretations of the current process model at different sites make the development process complex. Both companies are hardware oriented, meaning that a cultural shift is necessary in order to move further towards continuous integration. In both these companies the mechanical part has been the major part of the process so far and while it will always be critical it will have to successfully co-exist with important software functionality in development of future products. As can be seen in our interviews, this cultural shift is challenging and it requires a transformation of previous traditions and values. Furthermore, the companies find the variety of tools and the lack of transparency problematic. While company B notes that the many tools make learning and efficiency difficult, company C finds the lack of transparency problematic. Finally, and as noted in literature [196], both companies emphasize the test activities as one of the major challenges when moving towards continuous integration. The need for automated test processes is well understood but still difficult to fully implement.

To address the barriers mentioned above, the companies in our study mention a number of actions. What is most important, and something that is also noted in previous research [7, 196], is the need to develop complete test suites including automated tests that are well integrated with system validation. In both company B and C development of automated tests is an on-going activity and the aim is to increase the number of automated tests significantly within a short period of time. Both companies find this the most important activity in order to consolidate the concept of continuous integration and make possible for a culture shift among developers who believe things "only when they see it happen" as mentioned by one of the developers in company C. Furthermore, and in order to reduce complexity, code needs to be checked into a main development branch, i.e. the production line. If so, companies can avoid having several branches that will only add to the complexity and lead-time described by our interviewees. As a result of this, the transparency between teams will also improve and the barrier with lack of transparency can be reduced. Finally, company B and C both touch upon the fact that lead-time is long and that the dependency on suppliers as well as mechanical parts is problematic. In order to at least to some extent address this situation, development needs to be modularized into smaller units, i.e. the build process needs to be shortened so that tests can be run more frequently and hence, quality can be reviewed at an earlier stage. This will allow for more frequent deliveries to customers and an opportunity to learn from customer feedback earlier.

To summarize, the key focus area in this transition stage is to develop a fully automated testing infrastructure that continuously verifies the product as it evolves during development.

1.7.3 From Continuous Integration to Continuous Deployment

Our last company, i.e. company D, is the company closest to continuous deployment of software. In this company, continuous integration is a well established practice and there are already attempts to involve pro-active customers in continuous deployment of certain software functionality. However, there are a number of barriers that need to be addressed also for company D. What is most evident from our interviews is the complexity that arises in different network configurations at customer sites. While the product has its standard configurations there are always customized solutions as well as local configurations that cannot be fully counted for. Furthermore, the internal verification loop needs to be shortened in order to not only develop functionality fast but too also deploy it fast at customer site. Third, several of the companies mentioned lack of transparency as a barrier when moving closer towards continuous deployment of software. Depending on company, this barrier takes different forms but in common is the need to get an overview of the current status of development projects. This is evident in company D where one of the product line maintenance managers expressed a need to get better status reporting from teams in order to increase transparency and further improve speed. To address the barriers mentioned above, there are a number of actions that can be taken. In company D, one major action has been to involve not only the R&D units but also the product management units in the vision of delivering smaller features more frequently to customers. In similar with introducing agile practices to different parts of the organization as the very first step when moving from traditional development to agile development, the transition towards continuous deployment requires involvement of different organizational units in order to fully succeed. Especially, product management needs to be involved as they are the interface towards customers. In company D, we learnt from product managers that their involvement was important and that their insight into the R&D organization had increased when working towards continuous deployment. This is in line with previous research, which emphasizes the importance of having the R&D organization and the product management organization sharing the same goal when moving towards continuous deployment [404]. Finally, finding a pro-active customer who is willing to explore the concept of continuous deployment is critical. Here, the concept of 'lead customer' is useful and what is important is to find mechanisms to facilitate for fast customer feedback and mechanisms for translating this feedback into improved software functionality.

To summarize, in transitioning towards continuous deployment the internal action is to involve product management in the short, agile cycle of product development. The external action is to develop a new engagement model with lead customers to facilitate for continuous deployment.

1.7.4 From Continuous Deployment to Innovation System

In this study, we have not been able to explore the final step in the "stairway to heaven", i.e. the move from continuous deployment to R&D as an 'experiment system'. Based on earlier research with other companies, we anticipate that the key actions in this transition are twofold. First, the product needs to be instrumented so that usage and other data can be automatically collected from the installed product base. Second, the overall R&D organization needs to develop the capability to effectively use the collected data to test new ideas with customers. In our future research, we see the transition between the final steps in the "Stairway to Heaven" as our main interest to explore further.

1.8 Conclusions

In this study, we explored how software development companies evolve their practices over time. Based on a conceptual model presented as the "Stairway to Heaven" we presented the transition process when moving towards continuous deployment of software. In doing so, we identified the key barriers for such a transition as well as actions that address these.

   While the details in our study relate to each specific company, there are a number of implications that we think apply to more companies than those we studied. First, the transition towards agile development requires a careful introduction of agile practices into the organization, a shift to small development teams and a focus on features rather than components. Second, the transition towards continuous integration requires an automated test suite, a main branch to which code is continually delivered and modularized development. Finally, the move towards continuous deployment requires organizational units such as product management to be fully involved and a pro-active lead customer to work closely with when exploring the concept further. For the last transition, i.e. from continuous deployment towards R&D as an 'experiment system' the barriers are still to be explored. While our study does not cover this final transition, we believe that the empirical insights presented will be important for companies with an attempt to reach also this final and highly innovative step.

Chapter 2
Modeling Continuous Integration Practice Differences in Industry Software Development

Daniel Ståhl and Jan Bosch

Abstract Continuous Integration is a software practice where developers integrate frequently, at least daily. While this is an ostensibly simple concept, it does leave ample room for interpretation: what is it the developers integrate with, what happens when they do, and what happens before they do? These are all open questions with regards to the details of how one implements the practice of continuous integration, and it is conceivable that not all such implementations in the industry are alike. In this paper we show through a literature review that there are differences in how the practice of continuous integration is interpreted and implemented from case to case. Based on these findings we propose a descriptive model for documenting and thereby better understanding implementations of the continuous integration practice and their differences. The application of the model to an industry software development project is then described in an illustrative case study.

2.1 Introduction

Continuous integration has, not least as one of the Extreme Programming practices [31], become popular in software development. It is reported to improve release frequency and predictability [154], increase developer productivity [326] and improve communication [94], among other benefits. In previous work we found that the proposed benefits of continuous integration are disparate not only in literature: there are also great differences in the extent to which practitioners in industry software development projects have experienced those benefits [418]. Consequently, we asked ourselves whether this disparity might be because of differences in the way the continuous integration practice itself had been implemented in different projects, be it because the concept had been interpreted differently or because the project context

Reprinted with permission from Elsevier. Originally published in Journal of Systems and Software Volume 87, January 2014, Pages 48–59 DOI: https://doi.org/10.1016/j.jss.2013.08.032

J. Bosch et al. (eds.), *Accelerating Digital Transformation*,
https://doi.org/10.1007/978-3-031-10873-0_3

restricted the freedom of that implementation. Indeed, among the four projects included in the study there were indications that this may be the case, but as that study was not intended for this new research question it did not contain sufficient data to satisfactorily answer whether such differences manifest in software development at large.

Consequently, we decided to establish whether there are also differences in continuous integration descriptions found in literature, and if so, in which regards the described implementations differ. In this paper we show the results of the systematic review conducted in order to answer this question, along with a proposed descriptive model for continuous integration practice variants based on its findings.

In this work we have focused on process related differences, rather than differences in tooling. While we recognize that tooling may improve or otherwise affect a continuous integration implementation, the practice of continuous integration itself requires no particular tools at all [135]. Consequently we regard tools to be of secondary importance, but not of primary interest. Furthermore, we have not included contextual factors such as the size and longevity of the projects, the business environment or similar parameters. While they may conceivably correlate with variations in continuous integration practice — indeed, we consider the investigation of such correlations an important field of study in itself — they are not themselves aspects of continuous integration.

The contribution of this paper is twofold. First, it shows that there isn't one homogeneous practice of continuous integration. Rather there are variation points — those evident in literature are presented and discussed individually in this article — with the term continuous integration acting as an umbrella for a number of variants. This is important, because when consequences of continuous integration are reported and discussed, it must be understood that such consequences potentially may not apply to the practice of continuous integration as a whole, but rather be related to a particular variant of it. Therefore, the second contribution of this article is that a descriptive model that addresses all the variation points uncovered in the study is proposed. Such a model enables better study and evaluation of continuous integration and can thereby bring a finer granularity to our understanding of the practice.

The remainder of this paper is structured as follows. In the next section the research method is described. Then the aspects of continuous integration described in literature, and the statements pertaining to those aspects, are presented and analyzed in Sect. 2.3. In Sect. 2.4 the proposed model is described, and then applied to a software development project in an illustrative case study in Sect. 2.5. The paper is then concluded in Sect. 2.6.

2.2 Research Method

The research was conducted by first reviewing existing articles on continuous integration to find differing descriptions of the practice, with the purpose of identifying aspects where there is contention in published literature. In other words, we searched for aspects (represented by clusters of statements, see Sect. 2.2.2) where different attributes or characteristics of the practice are evident, as such areas can then be considered to constitute potential variation points. To exemplify, some sources describe how checks and barriers are implemented to prevent non-correctional changes to be integrated on top of a broken build, whereas others relate how anyone is able to contribute anything at any time (see Sect. 2.3.2.8). As these are clearly differing views, this area is considered a variation point in the practice of continuous integration.

In contrast, aspects where differing views are either not evident (see e.g. Sect. 2.3.1.4) or only addressed by a single source (see e.g. Sect. 2.3.1.5) are not regarded as potential variation points, the reasoning being that there appears to be consensus in the industry or that there is insufficient source material to reliably assess them.

Based on this literature review a model for the description and documentation of continuous integration implementations was then constructed, intended as a guide to help ensure that the variation points discovered in the literature review are covered.

2.2.1 Systematic Review

As a result of observations of dramatically different experiences of continuous integration benefits [418], and our assumption that this may be caused by differences between industry software development projects in how the concept of continuous integration is interpreted and implemented, we wanted to find an answer to the question of "Is there disparity or contention evident in the descriptions of various aspects of the software development practice of continuous integration found in literature?". To answer this question we conducted a systematic review [245], where a review protocol was created and informally reviewed by colleagues. The protocol described the research question above, the sources to be searched (the IEEE Xplore and Inspec databases), the exclusion and inclusion criteria of the review (see Table 2.1) and the method of extracting and clustering descriptive statements found in the publications (see Sect. 2.2.2). Following this the sources were searched (October 2012), with ACM subsequently being added for completeness, for publications relating to the software practice of continuous integration.

The search terms yielded 64, 79 and 45 results in IEEE, Inspec and ACM respectively. Combined, these result sets contained 112 unique items. Exclusion criteria EC1, EC2 and EC3 (see Table 2.1) were applied to this set, and the abstracts of the remainder were studied to determine whether they dealt with the software practice of continuous integration, or pertained to other fields of research (exclusion criterion EC4). This left a set of 76 publications.

Finally, these 76 publications were reviewed in full in search of descriptions of continuous integration practices (exclusion criterion EC5). Such descriptions were found in 46 of the reviewed articles.

Table 2.1 Inclusion and exclusion criteria of the literature review

Inclusion criteria	
IC1	Papers, technical reports, theses, industry white papers and presentations with the terms "continuous integration" and "software" in their titles or abstracts

Exclusion criteria	
EC1	Where studies were published multiple times (e.g. first as a conference paper and then as a journal article) only the most recent publication was included
EC2	Material not available to us in English or Swedish
EC3	Posters for industry talks lacking content beyond abstract and/or references
EC4	Material that does not address the software practice of continuous integration, or only mentions it in passing
EC5	Material that does not describe one or more aspects of how continuous integration practices are, can or should be implemented

2.2.2 Analysis of Literature

Statements as to the nature of continuous integration found in the 46 publications of the literature review were extracted and clustered in groups addressing similar aspects, where one statement may be included in more than one cluster. This yielded 180 discrete, descriptive statements pertaining to one or more aspect of continuous integration and 22 clusters (see Table 2.2). Following this, any group not containing any disparity in their statements were culled. In other words, only groups of statements describing aspects of continuous integration where contention was evident were preserved. This could either manifest as multiple statements in disagreement, or as statements themselves identifying disparity. Additionally, clusters containing statements from only one unique source were culled.

It shall be noted that determining what in this context constitutes an aspect of continuous integration practice — and thereby a cluster — is ultimately a call of judgment. Particularly, automation is not included, even though it is frequently brought up by papers discussing continuous integration, e.g. stating that "test cases [...] will be folded into the automated regression test suite" [443], that "an automated integration server not only makes integration easy, it also guarantees that an integration build will happen" [380], "the build process has to be fully automated" [93] or that "the build process is initiated automatically" [357] to mention a few. For the purposes of this study, we have taken the position that the practice of continuous integration is by definition automated, as described my Martin Fowler: "Each integration is verified by an automated build" [135]. Indeed, from the literature included in this study, we have not found reason to reconsider this position. One source goes so far as to consider it a criterion for success that "all [continuous integration] steps pass without error or human intervention" [371], and so questions of e.g. whether test cases are included in automated test suites rather becomes a matter of the scope of continuous integration, which is covered by its own statement cluster (see Sect. 2.3.2.13).

Table 2.2 Clusters of descriptive statements extracted from literature, shown alongside the number of constituent statements, the number of unique sources from which those statements were extracted, whether there exists contention between the sources and whether there are within the cluster single sources claiming disparity of implementations, respectively

Cluster		Statements	Unique sources	Contention	Claimed disparity
C1	Build duration	10	9	Yes	Yes
C2	Build frequency	10	8	Yes	No
C3	Build triggering	32	29	Yes	Yes
C4	Build version selection	2	2	No	No
C5	Component dependency versioning	6	3	No	No
C6	Definition of failure and success	8	6	Yes	No
C7	Fault duration	5	5	Yes	Yes
C8	Fault frequency	1	1	No	Yes
C9	Fault handling	9	9	Yes	No
C10	Fault responsibility	6	5	No	No
C11	Integration frequency	7	7	No	Yes
C12	Integration on broken builds	6	6	Yes	No
C13	Integration serialization and batching	6	6	Yes	Yes
C14	Integration target	8	6	Yes	Yes
C15	Lifecycle phasing	1	1	No	Yes
C16	Modularization	17	11	Yes	Yes
C17	Pre-integration procedure	16	12	Yes	Yes
C18	Process management	1	1	No	No
C19	Scope	50	40	Yes	No
C20	Status communication	19	16	Yes	Yes
C21	Test separation	11	9	Yes	Yes
C22	Testing of new functionality	10	9	Yes	Yes

2.2.3 Proposing a Model

Based on the analysis of the literature review, a model for documenting continuous integration was created. The purpose of this model was to cover all the statement clusters displaying contention or disparity, thereby answering all the relevant questions that may set one particular instance of continuous integration apart from another, yet at the same time being practical to use.

The benefit to researchers from using such a model is that it may help focus attention on the aspects of continuous integration that act as differentiators, and it provides a method for managing the multitude of continuous integration variants in existence. The benefit to software development professionals — to practitioners of continuous integration — is that it lists choices that they can make — and possibly have already made, consciously or unconsciously — with regards to implementing continuous integration. Such information can be an important factor in successfully improving one's development process.

2.3 Statement Clusters

This section describes each of the clusters of statements found in literature (see Sect. 2.2). In Sect. 2.3.1, those clusters that were culled from the set are presented. Then, in Sect. 2.3.2, the preserved clusters are discussed.

2.3.1 Culled Clusters

Clusters either not containing more than one unique source, or not found to display disparity or contention were culled from the set. These are described and discussed below.

2.3.1.1 Build Version Selection

It is pointed out in [468] that "the continuous integration system should always attempt to build the latest version of the software", while [467] states that "if the latest build of a component has failed [...] an earlier successful build is used instead". While these perspectives seem to differ, it shall be understood that they deal with different contexts: one discusses source code revision, while the other concerns itself with handling component failures in a modularized environment. Therefore there is no contention between them — indeed, they are entirely compatible with each other — and this cluster was therefore culled.

2.3.1.2 Component Dependency Versioning

One topic found in several of the papers is that of modularization of the product, and whether to rebuild the entire product upon integration of new changes, or only those components affected by the change (see Sect. 2.3.2.11). In the latter case, some articles discuss version handling of such components. It is stated that each component shall be built individually, with new versions made available for every such build [375]. It is also said that component dependencies shall be on the latest available version and that only one version of any one component may occur in a system configuration [468]. Furthermore, if a component build fails, then the latest working version shall be used for dependencies in its stead [467].

There is only a small number of articles addressing this aspect — which is not altogether surprising, as it is only relevant in a component oriented continuous integration setup — and no direct contention between them.

2.3.1.3 Fault Frequency

The issue of fault frequency in continuous integration is discussed by [57], where two development teams have been compared. Among other findings, it is pointed out that one team suffered much more frequent build failures than the other. It is readily conceivable that, while being a complex factor dependent on multiple parameters, the frequency of errors in continuous integration can have an impact on the development effort. Lacking additional sources, however, this cluster was culled from the set.

2.3.1.4 Fault Responsibility

Multiple sources describe how developers causing faults in continuous integration are also responsible for correcting those faults [326, 495], e.g. stating that it is "the responsibility of [the last person who checked in code] to ensure that a reported bug is resolved immediately" [1]. Additionally, the practice of developers not leaving work until their changes have been successfully verified is mentioned [326, 380]. No statements contradicting these stated practices were found in the study, with the exception of [212], describing how a "Quality Manager" interprets the produced code analysis metrics. This, however, is only for non-critical violations of coding standards, and so we find that this cluster does not display any contention or disparity.

2.3.1.5 Lifecycle Phasing

It is stated in [187] that continuous integration may be performed "during a phase of integration and tests; or it may be part of iterative methods". While other sources in the study do not explicitly discuss this — causing this cluster to be culled — it shall be noted that, in our understanding, it is implicit in many of the studied publications that continuous integration takes place during, if not necessarily limited to, development.

2.3.1.6 Process Management

In [187] it is noted that the degree of control over continuous integration processes differs, giving examples of projects using "less structured processes" as opposed to "central management of the build process". This aspect was, however, not highlighted by other sources in study.

2.3.2 Preserved Clusters

Statement clusters containing more than one unique source and either displaying contention between sources, or containing sources themselves acknowledging diversity in implementations were preserved. These clusters are presented and discussed below.

2.3.2.1 Build Duration

Some publications in the study give more or less exact figures for the duration of "builds" (where the scope of what a build entails varies, see Sect. 2.3.2.13); time from check-in to notification of verdict can be "several minutes" [94] or "a few minutes" [487], or the time required to compile and run tests can be over an hour [495]. Some articles highlight that build duration does vary from project to project [57] and that this can be of some importance, as a too long duration means that "continuous integration starts to break down" [380] and the build time must be quick enough to "allow the CI server to keep up with the changes and return feedback to the software engineers while their memory of the changes is still fresh" [93]. Others discuss separating quick test suites from slower ones to provide incremental feedback [375], removing slow tests altogether from the regular continuous integration builds and instead running them on a separate schedule [188], or how parallelism caused by modularization can affect build durations [468], as it is remarked that "the primary factor influencing the build time is the increasing number of tests" [380].

From this it is clear that not only is build duration a variation point for continuous integration and considered to be of great importance; it is also not an independent variable. Instead, it is highly dependent on what is included in the build. This would pose a problem if one were to attempt classification and comparison of continuous integration implementations, as any measurement of build duration would also have to take into account what is actually achieved in that duration. The abstract concept as such, represented by this statement cluster, however, is preserved for the purposes of this study.

2.3.2.2 Build Frequency

It shall be noted that for the purposes of this study, we make a distinction between build frequency and integration frequency (see Sect. 2.3.2.7). By the former we mean the frequency at which continuous integration "builds" (regardless of the scope of those builds) are performed, while the integration frequency refers to how often changes are brought into the product development mainline (typically in the form of source code changes). We consider these to be two crucially different activities which may or may not be synchronized.

The build frequencies described in literature vary. Some mention "multiple builds per day" [442] or "every few hours" [379], in contrast to the daily builds practiced by others [187]. Yet the frequency doesn't just vary between projects, it may also vary within the same project. Separation of slow activities into more infrequent cycles is described [94, 188, 284, 487] as well as performing "weekly integration" builds while modules are tested in isolation "several times a day" [454].

2.3.2.3 Build Triggering

The vast majority of statements on how continuous integration builds are triggered describe how source code changes cause a build to start [1, 50, 74, 93, 143, 148, 188, 212, 241, 242, 280, 307, 357, 379, 380, 442, 443, 466, 467, 487]. This is not always the case, however: builds can be executed at a certain time each day [187], or a mixed approach where some activities run on a fixed schedule while others are triggered by source code changes can be used [94, 185, 454, 487].

Another setup is where multiple activities are chained together in a sequence. A source code change triggers the first activity [495], while subsequent activities are triggered by "successful execution and evaluation of prior events" [182]. There is reason to believe that this may be more common than the number of explicit statements suggests, as it is sometimes hinted at or implied, e.g. stating that when "a step in the process fails, further process steps are skipped" [93]. Though such a statement is not unambiguous enough to be counted to the statement cluster total, it does imply that there are process steps which are triggered by the success of upstream steps.

In a modularized scenario, where each component has its own continuous integration, a build can also be triggered by a new version of a component dependency being made available [375, 467].

2.3.2.4 Definition of Failure and Success

What is considered a failure in a continuous integration build is touched upon by several sources. Commonly, if any test fails during the build, then the build as a whole is failed [1, 371], with some sources explicitly mentioning that compilation must also succeed [94, 212, 495] (although it may be argued that compilation errors are implicitly not allowed, even where the source does not explicitly state it).

This zero tolerance towards test failures isn't ubiquitous, however: it is put forward that for most teams "it is fine to permit acceptance tests to break over the course of the iteration as long as the team ensures that the tests are all passing prior to the end of the iteration" [380]. Yet others impose additional requirements before they will consider a build to be successful, such as a certain level of test coverage [495] or the absence of severe static code analysis warnings [212].

2.3.2.5 Fault Duration

Fault duration — that is, how long a detected fault persists before it is successfully addressed — isn't extensively discussed in the studied sources, but there are statements indicating differences. One example is a comparatively strict approach where "if any compilation errors or any test failure occurs, the relevant developer should solve the problem in less than 30 minutes or revert the check-in" [495], whereas another notes that "the great majority of build breaks were fixed within an hour" [326], without explicitly stating any similarly precise rules. Much longer fault durations are also described: "there were several occasions when [...] the code was broken for up to two weeks" [454]. Indeed, [57] recognizes that build failure length differs: while some would be "stuck for hours because of a broken build", others have "very few of these problems".

Yet the question of fault duration is dependent on that of the definition of failure and success, as demonstrated by one source claiming that typically not all types of test failures need to be fixed immediately, but can be left until "the end of the iteration" [380]. Consequently, the question of fault duration only really becomes meaningful in a context where "fault" is well defined. That being said, there are clear differences in fault duration as it is described by the sources in our study, and consequently the cluster is preserved.

2.3.2.6 Fault Handling

How faults, once detected, are handled (e.g. given what priority by whom) is touched upon by a number of sources. Several describe a policy of fault fixing being given top priority, either as the personal responsibility of the developer committing the fault [495] (a policy which would arguably presume that the offending commit can always be identified), as the responsibility of the developers "that have committed Source Code since the last successful integration" [212], or as the responsibility of the last developer to check in code, who is then responsible "to ensure that [the fault] is resolved immediately, for example by reverting to an older version or by fixing the problem in another way" [1]. Another source describes how "after an initial investigation, one developer would fix the build while the rest of the team continued with their work" [326], hinting at a more flexible delegation of work.

Some sources display a slightly more relaxed attitude with regards to faults, however. It is stated that there's a difference between types of tests, some of which may not be a priority to fix [380]. One source describes a development team displaying a certain extent of ambivalence: while fixing faults isn't a top priority, broken builds cause a number of problems unless fixed quickly — e.g. promoting a "laissez-faire attitude" and hiding other problems — and it is suggested that perhaps "a team policy could be instituted to make the broken build the highest priority, ahead of any other work items" [94]. In a multi-step integration setup it is furthermore stated that if one step fails, then "further steps are skipped" [93].

In other words, while sources take a similar position on the question of responsibility per se (see Sect. 2.3.1.4), there are different views on the methods used and priority given to addressing these faults.

As something of a special case in this context, if one uses a modularized continuous integration implementation with separate builds per component, it is mentioned that if a component build fails, then the latest successful build of that component is used by downstream dependencies [467].

In conclusion, there are clear differences in how one reacts to and handles a continuous integration fault once it has been detected, even though this, as is indeed the case with other aspects, is not an independent variable. As the definition of a fault (see Sect. 2.3.2.4) or whether one uses modularized continuous integration (see Sect. 2.3.2.11) varies, so the very meaning of fault handling isn't constant.

2.3.2.7 Integration Frequency

Integration frequency, as opposed to build frequency (see Sect. 2.3.2.2), is described by a number of sources. It is claimed that "on average developers check in once a day" [326], and that while the integration frequency "will vary from project to project, from developer to developer, and from modification to modification [...] a good rule of thumb [is that] developers should integrate their changes once every few hours and at least once per day" [380]. Other sources conclude that this implies that there will be multiple integrations per day [473], relating how "on average, a version was submitted to the source control system every hour over the period studied" [143], although presumably this would depend on the number of developers co-existing in the same source context.

While not mentioning any figures, other source simply claim that integration should be "frequent and timely" [29] or "[performed] regularly and early" [93]. Meanwhile, [468] states that even though current usage of the term continuous integration often doesn't consider the frequency at which check-ins are made, "continuous integration proper [...] includes the continuous checking in of changes, however small they may be".

To conclude, we do not consider contention to be evident in this cluster — not least because several of the sources are very vague — but it still fulfills the preservation criteria, as disparity is claimed.

2.3.2.8 Integration on Broken Builds

There are different approaches as to whether commits on top of revisions that failed in continuous integration are acceptable or not. Several sources describe how commits are not allowed unless the latest continuous integration build was successful

[468], saying that "once the build is broken other developers cannot check in their work" [326], that "all merge requests [are refused] unless they contain a special tag [identifying them as fixes]" [261] and that "developers not working directly on fixing the problem are not permitted to commit their changes [because] it could greatly complicate the problems for the people engaged in fixing the build" [380].

Others are less concerned. In "decentralized" continuous integration, developers are allowed to "add contributions to the development version at any time" [187]. In another case, check-ins on broken builds were not prevented, even though it was suggested that this sometimes caused problems, since "new code could conceivably be problematic too, but the confounding factors would make it difficult to determine exactly where the problem was" [94].

To summarize, the consensus appears to be that code commits on broken builds can be problematic, but whether enough so to actively try to prevent it (by process or by automated blocking of unwanted check-ins) is contended.

2.3.2.9 Integration Serialization and Batching

While it is common to let committed changes trigger new builds (see Sect. 2.3.2.3), it's an open question how one handles a situation where multiple changes are made during the timespan of a single build. This can be particularly relevant in a context of slow build times and high integration frequency. This is discussed by [371], pointing out that there are different approaches to serialization and batching: the check-in process can be serialized in order to minimize failures and "avoiding all integration conflicts", as opposed to "the more normal free flowing practice whereby any developer can optimistically check-in as soon as they have run the build locally and all tests pass". One source states that polling for changes implies "batching the revisions to be tested" [261], while another claims that "every commit should build the mainline on an integration machine" [442], with references to tooling used for achieving this.

It shall also be noted that in a situation where activities (particularly tests, see Sect. 2.3.2.15) are separated into stages it is possible that those stages are not executed at the same frequency [94, 185, 454], in effect batching changes in between different integration activities.

2.3.2.10 Integration Target

The integration target aspect concerns where developers check in their changes. Most of the publications in the study do not explicitly deal with this, but rather state that, for example, a change in source code repository triggers a build (see Sect. 2.3.2.3) without specifying where in the repository those changes are made. There are, however, some that go into details.

One method is that of every commit resulting in a new build on the product "mainline" [442] and letting developers check in to the development version at any time [187]. It is described how "all the development teams [were moved] into one common code branch — no private branches" and "each code check-in is now immediately integrated" [154].

Multiple branches are also used, however. One variant is the pattern of a single development branch into which new changes are merged, and a "stable" branch into which "all the revisions vetted by [the continuous integration] are pushed", the latest version of which is used for deployment [261]. Another variant is to let each team in a multi-team project integrate internally, using their own integration server, before integrating with the project at large (as a response to problems encountered when attempting to scale continuous integration) [380]. However, the same source continues, this "creates the problem of cross-team integration" where "teams are potentially building up an integration debt". Indeed, another source relates how, when implementing continuous integration, the initial decision was made "that each individual Scrum team should have a dedicated and private server", but "as integration issues were being discovered very late" they put "all teams onto a single server environment again" [450].

2.3.2.11 Modularization

While there are sources making explicit statements that their continuous integration is not modularized [371], e.g. claiming that "the entire software is built [and] tested" upon changes [1] or that "testing in the CI process focuses only on 'local' projects" [93], it is our understanding that sources where this topic is not discussed generally presume a non-modularized approach. For the most part, the sources that do deal with modularization are positive examples, in that they either explain how continuous integration can be modularized or describe examples of such modularization.

In such sources, it is related how products can be composed of "hundreds of components with complicated dependency relationship[s]" and "the source code of each [component] is controlled independently" [244]. Expanding on this concept, another source describes how components rely on pre-built artifacts of their dependencies, and "integrating the whole application then means building the topmost component in the dependency hierarchy" [468]. Furthermore it is stated that each component has its own continuous integration cycle, following which it is published to be tested in combination with other components [375], that "continuous integration can be seen as a [directed acyclic graph], where nodes correspond to package builds and edges correspond to dependencies among packages" [30] and that components are rebuilt if they themselves are changed, or one of their dependencies change [467]. Similar concepts are also discussed by [380].

Additionally, a modularized approach to continuous integration is claimed to impact feedback times. It is described how "modules were tested in isolation and embedded into the program" [454] and that such a practice enables faster feedback, because "instead of building the complete system on every change, only the components that have affecting changes are rebuilt [468]. In a similar vein, it is claimed that while a single source repository is often assumed in continuous integration, this in fact scales poorly, thus motivating a modularized approach [375]. To facilitate testing of components in such an environment, "surrogates" can be used "to simulate the behaviors of unavailable components" [280], and it is described how tests can be executed in several steps: first by component, then for the system at large [244].

It is noteworthy how, unlike most continuous integration aspects in this study, statements pertaining to modularization are mostly found in sources explicitly focused on that very problem. In contrast, few other sources mention it at all. This leads us to the conclusion that in many cases, non-modularized continuous integration is the default alternative, possibly even adopted without being consciously chosen.

2.3.2.12 Pre-integration Procedure

The pre-integration procedure of continuous integration refers to which actions are prescribed prior to performing an integration, e.g. by checking in source code. In some cases, these procedures can be practically non-existent, with one source arguing that the benefit of continuous integration can be measured as the time saved by developers not compiling and testing before checking in [326]. Others offer the option without prescribing any mandatory process, with developers running small subsets of tests rather than waiting for the centrally executed test suite [188]. It is also related how developers "typically [...] run tests before checking in changes" [57] and that "developers could ensure their check-in [...] both by manually compiling the code [...] and by executing the set of unit tests, [but] few did so" [94]. These examples appear to share the sentiment that "fundamentally, it needs to be acceptable to break the build" [380].

Other sources provide examples or mandatory pre-integration procedures, where developers are obliged "to integrate their own contributions properly" [187]. This can take various forms, such as reviews before checking in [94, 212], running light-weight "developer builds" [371], performing "a pre-check [...] before committing" [487] or "[ensuring that] all corresponding unit tests are successful" [12]. One source stresses the importance of testing before integration, fearing that the alternative "would be a nightmare" [261], while [495] describes a checklist of mandatory activities, where before committing any code, the developers must compile the whole system, design and code the needed unit and integration tests, and finally execute the entire unit and integration test suites.

Clearly, there are stark contrasts in what procedures are required before integrating. One source remarks on this, stating that it is "a common approach [to] institute a strict and thorough precommit procedure that will make it as hard as possible for developers to break the build", but that such procedures also have negative side effects [380]. The automation of pre-integration procedures is also discussed, since the developers "may forget [or] may not follow the practices" [12].

2.3.2.13 Scope

By scoping of continuous integration we refer to the amount and type of activities included in the practice, either as part of a single "build", or separated into several stages (see Sect. 2.3.2.15). Typically the compilation (where applicable) of source code followed by testing is included [1, 12, 30, 50, 57, 65, 74, 94, 154, 182, 185, 187, 188, 193, 212, 241, 242, 244, 272, 280, 307, 318, 326, 357, 371, 375, 379, 380, 442, 443, 445, 454, 467, 468, 495] — even in sources that do not explicitly state this, it is to our understanding often implicitly the case. The tests are frequently combined with static and/or dynamic code analysis [65, 182, 188, 241, 318, 326, 487], even though this can be considered to be "Continuous Measurement" and therefore not part of the scope of continuous integration itself [212].

The types of tests executed varies: some only run automated unit test suites [50, 182, 318, 326], others also run integration tests [12, 29, 94, 188, 193, 280, 473, 487], functional and/or non-functional system tests [29, 65, 188, 443] and/or acceptance tests [65, 188, 375, 442, 473]. Continuous integration can also involve creating installation packages [74, 148, 326, 357], so that a release "boils down to selecting the desired build" [467], and deploying the project [1, 74, 93, 148, 154, 272, 318, 357, 379, 442, 445]. It shall be noted, however, that the term "deployment" in this context is loosely defined and may refer to different activities.

In conclusion, we consider merely compiling and unit testing to be the basic continuous integration "build" activities. Then, other activities can be added on top of this, including but not limited to various types of more advanced testing, code analysis, packaging and deployment. Indeed, it's essentially possible "to chuck everything into [the build], including the kitchen sink" [380].

2.3.2.14 Status Communication

There are various approaches to communicating the continuous integration status, e.g. sending notifications of build failures [93, 307], in development projects. Dispatching e-mails is common [94, 148, 185, 241, 242, 442, 443], either notifying the last person to check in [1], "relevant developers" [495] or "the whole development [project]" [261]. Other communication methods can be used, such as RSS [442], web pages [466] or dashboards [29]. This may then be displayed on "information radiators" [1, 94, 154, 185], making the current status visible to all in the vicinity. Other methods include differently colored lava lamps and robotic dogs walking up to the responsible developers, "[displaying] to the team that it is not happy with that developer, in a friendly, funny and playful way" [1].

One source extensively discusses and evaluates differences in notification methods, and concludes that a combination of multiple communication channels can have a great impact on awareness of and responsiveness to broken builds [95].

2.3.2.15 Test Separation

Test separation refers to the practice of segmenting test suites into multiple parallel or sequential activities. Similar to the case of modularization (see Sect. 2.3.2.11), sources that touch upon this issue tend to be positive examples, and it is difficult to find explicit statements to the effect that testing is *not* separated, although to our understanding this is the case in a number of the articles in the study. That being said, one source argues that even though it's common to have "a single integration process that compiles the code, runs the unit tests and the acceptance tests, builds deployment packages for QA and the customer, validates code coverage and checks coding standards amongst other things" [380], this isn't necessarily a good thing, as they increase the build duration (see Sect. 2.3.2.1) and thereby delay feedback. Consequently, tests are sometimes separated into multiple activities.

One separation approach is to "segment tests by functional area and to only run those tests thought to be affected by the code change" [57] or to split test suites by components [244]. Commonly tests are separated into sequential stages based on the time it takes to execute them and the context in which they run [57, 443, 445, 495], e.g. "one an 'express build' that just runs unit tests to give a basic idea of the success of an integration; another a longer 'full' build that actually runs database processes, acceptance tests, deployments, etc." [375], or slower tests are performed on a different schedule altogether [454, 487]. Another source states in passing that continuous integration "is the automation of sequential build process steps" [93], which could be interpreted as implying that automated steps are linked together in a chain of sequential stages, but is ultimately too ambiguous to be included in the statement cluster.

2.3.2.16 Testing of New Functionality

Some sources in the study describe testing in continuous integration as primarily safe-guarding legacy functionality [94] by "[testing] against a suite of automated regression tests" [1]. Continuous integration can, however, be used for validating new functionality as well, by creating the automated test cases before the production code is implemented [188, 280, 495], or in parallel with the implementation [154, 442, 443, 454].

Some sources discuss the use of test-driven development, e.g. stating that "writing failing unit tests prior to writing any production code, then writing only enough production code to make the test pass" is required practice [148], yet do not explicitly describe the practice in relation to continuous integration and could therefore not be included in the statement cluster.

2.4 A Descriptive Model

It is apparent that continuous integration implementations vary in a multitude of ways. Consequently, we conclude that to derive more value from studies and discussions on continuous integration and its effects, more comprehensive information about the actual particular implementation or implementations at hand is required. In this section we propose a model, or guide, for how to better document the practice, that is designed to address every one of the variation points discovered in the systematic review (see Sect. 2.3.2). The model consists of two parts: the Integration Flow Anatomy — depicting activity and input nodes and their relationships (see Sect. 2.4.1) — and the Node Attributes applying to those nodes (see Sect. 2.4.2). Both of these parts, together forming the complete descriptive model, are detailed in turn below, as well as how they were designed and which variation points they cover. Following this there is a discussion on how to use a sub-set of the attributes and possible constraints (see Sect. 2.4.3).

As an alternative to defining a new model, existing ways of representing variability were also considered, with particular attention paid to the COVAMOF framework [413]. We consider the problem of representing activities, their scope, relationships and characteristics in a software integration process, however, to be a much simpler one than that of modeling e.g. variability, dependencies and interactions of software components. In addition, not all concepts (e.g. dependencies and realizations) necessarily translate well across the problem domains. Consequently, we have opted for the model described in this section.

2.4.1 Integration Flow Anatomy

A number of statements found in the systematic review touch upon how a "build" may consist of large numbers of interconnected steps, performing various tasks, which conditionally trigger each other. These steps may be executed in parallel or in sequence, or run on different schedules altogether. They may concern themselves with the entire product, or with separate components. As one of the articles in the study explains, this can be thought of as a directed acyclic graph (DAG) [30].

We find that by using such a DAG to depict the steps, or activities, of an integration process, several questions can be answered. Therefore, a meta-model was constructed with the aim of being able to accurately reflect all the variants possible from the variation points discovered in the systematic review. This meta-model is shown in Fig. 2.1. It consists of two types of nodes: Input (e.g. source code) and Activity (e.g. execution of test cases). Activities may be triggered by either input or activity nodes, with the conditions under which the trigger is activated (e.g. the source activity succeeded or failed) documented. Furthermore, both activity and input nodes contain a set of attributes describing their scope and characteristics.

The nodes themselves and their triggering relationships can be used to answer questions pertaining to the variation points of modularization and build triggering (see Sects. 2.3.2.11 and 2.3.2.3 respectively). Section 2.4.2 describes how the remainder of the variation points are covered by adding attributes to the nodes.

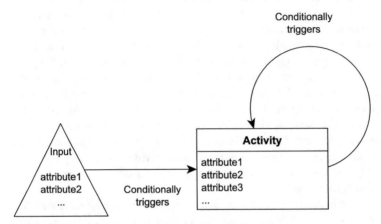

Fig. 2.1 The meta-model of the descriptive model. Note that the attribute set of either node type is flexible: the depicted model contains all attributes required to address the uncovered variation points (see Sect. 2.4.2), but both sub-sets and super-sets are conceivable

2.4.2 Node Attributes

This section presents a set of attributes, grouped into themes, for the activity and input nodes of the Integration Flow Anatomy (see Sect. 2.4.1). These attributes are derived from the variation points uncovered in the literature review (see Sect. 2.3.2). As each group of attributes is presented below the reasoning behind it and the variation points addressed by each attribute is explained.

It shall be noted that, when applying the model, the actual attribute set used may vary — with the information conveyed by the descriptive model varying accordingly — depending on the scope and purpose of the application of the model. A study focusing, for example, solely on the communication aspects of a particular integration flow may choose to exclude attributes deemed irrelevant to that purpose. This is further discussed in Sect. 2.4.3.

2.4.2.1 Scope Attributes

The scope theme of attributes applies to the activity nodes and addresses the scope (see Sect. 2.3.2.13), test separation (see Sect. 2.3.2.15) and testing of new functionality (see Sect. 2.3.2.16). The following attributes are designed to fully cover these variation points:

- legacy-testing: A list of testing activities applied to legacy code. Different nomenclature is used by different sources — testing activities mentioned by articles in the study include e.g. unit, acceptance, system, integration, performance and function tests.
- new-functionality-testing: A list of testing activities applied to functionality that is not yet fully implemented or considered legacy. Definitions of what constitutes legacy may vary.
- analysis: A list of analysis activities carried out, e.g. static code analysis or test coverage measurements.
- packaging: A boolean signifying whether the product is packaged and made ready for deployment.
- deployment: A list of environments (e.g. a lab environment or live customer systems) to which the product is deployed as part of this activity.

The legacy-testing and new-functionality-testing attributes are derived from both the test separation and testing of new functionality variation points. Since test activities may be split across multiple different steps, it's important to document in the DAG which nodes contain which types of testing. Also, since it's evident that projects treat testing of new functionality differently, the test activities need to be documented in two separate attributes for legacy and new functionality respectively.

The analysis, packaging and deployment attributes all address the scope variation point. Apart from testing, these are the three areas where the systematic review shows that the scope differs, and so these attributes are included in order to clearly show which, if any, of the tasks of analysis, packaging and deployment are performed in any given activity node.

2.4.2.2 Build Characteristics Attributes

The build characteristics theme contains questions pertaining to build duration (see Sect. 2.3.2.1), build frequency (see Sect. 2.3.2.2), integration frequency (see Sect. 2.3.2.7), integration on broken builds (see Sect. 2.3.2.8) and integration serialization and batching (see Sect. 2.3.2.9). To answer these questions, we propose that the following attributes shall be applied to the activity nodes:

- duration: The average duration of the activity.
- execution-frequency: The execution frequency of the activity.
- trigger-frequency: The triggering frequency of the activity.
- batching-allowed: A boolean signifying whether integrations may be batched into single builds.
- trigger-modifiers: A list of descriptions of possible modifiers to the activity's triggering behavior.

The duration attribute reflects the time required to execute an activity and addresses the build duration variation point. Similarly to the scope of the entire continuous integration being equal to the union of its constituent parts, its duration is then equal to the total duration of the activity nodes on its critical path.

Furthermore, though seemingly similar, execution-frequency and trigger-frequency are treated as separate attributes, corresponding to the separate variation points of build frequency and integration frequency. The former documents how often an activity is *executed*, whereas the latter how often it is *triggered*. Depending on the type of trigger this metric obviously has different meanings: in a situation where the trigger is a source code change it shows the frequency at which new content is integrated, whereas if it's a new version of a component being published it shows the frequency at which that component is being made available for integration with the larger system. Regardless it's informative — in particular, it's relevant to the batching-allowed attribute (corresponding to the variation point of integration serialization and batching): where the integrations frequency is higher than the build frequency, does one batch those integrations into a single build or not?

Finally, the trigger-modifiers attribute is derived from the variation point of integration on broken builds. Here any impact of the activity's state or context on the trigger, e.g. failures blocking new incoming changes unless they are flagged as fixes, should be documented.

2.4.2.3 Result Handling Attributes

Like the build characteristics theme of attributes (see Sect. 2.4.2.2), result handling attributes apply to each individual activity node (see Sect. 2.4.1). This theme covers the definition of failure and success (see Sect. 2.3.2.4), fault handling (see Sect. 2.3.2.6), fault duration (see Sect. 2.3.2.5) and status communication (see Sect. 2.3.2.14). In order to address these variation points, we propose the following attributes:

- result-definition: A list of possible results and their definitions.
- status-communication: A description of when, how and to whom the activity's status is communicated.
- fault-handling: A description of how discovered faults are addressed: by whom, and given what priority.
- fault-duration: The average duration of unbroken faulty status of the activity.

The result-definition attribute describes what is considered e.g. a faulty or successful execution of the activity. As possible outcomes may vary, a description shall be given per outcome. Status-communication, fault-handling and fault-duration all address their corresponding variation points.

2.4.2.4 Input Node Attributes

This section describes the proposed attributes that apply to the input nodes of the model. The relevant variation points in this context are pre-integration procedure (see Sect. 2.3.2.12) and integration target (see Sect. 2.3.2.10). From these the following two attributes are derived:

- pre-integration-procedure: A description of the procedure required before integrating changes.
- integration-target: A description of where the integration takes place (e.g. which branch and the rules governing it).

The pre-integration-procedure attribute describes what, if anything, the developer must do in order to integrate, and thereby create the change-set that serves as input to the activities of the integration flow. The integration-target attribute, on the other hand, describes whether the context of that integration is e.g. a team branch or a "mainline" branch.

2.4.3 Attribute Selection and Constraints

We recognize that it is not always desirable, practical or even possible to assemble all the data required by the full list of attributes proposed above. This is the reason why the meta-model does not prescribe any mandatory attributes. Obviously, the more complete the model, the more information and potential value it brings, but none of the proposed attributes explicitly requires any of the other in order to be valid or meaningful. A hypothetical descriptive model containing only a sub-set of attributes is shown in Fig. 2.2 to serve as a simple illustrative example.

On a further note, we have not identified any definite constraints in the sense of invalid or impossible attribute combinations creating invalid areas in the attribute space. However, this does not rule out that such areas, or areas that in practice are unpopulated, exist. In future work, we intend to investigate this further by means of gathering empirical data through multiple-case studies (see Sect. 2.6.4.3).

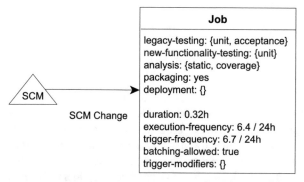

Fig. 2.2 A descriptive model, containing all proposed scope and build characteristics attributes, of a hypothetical simple integration flow

2.5 Illustrative Case Study

This section describes how the model proposed in Sect. 2.4 was applied to a development project, in this article referred to as Project A, within Ericsson AB. The assembled model and its data is not presented in its entirety in this article — instead, the purpose is to illustrate the steps involved in assembling the model and to present an example of how those steps may play out and the insights such an exercise may provide.

It shall be understood that the descriptive model (see Sect. 2.4) is not based on this case study, but on a systematic review (see Sect. 2.2.1). Neither is it intended as a complete validation of the model, beyond demonstrating that it can be applied with positive results. Furthermore, conducting the case study did not give cause for revising the model.

2.5.1 Project A

In Project A, multiple development teams are responsible for developing one of the components of a network node, with non-trivial integration dependencies to the other components of the node. The project was chosen as a case study candidate when one of the authors was invited to assist in improving its continuous integration implementation. In that situation, the model was used in order to establish the baseline implementation, and as a basis for identifying and planning improvement activities. Based on the multiple continuous integration case studies conducted in previous work [418] and our experience of industry software development, we deemed the project representative of industry practice and therefore suitable to serve as an illustrative example of application of the model.

2.5.2 Sketching the Integration Flow Anatomy

The first step of building the model was to sketch the Integration Flow Anatomy. This was done in front of a whiteboard, in collaboration with engineers working in the project, by analyzing the actual activities configured in Jenkins [213], their continuous integration tool. By studying how the Jenkins activities, or Projects, related to each other and their contents we were quickly able to create a graph of the component's entire flow (see Fig. 2.3), including its internal delivery to another part of the organization, and also determine the scope attributes of the activity nodes. During this work it soon became evident that the emerging anatomy had not been entirely clear to the project members themselves beforehand, which shows that this in itself can be a rewarding exercise from an educational point of view. It was also discovered that the delivery from D1 (see Fig. 2.3) to the receiving organization was done manually and that not much data on this was available. Consequently this was identified by the engineers as a prioritized area of the project's integration to improve.

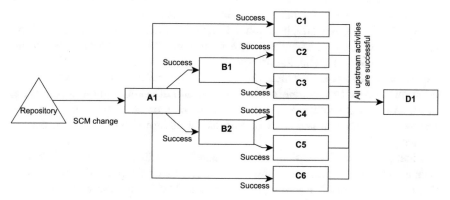

Fig. 2.3 The Integration Flow Anatomy of Project A. Activity D1 was followed by a manual delivery to another part of the organization, which was outside the scope of the case study. The figure only shows the anatomy itself, with all node attributes deliberately left out

2.5.3 Determining the Input Node Attributes

Following the Integration Flow Anatomy, the attributes of the input node was discussed. This took the form of an unstructured interview between the authors and the project's engineers, with the authors asking for descriptions of the current pre-integration-procedure and integration-target (see Sect. 2.4.2.4) in Project A. With regards to the integration-target attribute, it was suggested by the engineers themselves that the current implementation, where a "develop" branch was used both as the integration branch for all the developers and as the release branch from which deliveries were picked, might prove to be unsuitable in the future. It was agreed, however, that in the project's current early stage of development this solution was adequate, but that it may have to be revised in the future.

2.5.4 Determining the Activity Node Attributes

All the build characteristics attributes (see Sect. 2.4.2.2) for the activity nodes could be gathered by the authors themselves by analyzing the configuration of the project's continuous integration tool, Jenkins. One insight gained while collecting the trigger-modifiers information was that the first activity, A1, was in Jenkins configured as being part of the same "Project" (the entity used to configure an activity in Jenkins) as D1, meaning that A1 wouldn't be ready to start work on new changes until all other activities had finished. The consequence of this was that the entire flow became serial, in the sense that it was unable to work on more than a single change-set at any given time. It was concluded that this was a problem that should be addressed, not least because it caused under-utilization of available hardware.

Furthermore, this example illustrates how activities in the Integration Flow Anatomy may not necessarily map directly to e.g. Jenkins Projects — rather, the activities in the model should correspond to how the project members themselves would conceptually describe their integration flow. It may be argued, then, that if that description doesn't easily translate into how the activity entities of one's continuous integration tool are configured, then this should be seen as an indication that there may be a problem with said configuration, as indeed turned out to be the case in the studied project.

Finally, in a second session, the result handling attributes (see Sect. 2.4.2.3) of each activity in the integration flow was discussed with the project's engineers. In this project, the Result Handling of all the activities in the flow were similar — for instance, the status of all activities considered relevant were visualized in real time using a special information radiator functionality in the continuous integration tool, thereby made available to all stakeholders. Also, while failure in any activity would cause mails to be sent out to all developers and project support staff, it was a dedicated team's responsibility to act on those failures, and then escalate to developers if deemed necessary. Though it was said that this may not be the best solution, and that it would be better if the developers themselves had the mindset to take that responsibility directly, the result handling in the project was considered satisfactory and no urgent improvement needs were identified.

2.6 Conclusion

This section presents the conclusions of the conducted literature review, the model proposal, the illustrative case study and remaining questions left unanswered.

2.6.1 Disagreements in Related Work

It is clear from the conducted literature review that there is currently no consensus on continuous integration as a single, homogeneous practice. Out of the 22 statement clusters synthesized from statements extracted from the included articles, differences and/or disagreements were evident in all but six (see Sect. 2.3). Not only does this mean that, in order to make a meaningful comparison of software development projects, simply stating that they use continuous integration is insufficient information as we instead need to ask ourselves what kind of continuous integration is used. It also means that, taking into account the dramatic differences in experienced continuous integration effects [418], we need to ask which aspects or variants of continuous integration any proposed benefit (or disadvantage) is an effect of. For this purpose, based on the findings in our study, we have proposed a descriptive model for better documentation of continuous integration variants.

2.6.2 Model Proposal

In this paper we have proposed a descriptive model of continuous integration implementations, based on variation points evident in literature. We believe that using this model will enable us to better understand implementations of continuous integration and how they compare to each other. This in turn is a prerequisite for studying correlations between differences in those implementations and differences in their experienced effects. If we are to reach a level understanding where a development project is able to pro-actively and confidently design its continuous integration according to the benefits it wishes to maximize, then this is an important step on that path. That being said, it is also clear that applying the model to one's own integration flow, with or without comparing it to others, can be a valuable and educational experience, as it may provide insights into one's own development process.

2.6.3 Model Validation

We have demonstrated through an illustrative case study the applicability of the model proposed in this article to an industry development project, and that tangible benefits can be derived from it. Not only did the model bring to light the actual anatomy and characteristics of the integration flow in the project — something that had thitherto been an opaque part of the environment for a number of the project members — but it was also able to indicate areas where opportunities for improvement could be found and served as a basis for the planning of activities to pursue those improvements.

That being said, however, while the research presented in this article demonstrates that disparity in multiple areas exists, the sample size is insufficient to fully understand their distribution and consequently the actual space of variations. Also, we do not assume that we have identified every possible variation point in this research. There may still be important differentiators not yet included in the model, particularly as continuous integration as exercised by practitioners may well evolve in the future. Therefore, additional data provided by further case studies would help in improving our understanding of not only the value ranges and statistical distribution of the model's attributes, but could also uncover attributes that are as of yet missing. Based on the case studies conducted in previous work [418] and our professional experience we expect such case studies to allow refinement of the proposed model, but not lead to major disruption.

In conclusion, we would consider future case studies applying the model to a larger number of industry software development projects to be an important contribution, both in that they would serve to further validate and refine the model and at the same time provide additional data points in the study of continuous integration itself — in particular, we find that comparative case studies of multiple implementations are lacking in contemporary literature.

2.6.4 Open Questions for Further Research

A number of questions still remain unanswered in the field of continuous integration.

2.6.4.1 Correlations Between Differences in Practice and Differences in Experience

In previous work [418] we have identified disagreement among software development professionals as to the benefits of continuous integration experienced in their projects. In the research presented in this article we have further demonstrated that continuous integration implementations themselves may differ. Consequently, what we ask ourselves is whether there is a correlation between these differences in experience on the one hand, and differences in implementation on the other. Would it be possible to improve our understanding in such a way that we can not only present a model for describing variants of the practice, but also demonstrate that these variants allow for different effects? If so, could that be used to allow industry professionals to decide which flavor of continuous integration they should strive for, based on the benefits they prioritize?

We are still far from such an understanding of the practice. In order to get there we need a sufficient body of data detailing both experienced effects and the variation points of continuous integration in a number of projects utilizing continuous integration. We therefore propose that case studies be performed in this area.

2.6.4.2 Contextual Differences

Software development projects obviously differ in more ways than in how they have chosen or been able to implement continuous integration. They may be of varying size, longevity, budget, organizational structure, competence setup, geographic distribution etc. While the number of such conceivable variation points may be nearly infinite, it is nevertheless possible that some of them interact with the variation points of continuous integration. It may be that certain contextual factors enable or are enabled by particular variants of continuous integration, or that they influence the very interpretation of the continuous integration concept.

We believe that case studies investigating such relationships in the industry would be a valuable contribution in this area.

2.6.4.3 Internal Constraints and Correlations of the Model

We have proposed a model containing a number of attributes, grouped into themes, covering the variation points where we have shown that continuous integration implementations can and do differ. What is not understood is how, if at all, these variation points correlate. It is conceivable that some variants enable or disable each other, or certain variants tend to manifest together, allowing us to cluster them an identify "typical species" of continuous integration. Conversely, it is possible that constraints exist such that certain areas of the combinatorial space created by these attributes are invalid, or unpopulated in practice.

It could also be that some of the variation points identified in this research are so tightly coupled that they can be better understood as different manifestation of the same underlying practice, thereby allowing variation points to be merged and the model simplified.

Our understanding of these questions would be furthered by access to larger sets of empirical data. To this end, we propose multiple-case studies to be conducted, where the proposed model is applied and any constraints and correlations are searched for.

Acknowledgements

We would like to thank Ericsson AB for allowing us to study one of their software development projects and publishing our findings. We also want to thank our colleagues for all their feedback and the patience they have demonstrated during our research.

Chapter 3
Efficient and Effective Exploratory Testing of Large-Scale Software Systems

Torvald Mårtensson, Daniel Ståhl, Antonio Martini, and Jan Bosch

Abstract

Context: Exploratory testing plays an important role in the continuous integration and delivery pipelines of large-scale software systems, but a holistic and structured approach is needed to realize efficient and effective exploratory testing.

Objective: This paper seeks to address the need for a structured and reliable approach by providing a tangible model, supporting practitioners in the industry to optimize exploratory testing in each individual case.

Method: The reported study includes interviews, group interviews and workshops with representatives from six companies, all multi-national organizations with more than 2,000 employees.

Results: The ExET model (Excellence in Exploratory Testing) is presented. It is shown that the ExET model allows companies to identify and visualize strengths and improvement areas. The model is based on a set of key factors that have been shown to enable efficient and effective exploratory testing of large-scale software systems, grouped into four themes: "The testers' knowledge, experience and personality", "Purpose and scope", "Ways of working" and "Recording and reporting".

Conclusions: The validation of the ExET model showed that the model is novel, actionable and useful in practice, showing companies what they should prioritize in order to enable efficient and effective exploratory testing in their organization.

Reprinted with permission from Elsevier. Originally published in Journal of Systems and Software Volume 174, April 2021 DOI: https://doi.org/10.1016/j.jss.2020.110890

J. Bosch et al. (eds.), *Accelerating Digital Transformation*,
https://doi.org/10.1007/978-3-031-10873-0_4

3.1 Introduction

3.1.1 Background and Related Work

Continuous Delivery was popularized as a term by Humble and Farley [196], who state that in continuous delivery "every change is, in fact, a release candidate". Even though we in our previous work [424] have found that there is some confusion around the terminology, we find that the most common interpretation is that continuous delivery is about ensuring that the software can be released and deployed to production at any time, but may not actually be thus released and/or deployed. Humble and Farley [196] describe the principles behind continuous delivery, and the practices necessary to support it. The central paradigm of the book is the integration pipeline (also referred to as the deployment pipeline). The pipeline, as described by Humble and Farley, consists primarily of automated test activities, but also includes usability testing and exploratory testing.

Exploratory testing was coined as a term by Cem Kaner in the book "Testing Computer Software" [226], and was then expanded upon as a teachable discipline by Cem Kaner, James Bach and Bret Pettichord in their book "Lessons Learned in Software Testing" [227]. Exploratory testing combines test design with test execution, and focuses on learning about the system under test. The test technique is focused on learning, shown in for example Hendrickson's [178] definition of exploratory testing: "Simultaneously designing and executing tests to learn about the system, using your insights from the last experiment to inform the next". Gregory and Crispin [161] describe how exploratory testing and automated testing complement each other: "Exploratory testing and automation aren't mutually exclusive but rather work in conjunction. Automation handles the day-to-day repetitive regression testing (checking), which enables the exploratory testers to test all the things the team didn't think about before coding".

James Bach emphasizes that exploratory testing should not be mistaken for unstructured testing [22]. Different setups have been presented for planning, execution and reporting exploratory testing: testing can be organized as charters [161, 178] or tours [161, 477] which are conducted as sessions [161, 178] or threads [161].

3.1.2 Research Question

In our previous work [294] we have shown that exploratory testing plays an important role in the continuous integration and delivery pipeline for a large-scale software system. Whereas automated test activities in the pipeline are able to rapidly provide feedback to developers and to verify requirements, exploratory testing can provide more in-depth insights about the system under test. In a study based on both quantitative and qualitative data, we developed a test method for exploratory testing of large-scale systems, validated in a large-scale industry project [294].

Since our previous study on exploratory testing, we have identified a growing interest in exploratory testing from several of the companies we as researchers work with, and an interest to improve how the test technique is used in the companies. A holistic and structured approach is lacking that can point out the most important problem areas in each individual case. Based on this, the topic of this research paper is to answer the following research question:

- *RQ1: How can efficient and effective exploratory testing be realized in industrial organizations?*

In order to work with RQ1 in a step-by-step approach, the research question was during the study broken down into the following detailed research questions:

- *RQ1.1: How are key factors that enable efficient and effective exploratory testing of large-scale software systems described in literature?*
- *RQ1.2: What are, according to practitioners in industry, the key factors that enable efficient and effective exploratory testing of large-scale software systems?*
- *RQ1.3: How can a model be constructed to support practitioners in the industry to optimize exploratory testing in each individual case?*

3.1.3 Contribution

The contribution of this paper is two-fold: First, it presents results from interviews and workshops with participants from six case study companies, that can give researchers and practitioners an improved understanding how exploratory testing is used in large-scale industry projects. Second, it presents a new model (the ExET model) that can be used by practitioners in industry to identify and visualize strengths and improvement areas, which can be used to optimize exploratory testing in each individual case.

In this paper, we have built upon our previous work [293], introducing the ExET model (Excellence in Exploratory Testing) based on the nine identified key factors. The model is presented with a two-step process describing how the ExET model is used, and the validation of the ExET model (industrial evaluation). This paper also includes a more extensive presentation of the research method and a more extensive analysis of threats to validity. The five steps in the reported study and the results from each step are further described in Sect. 3.2.1.

The remainder of this paper is organized as follows: In the next section, we present the research method. This is followed in Sect. 3.3 by a study of related literature. In Sect. 3.4 we present the analysis of the interview results (the list of key factors), followed by a summary of the follow-up interviews and the cross-company workshop in Sect. 3.5. The ExET model is presented in Sect. 3.6, followed by a presentation of the validation of the ExET model in Sect. 3.7. Threats to validity are discussed in Sect. 3.8. The paper is then concluded in Sect. 3.9.

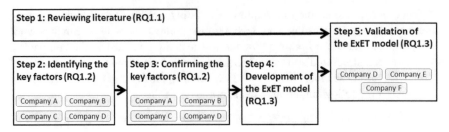

Fig. 3.1 An overview of the research method

3.2 Research Method

3.2.1 Overview of the Research Method

The research study reported in this paper consists of five major steps:

- *Step 1: Reviewing literature:* A literature review to investigate if any key factors that can enable efficient and effective exploratory testing have been previously presented in literature (presented in Sect. 3.3).
- *Step 2: Identifying the key factors:* A series of interviews to identify key factors that enable efficient and effective exploratory testing of large-scale software systems (presented in Sect. 3.4.
- *Step 3: Confirming the key factors:* A second series of follow-up interviews and a cross-company workshop in order to confirm the interpretation of the first series of interviews, as well as looking for negative cases (presented in Sect. 3.5).
- *Step 4: Development of the ExET model:* Analysis of the results from the two series of interviews, and development of the Excellence in Exploratory Testing (ExET) model (presented in Sect. 3.6).
- *Step 5: Validation of the ExET model:* Validation of the ExET model: Validation of the ExET model in interviews and workshops, and a comparison with the literature reviews (presented in Sect. 3.7). ·

An overview of the research method is presented in Fig. 3.1: As a first step, a literature review was conducted in order to look for solutions in published work. In parallel, a series of interviews was conducted to identify key factors that enable efficient and effective exploratory testing of large-scale software systems. This was followed by follow-up interviews and a cross-company workshop, to confirm the results from the first series of interviews. The development of the ExET model was based primarily on the results from the two series of interviews, as the literature review did not result in a comprehensive set of key factors. As the final step, the ExET model was validated with interviews and workshops, and a comparison with the literature review.

Figure 3.1 also shows how the steps of the study addresses the detailed research questions (defined in Sect. 3.1.2) and how the case study companies were included in the different steps of the study. The research method for each part of the study is further described in Sects. 3.2.2–3.2.6.

The study includes six case study companies, referred to as Company A, Company B, Company C, Company D, Company E and Company F. This study focuses on testing of functions fully or partly implemented in software. The six companies operate in the following industry segments:

- Company A: Automotive products and services
- Company B: Transport solutions for commercial use
- Company C: Video surveillance cameras and systems
- Company D: Services and solutions for military defense and civil security
- Company E: Communications systems and services
- Company F: Development, manufacturing and maintenance of pumps

The studied companies are all multi-national organizations with more than 2,000 employees. All companies develop large-scale and complex software systems for products, which also include a significant amount of mechanical and electronic systems. The companies were considered to be suitable for the study, as they have similar characteristics, but at the same time are operating in different industry segments.

The companies were selected as they wanted to increase the amount of exploratory testing in their organization, and improve the ways in which exploratory testing was used. The validation cases in Company D, Company E and Company F were purposely selected for the external validation, as they were separated from the primary studies.

3.2.2 Reviewing Literature

To investigate whether solutions related to the research question have been presented in published literature, a literature review was conducted, following the guidelines established by Kitchenham [245]. A review protocol was created, containing the question driving the review ("How are key factors that enable efficient and effective exploratory testing of large-scale software systems described in literature?") and the inclusion and exclusion criteria (see Table 3.1). The review was purposely designed to search for key factors that can enable efficient and effective exploratory testing (i.e. not necessarily presented as a method or a model) in order to include all types of material that could be relevant to the research question defined in Sect. 3.1. The stages of the review (according to the guidelines from Kitchenham) were:

- *Identification of research:* Iterative analysis of title, abstract and keywords of publications from trial searches using various combinations of search terms.
- *Selection of primary studies:* Exclusion of duplicates and conference proceedings summaries.
- *Study quality assessment:* The relevance of the selected research papers was assessed in a first review of each paper, and papers considered to be not relevant were excluded.

- *Data extraction & monitoring:* Characteristics and content of the remaining research papers were documented in an iterative process.
- *Data synthesis:* The results from the review were collated and summarized.

The analysis of the results from the literature review was conducted iteratively in a two-step process, involving three of the researchers in order to secure quality and correctness.

The results from the literature review was a better understanding of previously published literature related to the research question, which later in the study was used as input to the validation of the ExET model.

Table 3.1 Inclusion and exclusion criteria for the literature review

Inclusion criteria	Yield
Publications matching the Scopus search string TITLE-ABS-KEY ("exploratory testing") on October 27, 2018	129

Exclusion criteria	Remaining
Excluding duplicates and conference proceedings summaries	122
Excluding publications not related to development of software systems	71
Excluding publications with no available full-text	65

3.2.3 Identifying the Key Factors

In order to find a solution for the research question presented in Sect. 3.1, a series of interviews were conducted to identify a set of key factors that enable efficient and effective exploratory testing of large-scale software systems. The interviews included 20 individuals from four of the case study companies (Company A, Company B, Company C and Company D). Five interviewees participated from Company A, three from Company B, six from Company C and six from Company D. All of the interviewees had experiences from exploratory testing as testers, and in some cases also as test leaders. The interviews lasted from half an hour up to (in most cases) one hour. They were conducted as semi-structured interviews, using an interview guide with pre-defined specific questions (interview guide 1 in Appendix). The interview questions were designed to provide information leading to the identification of key factors, but also to provide background information about the interviewee and how exploratory testing was used in the interviewee's organization. The interviewer was summarizing and transcribing the interviewee's response during the interview, and each response was read back to the interviewee to ensure accuracy. The interview questions were sent to the interviewee at least one day in advance.

The main question in the interview guide (Q1.6) asked the interviewees to describe the key factors they believed can enable efficient and effective exploratory testing of large-scale software systems. The responses for Q1.6 included a large amount of statements and comments. The interview results were analyzed based on thematic coding analysis as described by Robson and McCartan [376], outlined in the following bullets:

- *Familiarizing with the data:* Reading and re-reading the transcripts, noting down initial ideas.
- *Generating initial codes:* Extracts from the transcripts are marked and coded in a systematic fashion across the entire data set.
- *Identifying themes:* Collating codes into potential themes, gathering all data relevant to each potential theme. Checking if the themes work in relation to the coded extracts and the entire data set. Revising the initial codes and/or themes if necessary.
- *Constructing thematic networks:* Developing a thematic 'map' of the analysis.
- *Integration and interpretation:* Making comparisons between different aspects of the data displayed in networks (clustering and counting statements and comments, attempting to discover the factors underlying the process under investigation, exploring for contrasts and comparisons). Revising the thematic map if necessary. Assessing the quality of the analysis.

The process was conducted iteratively to increase the quality of the analysis, reaching consensus within the group of researchers through discussions and visualization in diagrams and text. Comments and statements from the interviewees were as a first step sorted into categories, which during the process were reorganized into new structures. For example, statements regarding a test environment suitable for debugging and statements regarding tools for recording for were originally handled separately, but were then merged into the same category. The remaining nine themes were then described, with two or three representative quotes selected from the transcripts included in the descriptions. Special attention was paid to outliers (interviewee comments that do not fit into the overall pattern) according to the guidelines from Robson and McCartan [376] in order to strengthen the explanations and isolate the mechanisms involved.

The results from the analysis of the first series of interviews was a list of identified key factors which can enable efficient and effective exploratory testing.

3.2.4 Confirming the Key Factors

The next step of the study was follow-up interviews with the same 20 individuals as the first series of interviews, to collect feedback on the identified key factors. The purpose of the follow-up interviews was to confirm that the interpretation of the first series of interviews was correct, as well as looking for negative cases.

The interviews in the second series of interviews lasted for about half an hour, and were conducted in a similar way as the first series of interviews: The interviews were semi-structured interviews, using an interview guide with pre-defined specific questions (interview guide 2 in Appendix). The interview questions were designed to provide information about how the identified key factors were received by the interviewee. The interviewer was summarizing and transcribing the interviewee's response during the interview, and each response was read back to the interviewee to ensure accuracy. The interview questions were sent to the interviewee at least one day in advance.

In order to achieve method and data triangulation [384], the follow-up interviews were complemented with a cross-company workshop with 14 participants representing all four case study companies participating in the two series of interviews (Company A, Company B, Company C and Company D). The participants at the workshop had roles in their companies as tester, test leader, test specialist and line manager. At the workshop, two of the researchers presented the results from the literature review and the two series of interviews. The workshop participants discussed the presented key factors, and discussed the identified differences between the companies.

Researcher bias could be a threat to reliability during the interpretation of interview results. This threat was mitigated with member checking (the follow-up interviews) and a focus group (the cross-company workshop) as described in Sect. 3.5, following the guidelines from Robson and McCartan [376] who consider this to be "a very valuable means of guarding against researcher bias" and a good way to "amplify and understand the findings".

The results from the analysis of the follow-up interviews and the cross-company workshop was a better understanding of the identified key factors, and confirmation of the validity of the key factors in the case study companies.

3.2.5 Development of the ExET Model

The Excellence in Exploratory Testing (ExET) model was developed primarily based on the analysis of the results from the two interview series described in Sects. 3.2.3 and 3.2.4, which included interviewees from Company A, Company B, Company C and Company D. The analysis and design process was conducted iteratively to increase the quality of the results.

The ExET model is a representation of strengths and improvement areas in an organization, which can be used to improve exploratory testing. The ExET model was designed to provide as much information as possible about the strengths and possible improvement areas in the organization. One factor (factor six) represents balance between freedom and structure, and was therefore split into two statements (6a and 6b) in order to isolate the root causes as much as possible.

The ExET model is used in a simple two-step process, in order to both involve the testers and the stakeholders for the test activities. A simplistic approach was purposely selected, based on our experiences and positive feedback received in the validation phases in our previous studies [295, 296].

The results from this part of the research study was a model (the ExET model) which can show companies what they should prioritize in order to optimize exploratory testing in their organization.

3.2.6 Validation of the ExET Model

The ExET model was validated using the following methods to achieve method and data triangulation according to the guidelines from Runeson and Höst [384]:

- *Validation interviews and workshops:* Interviews and workshops in five validation cases in three companies (Company D, Company E and Company F). The interviewees and workshop participants used the ExET model to evaluate the status in their organization to identify improvement areas. The purpose of the validation interviews and workshops was to evaluate if the ExET model was considered actionable and useful in practice.
- *Validation cross-company workshop:* A cross-company workshop with participants from all six companies in the study (Company A, Company B, Company C, Company D, Company E and Company F). The workshop participants discussed the results from the validation cases, further strengthening the reliability of the results from the study.
- *Comparison with literature review:* Comparison of the ExET model and related work found in literature, primarily to discuss the novelty of the ExET model.

The validation cases in Company D, Company E and Company F were purposely selected for the external validation as they are separated from the primary studies (resulting in the ExET model). The organization in each validation case wanted not just to improve how they used exploratory testing, but also to increase the amount of exploratory testing in the organization. The design of the validation of the ExET model is described in-depth in Sect. 3.7.1.

The validation interviews and workshops (in all validation cases) were held within a time-frame of three months, and the validation cross-company workshop about one month later. Altogether, all validation activities were conducted within a time frame of four months.

The results from the validation of the ExET model was an industrial evaluation of how the model delivers value to the industry, and identified suggestions for how the model can be improved.

3.3 Reviewing Literature

3.3.1 Criteria for the Literature Review

In order to investigate if any key factors that can enable efficient and effective exploratory testing have been previously presented in related work, a literature review [245] was conducted. The question driving the review was "How are key factors that enable efficient and effective exploratory testing of large-scale software systems described in literature?" The inclusion criterion and the exclusion criterion for the review are shown in Table 3.1. To identify published literature, a Scopus search was conducted. The decision to use only one indexing service was based on that we in previous work [420, 421, 423] have found Scopus to cover a large majority of published literature in the field, with other search engines only providing very small result sets not already covered by Scopus. This threat to validity is also discussed in Sect. 3.8.1.

Our previous work [294] includes a similar literature review, covering 52 publications. For the literature review in this study we expanded the search scope, which yielded 129 publications. After removing duplicates and conference proceedings summaries, the abstract of the remaining 122 publications were reviewed manually. Publications not related to development of software systems were excluded, i.e. removing publications related to archeology, chemistry et cetera. As a final stage, publications for which we could not find any available full-text were excluded from the literature review.

Characteristics and content of the remaining 65 research papers were then documented in a consistent manner in a data extraction protocol: for each paper a summary of how the paper was related to the research question, and representative keywords and quotes (sorted into categories which emerged during the process). The process was conducted iteratively to increase the quality of the analysis. Finally, the results from the review were collated and summarized.

3.3.2 Results from the Literature Review

An overview of the publications found in the literature review is presented in Table 3.2. The review of the 65 publications retrieved from the search revealed that nine of the publications were not directly related to exploratory testing (only mentioning exploratory testing in passing while discussing other test techniques).

Ten of the publications are comparing exploratory testing and other test techniques, typically comparing exploratory testing and scripted testing (also referred to as test case based testing, specification based testing or confirmatory testing). The comparisons were based on literature reviews, true experiments, and case studies from industry projects. The papers describe or touch upon the strengths and weak-

Table 3.2 An overview of the publications found in the literature review

Topic of the publications	Number of papers
Not relevant	9
Comparing exploratory testing and other test techniques	10
Methods	20
Tools	7
How exploratory testing is used	9
Reporting experiences	10
Summary	65

nesses of exploratory testing (e.g. Shah et al. [401]), but do generally not define key factors for efficient or effective exploratory testing.

Twenty publications propose new methods that in different ways involve or include a reference to exploratory testing. Eleven of those publications present new methods or approaches, which combine exploratory testing and another test technique [27, 63, 136, 144, 177, 195, 240, 256, 324, 370, 390]. These methods try to combine the flexibility of exploratory testing with the structure provided by scripted test cases. As one example, Frajtak et al. [136] describe that the testers can use "their skills and intuition to explore the system", but "it is hard to measure the effectiveness of the [exploratory] testing". As a solution, Frajtak et al. propose a technique where recording of the (exploratory) testers actions are used to create test case scenarios. Ghazi et al. [149] provide a different kind of structure, aiming to support practitioners in the design of test charters through checklists. Sviridova et al. [451] discuss effectiveness of exploratory testing and propose to use scenarios. The level of freedom in exploratory testing is discussed by Ghazi et al. [150], presenting a scale for the degree of exploration and defining five levels. Raappana et al. [363] report the effectiveness of a test method called "team exploratory testing", which is defined as a way to perform session-based exploratory testing in teams. One of the papers is our previous work [294], presenting a test method for exploratory testing of large-scale systems (as described in Sect. 3.1). Finally, Shah et al. [402] take a somewhat different approach, describing exploratory testing as a source of technical debt, and propose (as a solution to this problem) that exploratory testing should be combined with other testing approaches.

Seven of the publications present different types of tools, developed to increase the efficiency in exploratory testing. However, three of the papers does not include any validation of the presented tool. The remaining four papers describe tools developed to visualize how the executed testing covers the system under test [62, 137], visualize code changes in the system under test [372], and refine system models based on recorded testing activities [145].

Nine publications describe in different ways how exploratory testing is used by the testers. Four of those publications [146, 209, 210, 323] focus on the tester's knowledge and experience: Itkonen et al. [210] discuss how testers recognize failures based on their personal knowledge without detailed test case descriptions ("domain knowledge, system knowledge, and general software engineering knowledge"). Gebizli and Sözer [146] present results from a study showing that both educational background and experience level has "significant impact" on the efficiency and effectiveness of exploratory testing. In contrast to that, two papers [361, 407] focus on the tester's personality: Shoaib et al. [407] simply conclude that "people having extrovert personality types are good exploratory testers". Pfahl et al. [361] analyzes the results from an online survey, and finds that exploratory testing "is as an approach that supports creativity during testing and that is effective and efficient". Tuomikoski and Tervonen [460] embrace both approaches, stating that "the effectiveness of exploratory testing is strongly based on individual test engineer's skills and ability to analyze system and its behavior" but also that "exploratory testing doesn't fit for everyone, and really requires experienced test engineers".

Finally, ten papers report experiences from exploratory testing in industry, but without presenting any documented quantitative or qualitative data. Pichler and Ramler [362] present experiences from development of mobile devices, and find that "tool support enhances the capability of human testers". Kumar and Wallace [258] describe that for the exploratory tester, it is "easy to get lost in a thicket of well-intentioned heuristics", and proposes the use of "problem frames" as a solution for this problem.

In summary, we found no publication summarizing key factors that enable efficient and effective exploratory testing. Some of the identified papers discuss isolated factors, e.g. how the effectiveness of exploratory testing is based on the testers' knowledge and personality, or how tools can increase the efficiency in exploratory testing. However, the results from the literature review shows that previously published work lacks a holistic perspective and instead tend to focus on one aspect, leaving out areas that other authors consider to be the core issues.

3.4 Identifying the Key Factors

3.4.1 Background Information

The literature review (presented in Sect. 3.3) did not result in a comprehensive set of key factors. In order to find a solution for the research question presented in Sect. 3.1, a series of interviews were conducted to identify a set of key factors that enable efficient and effective exploratory testing of large-scale software systems. The key factors were later in the study used in the development of the ExET model, which is described in detail in Sect. 3.6.1.

The interviews were based on an interview guide with pre-defined specific questions (interview guide 1 in Appendix). Twenty individuals participated in the interviews, with an average of 13 years of experience of industry software development (spanning from 4 to 46 years). The interviewees all had experiences from exploratory testing as testers, and in some cases also as test leaders. The interviewees had a very positive attitude towards exploratory testing, rating "the value of exploratory testing as a test technique for large-scale software systems" as 4 or 5 on a Likert scale from 1 ("very low") to 5 ("very high").

Interviewees from all four case study companies described that exploratory testing was used for two purposes in their organization: to find bugs during development of new functions and systems, and for testing of the complete system. The interviewees described that exploratory testing was used primarily for new functions, whereas automated testing and manual scripted testing was used primarily for regression tests.

The interviewees were also asked to describe strengths and weaknesses with exploratory testing. Generally, the interviewees described that exploratory testing is a good way to find problems quickly and efficiently. Exploratory testing is also a more creative way to work for the testers, and was therefore considered to make better use of the testers. Exploratory testing was also described as a good way to test system-wide and to test large-scale systems, especially exploratory testing with an end-user perspective. The interviewees also described a few weaknesses with exploratory testing: Some interviewees described that they believed that exploratory testing was more difficult for new testers (as experience is more important). Another viewpoint was that it could be more difficult to describe what you have tested, compared to if you follow a scripted test case.

3.4.2 Key Factors for Efficient and Effective Exploratory Testing

The main question of the first series of interviews was: "What are the key factors that you think enable efficient and effective exploratory testing of large-scale software systems?" The responses for this question included a large amount of statements and comments. Extracts from the interview responses were sorted into categories, which during the process were reorganized into new structures (as described in Sect. 3.2.3). A thematic network were constructed [376], resulting in a thematic map with four main themes, which in turn consist of several sub-themes: a list of key factors which can enable efficient and effective exploratory testing.

The four main themes (groups of key factors) and their sub-themes (the key factors) are shown in Table 3.3, together with information about of how many interviewees that provided statements supporting each factor and group of factors.

All 20 interviewees talked about the importance of the *testers' knowledge, experience and personality*. In order to test the system, the testers must *know how the system is built, and the correct behavior of the system*. One interviewee asked for "testers with different types of experiences". Another voice asked for "good system knowledge". One interviewee described that the tester must have "test confidence", meaning that as a tester you should "trust your instinct that this is wrong". The testers must also *know how the product is used by the end-user* (or the end user should be represented in the test team). To quote one of the interviewees: "If you have the end-user perspective, then you know if a problem is a problem". One interviewee

Table 3.3 The nine key factors that can enable efficient and effective exploratory testing, and the number of interviewees that provided statements supporting each factor and group of factors

	Interviewees
The testers' knowledge, experience and personality	**20**
1. The testers know how the system is built, and the correct behavior of the system	14
2. The testers know how the product is used by the end-user (or the end user is represented in the test team)	12
3. The testers are curious and want to learn about the system	16
Purpose and scope	**18**
4. A well-defined purpose and scope for the tests (system functions ready to be tested) which the testers can transform into e.g. scenarios or focus areas	10
5. Regression testing secure basic stability and integrity in the system (before exploratory testing)	11
Ways of working	**14**
6. An established way of working, including e.g. planning meetings, preparations, test strategies and heuristics (a balance between structure and freedom)	10
7. Testers with different experiences and competences work together as a team, helping each other with new ideas and knowledge about different parts of the system	12
Recording and reporting	**17**
8. Test environments that support debugging and recording	10
9. A well-defined way to report the test results, including a description of areas covered by the tests and a list of identified problems	12

even stated that "you should always have the end-user perspective". The testers must also *be curious and want to learn about the system.* This means that even if the tester has good system knowledge, he/she still wants to learn more. The interviewees described that this calls for certain types of personalities, e.g. "the right personality, to be interested in new perspectives, curiosity, imagination". Some of the interviewees also described this as an interest in tracking down the problems in the system, e.g. "someone who want to find the bugs – curious and creative people".

As many as 18 interviewees did in different ways talk about the *purpose and scope* of the tests. This includes a *well-defined purpose and scope for the tests (system functions ready to be tested)* which the testers can transform into e.g. scenarios or focus areas. One interviewee described that "you should have a list of functions that should be tested". Several interviewees clarified that this should not be interpreted as that exploratory testing only could be used at a final stage of a project, and that this also affect development planning: "Test when the function is ready, and not too early. You must build the function in steps so it can be tested". Another interviewee had a similar comment: "Do exploratory testing early, but test complete functions". A related area is *regression testing to secure basic stability and integrity in the system* (before exploratory testing). Efficient regression testing finds problems in legacy functions (introduced due to dependencies between functions or systems). If this works well, skilled exploratory testers will not waste their time investigating and reporting problems with legacy functions, but can instead focus on testing the new functions. As one of interviewees put it: "Simple problems should be identified and corrected from automated testing". In the same way, the testers' time is not wasted at trouble-shooting problems that has already been analyzed. To quote one of the interviewees: "what is the status of the product, what are the known errors or problems".

Ways of working were discussed by 14 of the 20 interviewees. The interviewees requested *an established way of working*, including planning meetings, preparations, test strategies and heuristics (a balance between structure and freedom). The statements from the interviewees were quite general, e.g. "some kind of structure for the testing". However, the interviewees also emphasized that this structure should never be at the same detailed level as manual test-case-based testing, described e.g. by one of the interviewees as to "find the balance between freedom and traceability". One interviewee stated that "You must have fun – play around with things". The interviewees particularly emphasized advantages from that *testers with different experiences and competences work together as a team*, helping each other with new ideas and knowledge about different parts of the system. Some interviewees asked for that the testers should do the testing together ("test together with colleagues"). Others focused on that testers should help each other with new ideas, preparations et cetera ("a structure for how testers should support each other"). Generally, the interviewees asked for individuals with different knowledge and experience ("a team with a mix of individuals").

Seventeen of the 20 interviewees talked about *recording and reporting*. The interviewees described *test environments that support debugging and recording* as a prerequisite for efficient testing, in order to provide detailed data about the identified problems. The interviewees also asked for recording in order to document the testing. Quoting one of the interviewees: "An efficient way of documenting what you do". The interviewees also asked for *a well-defined way to report the test results*, including a description of areas covered by the tests and a list of identified problems. Reporting should not be limited to only problem reports, as it is also important to describe which areas of the product that has been tested. This is important in order to avoid that testers (or test teams) spend time testing the same things, and to secure that the purpose and scope of the testing is fully covered. As one of the interviewees phrased it: "You must document in a good way what you have done, otherwise you might miss important areas". There were different opinions about how the results from the testing should be reported. One interviewee explained that test results should be visualized, i.e. not only described in text. Another interviewee argued that the best way is to "involve the people interested in the test in the test".

In summary, we find that the thematic coding analysis of the interview results resulted in nine factors, all supported by statements or comments from at least ten of the interviewees. The nine factors were arranged in four groups, each group supported by between fourteen and twenty interviewees.

3.5 Confirming the Key Factors

3.5.1 Follow-Up Interviews

In order to strengthen the validity of the findings from the first series of interviews, a second series of interviews was conducted (interview guide 2 in Appendix). The list of key factors (presented in Table 3.3) were presented to the interviewees. The interviewees were then asked to rate the importance of each factor on a Likert scale from 1 ("not important") to 5 ("very important"). This means that the interviewees did not only provide feedback on the interpretation of their own responses, but were also providing feedback on the input from 19 other interviewees from four companies.

The interviewees confirmed the list of factors, rating the importance of each factor as 4 or 5. The interviewees often added comments like "All factors seem to be very important" or "All factors are relevant and good – they describe prerequisites for good testing". The interviewees were also asked to explain if they had not for example talked about e.g. test environments in the first interview, but now rated this factor as very important. Generally, the interviewees explained this with e.g. "the things I did not talk about [at the first interview] was what I took for granted" or similar comments. Even though the interviewees described all of the factors as relevant and important, some of the interviewees did also in different ways emphasize the importance of one or several of the factors:

- Four interviewees emphasized the importance of the testers (the first three factors)
- Four interviewees commented on the importance of balance between structure and freedom (factor six)
- One interviewee described "working together" as most important (factor seven)
- Two interviewees described reporting of test results as difficult, and how a good test report is depending on a good test environment (factor eight and nine)

Three interviewees commented on the fact that the factors seem to be correlated, e.g. to work together as a team is less important if every single tester covers all types experiences and competences. One interviewee rated five of the factors as 2 or 3, and suggested changes such as "I want to include the term domain knowledge in this factor". However, the same interviewee concluded with "the list is great, but it can be better".

In summary, we find that all of the interviewees confirmed the list of key factors, often with positive or very positive comments. We find that the second series of interviews confirm the results from the first series of interviews, showing that the key factors presented in Table 3.3 in a good way reflect the interviewees' positions and viewpoints.

3.5.2 Cross-Company Workshop

To complement the second series of interviews, a cross-company workshop was organized with participants from all four case study companies. Fourteen individuals participated in the workshop, five of them with roles as manager, test leader or test specialist. Four of the participants at the workshop had also been participating as interviewees in the two series of interviews. At the workshop, two of the researchers presented the results from the literature review and the two series of interviews. The workshop participants discussed the presented key factors (from Table 3.3) but had only minor comments regarding the factors (e.g. "to talk to the developers is probably better than just to write a problem report").

The researchers also presented a summary of differences between the case study companies: All factors were supported by comments or statements from interviewees from all case study companies, except for the factor "A well-defined purpose and scope for the tests" (coming from three of the four companies). However, workshop participants from the fourth company described that they also work with purpose and scope, and considered this to be important. Another difference between the companies identified in the first series of interviews was that "Work together as a team" was implemented differently in the case study companies: In two of the companies the testers worked together in the test facilities. In the other two companies the testers tested separately, but worked together and supported each other as a team in other ways, e.g. with planning and preparations.

The workshop participants were asked to rate their current situation with regards to each factor. This revealed differences between the companies, and encouraged discussions related to some of the factors, e.g.:

- Should the exploratory test teams cover all types of end-users (such as e.g. a service technician), or focus only on the primary user (e.g. the driver of the car)?
- How are stability and integrity best maintained in the system — with e.g. 100% code coverage on component level, or a mix of component tests and system tests?
- What does reporting actually mean — does it include to follow up that the information has actually been received by the R&D department?

Participants representing all four case study companies showed interest in a continued study, with the purpose to construct a method or a model based on the identified nine key factors. The method/model could then be used to evaluate the current situation in an organization, and provide input to improvement initiatives related to exploratory testing. The workshop participants discussed if such a model could include the stakeholders who can enable solutions for the different key factors. It then became evident that the workshop participants had quite different opinions, also among participants from the same company. As it seems, it is difficult to identify one single role who can enable a factor. Instead, many roles are involved, or it could be difficult to identify any relevant role or part of the organization.

The workshop participants also discussed how the key factors are correlated, e.g. if the testers have the right knowledge, experience and personality (the first three factors), they probably need less support from an established way of working (the sixth factor). Generally, almost all of the identified connections pointed towards the first two key factors (related to the testers' knowledge and experience). We interpret this as that factors related to "the right people" should be considered to be more important than factors related to "the right structure".

Finally, the workshop participants discussed how exploratory testing is related to Agile methodologies. The individuals participating at the workshop expressed very different opinions. One of the workshop participants had the opinion that exploratory testing harmonize well with Agile development ("exploratory testing is enabling Agile"). Another individual had a somewhat opposite opinion ("Agile is killing exploratory testing") based on that Agile methodologies often tend to focus on automated testing.

We find that the cross-company workshop confirmed the findings from the two series of interviews, and that the identified key factors are valid for all four case study companies. The interest from the workshop participants in the construction of an actionable method or model based on the nine key factors shows that the results from the study are considered to be useful in practice. One workshop participant concluded the workshop with the words "It was good to see the nine factors, and to see that also other companies find these things to be important. This makes it easier for us to change things back home".

3.6 The ExET Model

3.6.1 A Description of the ExET Model

In the studies of related work (presented in Sect. 3.3) we found several publications presenting material related to the efficiency and effectiveness of exploratory testing. However, all of the reviewed publications tend to focus on one aspect, leaving out areas that other authors consider to be the core issues. In response to this, we developed the ExET model (Excellence in Exploratory Testing) based on the analysis of the interview results presented in Sects. 3.4 and 3.5.

The ExET model is a representation of strengths and improvement areas in an organization, which can be used to optimize exploratory testing in each individual case. The ideal situation in the model is represented by set of statements (presented in Table 3.4). At an ExET assessment, the participants compare their current situation to the ideal situation (as shown in Fig. 3.2). The result is a representation in the ExET model of the current status in the organization. The procedure to use the model is further described in Sect. 3.6.2, including an example of visualization of the results from an ExET assessment (Fig. 3.4).

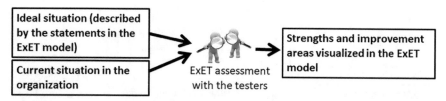

Fig. 3.2 Strengths and improvement areas for exploratory testing visualized in the ExET model

Table 3.4 Statements representing the ideal situation in the ExET model

1.	The testers know how the system is built, and the correct behavior of the system
2.	The testers know how the product is used by the end-user (or the end user is represented in the test team)
3.	The testers are curious and want to learn about the system
4.	We have a well-defined purpose and scope for the tests (system functions ready to be tested) which the testers can transform into e.g. scenarios or focus areas
5.	We have regression testing to secure basic stability and integrity in the system (before exploratory testing)
6a.	We have a structured way of working, e.g. planning meetings, preparations, test strategies
6b.	Our way of working (e.g. planning meetings, preparations, test strategies) provide sufficient freedom for the tester
7.	Testers with different experiences and competences work together as a team, helping each other with new ideas and knowledge about different parts of the system
8.	We have test environments that support debugging and recording
9.	We have a well-defined way to report the test results, including a description of areas covered by the tests and a list of identified problems

In the ExET model, the key factors from the thematic coding analysis (presented in Sect. 3.4.2) have been transformed into a list of statements. The statements, representing the ideal situation in the ExET model, are presented in Table 3.4. A simplistic approach was purposely selected in the design of the ExET model, based on our experiences and positive feedback received in the validation phases in our previous studies [295, 296]. The statements in the ExET model were designed to provide as much information as possible about the strengths and possible improvement areas in an organization. To a large extent, the statements in the ExET model are mirroring the key factors from Table 3.3 in Sect. 3.4.2. One of the factors (factor six) speaks about balance between freedom and structure, and is therefore split into two statements (6a and 6b) in order to isolate the root causes as much as possible.

The analysis of the first series of interviews in this study (presented in Sect. 3.4) showed that efficient and effective exploratory testing depends on many different things, spanning from recruitment and training of the testers to ways of working and the characteristics of the test environment. From the interviews, we also learned that companies struggle with different problems. For example, the testers' competence about the product could be a huge problem in one company, but this could be working

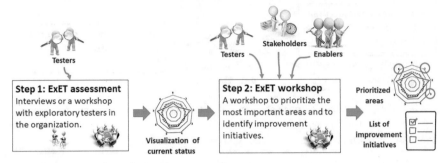

Fig. 3.3 Using the ExET model to identify a list of improvement initiatives to enable efficient and effective exploratory testing in the organization

well in other companies (which instead brought forward other problem areas). Here the ExET model plays a role, pointing out on the most important problem areas of each individual case.

3.6.2 How to Use the Model

The model is used in a simple two-step process (presented in Fig. 3.3) resulting in a list of improvement initiatives for the most prioritized problem areas in the organization.

Step 1 – ExET assessment: At the ExET assessment, the exploratory testers rate to which degree (on a Likert scale) each of the statements in the ExET model mirrors the situation in their organization. That is, the participants compare their current situation to the ideal situation (as shown in Fig. 3.2), and thereby identifies the strengths and potential improvement areas in the organization. The assessment can be conducted as a series of individual interviews, or a group interview (but still with individual responses from each tester). The participants are asked how each statement reflects the current situation in their organization, and are asked to respond on a Likert scale: *Strongly Agree, Agree, Somewhat Agree, Somewhat Disagree, Disagree* and *Strongly Disagree.*

Step 2 – ExET workshop: The purpose of the ExET workshop is to prioritize the most important problem areas and to identify improvement initiatives. The workshop participants are representatives for the exploratory testers, stakeholders (e.g. a line manager) and enabling functions (e.g. responsible for the test environment). The results from the ExET assessment are visualized in the ExET model, and presented at the ExET workshop, in order to promote discussions. An example of a visualization in the ExET model is shown in Fig. 3.4. The responses from the interviewees from the ExET assessment are shown as bullets in the cells corresponding to the interviewees' responses (Strongly Agree, Agree, etc.). Identified strengths and improvement areas are emphasized, in the example in

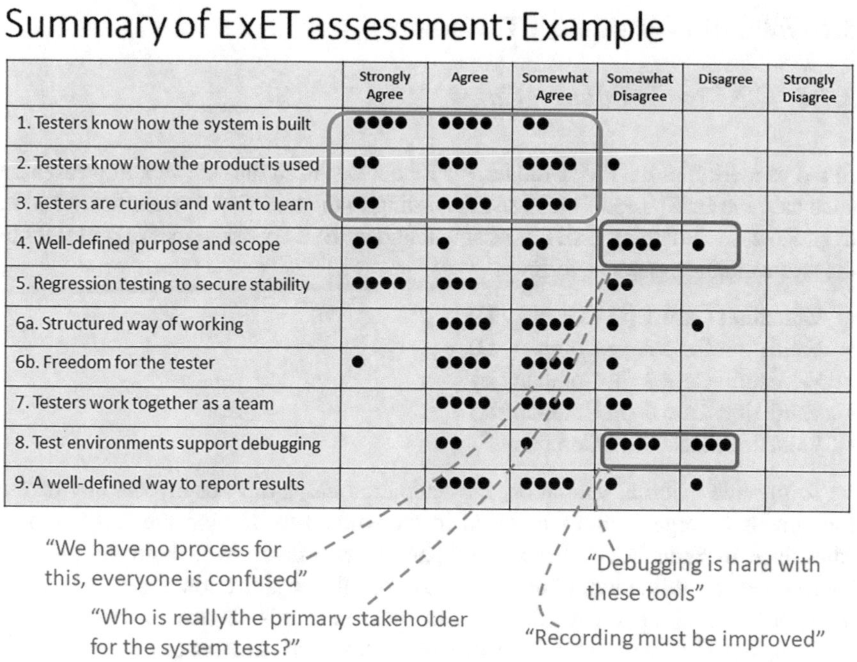

Summary of ExET assessment: Example

	Strongly Agree	Agree	Somewhat Agree	Somewhat Disagree	Disagree	Strongly Disagree
1. Testers know how the system is built	●●●●	●●●●	●●			
2. Testers know how the product is used	●●	●●●	●●●●	●		
3. Testers are curious and want to learn	●●	●●●●	●●●●			
4. Well-defined purpose and scope	●●	●	●●	●●●●	●	
5. Regression testing to secure stability	●●●●	●●●	●	●●		
6a. Structured way of working		●●●●	●●●●	●	●	
6b. Freedom for the tester	●	●●●●	●●●	●		
7. Testers work together as a team		●●●●	●●●●	●●		
8. Test environments support debugging		●●	●	●●●●	●●●	
9. A well-defined way to report results		●●●●	●●●●	●	●	

"We have no process for this, everyone is confused"

"Who is really the primary stakeholder for the system tests?"

"Debugging is hard with these tools"

"Recording must be improved"

Fig. 3.4 Strengths and improvement areas visualized in the ExET model, showing how exploratory testing can be improved in the organization (example)

Fig. 3.4 with one green circle (emphasizing the testers' competence and personality as strengths) and two red circles (marking purpose and test environments as improvement areas). Selected quotes from the interviews are shown to the right, highlighting representative comments and statements from the exploratory testers. The values in Fig. 3.4 are fictitious, and are not related to any of the case study companies in the study.

The expected result from the ExET assessment and the ExET workshop is a list of prioritized improvement areas (which can enable efficient exploratory testing in the organization) and/or a clearly defined list of improvement initiatives. We recommend to schedule a new ExET workshop (e.g. six months after the first one) to follow up the improvement initiatives. If significant improvement have been done in the organization, we recommend to also schedule a new ExET assessment, as it is conceivable that new problems can be identified (not evident in the organization at the time of the first ExET assessment).

3.7 Validation of the ExET Model

3.7.1 The Five Validation Cases

In the validation of the ExET model, the model was used in five validation cases. In each case the ExET model was used according to the two-step process described in Sect. 3.6.2, including an ExET assessment and an ExET workshop. We will refer to the five validation cases as follows:

- Validation Case 1 (in Company D)
- Validation Case 2 (in Company D)
- Validation Case 3 (in Company E)
- Validation Case 4 (in Company E)
- Validation Case 5 (in Company F)

To provide external validation, the validation cases did not involve any of the individuals or organizations involved in the studied to develop the ExET model (described in Sects. 3.4 and 3.5). Company D was involved in both the primary studies and the validation, but different parts of the organization were selected for the primary studies and the validation. In addition to this, the two validation cases in Company D (Case 1 and Case 2) were located in different cities and worked with different products in the company (an airborne product and a ground-based product). The same circumstances applied to Validation Case 3 and 4 in Company E (a platform system and a mobility system). Validation Case 5 in Company F covered the main product in the company. The organization in each validation case wanted not just to improve how they used exploratory testing, but also to increase the amount of exploratory testing in the organization.

The ExET assessments were done with individual interviews in four of the cases, and as a group interview in the fifth case in order to compare the different formats. The group interview format enabled discussions between the participants, but at the same time the individual interviews gave every participant the same opportunity to be heard. The interviewees had roles in their companies as tester, test leader, test architect or manager. They were all in different ways directly involved in the exploratory testing activities in their organization. The 36 interviewees had an average of 13.5 years of experience of software development in industry, spanning from 1 to 33 years. Figure 3.5 presents the distribution of the interviewees regarding years of experience and the interviewee's role in their company. The number of participants at the ExET assessments in each validation case are summarized in Table 3.5 in Sect. 3.7.3.

The results from the ExET assessment in each of the cases were summarized and visualized in the ExET model (similar to the example in Fig. 3.4). All validation cases had generally more positive responses (Strongly Agree, Agree and Somewhat Agree) than negative responses. At the same time, responses in all companies pointed at improvement areas in each company. No pattern could be found in all companies with regards to identified problems, i.e. what was considered to be a major problem in one or several of the companies were found to be working well in other companies.

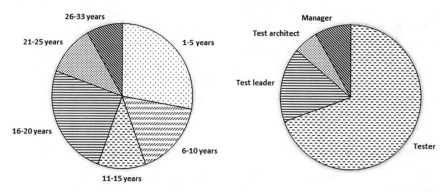

Fig. 3.5 Distribution of the 36 interviewees in the ExET assessments with regards to years of experience (left) and the interviewee's role in their company (right)

Each participant in the ExET assessments was asked how well the ExET Model succeeded in summarizing the status in their organization, and were asked to respond on the Likert scale from Strongly Agree to Strongly Disagree. All the participants responded Agree or Strongly Agree. The participants were also asked if they thought that there is something important that is not covered by the factors in the model, or if any of the nine factors do not belong in the list. Generally, the responses were that nothing needed to be changed. The other responses were found to be not related to the ExET model, e.g. "the testers should have more time for exploratory testing". There were also many positive, or even very positive comments on the ExET model. Comments such as "very good questions" or "the nine factors are spot on" showed that the factors in the ExET model were well received by the participants. The participants also found the results from the assessment to be valuable (e.g. "This was great, a good summary for management: to show them what needs to be done in order to make things work").

The ExET workshops were conducted in the same way in all the five validation cases. The visualization of the results from the ExET assessment were presented for the workshop participants, who all had roles as tester, test leader, test architect, test manager or line manager (for a group of testers). The number of participants at the ExET workshop in each validation case are summarized in Table 3.5. The workshop participants were generally confirming the strengths and problem areas presented in the visualization, and discussed root cases as well as solutions for the exposed problems. The workshop participants found that many problems could not be easily solved, especially issues related to the testers' competence and/or personality. The participants also discussed how the presented results applied to that their organization wanted to increase the amount of exploratory testing, e.g. how new testers should be onboarded.

The participants at each ExET workshop were asked to evaluate the workshop and the ExET model. The participants were also asked if they thought that there is something important that is not covered by the factors in the model, or if any of the nine factors not belong in the list. In all cases, the workshop participants

Table 3.5 Number of participants in each ExET assessment and ExET workshop

Validation case	Interviewees at ExET assessments with individual interviews	Interviewees at ExET assessment with group interviews	Workshop participants at ExET workshop
Case 1 (Company D)	5	–	5
Case 2 (Company D)	–	10	6
Case 3 (Company E)	12	–	13
Case 4 (Company E)	4	–	6
Case 5 (Company F)	5	–	16
Summary		36	46

found that the workshop had resulted in good discussions and ideas for improvement initiatives. The ExET model was well received, and the only improvement comments were related to how the model could be expanded to cover testing in general (not only exploratory testing). The two-step process to use the model was well received by the participants at the ExET workshops, expressed in comments such as "the method was very good" or "very much information for very little effort". Participants at three of the ExET workshops described how they should use the results from the ExET workshop, adding comments such as "I look forward to discussing this with management".

3.7.2 Validation Cross-Company Workshop

As a complement to the validation of the ExET model in the five validation cases presented in Sect. 3.7.1, we facilitated a validation cross-company workshop including participants from all six companies in the study. The validation cross-company workshop included 29 participants: six from Company A, three from Company B, three from Company C, five from Company D, six from Company E, three from Company F, and three of the researchers. The participants had roles in their companies as senior tester, test manager, test specialist or line manager (for a group of testers).

At the validation cross-company workshop, the researchers took turns in presenting the results from the study, from the studies to identify the key factors (presented in Sects. 3.4 and 3.5) to the development of the ExET model (presented in Sect. 3.6) and the validation of the model (presented in Sect. 3.7.1). The presentations worked as a catalyst, promoting good discussions among the workshop participants.

Especially two topics generated longer discussions: The workshop participants discussed the fact that the ExET assessments in the five validation cases had emphasized different problem areas, without any clear common pattern (as described in Sect. 3.7.1). Some of the participants expressed that patterns will probably emerge based on the characteristics of the product, e.g. proximity of hardware. Large-scale was also brought forward as a root cause for several of the identified problems, e.g. one participant commented that "scale is a problem for many factors, especially factor 1–4"). The workshop participants did not succeed in agreeing on a list of root causes or patterns, but seemed to agree that ways of working probably are more important than characteristics of the product when it comes to identifying such patterns. The workshop participants also had a longer discussion where they compared exploratory testing in a development team and exploratory testing of the complete product. Different opinions were expressed on the issue of biased testers. Some of the participants argued that exploratory testers in the development team always get biased, making them find less bugs in the product. Other participants at the workshop argued that the most effective and efficient testers are the ones who work close to the development teams.

The ExET model was well received also by the participants from Company A, Company B and Company C (who had not been involved in the validation of the model). Participants from two of the companies asked for ExET assessments to be scheduled in their organization, which we argue further strengthens that the model is considered to be novel, actionable and useful in practice.

3.7.3 Summary and Analysis of the Validation

In the validation of the ExET model, the model was used in five validation cases to identify what each company should prioritize in order to enable efficient and effective exploratory testing. In each case the ExET model was used according to the two-step process described in Sect. 3.6.2, including an ExET assessment and an ExET workshop. The number of participants in the ExET assessment and the ExET workshop in each validation case is summarized in Table 3.5.

In total, the ExET model was used in ExET assessments involving in total 36 exploratory testers, and ExET workshops involving in total 46 participants (as described in Sect. 3.7.1). The model was well received in all five validation cases. The participants at the ExET assessments found that the ExET model in a good way summarized the strengths and improvement areas in their organization. The ExET workshops resulted in good discussions and identified improvement initiatives. The participants at the ExET workshop described the results from the model as valuable and useful, expressed in comments such as "very much information for very little effort" or "I look forward to discuss this with management".

The results from the validation cross-company workshop (presented in Sect. 3.7.2) show that the ExET model was well received by all six companies in the study, which supports the generalizability of the model. The only suggested improvements from the participants in the validation were related to how the model could be expanded to cover testing in general (not only exploratory testing). We argue that this supports the completeness of the model.

In the literature review (presented in Sect. 3.3) we found no publication summarizing key factors that enable efficient and effective exploratory testing. Instead, published work tend to focus on one aspect, and are leaving out areas that other authors consider to be the core issues. Based on this, we find that although the different characteristics of the ExET model is mirrored in published literature, we have found no other publication that presents a model that can help a company to enable efficient and effective exploratory testing. We argue that this also supports the novelty of the ExET model.

In summary, we find that the validation of the ExET model has showed that the model is novel, actionable and useful in practice.

3.8 Threats to Validity

3.8.1 Threats to Construct Validity

The fact that only one search engine was used for the literature review (reported in Sect. 3.3) could be seen as a threat to construct validity. However, the literature review was primarily used to motivate a continued research study, and not used as the primary source for the construction of the ExET model. In Sect. 3.7.3, we also use the results from the literature review to discuss the novelty of the results from the study. As the decision to use one search engine is clearly described in Sect. 3.3.1, we consider this threat to be mitigated.

Other threats to construct validity are related to the two series of interviews described in Sects. 3.4 and 3.5: It is plausible that a different set of questions and a different context for the interviews can lead to a different focus in the interviewees' responses. In order to handle this threats against construct validity, the interview guides were designed with open-ended questions. It is conceivable that the interviewees' perception of the key factors for effective and efficient exploratory testing is affected by the current situation in the case study companies (e.g. which type of questions or topics that are currently in focus in each company). Therefore, it is plausible that the exact description of the key factors would have been different if the study had included other case study companies. However, all factors are based on comments and statements from at least 10 of the 20 interviewees. Due to this, we argue that this threat to construct validity can be viewed as acceptable.

In this paper, we also present background material for both the interviewees and the case study companies in order to provide as much information as possible about the context and enable reproducibility of the study.

3.8.2 Threats to Internal Validity

Of the 12 threats to internal validity listed by Cook et al. [75], we consider Selection, Ambiguity about causal direction and Compensatory rivalry relevant to this work:

- *Selection:* All interviewees and workshop participants were purposively sampled (selected as good informants with appropriate roles in the companies) in line with the guidelines for qualitative data appropriateness given by Robson and McCartan [376]. Based on the rationale of these samplings and supported by Robson and McCartan who consider this type of sampling superior for this type of study in order to secure appropriateness, we consider this threat to be mitigated.
- *Ambiguity about causal direction:* While we in this study in some cases discuss relationships, we are very careful about making statements regarding causation. Statements that include cause and effect are collected from the interview results, and not introduced in the interpretation of the data.
- *Compensatory rivalry:* When performing interviews and comparing scores or performance, the threat of compensatory rivalry must always be considered. The questions in our interviews described in Sects. 3.4 and 3.5 were deliberately designed to be value neutral for the participants, and not judging performance or skills of the interviewee or the interviewee's organization. Generally, the questions were also designed to be opened-ended to avoid any type of bias and ensure answers that were open and accurate. However, our experiences from previous work is that we found the interviewees more prone to self-criticism than to self-praise.

3.8.3 Threats to External Validity

The list of key factors presented in Sect. 3.4 was confirmed by series of follow-up interviews and a cross-company workshop with participants from the same case study companies as the first series of interviews (as described in Sect. 3.5). Due to this, it is conceivable that the findings from this study are only valid for these companies, or for companies that operate in the same industry segments and have similar characteristics (presented in Sect. 3.2). The follow-up interviews and the cross-company workshop (described in Sect. 3.5) showed that the list of key factors is valid for all four case study companies. Because of the diverse nature of these four companies, the case study companies represent a good cross-section of the industry (as described in Sect. 3.2). Based on analytical generalization [384, 478] it is reasonable to expect that the identified key factors that can enable efficient and effective exploratory testing are also relevant to a large segment of the software industry at large.

The validation of the ExET model (presented in Sect. 3.7) included interviews with 36 individuals and six workshops with in total 72 participants from the six companies participating in the study. The only suggested improvements from the

participants in the validation were related to how the model could be expanded to
also cover other types of testing. This supports the completeness of the model. The
validation of the ExET model is primarily based on the external validation in the
five validation cases, which were separated from the primary cases in the study.
The validation showed that the model and the list of key factors is valid for all
six companies in the study, which further strengthens the generalizability of the
findings from this study. Obviously, we see further validation of the ExET model
as an interesting area for future work, especially including companies in different
industry segments.

3.9 Conclusion and Further Work

3.9.1 Conclusion

In this paper, we have presented interview results from two series of interviews with
20 interviewees from four case study companies, all developing large-scale software
systems. The interviewees had generally good experiences from using exploratory
testing. According to the interviewees, exploratory testing is a more creative way to
work for the testers, and was therefore considered to make better use of the testers.
Exploratory testing was also described as a good way to test system-wide and to test
large-scale systems, especially exploratory testing with an end-user perspective.

In the analysis of the results from the two series of interviews (presented in
Sects. 3.4 and 3.5) we identified *nine key factors that enable efficient and effective
exploratory testing*, grouped in four themes:

- *The testers' knowledge, experience and personality:*

    - The testers know how the system is built, and the correct behavior of the system
    - The testers know how the product is used by the end-user (or the end user is
      represented in the test team)
    - The testers are curious and want to learn about the system

- *Purpose and scope:*

    - A well-defined purpose and scope for the tests (system functions ready to be
      tested) which the testers can transform into e.g. scenarios or focus areas
    - Regression testing secure basic stability and integrity in the system (before
      exploratory testing)

- *Ways of working:*

    - An established way of working, including e.g. planning meetings, preparations,
      test strategies and heuristics (a balance between structure and freedom)
    - Testers with different experiences and competences work together as a team,
      helping each other with new ideas and knowledge about different parts of the
      system

- *Recording and reporting:*
  - Test environments that support debugging and recording
  - A well-defined way to report the test results, including a description of areas covered by the tests and a list of identified problems

Based on the results from the two series of interviews (in total 40 interviews) and a cross-company workshop with 14 participants, we developed *the ExET model (Excellence in Exploratory Testing)*. The ExET model (described in Sect. 3.6) allows companies to identify and visualize strengths and improvement areas, which can be used to optimize exploratory testing in each individual case. The model is used in a simple two-step process (the ExET assessment and the ExET workshop) resulting in a list of improvement initiatives for the most prioritized problem areas in the organization.

In the *validation of the ExET model*, the model was used in five validation cases in three case study companies (described in Sect. 3.7). In each case the ExET model was used according to the two-step process, including an ExET assessment and an ExET workshop. In total, the ExET model was used in ExET assessments involving in total 36 exploratory testers, and ExET workshops involving in total 46 participants. The results from the five validation cases were presented at a validation cross-company workshop with 26 participants from all six case study companies in the study, which further strengthened the generalizability of the model. The model was well received in all five validation cases, and was considered to be actionable and useful in practice.

The literature review (presented in Sect. 3.3) identified 129 publications related to exploratory testing, with 65 publications related to exploratory testing of software systems. No publications were found that presents a model that can help a company to enable efficient and effective exploratory testing, which supports the novelty of the ExET model.

In summary, we find that *the validation of the ExET model has showed that the model is novel, actionable and useful in practice*, showing companies what they should prioritize in order to enable efficient and effective exploratory testing in their organization. The ExET model is based on interview results from four case study companies and has been validated in five validation cases in three case study companies. As the six case study companies included in this study operate in different industry segments, it is reasonable to expect that the ExET model can be applied to a large segment of the software industry.

We believe that the ExET model will be valuable for both researchers and practitioners as it provides a systematic approach, based on the key factors that enable efficient and effective exploratory testing.

3.9.2 Further Work

In addition to the results presented in the analysis and the conclusions, we believe that this study also opens up several interesting areas of future work. The validation of the ExET model in this study showed very promising results (as described in Sect. 3.7). Further validation should encourage more companies to use the model, including companies in different industry segments than the case study companies in this study. Further validation could also include other validation methods, e.g. using quantitative data.

The ExET model was well received in all five validation cases (as described in Sect. 3.7.1), and the only improvement comments were related to how the model could be expanded to cover testing in general (not only exploratory testing). A future study could expand the studies reported in Sects. 3.4 and 3.5 to include a wider scope of test activities. If the study succeeds in isolating a list of key factors, a model could be constructed similar to the ExET model — but applicable also to other types of test activities than exploratory testing.

At the validation cross-company workshop, the workshop participants discussed the fact that the ExET assessment had emphasized different problem areas, without no clear common pattern (as described in Sect. 3.7.2). Another area of further work could be to further investigate root causes for the identified problem areas, defining patterns for how different industry segments or other types of characteristics are related to different types of problem areas.

The participants at the validation cross-company workshop also had a longer discussion where they compared exploratory testing in a development team and exploratory testing of the complete product (described in Sect. 3.7.2). A future study could continue to investigate pros and cons with exploratory testing on different levels, e.g. discussing the role of the independent tester as a member of a development team.

Another topic for further work is to analyze the relation (described in Sect. 3.5.2) between exploratory testing and Agile methodologies: is it so that "exploratory testing is enabling Agile" or is it "Agile is killing exploratory testing"?

Acknowledgments

The authors would like to thank all the participating engineers for their insights, patience and willingness to share their experiences and data with us.

Appendix: The Interview Guides

Appendix presents the questions in the interview guides for the two series of interviews which are reported in Sects. 3.4 and 3.5 of this paper.

- Interview guide 1: Interviews to identify the key factor (described in Sect. 3.2.3)
- Interview guide 2: Interviews to confirm the key factors (described in Sect. 3.2.4)

Interview guide 1: the interview guide for the *interviews to identify the key factors that enable efficient and effective exploratory testing of large-scale software systems* included the following questions:

- Q1.1: How many years of industry experience with regards to software development do you have?
- Q1.2: How would you describe your individual role and responsibilities?
- Q1.3: How, and for which purpose do you currently use exploratory testing in your company?
- Q1.4: How do you on a scale from 1 (very low) to 5 (very high) value exploratory testing as a test technique for large-scale software systems?
- Q1.5: How would you describe the primary strengths and weaknesses of exploratory testing?
- Q1.6: What are the key factors that you think enable efficient and effective exploratory testing of large-scale software systems?
- Q1.7: Which of the things you have described in your response to Q6 are currently implemented in your company?

Interview guide 2: the interview guide for the *interviews to confirm that the interpretation of the first series of interviews was correct, as well as looking for negative cases* included the following questions:

- Q2.1: Is there anything that you would like to change in the presented key factors?
- Q2.2: How would you rate the importance of each of the key factors with regards to "efficient and effective exploratory testing"?
  - 5 (very high)
  - 4
  - 3
  - 2
  - 1 (very low)

Part II
Continuous Architecture

Introduction to the Continuous Architecture Theme

Christian Berger (Theme Leader 2016–) and Jan Carlson (Theme Leader 2017–)

Development of high-quality complex software, in particular in modern embedded and cyber-physical systems, requires careful attention to the software architecture and design in order to achieve the desired quality attributes. Generally speaking, the evolution in software development methods during the last decade, towards more agile practices with short iterations and early feedback, has focused more on implementation and validation activities than architectural design. It is sometimes argued, even, that the concept of architecture is obsolete in modern software development. However, architectural decisions still have a significant impact on software quality, including crucial aspects like performance, safety, and security. Moreover, although architecture can, and should, evolve over time, it does so at a slow pace compared to implementation changes, meaning that the architecture impacts how quickly new functionality can be implemented in response to changed market needs. Thus, for any long-lived systems, but in particular for systems where for example safety assurance is critical, there is definitely a need to document and reason about architecture. Architectural documentation no longer plays the role of a static, a priori, specification for developers to follow but should rather be viewed as an artifact that continuously evolves together with the implementation.

An overall characterization of the research carried out within the *Continuous Architecture* theme over the last 10 years is that it to a large extent addresses the challenges that arise when balancing the need for architectural quality and more agile ways of working, with shorter development cycles: How do we balance quick fixes and long-term quality? How can the agile principles be extended from pure software to mechatronic products? How do we work efficiently with other evolving artefacts than code, including models and documentation? How can safety and security assurance be done more incrementally? Although the high-level concerns of the theme have stayed the same, as the maturity of both the research area and companies' awareness have increased over time, the research has gone from initial state-of-practice investigations to also include development of concrete methods and tools, evaluated in industrial contexts.

J. Bosch et al. (eds.), *Accelerating Digital Transformation*,
https://doi.org/10.1007/978-3-031-10873-0_5

The first chapter in this collection, "Technical Debt Tracking: Current State of Practice: A Survey and Multiple Case Study in 15 Large Organizations" by Antonio Martini, Terese Besker, and Jan Bosch, represents a line of research that has been active since the start of Software Center, investigating how companies are affected by technical debt and proposing new means of identifying, visualizing, and prioritizing technical debt. The chapter investigates the state of practice, captured through a survey and interviews, focusing on the cost of managing technical debt and how it is tracked. It reports that a substantial part of development time is dedicated to managing technical debt, but that it is mostly not done in a systematic way. Based on these findings, a strategic adoption model is proposed to facilitate technical debt tracking in software organizations.

In the second chapter, "Expectations and Challenges from Scaling Agile in Mechatronics-Driven Companies – A Comparative Case Study," Ulrik Eklund and Christian Berger systematically investigate expectations and challenges from scaling agile in organizations dealing with mechatronics development. From a comparative case study with participants from three companies, they identify faster time-to-market to be the main expected benefit, with the two main challenges being inflexible test environments that inhibit fast feedback and existing organizational structures that need to be adjusted to agile principles.

The third chapter, "Lightweight Consistency Checking for Agile Model-Based Development in Practice" by Robbert Jongeling, Federico Ciccozzi, Antonio Cicchetti, and Jan Carlson, represents a more recent research topic focusing on the interplay of, on one hand, system and software modeling and, on the other, continuous development practices. The chapter describes a generic framework assisting developers in the context of agile model-based development, through frequent consistency checks between heterogeneous models. The checks are lightweight in the sense that they are easy to create, edit, use, and maintain, and since they are limited to identification of inconsistencies rather than aiming for automatic resolution. Building upon these ideas, later Software Center research has investigated specific mechanisms for detecting and managing inconsistencies between different, individually evolving, development artifacts.

Considering the future, the current research directions remain relevant and far from exhausted, but we also see a number of new areas of interest. Recently, we have started a project addressing incremental safety assurance and the relation between safety and continuous deployment, which has been the topic for a series of industry workshops. There is also a recent initiative, together with the metrics and continuous delivery themes, to start new research in the area of cybersecurity. Another topic of interest is how to achieve seamless integration of software on a device, on edge nodes, and in the cloud, as well as how to support the decisions of where to allocate functionality. There are also plenty of opportunities for additional collaboration between the themes, including architectural concerns in industrial-quality AI systems, artefact consistency from a metrics perspective, and synergies with testing and with advanced continuous integration pipelines.

Chapter 4
Technical Debt Tracking: Current State of Practice: A Survey and Multiple Case Study in 15 Large Organizations

Antonio Martini, Terese Besker, and Jan Bosch

Abstract Large software companies need to support continuous and fast delivery of customer value both in the short and long term. However, this can be hindered if both the evolution and maintenance of existing systems are hampered by Technical Debt. Although a lot of theoretical work on Technical Debt has been produced recently, its practical management lacks empirical studies. In this paper, we investigate the state of practice in several companies to understand what the cost of managing TD is, what tools are used to track TD, and how a tracking process is introduced in practice. We combined two phases: a survey involving 226 respondents from 15 organizations and an in-depth multiple case study in three organizations including 13 interviews and 79 Technical Debt issues. We selected the organizations where Technical Debt was better tracked in order to distill best practices. We found that the development time dedicated to managing Technical Debt is substantial (an average of 25% of the overall development), but mostly not systematic: only a few participants (26%) use a tool, and only 7.2% methodically track Technical Debt. We found that the most used and effective tools are currently backlogs and static analyzers. By studying the approaches in the companies participating in the case study, we report how companies start tracking Technical Debt and what the initial benefits and challenges are. Finally, we propose a Strategic Adoption Model for the introduction of tracking Technical Debt in software organizations.

4.1 Introduction

Large software companies need to support continuous and fast delivery of customer value both in the short and long terms. However, this can be hindered if both the evolution and maintenance of the systems are hampered by Technical Debt.

Reprinted with permission from Elsevier. Originally published in Science of Computer Programming, Volume 163, 1 October 2018. DOI: 10.1016/j.scico.2018.03.007

Technical Debt (TD) has been studied recently in the software engineering literature [58, 79, 271, 455]. TD is composed of a debt, which is a sub-optimal technical solution that leads to short-term benefits as well as to the future payment of interest, which is the extra cost due to the presence of TD (for example, slow feature development or low quality) [36]. The principal is regarded as the cost of refactoring TD. Although accumulating Technical Debt might prove useful in some cases, in others, the interest might largely surpass the short-term gain, for example, by causing development crises in the long term [303].

There are several kinds of TD, such as Architecture TD, Testing TD, Source Code TD, and so on [271], depending on what artifact and what level of abstraction the sub-optimality has occurred. TD can be measured only partially by static analysis tools; the rest of TD needs to be tracked; otherwise it will be invisible, as outlined in a quadrant by Kruchten et al. [255] In 2011, Guo et al. proposed an initial portfolio approach, with the creation of TD items to be tracked and managed, which was empirically studied [164]. Seaman et al. have identified the theoretical importance of TD as a risk-assessment tool in decision-making [395]. However, current literature does not cover a number of aspects related to TD: how teams manage (and track) TD, what tools are used in practice, and how TD management is introduced in large organizations. Finally, current literature lacks any estimation of the effort spent by the practitioners for managing TD.

In this paper, we therefore aim at addressing the following RQs:

RQ1:   How much of the software development time is estimated to be employed in managing TD? It is also important to understand how a TD tracking process is introduced and implemented in large software companies:

RQ2:   To what extent are software practitioners familiar with the term Technical Debt?

RQ3:   To what extent are software practitioners aware of the TD present in their system?

RQ4:   To what extent do software organizations track TD?

RQ5:   Is there a difference between individual and collective management of TD?

RQ6:   Does the background of the respondents influence the way in which TD is managed?

RQ7:   What tools are used to track TD?

RQ8:   How do software organizations introduce a TD tracking process?

RQ9:   What are the initial benefits and challenges when large organizations start tracking TD?

To shed light on these questions, we have conducted a survey in 15 organizations with 226 participants, and we have carried out a multiple case study in three companies that have started tracking TD: In this context, we have interviewed 13 practitioners responsible for tracking TD and analyzed 79 TD items from a pool of 597 improvements. Our findings include the following contributions:

1. The cost of managing TD in large software organizations is substantial, and it is estimated to be, on average, 25% of the whole development time.

2. We list the tools that are currently used to track TD, and we provide a first assessment of which ones create less management overhead.
3. We report the state of practice related to the introduction of a TD management process in 15 Scandinavian organizations
4. We report the lessons learned from three companies that have started tracking Technical Debt: their starting process, the perceived benefits, and the challenges.
5. We propose a Strategic Adoption Model for Tracking Technical Debt (SAMTTD), aimed at helping companies assess their Technical Debt management process and make decisions on its improvement. The model also defines the next research challenges to be addressed in theory and to be evaluated in practice.

This paper adds new and more in-depth results to the findings reported in a previous paper [298]. In particular, we address new research questions (RQ2, RQ3, RQ5, RQ6, RQ7), while we add new insights related to the relationship between RQ4 and RQ7 (or else, we study how the practitioners' perception of tracking Technical Debt is related to their usage of tools).

The remainder of the paper reports our methodology in Sect. 4.2, the results in Sect. 4.3, and then we discuss the results in Sect. 4.4, concluding in Sect. 4.5.

4.2 Methodology

For the execution of this study, we aimed at combining different sources of data (source triangulation) and different methodologies (methodology triangulation) to obtain reliable results [384]. To fulfill these triangulation strategies, we surveyed 226 participants. The different sources included 15 large organizations and different roles, that is, developers, architects, and managers. To complement such quantitative investigation, we followed up with a qualitative, in-depth multiple case study at three of the companies involved in the survey and that have started tracking TD. Here, we conducted interviews with 13 employees, and we analyzed documents including 79 TD issues out of a pool of 597 improvements present at the companies.

4.2.1 Survey

In this study, we have involved 15 software organizations belonging to eight distinct large software companies. We consider a large software company an organization with more than 250 employees. As shown in the descriptive statistics in Table 4.2, 91.6% of the respondents reported working for an organization bigger than 250 employees. The remaining 8.6% were consultants from small/medium organizations working on the same systems and projects developed by the large organizations participating in the survey. The latter can, therefore, be considered as working in the same context as the other 91.6% of the participants. Seven out of eight companies developed embedded software, while another one developed software for optimization (company D). The companies are anonymized and named A–H, and the sub-organizations are called B1, B2, F1–F4, and G1–G4.

4.2.1.1 Survey Data Collection

In the first part of the survey, we asked about the participants' background information:

- Software development experience: "< 2 years", "2–5 years", "5–10 years", "> 10 years"
- Role: "Product Manager", "Project Manager", "Software Architect", "Developer", "Tester", "Expert", "Other (Specify)"
- Gender
- Education
- Team size
- Organization size
- Size of their current project in MLOC (Millions of Lines of Code)

In the second part of the survey, we asked for and analyzed the data related to the effort caused by several Technical Debt challenges. To make sure that the respondents did not misinterpret the question, the challenges were listed as reported in current literature and not as generic "Technical Debt." Table 4.1 reports the different kinds of TD together with their scientific names and the related academic source. This assured that a better construct validity of our survey was achieved, as we reduced the subjectivity of the respondents interpreting "Technical Debt."

Table 4.1 Kinds of technical debt recognized in [271, 298, 395]

Survey entries	Source and literature term
Lack or low quality of testing	Test Debt [271]
Low code quality	Source Code Debt [271]
Lack or low quality of requirement	Requirement Debt [271]
Lack or low quality of documentation	Documentation Debt [271]
Dependency violations	Architecture Debt [271, 299]
Complex architectural design	Architecture Debt [271, 299]
Too many different patterns and policies	Architecture Debt [271, 299]
Dependencies on external resources/software	Architecture Debt [271, 299]
Lack of reusability in design	Architecture Debt [271, 299]
Uneasy/Tensed social interactions between different stakeholders	Social Debt [271, 452]
Lack of adequate environment and infrastructure during development	Infrastructure Debt [271]

It is important to notice that the details and the results from the questions in the second part of the survey are not included in this paper because the data has been used to cover a different scope and to answer different questions related to Technical

Debt in another work [37]. Therefore, the only questions overlapping between the papers are the ones related to the background of the respondents.

In the third part of the survey, we asked the following questions, some of which can be mapped directly to the RQs. Some of the following questions are instead statements. In those cases, we have asked the agreement of the participants to such a proposition.

Q1. "How much of the overall development effort is usually spent on TD management activities?"
Q2. "How familiar are you with the term 'Technical Debt'?"
Q3. "I am aware of how much Technical Debt we have in our system."
Q4. "All team members are aware of the level of Technical Debt in our system."
Q5. "I track (using tools, documentation, etc.) Technical Debt in our system."
Q6. "All team members participate in tracking Technical Debt in our system."
Q7. "I have access to the output of the tracking of the Technical Debt in our system."
Q8. "All team members have access to the output of Technical Debt in our system."
Q9. "If you track Technical Debt in your project, what kind of tool(s) do you use?"

The formulation of Q1 was slightly different, as we did not mention "TD," but we referred to the challenges mentioned in the second part of the survey (see Table 4.1). However, we use the formulation in Q1 in the rest of the paper for the sake of readability.

After question Q2, the survey included the following definition of Technical Debt:

> Technical Debt (TD) is constituted of non-optimal code or other artifacts related to software development that give short-term benefits, but cause a long-term extra cost during the software life-cycle.

This definition has been operationalized based on the explanations and definitions given by Cunningham [79] and McConnell (presentation given at the workshop at ICSE 2013 [313]). We could not include the most recent one from the dedicated Dagstuhl seminar [20] because it was held after the survey was conducted. However, the difference between our definition and the one given in Dagstuhl does not seem very distant, as visible below:

> In software-intensive systems, technical debt is a design or implementation construct that is expedient in the short term, but sets up a technical context that can make a future change more costly or impossible. Technical debt is a contingent liability whose impact is limited to internal system qualities, primarily maintainability and evolvability

In our definition, we omitted the second part of the Dagstuhl definition. However, by enumerating the different kinds of TD in the first part of the survey (excluding external qualities from the questionnaire), we can be sure that the second part of the Dagstuhl definition was also covered, although not explicitly mentioned.

This assures that we provided the participants with a good means to understand what Technical Debt meant when we asked about its management. However, we cannot guarantee that the practitioners read and understood the definition.

For question Q1, since we wanted to quantify the amount of effort related to TD faced by the companies, we provided a scale including the following options: "<10%," "10–20%"... "80–90%," and "I don't know." This question was aimed directly at answering **RQ1**.

For Q2, we provided the answers "Not at all familiar," "Slightly familiar," "Moderately familiar," "Very Familiar," and "Extremely Familiar." The answers were mapped on a 5-grade Likert scale, respectively 0–4. This question aimed directly at answering **RQ2**.

For Q5–Q8, we asked the respondents to report their agreement on a 6-grade Likert scale: "strongly disagree," "disagree," "somewhat disagree," and the symmetric scale for agreement. These statements were aimed at answering **RQ3**, **RQ4**, and **RQ5**. In particular, we wanted to understand if tracking Technical Debt was an individual activity (by asking the same questions for the individual and about the whole team) and if there was a discrepancy between the awareness of the practitioners and their tracking process.

As for question Q9, we asked the participants to report the tools used in a qualitative way (text-box). The input was then post-processed and compiled in the resulting word cloud. This question was used, together with the previous ones, to answer **RQ7**.

4.2.1.2 Survey Data Analysis

First, we analyzed the answers from Q1 to understand the magnitude of the estimated effort spent by the respondents on managing TD. We transformed the answers from categorical to numerical: for example, we parsed "<10%" to 5, "10–20%" to 15, and so on. After the calculations, we can reapply the tolerance interval of $+5/-5$, and the various means and so forth would not change. When calculating the means, we did not consider the "I don't know" answers. However, only a small portion of the answers was of this kind (11.5%).

To avoid the bias introduced by different roles answering the questionnaire, we ran a cross-tabulation chi-square test of independence to understand whether the role of the participants affected the answers.

The second step was to apply frequency analysis on questions Q5–Q8. To do so, we transformed the categorical data to a Likert scale (1–6), where "strongly disagree" was mapped to 1 and "strongly agree" to 6. As for Q5, we also reported the grouped answers in three main intervals, "No tracking" {1–2}, "Somewhat tracking" {3–4}, and "Tracking" {5–6}. We used these aggregated intervals only for the last results related to the adoption model SAMTTD.

For some of the results, we used a standard boxplot. The boxplot is a comprehensive way to visualize various descriptive statistics altogether at a glance. We used this method when we aimed at showing the difference about the distribution of the data with respect to two specific variables. For example, Fig. 4.4 shows the comparison, with respect to different companies, of the distribution of the management effort:

We can compare the medians (the black lines in the middle), but we can also see different percentiles (where most of the answers were concentrated) and outliers.

In other cases, we compared the different variables using statistical tests. For example, it seemed interesting to compare how much the respondents were aware of TD with respect to how much they were tracking it. To do so, we performed a number of tests for linear correlation using the tool R. Most of the numerical variables did not have a strong linear correlation with each other, except the answers for Q5, Q6, Q7, and Q8. This is not surprising because, if TD is not tracked by an individual, it is probably not tracked by the team, and the output will not be visible to the individual or to the others as well. The Pearson tests for linear correlation gave results from 0.72 up to 0.89 with p-value vastly lower than 0.05. This can be considered a good test for the reliability of the answers. Since these variables all strongly correlate, in the remainder of the paper, when studying different variables, we will use only the "tracking" variable without considering whether the output was available or not.

We also wanted to understand whether the results depended on a specific variable. For example, we tested whether developers answered differently from architects or managers. Thus, to answer RQ6, we ran several chi-squared tests of independence between the background variables of the participants and their answers related to questions Q5–Q8. For example, we wanted to know if the familiarity, awareness, tracking, and so on of the respondents would depend on their background, such as by their affiliation with a company, their education, and so on. This analysis was done to answer **RQ6**.

We finally analyzed the qualitative answers from Q9 to understand better the results answering **RQ7**. We selected the answers in which the respondents reported that tools were explicitly used (61/226, 27% of the respondents), and we compared the respective levels of awareness, tracking, and familiarity. This was done to understand better what the respondents meant by "tracking." We also created a word-cloud representation of the qualitative answers for Q10. This, we found, could represent quite well which tools were the most used and in what way. To do so, we processed the qualitative data, removing terms that would appear in the word cloud but would not make sense from the tool point of view, for example, "code" and "Technical Debt." Finally, from the coding of the qualitative answers, we could also identify the frequencies of the tools used. To do so, we manually coded the 61 answers in the following six categories:

- *Comments:* These are usually "TODO" comments, left by the developers in the code or other artifacts. These are useful for the developers to know that something is left to do, but it does not imply a systematic monitoring of the TD reported in the comments.
- *Documentation:* From the qualitative answers, this represents a text or spreadsheet where issues are listed and explained in a semi-systematic format. Another example could be a wiki. However, such documentation is different from a backlog as it is more difficult to monitor, and it does not use a specific technology to manage and perform operations on the backlog.
- *Issues:* using the same ticket system for bug fixing, but usually down-prioritizing the issues related to Technical Debt.

- *Backlog:* This is either a dedicated backlog for TD issues or the usual feature backlog where TD items are mixed with features. This practice usually involves a technology such as project management tools.
- *Static analyzer:* These are tools such as SonarQube, SonarGraph, Klockwork, and so on used to analyze the source code in search for Technical Debt. In a few cases, respondents report that they built their own metrics tools. These tools usually check (language-specific) rules or patterns that can warn the developers of the presence of TD. These tools are used as trackers by the developers, with the limitation that they cover only part of the TD.
- *Lint:* They are also static analyzers but are used more to find potential bugs and security issues rather than technical debt.
- *Test coverage:* Some of the respondents measure test coverage, and they consider a low test coverage as presence of test debt.

4.2.2 Multiple Case Study

To understand better to what extent companies tracked TD (**RQ4**) and how the tracking process was introduced (**RQ8–9**), we conducted a multiple case study, investigating some of the companies involved in the survey. We interviewed 13 employees from cases B1 (project manager, system architect, and two developers), F1 (three software architects responsible for TD management in three different teams), and F4 (two system architects, two project managers, and two developers). In particular, to understand what was considered "good tracking," we had the opportunities to interview the participants, belonging to company F1, who answered "strongly agree" (the highest level of tracking) to question Q5. This gave us an idea of what was considered as current best practices for tracking TD. To support the interviews, we also analyzed 79 out of 597 TD backlog items used for tracking improvements (and thus including TD items) in companies B1, F1, and F4.

4.2.2.1 Interviews

Data Collection

The interview questions were designed to cover taxonomies we found in the pre-study concerning the *reason for initiation*, the *activities* within the TD management process, and the *process implementation*. All interviews were audio-recorded, and the results of the interviews were organized by different questions and activities for later analysis.

We formulated the interview questions in three sections.

- The *first* section contains questions about the profile of the interviewees and their companies.
- The *second* section focused the questions on the initialization of the process for managing TD. "What was the main reason for implementing a TD manage-

ment process?" "Who decided that the process should be implemented?" "What negative effects did you experience in your system due to TD?" (**RQ8**).

- In the *third* section, we asked about the outcome of the implemented process (**RQ4**) and how the companies experienced the implementation of the process in terms of the most obvious benefits and challenges (**RQ9**).

Data Analysis

The data analysis used an inductive approach based on open coding [129]. We were looking for activities related to the introduction of a TD management process in the company. For this purpose, we followed the points in [328], which is a well-known study on change management in software engineering. The data were coded using a Qualitative Data Analysis (QDA) software tool called Atlas.ti. Such a tool supports keeping track of the links between taxonomies, codes, and quotations. Based on the taxonomies, we developed a coding scheme that contains a corresponding set of codes and sub-codes. Figure 4.1 shows an example of our code hierarchy and how the codes were mapped to the taxonomy. The graph is part of the overall data collection model (not completely displayed here for space limitations).

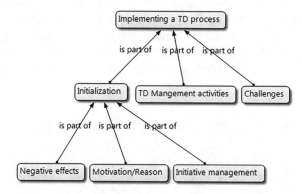

Fig. 4.1 The coding process

As an example of how the coding was conducted, we present a quotation from one of the interviewees which was mapped to the Motivation sub-code. *"We realized that for each and every release it took much time correcting or fixing problems with additional patches and it took more and more time adding new features on top of the system."*

4.2.2.2 Document Analysis

To gain more evidence on how the companies were tracking TD (**RQ4**), we investigated the existing documentation. Also, we had access to the TD backlogs of the studied teams: 26 items in the organization B1, 451 items in F1, and 20 items in F4. We analyzed the TD items' fields, values, and how they were ranked. We did not analyze all items in company F1, as 451 items also included improvements that were not TD. We randomly selected 30 items that corresponded to the definition of TD; we analyzed them, and then we tested our assumptions by randomly looking at other items in the backlog. We used the backlogs in the interviews (see previous section) to ask follow-up questions of the participants. Also, we analyzed the documentation that was created by the organizations to explain TD to the users of the tracking process.

4.3 Results

4.3.1 Demographics and Background of the Respondents

In total, we obtained 226 complete answers. The total respondents were 259, which gives us a completion rate of 87%. We aimed at having a similar number of respondents from each organization (Fig. 4.2). The participants were almost all experienced practitioners, since 156 respondents (69%) had more than 10 years of experience, while only 8 (3.5%) had less than two years of experience (the remaining 62, 27.5%, had between two and 10 years of experience). Several roles participated in the survey: 37 managers (16%), 52 software architects (23%), 105 developers (46%), seven testers (2.65%), 14 experts (5.75%), and nine system engineers (4%) completed the survey.

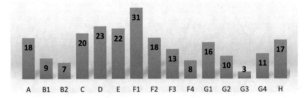

Fig. 4.2 Number of participants per organization

As shown in Table 4.2, we can infer the following characteristics of the studied sample:

- *Experience:* Most of the respondents had more than two years of experience, while 69% of them had more than 10 years of experience. The estimations can, therefore, be considered reasonably reliable, as they are made by expert practitioners used to estimating their work (more discussion in the threats to validity section).
- *Education:* Most of the respondents had a bachelor's or master's degree. The level of education is therefore quite high. However, the sample does not include many practitioners involved in research projects.
- *Team size:* Although many of the teams are small (1–10 members), the sample includes a substantial number of respondents working in large teams as well.

Table 4.2 Background data related to the respondents, with the percentage, the number of respondents, and the relative distribution

Option	%	Resp.	Distribution
Practitioners' Experience			
< 2 years	3,50%	8	
2 - 5 years	8,80%	20	
5 - 10 years	18,60%	42	
> 10 years	69,00%	156	
Gender			
Female	7,10%	16	
Male	92,00%	208	
Other / Don't want to share	0,90%	2	
Education			
No University education	7,10%	16	
Bachelor degree	24,80%	56	
Master degree	58,00%	131	
Ph.D. degree	4,40%	10	
Other:	5,80%	13	
Team Size			
1-5 team members	21,70%	49	
6-10 team members	38,10%	86	
11-20 team members	15,50%	35	
21-40 team members	5,80%	13	
> 40 team members	19,00%	43	
Organization Size			
< 50 employees	1,30%	3	
51-250 employees	7,10%	16	
251-1000 employees	15,00%	34	
1001-5000 employees	14,60%	33	
>5000 employees	61,90%	140	
Age of current system			
< 2 years	10,20%	23	
2-5 years	20,80%	47	
5-10 years	33,20%	75	
10-20 years	29,60%	67	
>20 years	6,20%	14	

- *Organization size:* As mentioned in the analysis made in Sect. 4.2.1, the organization of the respondents is large. This was chosen by design. We wanted to restrict our results to large organizations. This imposes a limitation on our study: we cannot generalize these results to small organizations.
- *Age of the current system:* The distribution of the different systems is quite even, as the sample covers almost equally all the different phases of the system. This raises the degree of generalizability of our results, as it assures that our data cover both "young" and "old" systems.

4.3.2 Estimation of Management Cost of TD (RQ1)

First, we report the answers to Q1 from the survey. In Fig. 4.3, we show the distribution of the respondents with respect to the different levels of estimated effort that were reported. By picking the middle values, as explained in the methodology section (e.g., 10–20% was transformed into 15), we calculated that the average cost of managing the TD was estimated by 215 respondents to be 25.9% with a median of 25% of the whole development time. From the results, we can see how most of the respondents answered between 0 and 40%, while half of them are between 10 and 30%. However, some respondents report spending more than 40% of their time managing TD.

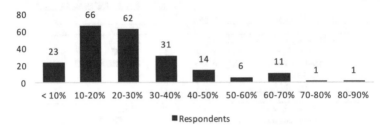

Fig. 4.3 Distribution of respondents for Q1: "How much of the overall development effort is usually spent on TD management activities?"

Looking at the comparison of medians (bold lines) and percentiles among the companies (boxplot in Fig. 4.4), we cannot see a big difference in how the respondents answered, apart for the slight difference for E, F1, and F3. This means that the amount of time spent managing TD is quite not dependent on the organization.

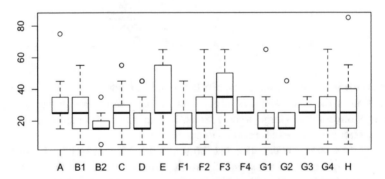

Fig. 4.4 Comparison of companies with respect to Q1: "How much of the overall development effort is usually spent on TD management activities?"

A chi-square test of independence, aggregating the intervals over 50% in the same category (the lack of values would have invalidated the chi-square test) yielded a p-value of 0.144, so we could not reject the hypothesis that the role of the respondents would influence their answer. This means that the answers did not vary significantly across the roles, contrary to what one might expect, considering different views and experiences of different roles in the organizations.

4.3.3 Familiarity with the Term "Technical Debt" (RQ2)

The respondents seem to be, in total, moderately familiar with the term Technical Debt. The mean is 2.26, while the median is 2. From the graph in Fig. 4.5, we can see that there are more respondents who are very familiar with respect to the other ones.

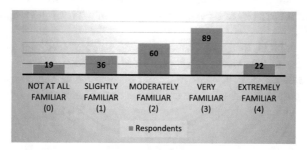

Fig. 4.5 Distribution of respondents according to their answers to Q2: "How familiar are you with the term "Technical Debt"?"

From the comparison among the companies, we can see how they are mostly on the same level: F4 is above all the rest, while the organizations B2 and G4 are not very familiar with the TD concept. However, since we did not have access to the practitioners working in these two organizations, we cannot tell what the cause of this lack of familiarity was. We omit the test of independence, as the results are clearly visible in Fig. 4.6.

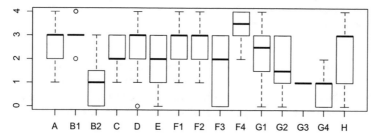

Fig. 4.6 Level of familiarity with the term Technical Debt for each organization (answering Q2: "How familiar are you with the term 'Technical Debt'?")

4.3.4 Awareness of Technical Debt Present in the System (RQ3 and RQ5)

When assessing the level of awareness of the TD present in their system, the respondents, on average, somewhat agree that they are aware of how much TD they have in their system (mean = 3.69, median = 4). Almost half of them (45%) *somewhat agree*, while only 21% feel more confident (they *agree* or *strongly agree*) and the remaining 32% *disagree* or *somewhat disagree*. Only 3% of the respondents were not aware of TD.

On the other hand, the practitioners seemed less convinced that the whole team would be aware of how much TD is present in the system. Here, the mean is 2.8, while the median is 3, both close to a mild disagreement. The comparison of the answers is reported in Fig. 4.7. The chi-square test of independence confirmed that the distributions are not dependent, with a p-value < 2.2e−16.

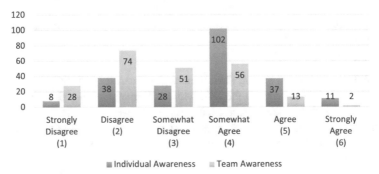

Fig. 4.7 Comparison of answers for Q3: "I am aware of how much Technical Debt we have in our system" (Individual Awareness) and Q4: "All team members are aware of the level of Technical Debt in our system" (Team Awareness)

For what concerns the different companies, they are quite aligned on the awareness among each other. Once again, B2 seems to have a somewhat lower level of awareness. The results suggest that belonging to one or the other organization would not have an impact on the level of awareness of their employees (Fig. 4.8).

4.3.5 Tracking Technical Debt (RQ4)

In this section, we report the results from Q5: "I track (using tools, documentation, etc.) Technical Debt in our system." The average tracking level, reported by 219 respondents, is 2.3 with a median of 2. On the team level, it seemed to be just slightly worse, as shown in Fig. 4.9 and discussed below.

Based on the results of a chi-square test of independence between the role and the tracking level, we could not reject the hypothesis (p-value 0.63) that the role of

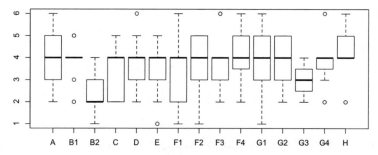

Fig. 4.8 Distribution of answers with respect to Q3: "I am aware of how much Technical Debt we have in our system." 1–6 correspond to "strongly disagree" to "strongly agree."

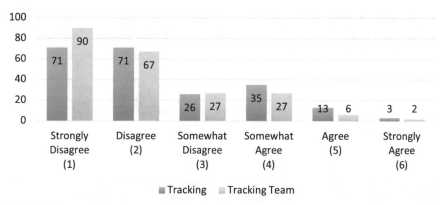

Fig. 4.9 Distribution of answers related to Q5: "I track (using tools, documentation, etc.) Technical Debt in our system" and Q6: "All team members participate in tracking Technical Debt in our system."

the respondents would influence their answer with respect to tracking. In Fig. 4.10, we show the comparison among different companies. We can see how the different companies answered similarly, apart from company F4 and partly company D. However, the test for independence did not show any significant relationship between the variable company and the answer given in the survey with respect to Q5 (tracking TD).

Finally, there is very little difference between tracking on an individual (Q5) or team level (Q6). Only some of the individuals track TD more than the rest of their team. This is strongly confirmed by a Wilcoxon test, which rejected the null hypothesis (p-value = 2.008e−05) that the difference in the two paired distributions is given by chance. In other words, the same participant answered very similarly when asked Q5 and Q6, and this is not because of randomness, which means that if someone in the team tracks TD, it is very probable that the whole team is involved in the tracking.

Finally, as observed in the methodology section, the results from Q7 and Q8 (related to who in the team has access to the outcome of TD tracking) very strongly

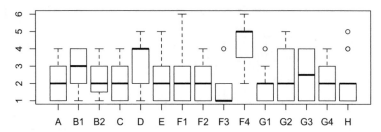

Fig. 4.10 Distribution of answers for Q5: "I track (using tools, documentation, etc.) Technical Debt in our system."

correlated with the answers to Q5, so we do not report the exact results here. In other words, this means that the respondents who track TD also have access to its output (e.g., backlogs, dashboards, etc.).

4.3.6 Influence of the Background of Respondents on the Management of TD (RQ6)

We have partly answered RQ6 ("Does the background of the respondents influence the way in which TD is managed?") in the previous sections, especially with respect to the variables roles and organizations. However, we had several other variables in the background section, and we investigated whether any of those variables would help in understanding what causes a more or less mature TD tracking. To answer this question, we ran several statistical chi-squared tests of independence between the background variables (education, team size, etc.) and the variables of interest (familiarity, awareness, and tracking of TD). However, none of the statistical tests yielded a significant answer. Technically, we could not reject any hypotheses for which the answers were dependent on the background of the respondents. Since the results would include several combinations of p-values that would not add any meaning to the manuscript, we decided to omit such a table.

In conclusion, the management of TD depends on some factors that have not been captured by the surveyed background variables. However, in the next sections, we provide some answers that could not be found in the quantitative data but seem to be related to the historical and social context where the participants work. More information is given in Sects. 4.3.8 and 4.3.9.

4.3.7 Tools Used to Track Technical Debt (RQ7)

In this section, we analyzed whether the respondents who used some tools to track TD were also more aware of TD or tracked it more than the others. To do so, we considered only the answers from the 61 participants (27%) who answered the qualitative question Q9 (specifying what tools they used). We also report the boxplot for the questions Q5 and Q3: we compared the answers of the participants who used a tool with the ones who did not. Figure 4.11 illustrates the results we found: *"Awareness"* is the awareness of the respondents who did not use a tool, while *"Awareness_Tool"* is the one for the ones using a tool (same for *"Tracking"*). It seems that, indeed, if the participants used a tool to track TD, then they would report a high perception of tracking TD. A chi-squared test of independence confirms a strong difference in the distribution of the answers (p-value < 2.2e–16), strongly confirming this claim. However, more surprisingly, their perception of the level of awareness of how much TD is present in the system would only slightly change. This is confirmed by a chi-squared test of independence (p-value of 0.59), which did not show any difference in the distribution of the answers between the participants using a tool or not. Very similar results were found at the team tracking level, so we do not report them in the boxplot below.

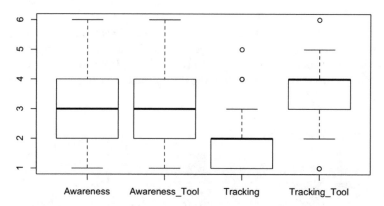

Fig. 4.11 Distribution of answers for Awareness and Tracking and comparison if a tool is used or not

Given the high difference in tracking between the respondents who claimed to use a tool and the ones who did not, we can safely claim that the respondents tracking TD also use a tool. This result confirms that we captured most of the respondents' answers related to the tool that they used. The respondents who did not input an answer for the tool also most probably don't use any tool, since they have in general a much lower level of tracking. Therefore, we can further validate the result that only 26% of the participants used a tool to track TD. This is also important for the reliability of our results related to the SAMTTD model explained in the next sections.

From the qualitative data, we could also report what tools were used in practice. After removing some of the words that would just create noise (such as "Technical Debt," see methodology section for more details), we obtained the word cloud presented in Fig. 4.12, which shows the distribution of tools used among the respondents.

Fig. 4.12 Word cloud of the tools used by the participants to track TD

By codifying the qualitative answers in comments, documentation, issues, backlog, static analyzer, lint and test coverage, we can also analyze the frequencies. We can see how the tool that was mostly used is a backlog (dedicated to TD or the same used for feature development), followed by documentation, static analyzers and issue trackers (Fig. 4.13).

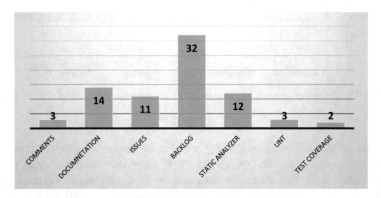

Fig. 4.13 Number of participants using a specific kind of tool

We then analyzed the distributions of the respondents for Awareness and Tracking levels (Fig. 4.14) with respect to the different kinds of tools. On the other hand, by analyzing the kind of used tool with respect to the mean amount of effort spent on management activities (Fig. 4.15), we can see a quite clear difference. Although this difference could not be statistically tested (the chi-square tests did not report significant difference, but this could be due to the small sample), backlog and static analyzers are the ones that seem to create less overhead.

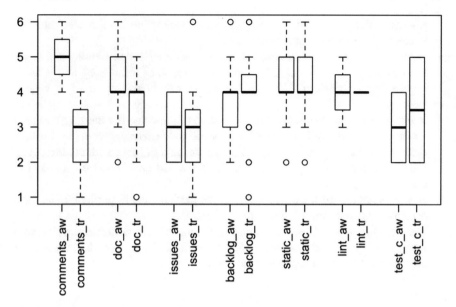

Fig. 4.14 Distributions of levels of TD tracking ("_tr") and awareness ("_aw") reported to the user of each kind of tool

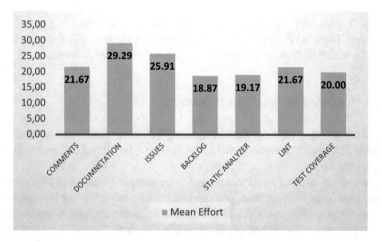

Fig. 4.15 Mean of management effort for each kind of tool

In conclusion, the following considerations on the tools can be made:

- Comments in the code help awareness, but they are not considered tracking, and they are used by just 1% of the respondents. This is probably because they are not used in a document that can be monitored by the team outside the code.
- Documentation increases TD awareness, but it is not considered as a high level of tracking, and it has the highest overhead. The main tools used here were

Microsoft Excel or Word. We can infer that this practice is not recommendable in comparison with the other ones.

- Using a bug system for tracking TD is not considered as contributing to a better level of awareness or tracking compared to the other techniques, and it has a slightly higher overhead. We would infer that this is also not the best way of tracking TD.
- Backlogs, static analyzers and "lint" programs all increase the tracking level, but we cannot see a big difference (although static code analyzers seem to contribute better to the participants' awareness). They are also the ones with the least overhead. They therefore seem to be considered the best practices at the moment to track TD.
- Backlogs are the most used tool among the participants. In particular, the most used backlog tools are Jira, Hansoft, and Excel.
- Test coverage does not seem to contribute too much to the awareness and tracking level, although it does not involve much overhead. This might be because test coverage is related to only a small part of TD.

4.3.8 Why and How Do Companies Start Tracking TD? (RQ3)

First, we report why the companies decided to start tracking TD, or else their motivation. Then, we found that the preparation activity was critical to start tracking TD, and we, therefore, report the main steps involved in this practice.

4.3.8.1 Motivation for Start of TD Tracking

The main reasons behind the start of tracking TD were related to experiencing the interest of TD, or else there were too many bugs to fix, decreased feature development, performance issues:

"Because we realized that for each and every release it took much time correcting or fixing problem with additional patches and it took more and more time adding new features on top of the system. [. . .] The system became more and more inefficient." These statements confirm our previous results [303], as one of the architects also mentioned: *"After some time the TD was increasing and we had a crisis situation,"*

In other words, the main motivation was related to the negative impact experienced by the practitioners, or else the perception of the interest associated to the TD.

4.3.8.2 Preparation of the Tracking Process

From the cases investigated, it was clear that adopting a TD tracking process requires some initial activities and time to implement the process. From B1, we understood that they *"Have done this for 1.5 years more or less, switching from reactive to more proactive. It's a better information about the status of the system."* The preparation includes the following aspects. Although we used [384] to code these results, we prefer to report them in a way that is more readable in the context of Technical Debt management:

- Initiative —— In all the three cases, the tracking process started from an individual initiative. A manager, a system architect, an experienced developer, and so forth. In other words, tracking TD requires a *champion* in the sub-organization who is aware of TD and is willing to promote the adoption of the practices.
- Budget —— Tracking TD needs both an initial effort and a continuous effort. Company B1 started with 150 hours, in the beginning, for a development unit (i.e., a sub-organization responsible for a sub-system, which includes a few teams). However, this was *"ok just to start the backlog, but not to go in depth investigation."* The continuous time allocated to tracking TD varied across our cases: it ranged from 10% (company F) to 30% (company A). The cases also show how the continuous allocation of resources to manage TD could be dynamic, and varying according to newly identified items, as suggested for Architectural TD in [301].
- Management involvement —— although the initiative can start from anyone in the organization, tracking TD requires an initial and a continuous investment (budget). This entails the need of involving a manager who understands the importance of TD and who can grant a budget for this activity.
- Benefits —— as the previous point entails, there is a need, for the management to understand the benefits of tracking TD given the initial and continuous budget allocation. Such benefits need to be communicated and continuously evaluated to justify such investment.
- Measurement set up —— according to company B1, an amount of time is needed to set up measurements (e.g., complexity) and TD identification (static code analyzers). In other companies, such as F1, we found that a developer set up a specific analysis tool to measure complexity and bug density: this activity was supported by a team dedicated to the measurements in the organization.
- Explanation and alignment —— The *Champion* for the TD tracking activity needs to communicate well to the teams what TD is and what needs to be reported (to avoid overhead). The interviewees mentioned that they conducted a first workshop for explaining TD and its tracking, and they also produced some documentation. It is also important to have a *validation* workshop in which the teams bring up some TD issues to align their understanding with the main TD concepts such as *Principal* and *Interest*.
- Appointing of a Sub-System TD Responsible (SSTR) —— TD tracking needs someone responsible across the organization who can take the initiative to support the tracking process. In all the studied cases, the people responsible for collecting and maintaining a list of TD issues were chosen as experienced developers on a given sub-system. The sub-system TD responsible, however, needs to be supported by the knowledge of the teams when tracking the issues because different practitioners have better and more detailed views of different parts of the system.

- Breaking down and distributing TD items —— The SSRT needs to allocate the TD items to the teams according to their competences and their responsibilities with respect to the system. Architecture items were explicitly appointed to an experienced developer to be analyzed and estimated.
- Communication of TD to management —— Once the first TD backlog was prepared, it was communicated to a manager connected to the evaluated (sub-)system. This was supposed to show management the risk associated with such a system due to TD.

In summary, quite a few activities are necessary to set up a TD tracking process; this requires the organizations to take the initial decision of allocating some budget to TD tracking.

4.3.9 What Are the Benefits and Challenges of Tracking TD? (RQ4)

4.3.9.1 Benefits

When we evaluated the tracking process together with the teams, they mentioned several benefits of tracking TD. The backlog gave them a long-term perspective, not only the short-term one given by the feature backlog. The respondents did not think that the TD backlog was hard to maintain. This is supported by the lower management overhead reported in the survey with respect to the other practices.

One of the architects in organization F4 mentioned that, after an important architectural TD item was refactored, *"The evidence was visible in the next release with positive impact when adding new features on top of the one we fixed. Easier to add and no side effect, cleaner architecture."* According to the project manager interviewed in company B1, the initiative was overall successful, but it needed to be continuously supported, to be really effective. *"Yes it was worth it, but it is important to follow it up now and to make sure that parts of the list are done [refactored]."*

Another benefit reported by the architect in company B1 was that the initiative and the weekly meeting promoted a discussion with teams working on other systems, for example, when an issue on the interfaces was revealed. The same architect reported that the TD backlog was a great way to receive feedback from the developers, as it made clear what, according to them, was important to refactor.

One of the interviewed SSTRs and a developer mentioned that focusing on TD was important in order to *"zoom out"* from their daily work, and it was an opportunity to check the system with a broader perspective. Finally, all the architects mentioned that, by using the tracking process, they learned issues that were not known before.

4.3.9.2 Challenges

Although the respondents mentioned several benefits, some issues with the current approaches were also reported. The most important one was the acceptance, from the managers, of the need for refactoring. Even with the list updated, the information about the risk and benefits of performing a refactoring was not always clear to the managers. This meant that, especially for large TD items, it was difficult to receive the needed budget for TD repayment.

One of the major problems in starting to track TD was that the first step needed a substantial amount of effort to collect all the existing items. Although this would be only a one-time effort, in some teams the managers would not concede the necessary budget. A challenge mentioned by all the participants was that the refactoring became more difficult to be prioritized and completely repaid when several items and several teams were involved. It required *"double"* the effort to prioritize the item with different managers (who could disagree on the necessity of refactoring) and the coordination of the refactoring was considering quite risky and as a dangerous overhead. For example, TD issues involving interfaces were more time-consuming to estimate and prioritize, because they required more discussions involving more stakeholders from more teams.

Another challenge in the prioritization activity was the difficulty of prioritizing *among* TD items, especially where an explicit risk/impact value was not calculated. The participants reported that it was generally difficult to show an actual gain from the cost/benefit analysis to the managers, even with a field explicitly represented in the backlog. In general, the intuitive values used for the risk/interest (but usually not including a systematic calculation) were working only sometimes, and more explanations and indicators were required by the managers to accept a costly refactoring.

The respondents mentioned the difficulty of coordinating the different teams in using a standardized process for tracking TD. In some cases, it was difficult to *"make them care"* about reporting TD, while for other teams the TD list was created with enthusiasm.

Finally, the participants mentioned that in some cases the TD backlog itself did not make the TD more convincing for the management to be refactored, but it served for the teams to remember to take care of TD, which would otherwise remain invisible and overlooked.

4.3.10 Strategic Adoption Strategy

As a final result from the combination of the various analyses performed so far, we aggregated the results and combined them with the roadmap related to the current literature on TD. This led to the Strategic Adoption Model for Tracking Technical Debt (SAMTTD, Fig. 4.16). The first four steps in the model represent the results from the survey on the current state of practice in the companies.

We used the results from Q4 to create the first step: If the respondents were not familiar with the TD concept, they could be on a higher level. Then, we defined three more levels of TD tracking maturity. To discern between the different levels, we mapped practices that we found used or not and that correlated with different levels of tracking (e.g., the usage of a tool). We additionally used the results from the interviews where it was clear what different practices were introduced to track TD.

- *Unaware:* There is no awareness of what Technical Debt is and therefore how to manage it. According to our survey data, only 8.4% of the participants are in this stage. This datum is related to the respondents that answered *"Not familiar at all"* with the term Technical Debt, as visible in Fig. 4.5.
- *No tracking:* In this stage, the software engineers are aware of the TD metaphor, and there is a general understanding of the negative effects brought by having TD in the system, but there is no initiative to track TD, which remains invisible. Around 65.6% of the respondents report being on this level, by (strongly) disagreeing about tracking TD. The percent was calculated by counting the total answers minus the answers from Q4, counted previously as the *unaware* respondents, and the ones who use tools, counted in the next levels (26%). Therefore, this yielded $100 - 8.4 - 26 = 65.6$.
- *Ad-hoc:* In this stage, the software engineers are aware of what TD is, and some of the individuals have started tracking TD on their own. This makes the TD management process ad-hoc, since, without a dedicated budget, such individuals use what is available, in terms of tools and processes, for other activities. For example, according to the qualitative answers related to Q3, the sprint or product backlog, a common issue tracker or a simple excel spreadsheet can be used for tracking TD. Static analysis tools might be in use but are limited to the individual usage. According to the survey, approximately 26% of the respondents are at least on this stage (61 participants, 26%, were using tools, see Sect. 4.3.6). However, from these ones, we need to take away around 7% that we place on the next level (see point). In total, we therefore report around 19% of respondents on this level.
- *Systematic tracking:* The company in this level has acknowledged the importance of tracking TD also on a management level (see *Preparation* section). Therefore, there is a budget generically associated with the management of TD. This amount usually ranges between 10% and 30%. According to the document analysis of the TD items from the case study, a specific backlog and documentation related to TD is necessary, with TD-specific values useful to analyze the principal and the risk/interest. The TD is understood by the participants, who have been instructed by a person responsible for the process (see *Preparation*). There is an iterative process in place to monitor TD (identify, estimate, prioritize, and repay it), and such process is subjected to *continuous improvement*. 7.2% of the respondents are on this stage, actively tracking TD. This is the maximum level achieved by the companies, as confirmed by the interviewees. This amount can be obtained when taking into consideration the respondents who answered "Agree" or "Strongly Agree" to Q5 (see Fig. 4.9).

We do not have evidence that companies have better processes and tools in place. However, based on current literature on TD [271] and related work on change management [328], we hypothesize future maturity steps that can be reached by the companies when the results of research would be put in place. We identify the following three steps:

- *Measured:* In this stage, identification tools for TD are in place, for example, the use of the tool SonarQube for source code TD (such as McCabe complexity) or, for example, dependency checkers on the architecture level (as reported in company F1). The measurement of the interest is also in place, for example, there are indicators that show the amount of interest paid or predicted if the refactoring is not conducted. Such tools are not employed in practice yet and should be integrated to provide overall indicators to provide help to the stakeholders to estimate and prioritize TD. The authors of this paper are actively working on introducing such tools and indicators, as explained in our recent work [300].
- *Institutionalized:* According to change management [328], a process is mature when it is spread and standardized across the whole organization. This would allow an aligned prioritization of TD across the system. This would also allow the practitioners to plan the allocation of resources according to the quality of the (sub-)systems in order to plan for the life-cycle of the product. As an example, the reader can consider a team who needs to build a feature on a sub-system developed by other teams: knowing how much TD is present in such sub-system would allow the team to estimate whether refactoring is needed or the lead time for the features to reach the customer.
- *Fully automated:* In this stage, the decisions on the refactoring are completely data-driven, making use of statistics collected on historical data or by benchmarking the system against a collection of reference systems. For this purpose, however, the previous steps are necessary.

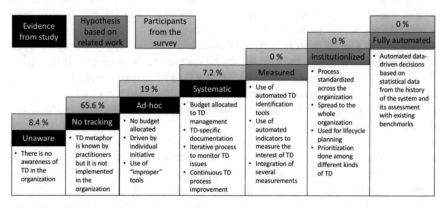

Fig. 4.16 The Strategic Adoption Model for Tracking Technical Debt: the main milestones and the state of practice (% of respondents per category)

4.4 Discussion

The combination of data from 226 participants in 15 large software organizations with the in-depth case study provided an overall picture of the current state of practice with respect to TD tracking. In this section, we discuss the contributions in this manuscript, with respect to practitioners and researchers, we compare our results with existing literature, and we report limitations and threats to validity related to our study.

4.4.1 Current State of Practice of Tracking TD and Implications for Practitioners and Researchers

The results related to RQ1 tell us that software companies spend, on average, around 25% of their development time on TD management activities. The boxplots (Figs. 4.4 and 4.10) show some consistency in the companies: The medians range between 15 and 25% of the effort. The 50-percentile also shows some consistency in the answers, but there we can find some variance as well: Different organizations and individuals dedicate divergent amounts of time to TD management. We could find some differences in the approaches used by the participants, which seems promising. For example, the usage of backlog and code static analyzers appear to be related to less management overhead. However, considering the quantitative analysis, we cannot infer that any background variable related to the respondents would have a significant impact on the overall management overhead.

The results related to RQ2, RQ3, and RQ4 tell us that only a few employees do not know what TD is (around 8%). However, despite the familiarity with TD, more than half of the participants still do not track TD (approximately 65%), and almost one out of five do it in an ad-hoc way (19%), that is, by using tools that are not made for TD tracking and therefore are not effective. Finally, only 7% of the participants tracks TD in a more dedicated way.

An interesting observation is that the results are not significantly affected by the background and the role of the respondents. This datum increases the reliability of the results: Independent of the organization and the background of the participants, we found very similar results across the respondents, which can be considered also more general. In other words, the means and the variance across different practitioners are similar in different organizations.

However, this also led us to consider the following: Different roles with different priorities and views (e.g., managers and developers) agreed on the estimated amount of effort done to keep TD at bay, as well as on the fact that such effort is not systematic (TD is mostly not tracked). Then, an unanswered question is: If TD is so painful, why do organizations not track TD more systematically? One possible answer is that employees do not know how to track TD effectively. This is supported by the fact that most of those who track TD do not use proper tools or documentation, while the few who systematically track TD still do so manually and rarely use basic measurements. For this reason, we found it important to propose the SAMTTD model, to help practitioners understand what it means to track TD and what is necessary to implement a tracking process in practice.

Another answer to the current lack of TD tracking, despite the management effort, might be found in the results related to RQ8 and RQ9 concerning the necessity of a *Preparation* phase and its cost, which is critical for the introduction of a TD tracking process in the companies. At the outset, the initiative needs to be conducted by one or more *champions* in the organization. An initial budget should be allocated to allow the first activities related to the TD inventory, and this entails a need for a commitment by management, which is achieved by communicating how a systematic TD management process would bring benefits to the organization. Unfortunately, this is one of the challenges reported by the practitioners, who claim that there is a lack of good instruments and publicly available results to advocate for the need of systematic TD management. Other activities include the communication and alignment of what should be collected as TD, the set-up of measurement systems, the appointment of a Sub-System TD Responsible (SSTR), and the breakdown and distribution of the TD items to the teams. Unfortunately, the first investment can be burdensome. For example, a trial of 150 initial hours for a unit with three teams was barely enough to identify preliminarily the initial TD list. It also did not leave time for the company to set up measurement systems and accurately estimate and prioritize the TD items, although updating the TD backlog becomes lightweight in the following iterations.

For tools to track TD, we found that many participants use backlogs, implemented in project management tools such as Jira and Hansoft, and static analyzers. The results also suggest that these approaches require less management effort, and they seem to give slightly more awareness of the TD in the system. However, it seems that, for most of the respondents, the awareness of the amount of TD present in the system is not affected by the tool in use, if not slightly. This means that TD tools are not only used by the teams to be aware of the TD, but also for communication, monitoring, and management purposes. The usefulness of these tools is shown by the fact that the participants using backlogs and static analyzers spent less than the average time (18–19% compared to 25.9%) on TD management. However, the tools seem not to help raise the awareness of the respondents: The mean awareness remains between "somewhat disagree" and "somewhat agree." Many qualitative answers, both from the survey and from the case study, also report the fact that many TD items cannot be automatically revealed because they are too context-specific and they cannot be represented by generic patterns. This leads to the conclusion that better and more specific tools for managing TD need to be developed.

In summary, managing TD requires a few investments that are not well known by the practitioners and are difficult to be motivated by a precise cost/benefits ratio. Consequently, without an investment in processes and tools to track TD, it is difficult to make TD visible, as well as to advocate for refactoring "invisible" TD. This represents a *vicious cycle*: companies suffer the negative effects of TD and try to contain it, but at the same time they do not find enough motivations to invest in a more systematic management process. By looking at the motivations for starting to track

TD, the results show that organizations do so when they experience the interest of TD: *slow feature development*, *quality issues*, and *performance degradation*. However, at such a point, the interest associated with TD is already high and, as explained in other recent papers —— [303], [299] —— from the authors of this manuscript, it is hard to refactor, as the cost has also increased and has become too expensive. In conclusion, the only way out the vicious cycle seems to be, for the practitioners, to *proactively start tracking TD*. Using backlogs and static analyzers help reduce the management overhead and increase (even if slightly) the awareness of TD. New tools need to be developed, in two main directions: allowing the developers to communicate the urgency of refactoring TD to the management, and better (semi-)automatic tools to identify and track TD to increase the awareness of the respondents.

4.4.2 Related Work

There are two survey-based studies regarding the familiarity and tool usage related to TD. In [110], the authors concluded that 50% of respondents said that no tools were used and only 16% said that tools gave enough details. Their study also shows that 27% of the respondents do not identify TD. Furthermore, Holvitie et al. [191] show that over 20% of the respondents (in Finland) indicated poor or no TD knowledge. However, in these studies, we cannot find an estimate of the effort spent on TD management, and there is no explanation of how a TD tracking process can be started or implemented. As a comparison with these studies, the results from our survey show that familiarity with TD and its tracking seems to be higher among the respondents who answered our survey. This may be related to the different size, culture, or domain of the organizations, but given that our study is more recent, we could speculate that the familiarity with TD is growing. In our results, only 8.4% of our respondents were not familiar with TD, and 27% of the respondents used tools. Both findings are higher than in the other surveys.

There are a few articles about industrial practices concerning Technical Debt, for example [73, 164, 497], but they are single case studies, and, in two cases, they were performed in small companies. Also, such work does not focus on the current state of practice of Technical Debt tracking, an estimation of the TD management effort, the motivations for starting to track TD, or the maturity evolution of tracking. This makes it difficult to compare the results with our survey, but we will take the topics one by one and discuss similarities and differences. As for the cost of tracking TD, [165] reports detailed results from a single case study. Some results are in line with the broad results reported here including, for example, that the effort might vary greatly, reaching even 70% of the development time, and starting the TD tracking is more expensive in the beginning but it becomes more lightweight when the process is repeated. In [493], the TD management process of several companies is analyzed with reported results similar to our cases, for example, the limited use of measurements and lack of a systematic process. However, in contrast with our work, the study does not focus on TD tracking; it reports a broad snapshot of current practices and does not take change management perspective into account. For example, we report information such as the quantified cost of managing TD, the reasons why organizations start tracking TD, and the preparation activities and costs necessary to track TD. We present a maturity model, SAMTTD, that, taking change management aspects into account, allows for the transfer of knowledge to practice. This is visible in the additional four levels added in our model. We can consider the fourth step in our model as an especially important addition to our work because we found evidence of a systematic process using TD-specific documentation not reported in [493]. Also, none of the cited studies reports quantitative answers from as many as 226 practitioners, which also show trends and statistical results reported here.

There are a few studies regarding Technical Debt tracking and tools in the literature. As for tools, most of the recent findings report tools created by researchers (e.g. [132, 190, 233]). The experience reports are usually related to the evaluation of the tool in a specific context and, therefore, cannot be considered as state-of-practice (at least, not yet). This is understandable as new tools are being developed while this manuscript is being written, and the attention to TD by software organizations is quite recent. As for tracking, three initiatives have been reported in the literature [190, 194, 302]. The first one, [190], presents a tool called DebtFlag, which allows tracking TD and its propagation. However, the evaluation of such a tool in practice has yet to be reported. The second one, [302], reports the evaluation of a tool (AnaConDebt) to assess and track TD. A first study has been done in an industrial environment, but more studies are needed to understand whether the tool is usable in practice. Finally, the last paper, [194], reports a new method to analyze the TD reported in code comments. Although some of the features of the semi-automatic approach seem interesting, it is not clear how many TD items are covered by comments and whether this approach can be used in practice (the paper does not report a practical use of the method with an evaluation from the practitioners). For example, if we look at the survey conducted in this paper, currently only around 1% of the participants (three) state that they track TD using comments.

4.4.3 Limitations and Threats to Validity

Here we report the main threats to validity regarding this study, according to [384]: *construct validity*, *internal validity*, *external validity*, and *reliability*.

Construct validity is concerned with the investigation device and the validity of the data with respect to the RQs that are investigated. In a survey, this is usually one of the main threats to the validity of the results, as participants might interpret definitions and other terms differently from each other. Although this phenomenon is unavoidable, we took a few approaches to mitigate the consequences. As for the misunderstandings related to the interpretation of what TD is, we have reported, before the questions, short definitions of the issues and management activities that are associated with TD according to the most up-to-date literature. In other words, we did not ask questions on "Technical Debt" directly but, instead, on more concrete issues that are associated with it. In our experience, this should have reduced the possibility that the respondents would consider TD as something else, for example, bugs or missing features (something that might happen in practice, according to our experience). We also provided, in the last part of the survey, a definition operationalized from the various existing formal definitions. We asked a question about whether the practitioners were familiar with TD according to the definition, and they mostly agreed. Although this does not ensure that the practitioners had answered with full knowledge of what Technical Debt is, we believe that the two mitigation strategies together contributed to reducing the threats to construct validity.

There is a threat of construct validity also when mapping the respondents to the levels in the SAMTTD, as we did not ask this question directly to the participants. To mitigate this threat, we used multiple evidences from various quantitative and qualitative answers, and we can reliably say that no company is using integrated measurements of TD, which place the respondents necessarily from level 1 to 4. We have thoroughly assessed the number of respondents for level 3 regarding the usage of a tracking tool. By definition, the respondents in level 1 do not know what TD is, and this datum comes directly from the answers related to their familiarity with TD. Level 4 includes the few practitioners who have confidently reported how they track TD. These practitioners have also been interviewed, which yielded a description of what systematic process they used. Consequently, level 2 contains the remainder of the respondents not included in levels 1, 3, and 4.

As for the results concerning testing hypotheses statistically, it is important to notice that, in most cases, we could not reject the null hypotheses that the results would depend on the background of the respondents (roles, company, etc.). This means that we could not find enough evidence in this dataset to support the rejection of the null hypotheses, but the reader should be warned that we also did not prove the opposite hypotheses. In summary, we cannot claim that the background played a role in the results.

Finally, it is important to report the threats to external validity. We investigated mostly large companies involved in the development of embedded systems and from the Scandinavian area. This entails three possible threats.

- It is possible that, in other domains (e.g., web development), the percent of the companies in the maturity steps would differ. To mitigate this threat, we have included a company developing "pure" optimization software. In this case, we did not find a statistical difference with respect to the other companies. However, more research is needed to understand if there is a difference.
- Companies in other countries, with different contexts and cultural backgrounds, might answer the survey differently or have different ways of managing Technical Debt. However, all the companies investigated in this study employ developers from all over the world and have distributed development. It is therefore likely that the background of the participants in the survey would actually be more heterogeneous than the organizations themselves, who are only Scandinavian.
- Small companies might behave very differently with respect to Technical Debt management.

Therefore, the reader must be aware that there are some limitations to the extent to which we can generalize from these results.

There are also threats to the reliability of the results, or else, the results might be biased depending on an interpretation given by the authors, method, or source of evidence (e.g., if we asked only developers but not managers), as reported below.

- There is a threat in the quantities estimated by the respondents with respect to Q1. We do not know what the given estimations are based on since most of the participants do not explicitly track TD and their time spent on it. However, as the demographic data show, many participants can count several years (more than 10) of software development experience. Estimations are based on experience, and they are referenced to the practitioners' last projects, which limits a possible retrospective bias. Practitioners are used to estimating the amount of work that has been done or that is upcoming, which mitigates the threat that the estimated effort would be very distant from the real one.
- As for the authors' interpretation, we have made sure that, especially for the qualitative data analysis, we have applied observer triangulation: Two or more authors have analyzed the interviews and either separately coded the statements or checked the other authors' codes. Although this does not remove the threat completely, it is the main strategy used when qualitative data analysis is involved in the study.
- Relying only on quantitative data might miss important details that are necessary to understand the results or might show correlations that are not related to any real causality. For example, we could not find reasons from the quantitative background data that would explain the variance in the amount of time that the participants are employing to manage TD. However, we could combine the quantitative results to qualitative answers coming from some of the organizations participating in the survey, which helped explain the factors related to their maturity by analyzing the interviews.
- Finally, there is a threat of reliability of the results, as the percentage of developers participating in the survey was larger than other roles. This means that the results might be skewed by the developers' biases. However, to mitigate this threat, we performed a chi-square test to understand if the distribution of the answers would depend on the roles of the respondents. The test did not support such a hypothesis, meaning that there was not a statistically significant difference between different responding roles (different roles gave similar answers). By having such roles participating in the survey, we could apply a mitigation strategy denoted as source triangulation.

4.5 Conclusion

According to 226 respondents in 15 software organizations, practitioners estimate spending, on average, a substantial amount of time trying to manage TD (25%), although such an amount is affected by some variance. Software companies in Scandinavia are more familiar with the TD metaphor with respect to previous studies, and they track TD more. The awareness of TD in the system seems to be somewhat known by the developers, independent of which approach is used. Tools such as backlogs (the most popular approach) and static analyzers help reduce the management overhead of approximately 7%. However, only 2% of the respondents use tools to track TD, and only 7.2% of them created a systematic process for doing so. These low numbers are due to a lack of knowledge of what must be implemented, in terms of tools and processes, to introduce a TD tracking approach in the organization, as well as a lack of awareness of what the negative effects of TD are before they occur. Moreover, we studied some approaches and found that an initial investment in *preparing* for the introduction of TD is necessary, which makes starting TD tracking less appealing for managers who need to fund the activities. However, although there are some obstacles to overcome, some of the companies are proactively and strategically implementing a solution to make TD visible, which shows that it is practical to introduce such approaches. To help this process for other practitioners, we propose a Strategic Adoption Model (SAMTTD) based both on the evidence collected across this study in combination with current literature. The model can be used by practitioners to assess their Technical Debt tracking process and to plan the next steps to improve their organization.

Acknowledgement

We thank the Software Center companies and Matthias Tichy for his valuable insights. The research leading to these results has received funding from the European Union's Horizon 2020 research and innovation programme under the Marie Skłodowska-Curie grant agreement No 712949 (TECNIOspring PLUS) and from the Agency for Business Competitiveness of the Government of Catalonia.

Chapter 5
Expectations and Challenges from Scaling Agile in Mechatronics-Driven Companies – A Comparative Case Study

Christian Berger and Ulrik Eklund

Abstract Agile software development is increasingly adopted by companies evolving and maintaining software products to support better planning and tracking the realization of user stories and features. While convincing success stories help to further spread the adoption of Agile, mechatronics-driven companies need guidance to implement Agile for non-software teams. In this comparative case study of three companies from the Nordic region, we systematically investigate expectations and challenges from scaling Agile in organizations dealing with mechatronics development by conducting on-site workshops and surveys. Our findings show that all companies have already successfully implemented Agile in their software teams. The expected main benefit of successfully scaling agile development is a faster time-to-market product development; however, the two main challenges are: (a) An inflexible test environment that inhibits fast feedback to changed or added features, and (b) the existing organizational structure including the company's mind-set that needs to be opened-up for agile principles.

5.1 Introduction

Developing high-quality software products that better match a customer's expectations is successfully supported by Agile [33]. Key advantages over other development approaches are short and fixed periods consisting of development, integration, and testing, small team sizes, and active communication within the software team while also including the customer. A flexible development approach allows a team to get frequent feedback to newly added features from the end-user but also enables reprior-

---

Reprinted with permission from Springer. Originally published in Agile Processes in Software Engineering and Extreme Programming. XP 2015. Lecture Notes in Business Information Processing, vol 212. Springer, Cham. DOI: 10.1007/978-3-319-18612-2_2

itization of user stories and feature requests whenever the stakeholders' needs change over time.

The typical habitat for adopting Agile are pure software-driven companies with prominent examples being Google and Amazon. Implementing Agile in environments where the final product combines software, hardware, and mechanics is more challenging considering the different nature of the involved artifacts.

5.1.1 Problem Domain and Motivation

In the mechatronics domain there are two opposing trends affecting R&D: Manufacturing and hardware development is a mature domain, which has been optimized for more than fifty years, but still having long lead-times, typically years. Focus during R&D is on predictability, i.e. meeting the start-of-production (SOP) with the required mechanical quality, which in practice is achieved by stage-gate/waterfall processes. In contrast, software development today is characterized by increasing speed and being more nimble while keeping quality. This typically enables lead-times of weeks or months, and many agile methods are a response to this. There are no established solutions to solve the intersection between the aforementioned trends, but the necessity to resolve them in the mechatronics domain motivates further studies.

5.1.2 Research Goal

The goal for this comparative study is to systematically investigate expectations and challenges from scaling Agile outside software teams on the example of three companies from the Nordic region developing and manufacturing embedded and mechatronic products. Specifically, we are interested in the following subgoals:

1. Unveiling expectations and challenges originating between teams, departments, and divisions,
2. Unveiling challenges from mechatronics-related development-, project-, and product-processes, and
3. Understanding expectations from key stakeholders like teams, managers, and organizations at large.

5.1.3 Contributions and Scope

We designed and conducted a comparative case study at three companies and report about our findings according to Runeson and Höst (cf. [384]). The main contributions of this work are:

1. Defining a methodology to systematically unveil and compare expectations and challenges for scaling Agile in mechatronics-driven organizations,
2. Presenting results from individual on-site workshops at the three different mechatronics companies, and
3. Summarizing results from a joint follow-up survey at all companies based on the results from the individual workshops.

5.1.4 Structure of the Article

The rest of the article is structured as follows: Sect. 5.2 presents related work in this field. Section 5.3 describes the design of the comparative case study and the embodied methods followed by the results from the comparative case study in Sect. 5.4. Section 5.5 presents conclusions from our study.

5.2 Related Work

Originally, agile methods evolved to meet the needs of small and co-located development teams [237]. They typically emphasize close customer collaboration, iterative development, and small cross-functional development teams. Also, team autonomy and end-to-end responsibility are reported as important characteristics permeating the methods [100]. Most companies introduce agile methods to increase the frequency in which they release new features and new products, and as a way to improve their software engineering efficiency. According to Dingsøyr et al. [92], agility embraces lean processes with an emphasis on realizing effective outcomes, and common for agile methods is that they entail the ability to rapidly and flexibly create and respond to change in the business and technical domains [92].

Due to many successful accounts [4, 189], agile methods have become attractive also to companies involved in large-scale development of embedded systems, and several attempts to extend agile methods to include development of embedded systems are seen [235, 262, 316].

While convincing success stories from industry help to further spread the adoption of Agile, there are few studies of agile development focusing on the mechatronics domain. There are examples of some companies successfully introducing agile practices at the team level, typically characterized by individual teams defining their own ways-of-working to facilitate speed, short iterations, and delivery quality when developing their components. The experiences thereof are generally positive according to two literature reviews by [9] and [406]. There are also some publications stating that a third of German and American automotive development teams using agile practices reported in a commercial survey [331]. However, with characteristics such as hardware-software interdependencies, heavy compliance to standards and regulations, and limited flexibility due to real-time functionality [225], the development of embedded and mechatronic systems seems to challenge common practices of agile development.

5.3 Comparative Case Study Design

We addressed the aforementioned research goal by designing a comparative case study, where we collected data from three different mechatronics-driven companies.

5.3.1 Research Questions

We derived the following research questions for the comparative case study:

RQ-1:   Which practices from Agile are in use in a mechatronics-driven organization?

RQ-2:   How is the current implementation of Agile perceived in a mechatronics-driven organization?

RQ-3:   What are the expectations from scaling Agile within a mechatronics-driven organization?

RQ-4:   What are the main foreseeable challenges when scaling Agile in mechatronics-driven organizations to achieve the expected benefits?

5.3.2 Case and Subjects Selection

We conducted our research in the context of the Software Center.[1] The Software Center is a cooperation environment where different companies from the Nordic region collaborate with selected universities on research topics and technology transfer from academia to industry. The participating companies in the Software Center cover domains like Automotive, Telecommunication, Mobile Phones, and Defense.

For our comparative case study, we selected three large companies who are mainly mechatronics-driven in their business to which we are referring to as company A, B, and C. The companies employ between approximately 18,000 and 93,000 people and their respective yearly manufacturing of mechatronic products ranges from 0.4 to over 16 million units according to their respective annual reports from 2013. These companies can be considered to be representative due to their individual market shares. Furthermore, all companies have already adopted Agile at team-level in their R&D departments and apply it since several years during the software development

---

[1] http://www.software-center.se.

of projects with varying sizes. For the workshops and surveys, participants covered experienced developers and managers from software development, hardware development, integration, and testing.

5.3.3 Data Collection Procedure

The data collection was conducted threefold: (a) We planned and conducted individual on-site workshops at the respective companies in the first phase; (b) the collected data from these individual workshops was analyzed to design a joint survey that was subsequently distributed to key stakeholders within the respective companies in a second phase to enlarge the population for data collection; (c) the feedback from the survey was used to plan and conduct a joint workshop with key representatives from all three companies in the third phase involving an external expert on Agile practices to follow-up on selected key challenges for scaling Agile and to identify topics where to proceed internally at the companies.

5.3.3.1 Individual On-Site Workshops

The individual workshops were conducted separately for each company. The respective workshop's duration was approximately 3 hours and was moderated by one researcher while the other researcher took notes during the discussion phases. The workshop addressed in a qualitative manner the following two main questions:

1. What would be the biggest benefits if your company successfully scales Agile?
2. What are the challenges for your organization to achieve these benefits?

The participants from different teams (software development, hardware development, and testing) had approximately 20 min to write their answers on two-colored sticky notes. The notes were subsequently collected, presented to the audience by the workshop moderator, and clustered during a joint discussion about the respective matter. The resulting topic maps were summarized to identify the key topics for the two aforementioned questions.

5.3.3.2 Survey

Afterwards, we designed a survey based on the results from three individual on-site workshops according to the guidelines by from Singer et al. published in Shull et al. [408]. The survey was realized as an online questionnaire to reach out to more participants who could not join the on-site workshops.[2] The questionnaire consisted of the following five sections:

1. General data about the role of the participant in the company
2. Use of Agile practices in the company
3. Evaluating the use of Agile in the company
4. Expectations from scaling Agile outside the software development teams
5. Expectations about challenges to be solved when scaling Agile

The first section contained three open-ended questions; the second section contained eight questions to be ranked as *Yes*, *No*, and *Not applicable* and an optional open-ended text field; the third section consisted of eight pairs that needed to be weighted on a scale from 1 to 7, where 1 means that the entire focus is on the left aspect of the pair and 7 that the entire focus is on the right aspect of the pair; additionally, an optional comment field was available. The fourth section consisted out of 16 expectations for benefits to be ranked on the 6-Likert-scale *very important, important moderately important, of little importance, unimportant,* and *not relevant*; this section was complemented with two optional questions asking for further benefits and drawbacks when scaling Agile. The last section consisted of 21 potential challenges collected during the workshops to be ranked on the same 6-Likert-scale as before; this section was also complemented with an optional question asking for further challenges.

The questionnaire was piloted with the single-points-of-contact (SPoC) from the involved companies to improve its logical structure and the overall understanding. The target group for this study contains the attendees of the on-site workshops extended in snowball manner (cf. Goodman [155]) by the SPoCs to reach out to more employees who are affected when scaling Agile.

5.3.3.3 Joint Workshop

After conducting on-site workshops and the survey, we organized a joint workshop where we invited delegates from all companies. These delegates covered different departments not only focusing on software development. The goal for the workshop was to present the findings from the separate workshops and the survey, to jointly discuss and complement with missing challenges, and to identify first steps towards initiating initiatives for scaling Agile outside software development teams. For the workshop, we invited an external Agile expert as moderator so that we could follow the discussions among the participants from an observer perspective according to the guidelines from Seaman as published in Shull et al. [408].

---

[2] The survey can be found as supplementary material here: http://goo.gl/yJNez1.

5.3.4 Analysis Procedure

5.3.4.1 Individual On-Site Workshops

Notes were taken during the separate on-site workshops alongside with capturing the resulting topic maps. The notes were structured and summarized as separate reports that were sent to the SPoCs afterwards. The collected clustered topics as well as key statements served as basis for designing the survey.

5.3.4.2 Survey

The survey was realized as online questionnaire that allowed post-processing of the data in the statistical environment R. The data was split according to the different sections in the survey and open-ended responses were separated. Likert-visualization was chosen for the range-, pair-focusing, and Likert-scale answers; for the pair-focusing answers, Fisher's exact test (cf. [126]) was chosen to test for differences pairwisely between all companies as this test is robust and applicable even to smaller data sets.

5.3.4.3 Joint Workshop with External Agile Expert

During the joint workshop, notes were also taken to complement and structure the existing data. The main results from the joined workshop were summarized and sent to attendees afterwards.

5.3.5 Validity Procedure

To ensure validity in our comparative case study, we applied both, method and data triangulation: For the former, (a) we initially conducted individual on-site workshops to explore the topic at the three different sites, followed by (b) separate surveys at the respective companies with a broad set of recipients, and complemented by (c) a joint workshop from the observer perspective, where we presented results from the first two steps. For the joint workshop, (a) we collected input from different, independent companies, and (b) let the final workshop be moderated by an external person to avoid influencing the workshop outcome.

5.4 Results

In the following, we are presenting the joint results from the three aforementioned data sources. As the notes from the individual on-site workshops were used to design and structure the survey, they are not reported here explicitly. The survey was completed by 11 respondents from company A, 19 respondents from company B, and 16 respondents from company C resulting in 46 responses in total.

Results to RQ-1

Figure 5.1 depicts the familiarity and usage of agile principles over all companies. While having *small teams* is apparently present to a large extent, test-driven development is only applied at one third of the respondents.

Results to RQ-2

The survey's next section asked to estimate where their own company puts its emphasis regarding pairs from opposite aspects regarding agile and non-agile values. Figure 5.1 visualizes the responses.

Fig. 5.1 Where do companies put their emphasis on? Respondents could express their emphasis on a scale from 1 to 7 to describe their level of favoring one topic over the other

We conducted a test to pairwisely compare the companies as shown in Table 5.1, and we could not observe any pairwise difference in the responses from the three different companies.

Table 5.1 Fisher's exact test with a p-value of 0.05: There is no difference in perceiving a company's emphasis between the responses from pairwisely comparing the companies

Where does your organization put emphasis on?	Companies		
	A/B	A/C	B/C
Individuals and interactions over processes and tools	$p = 0.691$	$p = 0.077$	$p = 0.072$
Working implementation over comprehensive documentation	$p = 1.000$	$p = 0.400$	$p = 0.272$
Customer collaboration over contract negotiation	$p = 0.433$	$p = 0.192$	$p = 0.694$
Responding to change over following a plan	$p = 1.000$	$p = 0.666$	$p = 0.476$
Product implementation over product delivery	$p = 0.380$	$p = 1.000$	$p = 0.440$
Product implementation over product integration	$p = 0.354$	$p = 0.642$	$p = 0.054$
Flexibility over predefined plan	$p = 0.679$	$p = 1.000$	$p = 0.452$
Teams over overall enterprise	$p = 0.411$	$p = 1.000$	$p = 0.710$

Results to RQ-3

The expected benefits when scaling Agile are presented in the following. As shown in Fig. 5.2, all companies expect with almost 90% a higher quality of the work products.

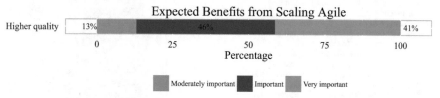

Fig. 5.2 Higher quality is expected from all companies

Figure 5.3 depicts further expected benefits when scaling Agile where the top responses expect faster time-to-market and shorter lead-times during the development.

Results to RQ-4

The expected challenges when scaling Agile are depicted in Fig. 5.4. The most difficulties are expected in the existing test facilities, which is in line with the low adaptation rate for test-driven development, followed by adapting the organizational structure.

The joint workshop with the external expert on Agile resulted after a discussion phase among the involved companies in the following four cluster areas for expected challenges when scaling Agile: Leadership, Collaboration, Focusing on System, and Focusing on Customer. From these four topic areas where different possible change initiatives were jointly identified, there was consensus between all companies for (a) *improving collaboration between all disciplines involved in product development*

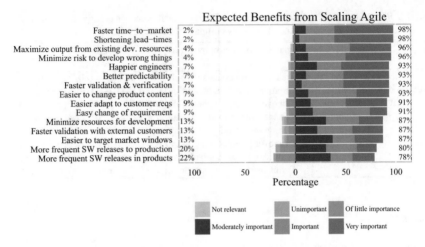

Fig. 5.3 Expected benefits from scaling agile over all companies

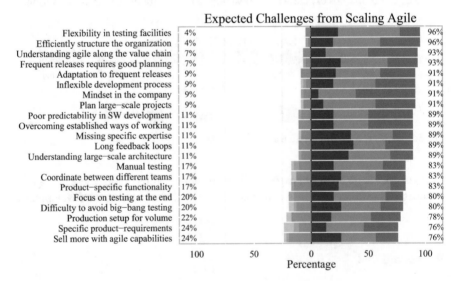

Fig. 5.4 Expected challenges when scaling Agile over all companies

and (b) *changing the overall mindset in the organization* as initial steps towards scaling Agile outside software development teams.

5.4.1 Threats to Validity

In the following, we are discussing threats to the validity of our comparative case study. Considering construct validity, our method triangulation reduced the risk of capturing incomplete data that would render in misleading results; in this regard, the plausibility of the findings from the different stages was validated with the SPoCs and the final joint workshop. A possible threat to the construct validity is that the survey was based on the underlying assumption that scaled agile development would actually have benefits for the organization, and that assumption may not be shared by respondents to the survey. Furthermore, the authors had only limited influence on the selection of the participants for the workshops.

Regarding internal validity, responses to the expected benefits from scaling Agile were gathered without associating implementation costs to them and thus, enforcing a prioritization. Thus, there might be a tendency from the respondents to wish or hope for all benefits from scaling Agile. As for initial initiatives to scale Agile, the most important challenges are of main interest, this risk, though, can be neglected.

Considering external validity, the selected companies reflect large scale enterprises with more than 15,000 employees and a volume-oriented production process. Furthermore, these companies are leading in their respective market segments and thus, the findings can be generalized to other companies in the mechatronics domains that have a lengthy and traditionally non-agile development process; this observation is also supported by the results from Fisher's exact test.

With respect to reliability, the iterative feedback of the company's SPoCs as well as the involvement of an external expert for Agile, the risk that the findings depend on the involved researchers was tackled.

5.5 Conclusion and Future Work

We presented a comparative case study conducted at three large-scale, mechatronics-driven enterprises to explore benefits and challenges from scaling Agile to non-software teams. The study consisted of individual on-site workshops, a large survey, and a joint workshop with all companies moderated by an external expert on Agile. While all companies have implemented elements from Agile, main findings are that (a) the expected main benefit is a faster time-to-market product development, (b) an inflexible test environment, though, inhibits fast feedback to changed or added features and thus, prevents scaling Agile outside the software development team, and (c) the existing organizational structure including the company's mind-set needs to be adapted to beneficially scale Agile.

Relation to Existing Evidence

Our results of the need for an agile mindset and the importance of the testing environment in mechatronics systems is confirmed by other studies. [290] concludes that observed resistance towards working agile was partially based on a lack of an agile mindset, caused by extensive experience with non-agile methods, something also common among the companies in our study. [360] also identified the challenge of realizing continuous integration testing with a wide variety of platforms. One example they mention is the difficulty to reproduce reported faults with the right testing environment including released hardware.

The other main challenge on adjusting the organizational structure confirms what many scaled methods aim for, and is also the topic of both recent research (e.g. [290, 471]) and of industrial frameworks such as Disciplined Agile Delivery [14].

Impact/Implications

This comparative case study is the first of its kind reporting about explorative results regarding expected benefits and challenges from scaling Agile at large scale, mechatronics-driven companies. Its findings have an apparent impact to companies with a similar development and manufacturing structure.

Limitations

All involved companies are at an comparable stage regarding scaling Agile. Thus, this comparative case study focuses primarily on the expected benefits and the foreseeable challenges when initiating initiatives for scaling Agile outside the software development teams.

Future Work

Future work needs to be done in continuously accompanying the enterprises during their initiatives for scaling Agile to collect and analyze more data towards guidelines and best practices for adopting and scaling Agile in mechatronics companies. Furthermore, comparisons with other domains would be possible to plan and guide such initiatives.

Acknowledgments

We are grateful to the companies who significantly supported this study in the context of Software Center.

Chapter 6
Lightweight Consistency Checking for Agile Model-Based Development in Practice

Robbert Jongeling, Federico Ciccozzi, Antonio Cicchetti, and Jan Carlson

Abstract In model-based development projects, models at different abstraction levels capture different aspects of a software system, e.g., specification or design. Inconsistencies between these models can cause inefficient and incorrect development. A tool-based framework to assist developers creating and maintaining models conforming to different languages (i.e. *heterogeneous models*) and consistency between them is not only important but also much needed in practice. In this work, we focus on assisting developers bringing about multi-view consistency in the context of agile model-based development, through frequent, lightweight consistency checks across views and between heterogeneous models. The checks are lightweight in the sense that they are easy to create, edit, use and maintain, and since they find inconsistencies but do not attempt to automatically resolve them. With respect to ease of use, we explicitly separate the two main concerns in defining consistency checks, being (i) which modelling elements across heterogeneous models should be consistent with each other and (ii) what constitutes consistency between them. We assess the feasibility and illustrate the potential usefulness of our consistency checking approach, from an industrial agile model-based development point-of-view, through a proof-of-concept implementation on a sample project leveraging models expressed in SysML and Simulink. A continuous integration pipeline hosts the initial definition and subsequent execution of consistency checks, it is also the place where the user can view results of consistency checks and reconfigure them.

Reprinted with permission from the authors. Originally published in Journal of Object Technology, Volume 18, no. 2 (July 2019). DOI:10.5381/jot.2019.18.2.a11

131

6.1 Introduction

The Model-Based Development (MBD) paradigm holds the promise of improving productivity of the development process by promoting models as core artifacts, particularly in early development phases, i.e., specification and design [392]. Further, models are also used for advanced development activities such as simulation and code generation. Besides, in industrial contexts, models as main project artifacts play an important role in documentation and communication between different development teams [446]. Models are becoming critical assets for development of industrial systems and software, not only within single projects but over several projects through model reuse. In modern industrial MBD practice, software systems are modelled through multiple views, using so-called *multi-view modelling* [70].

Views are represented by *heterogeneous* models, i.e., models conforming to different modelling languages (often created with different tools, which complicates consistency checking). Usually, these views are exploited by different teams and for different aspects of development. Consider the context shown in Fig. 6.1, where a system model, created by system designers to describe architectural matters, is refined into a set of software models by the software designers. In many cases, models across different views are closely related and they may partially overlap since they describe the same parts of a system. The use of multiple (often partially overlapping) views requires a careful checking and maintenance of consistency among them. Consistent models are in fact essential to ensure a coherent design as well as efficiency and correctness in the development process. While complete consistency (at any time in the development) may not be achievable or desirable, lingering inconsistencies can snowball into serious issues if not identified in early phases of development. A way to prevent this is to notify the developer about inconsistencies between models soon after their introduction, by means of consistency checking.

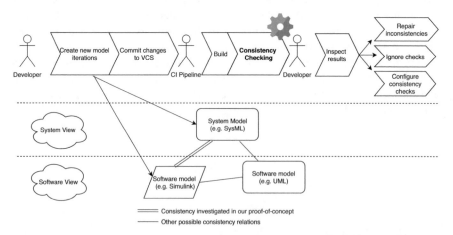

Fig. 6.1 Illustrating the scope of our approach, a tool performing inter-model consistency checking between heterogeneous models and notifying the developer about inconsistencies

Consistency checking within a model (i.e. intra-model consistency), or between models conforming to the same modelling language, is often available in modelling tools. We focus on checking inter-model consistency between heterogeneous models, which is a more complex endeavour for several reasons. Firstly, inter-model consistency often requires the ability to interact with a set of different modelling tools and processes in an industrial MBD context. Changes in this ecosystem are hard to make. Replacing a modelling tool to be able to perform inter-model consistency checks is often not feasible and any additional tool should not interfere with the existing ecosystem. Similarly, existing development processes are not easily changed, additional actions would be performed reluctantly in the best case, or skipped in the worst case, if they disrupt existing processes. Secondly, when consistency checks require a steep learning curve or excessive effort to create or maintain, the intended users may be discouraged from using them in the first place. Existing approaches, e.g. those based on Triple Graph Grammars [105] or link-models [123], are powerful but complex, hence requiring considerable effort to define and maintain consistency checks.

The context of this research is represented by an academia-industry collaboration called Software Center[1] and composed of 12 large companies and 5 universities. Among our industrial partners in Software Center, there is a clear trend of model-based development going agile. Very short cycles, typical of agile development, complicate consistency checking, especially if it requires a large effort in defining, maintaining and executing consistency checks. A consequence is that there is a need for a lightweight consistency checking approach. Lightweight means that it shall infringe minimally on existing development processes and tools, but aid developers in easily monitoring inter-model consistency. This kind of approach is currently lacking and much desired by practitioners.

In this paper, we show an application of consistency checking between heterogeneous models. We motivate requirements for a lightweight approach in Sect. 6.2, present a generic approach that satisfies these requirements in Sect. 6.3, and show an implementation of this approach in Sect. 6.4. Limitations and potential extensions to our approach are discussed in Sect. 6.5, a relevant portion of the extensive related work about consistency management is discussed in Sect. 6.6, while conclusions and some prospects of future work are included in Sect. 6.7.

6.2 Scope

We have already introduced the need for lightweight consistency checking. This section describes further our target industrial MBD context. From it, we derive a set of requirements for a lightweight consistency checking approach that is useful and usable in practice.

---

[1] www.software-center.se.

6.2.1 Industrial Context of Consistency Checking

Multi-view modelling refers to a practice in which a system is designed using multiple models (each of which representing a specific modelling view), potentially created in different tools and described by means of different languages [60]. Different models may describe the system under development, or just part of it, at different levels of abstraction and from different stakeholder perspectives, such as requirements engineer, system designer, or software developer. Yet, these models are commonly not disjoint, since they describe (parts of) the same system. There is often an explicit overlap, where multiple models describe, in the same or different levels of detail, the same parts of the system.

Kolovos et al. [254] classify the relationships between models that induce this overlap, of these, the most relevant in industrial practice are "uses", "refines", "complements", "alternative for", and "aspect of". Due to the nature of these relationships, they are highly correlated to the structure of the models. Kolovos et al. [254] go on to classify types of inconsistencies that can occur between overlapping models, the ones relevant to us are "incompleteness", "contradiction", "misuse", and "redundancy." Intuitively, a comparison of the structure of two overlapping heterogeneous models would show these types of inconsistency at a glance. While these relationships can occur between any pair of models, in our industrial context, we are primarily interested in consistency between models across different levels of abstraction, i.e., vertical inter-model consistency [198].

For example, let us consider a system model containing a SysML block B with two ports, P_1 and P_2. During system specification, the system designer might model parts of the system as a "black box", i.e., stop modelling at this level of abstraction and only care about the interfaces between blocks. Software designers on the other hand, as part of the system design, would model this as a "white-box", down to a more detailed level. They might, for instance, create a Simulink model S that describes B in more detail, with input and output ports corresponding to P_1 and P_2, and with additional details not included in B. This type of view relation between models S and B is commonly called *refinement* from S to B, or *abstraction* from B to S, respectively [356]. Other examples of these refinement relations include the one between a SysML model and an EPLAN[2] model to capture hydraulic schematics and between a SysML model and a Modelica model capturing the control system and dynamic behaviour, as exemplified in [400].

Figure 6.1 shows an overview of an industrial MBD context for which our proposed consistency checking is intended. Model inconsistencies across views, and thereby across e.g. specification, design, and implementation, complicate the development and evolution of systems. Inconsistencies shall never uncontrollably spread through the system design and one way to avoid this issue is by introducing consistency checks to support developers in identifying, at an early stage, possible inconsistencies in the system under development. Therefore, as shown in Fig. 6.1, the development team is aided, during development and evolution of the architectural

---

[2] https://www.eplanusa.com/us/home/.

and software models, in keeping these models consistent through lightweight checks that indicate discrepancies in the structures of the created models. Note that in the different views, several heterogeneous models could exist, for example UML models in the software view (as shown in Fig. 6.1). We highlight the generic applicability of our approach by choosing different languages in the example shown in Sect. 6.4.

To summarize, usable consistency checking, to ensure that models express overlapping concepts from different point of views without contradicting each other [351], is pivotal for multi-view modelling approaches to be efficient. For industrial adoption, tool support is vital, too. Next, we elaborate on which requirements an industrial application of such a consistency checking mechanism entails.

6.2.2 Requirements

Since models conforming to different languages are typically designed using different tools and ensuring consistency is often a manual task, inconsistencies between them could remain unnoticed for considerable time during development. This is particularly true when models are created in different views and for different aspects of the development. Let us exemplify in the context shown in Fig. 6.1. During the specification and design of a car, a system model denotes the overall design of the car and more detailed models are designed to describe software, electronics, braking system, etc. A possible inconsistency could be introduced between the structural model, conforming to SysML, and the refining functional model, conforming to Simulink, that fails to refine a particular block of interest as defined in the structural model. We aim to support the checking of vertical consistency between heterogeneous models in cases where models are related by one of the aforementioned relations and a certain overlap in the structure of the models exists. As already mentioned, notifying developers of possible inconsistencies of this type is considered as very helpful in industrial practice, given the complexity of the systems and the distribution of the development efforts.

Overlaps causing possible inconsistencies are, in most cases, not one-to-one relations between entire models, nor between model elements at the same granularity level. Rather, since different models describe the same parts of the system at different levels of abstraction, the overlap is more likely to spread across the different levels of granularity, e.g. an entire model refining a subsystem, or a package of multiple blocks refining a model. For example, in the case of SysML and Simulink models describing the same system, a Simulink subsystem might not map one-to-one to a SysML block, but rather the SysML block might be refined via an entire Simulink model, containing several subsystems. Our approach allows the definition of consistency checks between related model elements across different languages and granularity levels. Since model elements may represent complex sub-models (a model element being the container root of a sub-tree of contained model elements), our approach should be able to recursively execute consistency checks too, to account for hierarchical compositions and containments across models.

The need for consistency checking becomes more pressing when companies adopt agile multi-view modelling, in particular, when the development includes continuous integration (CI). CI refers to the practice in which developers integrate their work frequently, multiple times per day, in a shared repository [135]. In this context, inconsistencies between heterogeneous models are easy to overlook but nevertheless important to identify as soon as possible, to prevent them from rapidly spreading to related artefacts. Agile development implies that models are developed in short iterations and in parallel with other models. Consequently, any of the overlapping models can be seen as anticipating changes in the others at any time during development, e.g., the system model may not yet contain concepts already described in software models and vice versa. In these settings, inconsistencies are inevitable and almost required, since forbidding them would hinder the concurrent and incremental nature of agile. Automatic resolution is undesirable too, since in most cases it can not be determined which of the involved models should be reconciled in a scenario where any can be anticipating the others. Moreover, temporary inconsistencies are sometimes required to allow for particular development activities [335]. Therefore, we want to allow developers to choose if and how to act on detected inconsistencies. For this reason, we propose a consistency checking approach that identifies and indicates inconsistencies to the developers, without enforcing their resolution.

The frequency by which inconsistencies are presented to the developer, if not on-demand, is a sensitive matter: if too frequent, it becomes annoying, if too seldom, it becomes irrelevant. The CI pipeline provides a middle-ground, where inconsistencies can and should be presented at the time of pushing changes to the shared repository. Furthermore, it provides an environment independent of any particular modelling tool, where to configure consistency checks and view their results.

Industrial MBD practice typically involves many different tools, modelling languages, and development processes. Often, techniques fail because the process view is not taken into account. For example, because for the introduction of consistency checks, large changes to this environment, or to existing development process, are undesirable. Therefore, our approach should have a small footprint, i.e., be a minimal addition to existing MBD environment and a minimal added effort in existing development processes and ways of working. We aim for the application of consistency checks in an agile MBD process and in particular in a CI pipeline, so we must also minimize their interference with the developer flow. Consistency checks should thus also be lightweight with respect to the required effort to create, maintain, and use them. The checks themselves should be frequently executed, applicable to multiple languages and allowing for checking consistency across granularity and abstraction levels.

Table 6.1 summarizes the requirements described in this section and their motivation. Our goal is to provide an approach, and tool support, for detection and notification of inter-model inconsistencies, across heterogeneous models and in a CI pipeline for agile MBD projects. We focus on structural equivalence between model elements or parts of models, as well as for structural refinement between model elements and parts of models.

Table 6.1 Industrial practice (left) and the corresponding requirements (with ID) they entail (right)

During development, models are:	So, consistency checks should:
Created in different languages and tools	R1. Check inter-language consistency
Partly overlapping.	R2. Compare the structure of models
Related by refinement or equivalence at between model elements	R3. Allow consistency definition across model elements at different granularity
Purposefully, temporarily, inconsistent	R4. Not attempt automatic resolution
Changed continuously	R5. Be executed frequently
Created in complex environments	R6. Have a minimal impact to the existing environment
Created in complex processes	R7. Be easy to create, use and maintain

6.3 Our Consistency-Checking Approach

In this section we outline the constituents of our approach for checking consistency between models expressed in different views and languages.

The types of consistency interesting for the developer depend on the involved modelling languages and the system under development. Hence, the meaning of consistency cannot be decided a priori, but should rather be specified by the person defining the consistency checks. In some existing consistency checking approaches, the meaning of consistency is captured in an intermediate translation, like a case by case dictionary, formally defining how to compare model elements between different models (and languages). An example of fixed medium to express these 'dictionary entries' is Triple Graph Grammars (TGGs) [105]; this and other related mechanisms are discussed in more detail in Sect. 6.6.

In these approaches, each dictionary entry (mapping) describes two types of information. The first maps meta-model elements between different languages and how to check consistency between them. The second denotes model elements, across heterogeneous models, between which consistency should be checked. The user is expected to define both for each entry. In our approach, we propose to simplify the task of creating these entries by splitting the two information types as follows.

Mappings between meta-model elements across different languages and the definition of the various kinds of consistency that can be checked (e.g., name equivalence) are described in *language consistency mappings*. Mappings of model elements, across heterogeneous models, between which consistency should be checked and which specific kind of consistency to check are described in *model consistency mappings*. The user is only concerned with declaring and maintaining model consistency mappings, while the labor invested in creating language consistency mappings is limited to a one-time effort, unless the language undergoes changes. This makes the usage of our approach lightweight. Since we are dealing with heterogeneous models, in order to be able to compare them, and thereby check consistency, we need to represent them in a common notation.

---

[3] Note that in the paper we use 'language' and 'modelling language' interchangeably as synonyms.

A consistency check CC is composed of one language consistency mapping LC_{map} and one model consistency mapping MC_{map}. The remainder of this section presents LC_{map} and MC_{map} in detail and shows an overview of all the steps required for the definition and execution of consistency checks.

6.3.1 Language Consistency Mapping

A language consistency mapping LC_{map} consists of:

(1) a relation between different languages (at meta-element level), and
(2) the definition of consistency types.

As mentioned before, we aim at checking consistency by comparing models structure and their hierarchical nature. To structurally compare two heterogeneous models, we need to bring them to a common notation that highlights their structure. We opted for a tree-based notation since it permits to capture structures, and hierarchies, in a convenient and compact way. Furthermore, it is generic enough to represent models conforming to, potentially, any modelling language that entails structural modelling in a hierarchical fashion. Since we address in this case specifically comparisons of model structures, a tree structure suffices. In more general cases, more generic structures would be more appropriate. A tree is an abstract representation of a non-empty set of model elements, which precisely reproduces the model hierarchical structure. Model elements become nodes.

For example, in the case of Simulink models, blocks, subsystems and ports can be mapped to tree nodes, together with their hierarchical structure, whereas the operations inside blocks are not. Figure 6.2 shows an example of tree representation of a Simulink model, where "distiller" contains a subsystem "Distiller", which in turn contains subsystems "Heat_Exchanger" and "Boiler", which are in that hierarchy mapped to nodes in the tree.

Nodes inherit names from respective model elements and they are assigned an abstract type for comparison purposes (e.g., a Simulink inport and a SysML flowport become nodes of type 'port'). Types can be leveraged to check consistency in cases where name equivalence does not hold. For example, to check that two blocks, one in a SysML model and another in a Simulink model, contain the same number of 'ports', regardless of the names of these blocks and ports.

A LC_{map} between language L_A and language L_B consists of:

(1) two separate transpositions, from L_A and L_B to a tree-based notation TN, and
(2) a set of comparison rules between L_A and L_B (e.g. name equivalence) done at the TN level.

Figure 6.3 shows how a LC_{map} is used for comparing models. Technically, two models M_A conforming to L_A, and M_B conforming to L_B, are transposed into two corresponding trees T_A and T_B, conforming to TN, and comparisons are done between T_A and T_B.

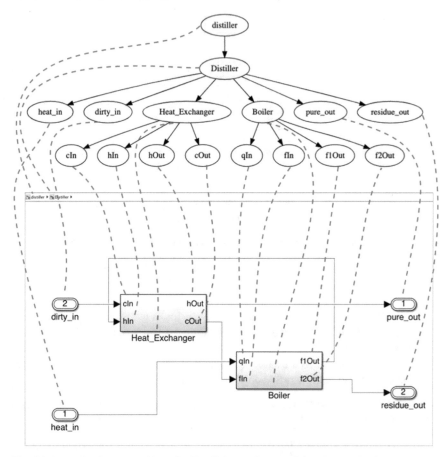

Fig. 6.2 Example of a transposition of a Simulink model to tree. Subsystems and ports are mapped to nodes in the tree, but not the simulation blocks inside the subsystems. The Simulink model is inspired by the well-known SysML Distiller example model [172]

Our proof-of-concept implementation provides two comparison rules, one for equivalence and one for refinement, exemplified in Fig. 6.4. Since we can do comparison based on node names, types, and structure of their tree representations, we defined three levels of consistency *strictness*:

- Strict: when comparisons are based on node names, types and structure;
- Intermediate: when comparisons are based on node types and structure;
- Loose: when comparisons are based on structure only.

Equivalence between nodes $n_A \in T_A$ and $n_B \in T_B$ is defined as follows, with respect to the strictness levels:

- Strict: n_A and n_B have the same name and type and the same number of children; in addition, each child of n_A has a *strict* equivalence to a child in n_B and vice versa;

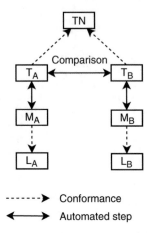

Fig. 6.3 LC_{map} consists of separate transpositions from both languages to a tree-based notation and a number of comparison rules. When executing a consistency check, automated model transformations transpose models into trees, between which automated comparison is run

- Intermediate: n_A and n_B have the same type, the same number of children; in addition each child of n_A has an *intermediate* equivalence to a child in n_B and vice versa;
- Loose: n_A and n_B have the same number of children; in addition, each child of n_A has a *loose* equivalence to a child in n_B and vice versa.

Refinement between nodes $n_A \in T_A$ and $n_B \in T_B$, where n_B refines n_A, is a directed relation defined as follows, with respect to the strictness levels:

- Strict: n_B has at least the same number of children of n_A and each child of n_A has a *strict* equivalence to a child in n_B.
- Intermediate: n_B has at least the same number of children of n_A and each child of n_A has an *intermediate* equivalence to a child in n_B.

Note that we do not define loose refinement, since its checking would not lead to meaningful inconsistencies.

Comparison rules – equivalence or refinement – can be defined between any pair of nodes $n_A \in T_A$ and $n_B \in T_B$, also when placed at different hierarchical levels in the respective trees. For two trees to be consistent (either through equivalence or refinement), their root nodes should be consistent. This also means that, if comparison rules are defined between roots of sub-trees, then all nodes above them would not be considered for consistency checking.

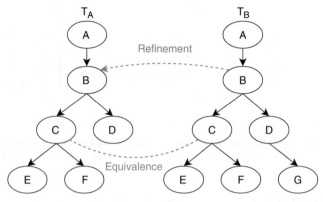

Fig. 6.4 Examples of an equivalence relation and a refinement relation between T_A and T_B. Node C in T_A is strictly equivalent to node C in T_B and node B in T_B strictly refines B in T_A

6.3.2 Model Consistency Mapping

A consistency check CC requires, in addition to a LC_{map}, a model consistency mapping MC_{map}, which consists of:

- two model elements, between which consistency should be checked,
- the type of consistency to check, and
- the level of consistency strictness.

To define MC_{map}, the user only needs to configure these three parameters. Automated mechanisms implementing LC_{map}, and the comparison rules defined in it, are then responsible for generating and executing the consistency checks. Once defined, CC can be executed at any time throughout the evolution of the entailed models, with the possibility to adjust its configuration if needed. Future extensions of our approach will reduce the effort of defining consistency checks by automated support, for instance by suggesting model consistency mappings based on potential matches identified through a similarity analysis between the heterogeneous models to be compared.

As mentioned in the explanation of language consistency mappings, the tree-based notation allows to easily compare models and their elements, also when placed at different hierarchical levels. Figure 6.5 illustrates examples of model consistency mappings. For instance, model B could be a refinement of model A, or parts of it, such as sub-model X or elements p or q. Similarly, parts of model B, for example sub-model Y, could refine sub-model X or element q. Lower level mappings are possible too: for example element r in model B refining element q in model A.

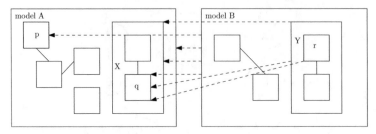

Fig. 6.5 Example of possible model consistency mappings between an abstract model A, refined by a model B. The dashed lines indicate possible refinement relations at different granularity levels

These model consistency mappings relate two model elements, but can be used to check consistency between more than two model elements, by chaining consistency checks. For example, to check that elements a, b, and c are equivalent, two consistency checks can be defined, one checking that a is equivalent to b and the other checking that b is equivalent to c. Future extensions of our approach will support grouping these checks such that one result summarizes all of them. For instance, if in the above example a is equivalent to b but b not to c, the grouped check would fail too.

6.3.3 Continuous Integration Pipeline

The execution of consistency checks is embedded in the CI pipeline, triggered by a model change that is pushed to a common repository, and executed after a build. A high-level description of the execution and configuration of a CC consists of the following steps:

1. MC_{map} is evaluated. Consider a mapping between model element e_A of model M_A in language L_A and a model element e_B of model M_B in language L_B

   a. LC_{map} between L_A and L_B is used to create trees T_A and T_B from models M_A and M_B, respectively.

   b. In T_A and T_B, nodes corresponding to e_A and e_B are compared using a comparison rule, corresponding to a combination of the type of check (equivalence or refinement) and the strictness level (strict, intermediate, or loose). Since comparison rules define a comparison between nodes by including, recursively, their children, technically the subtrees with root nodes represented by e_A and e_B are compared.

   c. The result of executing the CC is summarized as a binary outcome: pass or fail. In case of a failed check, a summary of the reasons behind the failure is shown to the user.

2. Configuration of existing model consistency mappings can be modified, including options to mute or skip checks in future runs.
3. The user can also add or delete model consistency mappings.

6.4 Proof of Concept

In this section we present a proof-of-concept implementation[4] of our approach. The approach is implemented as a plug-in for Jenkins,[5] a tool supporting automation of CI pipelines. In such a pipeline where a CI server is already in place and used to monitor the state of the development, including our consistency checks in both the process and toolset requires only a minimal overhead.

In the remainder of this section, we show the process of defining and executing consistency checks on the Distiller example [172] and applying it to one model consistency need that we identified exists in our industrial partners: a functional Simulink model refining a structural SysML model. Two models are created, one SysML model, shown in Fig. 6.6, and one Simulink model which refines selected subsystems of the SysML model, and which was shown earlier in Fig. 6.2.

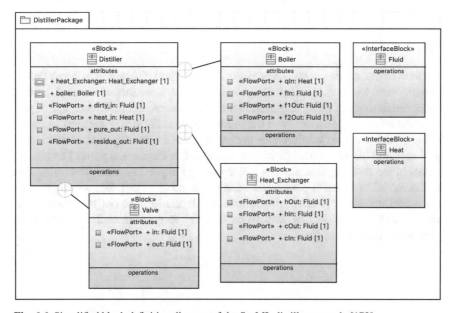

Fig. 6.6 Simplified block definition diagram of the SysML distiller example [172]

---

[4] For the interested reader, the implementation is available at: https://github.com/RobbertJongeling/consistency-plugin. A demo video https://github.com/RobbertJongeling/consistency-plugin/blob/master/Demo.mp4 showing the approach at work is available in the GitHub repository too.

[5] https://jenkins.io/.

Next, we briefly present the LC_{map} between the two entailed modelling languages and illustrate the implemented plug-in at work through an example of a consistency check definition and execution.

6.4.1 Language Consistency Mapping

To transform the structure of Simulink and SysML models to trees, we defined two model transformations, which map concepts from the respective modelling languages to a tree-based notation. Both transformations are implemented in Xtend,[6] to allow seamless integration with the Java implementation of the Jenkins plug-in. Transformations take in input the model files as they persist in the file system rather than requiring multiple interfacing with modelling tools. The models are then parsed and model elements of interest, as defined in the language consistency mappings, are added as nodes to a tree. In the current implementation, LC_{map} is embodied in the model to tree transformations. We are currently working on a more flexible implementation, where we will separate the definition of LC_{map} from the model transformation implementation. Once LC_{map} is defined, a set of higher-order model transformations will generate specific model to tree transformations based on LC_{map}.

SysML

A subset of SysML diagrams is represented by structural diagrams, i.e., block definition diagrams and internal block diagrams. In this work, we focus on SysML models described in terms of these diagrams. In our tree-based notation, the root node represents the entire SysML model and the tree hierarchy reflects the structural hierarchy of the model. The root's children are packages or blocks. Packages can contain other packages and blocks, while blocks can contain other blocks and ports. The SysML model in the running example was created using Eclipse Papyrus.[7] The translation of the model to a tree is performed taking in input the `.uml` file, which contains the model definition (without diagrammatic information). In our transformations, we leverage the `EMF Ecore Resource` facilities to programmatically access the contents of this type of file.

---

[6] https://www.eclipse.org/xtend/.

[7] https://www.eclipse.org/papyrus/.

Simulink

To parse Simulink models, from binary `.slx` or serialized `.mdl` format, we rely on CQSE's Simulink Library for Java.[8] As for the SysML model, the root node of the tree represents the Simulink model. The children nodes are then the SubSystems, Inports, and Outports contained in the models. SubSystems can contain other SubSystem, Inports and Outports. Note that we choose to omit certain types of blocks used to specifically implement Simulink simulations, such as logic operations and data conversions, since they do not affect the model structure.

6.4.2 A Consistency Checking Tool

In this section we detail the approach steps enumerated in Sect. 6.3.

Defining Model Consistency Mappings

Model consistency mappings are defined inside the Jenkins plug-in, by selecting the model elements between which consistency should be checked as well as the type and strictness of those checks. Figure 6.7 shows an example of consistency check definition. In our example, the type of model can be Simulink or SysML, but this can be extended to any language for which a transformation to the tree-based notation is implemented. When a modelling language is selected, the next drop-down box is populated with all model files of that language in the Jenkins workspace. When a file is selected, the next drop-down box is populated with all fully qualified names (FQNs) of model elements in the model, as represented in the related tree. Eventually, the strictness and type of check are selected. Note that, after checks are executed, the user can select to mute or skip them in future runs. Before executing the check, its result is set to *NYE* (Not Yet Executed), and no further comments are available.

Post-build: Run Consistency Checks

We have implemented the execution of our consistency checks as a post-build action in Jenkins. After the build step, the execution of the consistency checks is triggered and results are shown.

---

[8] https://www.cqse.eu/en/products/simulink-library-for-java/overview/.

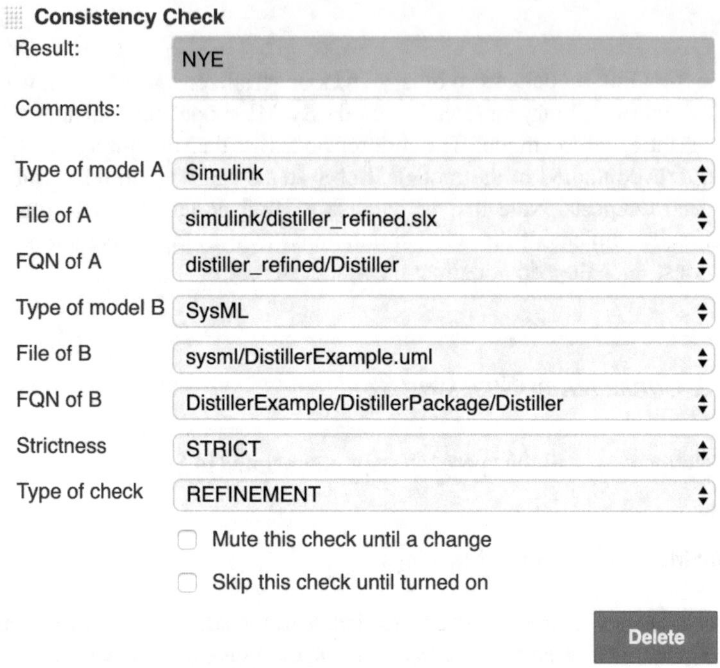

Fig. 6.7 Example definition of a model consistency mapping in the Jenkins plug-in. Here, the element Distiller of the Simulink model distiller_refined is said to strictly refine the element Distiller in package DistillerPackage in the SysML DistillerExample model

Comparing Trees

The first step in executing a consistency check is to transform the models to trees. Resulting trees for our running example are shown in Fig. 6.8, where the black nodes represent the model elements to be compared (their selection in the MC_{map} can be seen in Fig. 6.7. The refinement relation is now checked, not between the complete trees, but between the subtrees starting at the black nodes.

View Results and Manage Configuration

In this case, the consistency check fails, since the model element in model A is not a refinement of the model element in model B. The Valve is in fact missing in the Simulink model as compared to the SysML model. This short explanation is shown in the result field of the MC_{map} definition, as shown in Fig. 6.9. More detailed logs are available in the console output in Jenkins. A whole cycle of definition and execution of consistency checks is now completed. New consistency checks can be defined and existing ones edited or deleted. Model consistency mappings can also be left unaltered to be run again in future builds, or set to be skipped or muted.

a

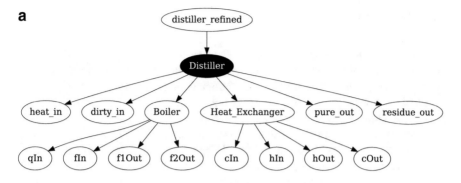

b

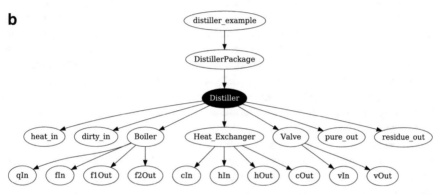

Fig. 6.8 (**a**) Tree representation of the Simulink model, only including *SubSystems* and *Ports*. (**b**) Tree representation of the SysML model, only including Blocks and Ports. The subtrees with root nodes indicated in black are compared

When a check is skipped, it is not executed in future builds, until the user enables it again. When muted, a check is executed but its results are hidden, unless they are different to previous results in its previous execution. This allows the user to mute reports on inconsistencies that are relevant but temporarily tolerated, for example when modifying a model and before propagating the changes to other related models.

Consistency Check	
Result:	FAIL
Comments:	Node: Distiller does not strictly refine Node: distiller_refined/Distiller. Missing: [Distiller/Valve, Distiller/Valve/vIn, Distiller/Valve/vOut]

Fig. 6.9 Result message of the failed strict refinement check

6.5 Discussion

In this work, we have focused on lightweight consistency checking to help developers discover structural inconsistencies between heterogeneous models. In particular, we have considered the requirements (Rx) summarized in Table 6.1. R1–R2–R3 are satisfied by choosing to construct an abstract tree representation from models. Indeed, this allows checking between models in different languages, since we compare their representations in a common format, but more importantly, this format represents the structural characteristics of the models, enabling their comparison. Comparison rules are defined between tree nodes, regardless of their position in the tree, so they enable consistency checking between model elements at different levels of granularity, for example an entire Simulink model can be compared to a single SysML block. R4 is fulfilled by providing detailed feedback on detected inconsistencies to the user, but not automatically resolving inconsistencies. R5–R6, regarding frequent execution and minimal impact on the existing ecosystem of consistency checks, are satisfied by the implementation of our approach in a CI pipeline. This provides a natural environment for executing the defined checks frequently, while not requiring a particular modelling tool nor notable changes to the development process. R7 states that our approach should consist of consistency checks that are easy to create, use, and maintain. This is satisfied by separating language consistency mappings from model consistency mappings, requiring the user to only input a small amount of information to generate and execute consistency checks. These checks are defined once and executed at each integration, unless they are skipped, muted, or deleted by the user.

Evidently, the proof-of-concept implementation only focuses on a limited industrial context characterized by multi-view modelling and consistency checking, but we have argued its applicability in broader context. We exemplify our approach by applying it to check consistency between a SysML and a Simulink model, but the approach is generic enough to deal with many different situations from industrial practice. For example, to check consistency between EAST-ADL models and AUTOSAR models, UML models and Modelica models, or even between architectural models and code. One of the powers of our approach and implementation is that it can be easily extended to accommodate such checks, requiring few extra things than a language consistency mapping for those languages.

Applying the approach in those different scenarios requires generalizing it beyond its main limitation, i.e., its entailed type of only structural consistency. Such generalizations can be supported by opting for a different intermediate notation than the current tree structure. When we consider a different metamodel in this place, also the comparison algorithms can be extended to detect more different types of inconsistencies. For example, when we consider not just the structure of models but also values of variables, the intermediate notation should also contain this information and then a comparison algorithm can be devised that utilizes that information for inconsistency detection.

A smaller limitation, intrinsic to our approach, is a decreased level of control over the case-by-case semantics of consistency checks. Instead, this has been for ease of use: the user relies on a global language consistency mapping created once and only specifies for each consistency check in a minimal way what elements are to be checked for consistency and what type of consistency should exist between them. The latter definition is reused throughout the evolution of the models, the consistency check is executed whenever the models are changed. The very limited effort required to use it together with the relevance of the entailed spectrum of identifiable inconsistencies and its non-disruptive nature, with regards to the development process to which it is applied, make our approach promising for use in industrial contexts.

In the current implementation, we have focused on a specific example relevant to industrial practice. To perform a full-scale industrial evaluation however, requires the implementation to be enhanced with additional language consistency mappings and capabilities to check other types of inconsistencies.

6.6 Related Work

Consistency among and within views is pivotal to ensure efficiency and correctness in the development process [207]. This work provides an approach to lightweight consistency checking between heterogeneous models in a multi-view modelling context. In particular, we study an industrial multi-view modelling environment [446] in combination with agile development practices.

Dajsuren et al. [83], also consider consistency between different views. Similarly to our approach, the authors prototype a tool for SysML structural diagrams aimed at the automotive industry, but the underlying approach is applicable to other languages as well. To enable comparison between models, both are first expressed at the same level of abstraction. The resulting models are compared as graphs to detect inconsistencies based on missing model elements or relations in one model that are declared in the other model. In their approach, model elements are annotated directly in the modelling tool to denote consistency between model elements at the same granularity level. Similarly, our approach aims to compare consistency between two different views with some structural overlap, but in addition it allows for checks across heterogeneous models and model elements at different granularity levels.

In this work, we create an abstract tree representation of models to enable comparisons between them. Other works employ other formalisms to achieve the same goal of being able to compare models in different languages. An often used mechanism is Triple Graph Grammars (TGGs), which allow a formal definition of the mapping of model concepts across different languages [105], for instance between SysML and Modelica as done by Johnson et al. [219]. As opposed to our approach, these approaches require a high effort in declaring and maintaining the consistency checks.

The consistency checking approach proposed by Egyed allows for the creation of consistency rules in any formalism [104]. Notably, in this approach, consistency checks are only executed when model elements they cover are changed, thus improving over approaches in which batches of checks are executed periodically. It can be a valuable future enhancement of our approach to similarly only execute those checks that relate model elements that have changed since the last execution.

Another means capturing the specific way of comparing particular model elements are link-models [123]. These link-models declare the relation between parts of models, and constraints on that relation, by relating model elements through particular types of links, equivalence, refinement or satisfies. The link-models are then used to derive validation rules that can be automatically executed. The applicability of this approach is limited to MOF-based models, whereas our approach is meta-metamodel independent.

Similar to our approach, also graph structures have been proposed as an intermediate representation of models as well as the starting point for detecting inconsistencies [179]. There, the graphs represent logical facts contained in the model, such that inconsistencies between graphs mean inconsistencies in the models. In our approach, the tree denotes not such logical facts, but rather focuses on the model structure.

In addition to approaches based on intermediate representations of models, others have proposed different means of comparison between models. For example, by declaring statements based on first-order logic to express facts that should be true about models [162]. Later, these ideas were more matured and generalized, for example in the Epsilon Object Language [253]. The advantage of our approach relative to these approaches is that the developer is not tasked with declaring such statements, since the meaning of consistency is captured in the language consistency mapping and the developer just specifies which model elements should be consistent.

The existing literature on consistency management in general is extensive [70], so necessarily, the included works cover only a small portion of it. Notably, Feldmann et al. categorize existing approaches as proof theory-based, rule-based, or synchronization-based [122]. Our approach can be categorized as synchronization-based, where the language consistency mappings define how model elements should be compared between languages, albeit not by a direct comparison but through an intermediary tree structure. Moreover, a plethora of approaches exists for consistency checking between UML models [285]. Even though there are numerous approaches presented, we are not aware of any approach satisfying the requirements with respect to lightweightness as listed in Sect. 6.2.

6.7 Conclusions and Future Work

In this work, we argued for inter-model consistency checks that are lightweight, i.e. easy to use and non-intrusive as they identify inconsistencies but do not strictly enforce consistency. The creation and maintenance of consistency checks is simplified by separating their definition in a globally reusable part, the language consistency mapping, and a simple specific definition, the model consistency mapping. The model consistency mapping can be used to notify the user throughout the (possibly parallel) evolution of involved models. We provided a proof of concept implementation and showed how the approach works on a simple example of inter-model consistency between models conforming to different languages.

While our approach is applicable to MBD in general, we showed its feasibility in agile MBD settings, by leveraging CI and related tools to implement consistency checks. Through our proof-of-concept, we showed the ease by which a user can define checks at different granularity levels and between heterogeneous models. Moreover, we showed the usefulness of lightweight checks for inter-model consistency in a CI pipeline, as well as possible interactions between a CI server, modelling tools and version control systems. In agile MBD settings, this approach allows simple explicit checking of consistency between a large number of model elements, thereby highlighting at a glance, and soon after their introduction, structural inconsistencies that may be costly to fix if detected at a later stage.

In our future work we plan to build upon the approach presented in this paper to enable the detection of additional and more complex inter-model inconsistencies, while maintaining its lightweight nature. Moreover, we will provide features to further simplify the manual definition of model consistency mappings, e.g. by having the tool to automatically suggest likely candidates. An evaluation of our approach in terms of an industrial case-study or controlled experiment will follow once the implementation will be more mature (and including the future enhancements listed in this paper).

Acknowledgment

This work is partially supported by Software Center[9] and by the Knowledge Foundation in Sweden through the MINEStrA project. The authors would like to thank Jagadish Suryadevara from Volvo Construction Equipment for his input in discussions about the work and his comments on early versions of the manuscript.

---

[9] www.software-center.se.

Part III

Metrics

Introduction to the Metrics Theme

Miroslaw Staron (Theme Leader 2011–)

1 Introduction

Measuring properties of software systems, organizations, and processes has much more to it than meets the eye. Numbers and quantities are at the center of it, but that is far from everything. Software measures (or metrics, as some call them) exist in a context of a measurement program, which involves the technology used to measure, store, process, and visualize data, as well as people who make decisions based on the data and software engineers who ensure that the data can be trusted.

The field of software measurement has been around since the first NASA conference on software engineering in 1968. It has been named as one of the subdisciplines of software engineering in 1976 with the publication of the book *Software Metrics* by Tom Gilb [152]. Over the years, this subdiscipline evolved from a simple "find-bug, record-bug" in the 1980s to a fully fledged AI-based analytics field of the late 2010s. Just beyond the corner, we can speculate that this AI-based measurement, machine learning, and continuous evolution of measurement will shape the next decade.

The challenges of the interconnected world play a significant role in what we measure. The recent focus on system safety, continuous integration, and cybersecurity will bring measures in these areas. AI will be a technology used for software measurement, and it will also be a technology that will need new measures – How to know that your deep learning AI-based software is safe? How do we know that it is trained sufficiently? When do we need to evolve the deep learning network to adapt to its new environment? Or how do we know that there is no adversarial code in deep learning systems? These are just examples of what the future can bring in the area of software metrics.

In the metrics theme, our focus has been to work collaboratively with Software Center companies, mostly on-site, to solve their challenges related to software measurement. We adopted a dedicated research methodology for that – Action Research [427]. This ability to be present at the premises of the companies is pivotal for

J. Bosch et al. (eds.), *Accelerating Digital Transformation*, https://doi.org/10.1007/978-3-031-10873-0_9

understanding their context and to deliver value to the collaborating companies, the academic community, and to the software engineering industry in general.

This part contains a synopsis of the 10 years of research in this area, focusing on the main contributions and the unique value provided by the metrics theme's research to Software Center and the software engineering community at large.

In this part of the book, we present three chapters that exemplify research studies conducted in Software Center's metrics theme. The first chapter demonstrates how to assess the quality of a measurement program. The assessment framework presented in this chapter includes a series of definition and explanations of what a measurement program is and why it is important for modern software organizations.

The second chapter presents how software measurement, combined with machine learning, can be used to improve the quality of software products. The chapter presents a method, a tool, and its application at two companies. It demonstrates the power of using machine learning to introduce flexibility in understanding the rules, create foundations for crowd sourcing of quality rules, and how to understand the evolution of software quality over time.

The third chapter shows how modern, biology-inspired algorithms can be used to quantify and monitor evolution of software processes. The chapter shows that applying this method provides software development companies tools to understand whether their process evolution happens "on paper" or "for real." The studies of software process evolution at one of the Software Center companies showed that process evolution happens over time.

Before we go through these specific chapters, let us take an overview of what we have accomplished over the last 10 years as well as take a peek as to what the future might hold.

2 Software Metrics in 2010, 2020, and Beyond

The metrics research in Software Center was initiated by the industrial needs to optimize the number of measures in an organization. In short, the organization collected a large number of measures but did not have control over how, when, and by whom they are used. The first collaborative practice was to introduce a common measurement language to the organization. We used the ISO/IEC 15939:2002 standard (which we later changed to version 2007) to establish a common, standardized nomenclature [208, 430]. After introducing the standard, we realized that the number of measures collected was unjustifiably large. Figure 1 shows how we visualized the set of measures for one software development program. The figure illustrates the vocabulary that we used in the company at that time – the notion of indicators, base, and derived measures.

Using the standard led us to the first contribution, which fundamentally changed the way we work with measures today – instead of focusing on what can be measured,

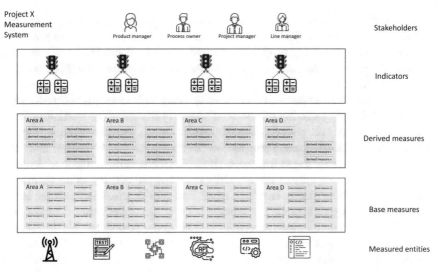

Fig. 1 Measures and indicators for one software development program. The names of the measures and indicators are obfuscated

we focused on the stakeholders and their information needs (what needs to be measured and why). This led to the reduction of the number of measures by an order of magnitude – as it is shown in Fig. 2.

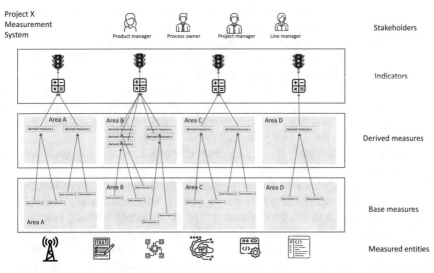

Fig. 2 Measures and indicators for one software development program. The names of the measures and indicators are obfuscated. The smaller number of measures illustrates the shift of focus from *What can be measured?* to *What do we need to know?*

In addition to the reduced number of measures, we can also observe that the top of the figure (the indicators) is now connected to the bottom (base measures and measured entities). By explicitly linking the measured entities, base measures, derived measures, indicators, and the information needs, we visualized what is measured and why.

An example of an impact of this kind of working with measures is transforming defect counting to predicting release readiness – [429, 438]. The starting point of the transformation was counting the number of defects reported at each stage of software testing (and by customers), as illustrated by Figs. 3–6. At the beginning, the focus of the company was to understand how the trends in the number of detected defects (a.k.a. defect inflow) are shaped during the project. By using regression techniques, we could extrapolate these trends and provide predictions for the entire project. These long-term predictions for the entire projects were useful, but they led us to discovering another industrial information need – how to predict the number of defects for the next few weeks in order to prioritize resources. To address that, we developed techniques for predicting the number of defects on a weekly basis and introduced them to the company. After a few months of the use of these predictions, the company wanted to focus on the trend rather than the exact number of defects, which led to the development of the first MS Windows Vista Gadget, shown in Fig. 5. When predicting the number of defects, we also understood that these predictions are based on the processes and data sources related to testing, defect removal, and release preparations. The company identified another information need – how to predict when their software is ready to release in their new, Agile, process. Together with a team of product, line, test, and quality managers from the company, we designed a measure of release readiness – Fig. 6. This measure helped the company to become more responsive and showed that it is possible to track progress of large software development projects using one, product-focused, indicator.

Figure 6 shows one of the visualizations of measures, which had a significant impact on the collaborating company. Over the course of our collaboration, we observed that visualization was one of the cornerstones of measurement programs – those measures and indicators which were supported by good visualizations were more impactful than others. The other were the notions of *measurement systems* [437], *information quality* [431], and *self-healing* [426].

In 2021, 15 years after the introduction of these methods, the measurement programs in the Software Center companies are more mature than the ones we started with. One of the companies established a fully fledged measurement program (including a measurement team) within 18 months. Another company introduced a measurement team and a basic measurement program already within 1 year.

We have learnt that challenges addressed by the measurement programs evolved significantly. The number of questions related to what should be measured has decreased. At the same time, the number of questions related to how to measure something specific (e.g., productivity, speed) and how to continuously improve has increased (e.g., how to increase the efficiency in code reviews) [440], still with the strong focus on delivering new methods, tools, and technologies to support Software Center companies.

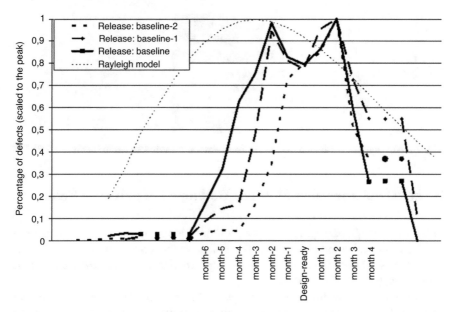

Fig. 3 An example of long-term defect inflow predictions – predicting defects on a monthly basis

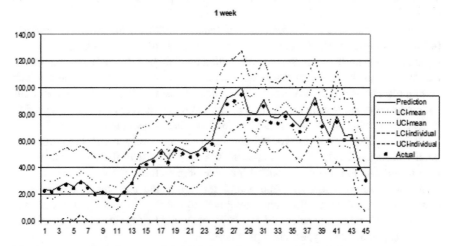

Fig. 4 An example of short-term defect inflow predictions – predicting defects on a weekly basis

Fig. 5 An example of defect trend prediction – predicting defects and the trend on a weekly basis

Fig. 6 An example of predicting release readiness – when the software will be ready

3 Industrial Tools and Methods Developed in Software Center

One of the unique strengths of Software Center is the open collaboration culture between companies and universities. This collaboration resulted in the co-creation of several results. Let us demonstrate a few examples of the most widespread innovations – methods, tools, and products.

One of the most widely spread concept was the concept of a *measurement system* [431, 437]. The framework was used to instantiate over 50,000 measurement systems and has opened up possibilities to address research problems of which measures to use [425] and how to design their visualizations [435].

One such measure is the *indicator of release readiness* for software products [438], as shown in Fig. 6. This indicator was used to monitor the agility of an organization. The development of this indicator demonstrates how co-creation of results leads to changes in software companies and to dissemination in the research community. In short, the novelty of the indicator was that it combined continuous data from software testing and defects to calculate the number of weeks required to release the product without any information from the project plan!

An example of another type of online system was the development of requirements quality model – Rendex [16]. The model was developed with three companies and later introduced as a feature in one of the development tools at one Software Center company. Rendex is a model and a tool for measuring and visualizing internal quality of requirements. Its main strength is the ability to quickly analyze over 10,000 requirements and select the top 100 that should be rewritten because of their vagueness, inconsistency, or incompleteness.

It is this ability to "find the needle in a haystack" that characterizes many of the metrics theme's projects. One more method and tool, which demonstrates this, has been developed in a project associated with Software Center, Quasar – Quantifying Architectural Changes in Automotive Software [98]. The tool has been used to monitor architectural changes when introducing new versions of the AUTOSAR standard into new car models. By using the tool, the collaborating Software Center company managed to shorten their analysis time from months to days.

4 The Future

The future of the metrics theme will be shaped by the trends in software development. We can take this opportunity and discuss what these trends are and how they can shape the area of software measurement and thus the metrics theme in Software Center.

First, and probably the most significant trend, is the fact that AI and ML have been established as fully valued tools to improve software engineering. Beyond the classical tasks of predicting defects, supporting code reviews, and similar, the AI and ML technology is used to off-load certain tasks of software engineers. CodeX, which is a neural network tool designed by Open AI, is on the verge of being released. From the announcements, this tool can be used to write programs from low level requirements. This may seem like a small step, but it is a significant one. This means that even non-programmers can get a possibility to write programs for data collection, processing and visualization. On the one hand, this will increase the use of measures, while on the other hand it will require new ways of governing and maintaining measurement programs.

Another aspect which will influence the software engineering industry, and the discipline of software measurement, is climate change (including the energy shortages). The focus of software companies shifts towards sustainable software, green software, and energy-efficient software. This shift brings the change in how software is designed and used. Diagnostic measurements, energy-efficient measurements, and optimization algorithms are just some of the areas which need new measures and measurement mechanisms.

The third trend which will shape software engineering in the coming decade is cybersecurity. When the Covid-19 pandemic emerged, work from home became one of the default modes of working. Many professions have shifted to that mode and started to use work infrastructure from home, which opened up new security threats, e.g., ransomware attacks. Since many believe that the work-from-home model is here to stay, software development companies will need to introduce new mechanisms to handle potential cybersecurity threats. This means that software engineers will require new measurements for potential attacks, vulnerabilities, and threats, as well as methods to tackle them (and to measure the effects of applying these methods).

Finally, wearables, Internet of Things, and automation will change the way in which we use software. Programs will become smaller but more interconnected. Software systems will become more distributed and consist of many interconnected programs. They will also become more safety critical – used in medicine, operating rooms, elderly care. This means that the measures used in software development will also change from internal, software construction measures (e.g., algorithm complexity) to external, connectivity measures (e.g., system connectivity).

Chapter 7
MESRAM – A Method for Assessing Robustness of Measurement Programs in Large Software Development Organizations and Its Industrial Evaluation

Miroslaw Staron and Wilhelm Meding

Abstract Measurement programs in large software development organizations contain a large number of indicators, base and derived measures to monitor products, processes and projects. The diversity and the number of these measures causes the measurement programs to become large, combining multiple needs, measurement tools and organizational goals. For the measurement program to effectively support organization's goals, it should be scalable, automated, standardized and flexible – i.e. robust. In this paper we present a method for assessing the robustness of measurement programs. The method is based on the robustness model which has been developed in collaboration between seven companies and a university. The purpose of the method is to support the companies to optimize the value obtained from the measurement programs and their cost. We evaluated the method at the seven companies and the results from applying the method to each company quantified the robustness of their programs, reflecting the real-world status of the programs and pinpointed strengths and improvements of the programs.

7.1 Introduction

Measurement programs in large software development organizations are subjects to constant changes [337], since as the software market changes, so do the software development organizations and their information needs. The evolution of measurement programs is natural and should be monitored and managed in order for the measurement program to remain effective and efficient for the organization. From the perspective of the measurement programs, these changes in the organization can cause its decay and in the end its failure if not institutionalized properly. However, a good measurement program has mechanisms that will assure its robustness to

Reprinted with permission from the copyright holder. Originally published in Journal of Systems and Software 113 (2016): 76–100. DOI: https://doi.org/10.1016/j.jss.2015.10.051

J. Bosch et al. (eds.), *Accelerating Digital Transformation*,
https://doi.org/10.1007/978-3-031-10873-0_10

changes – for example well-defined measures and well-accepted measurement organization. The robustness of the measurement program is important as it assures a structured approach to using measures and indicators over time, in presence of the changing conditions as indicated in previous work of Buglione and Abran [61] in the context of long-term software process improvement. In addition to these long-term improvements the robustness of the measurement programs is important when using them in large scale organizations over the long term – for example for the cost-efficiency as indicated by Baldasarre [23] who argues that the ability to balance the breadth of a measurement program (number of metrics and indicators) with the effectiveness of their use (comprehension) and inter-dependencies between the metrics can determine the cost of the maintenance of the measurement program. When establishing new measurement programs the aspects of breadth and effectiveness can be balanced as two success factors when following such processes as defined by Desharnais and Abran [86]. However, this initial balancing can change over time, which creates the need for a method that assesses the robustness of existing measurement programs. Therefore, in this paper we focus on addressing four research questions:

- *RQ1: How to assess the robustness of a measurement program?*
- *RQ2: To what extent do the measurement programs differ depending on process model?*
- *RQ3: To what extent do the measurement programs differ depending on product type?*
- *RQ4: To what extent do the measurement programs differ depending on in-house vs. outsourced development style?*

Addressing the first research question (RQ1) resulted in a method for assessing the robustness of measurement programs in industry. Conducting the assessment at seven large software development companies provided us with the possibility to study whether measurement programs differ depending on such factors as process model (RQ2 with Agile, Waterfall and V-model as factor levels), product type (RQ3 with infrastructure and customer products) and the in-house vs. outsourced development style (RQ3).

In the first research question (RQ1) we consider a measurement program to be *robust* when it can operate despite variations (where evolution is a special kind of such a variation) in measurement needs, infrastructure, organization and decision processes. This definition is a revised definition of robustness as a quality attribute from IEEE Standard Glossary of Software Engineering Terminology [364].

In order to be able to handle changes a robust measurement program has to be able to incorporate a broad set of measures, has a support organization which maintains the measurement program (and the know-how around it), has a solid infrastructure which is cost-efficient and flexible, and is used in an organization which uses the measures in decision processes. A robust measurement program is also open for changes by constantly learning from others – both from industry and academia.

In order to capture the technical and organizational aspects of measurement program we discuss two facets of them – the ability of the measures in the measurement program to accurately capture the measured quantities (empirical properties of measurands) and the acceptance of the measurement program in the organization. We use the theories from metrology (c.f. [5]) and empirical metrics validation (c.f. [124]) in the discussion of the accuracy and the organizational change theories by Goodman at al. [157] to discuss the institutionalization of the measurement program.

Based on these discussions we developed the robustness model and a method for assessing robustness of measurement programs, during an action research project at a large software development organization with a mature measurement program and measurement culture. The Measurement System Robustness Assessment Method (MeSRAM), which is the result of our work, has been evaluated through a pilot study at a software development company with a different, distributed metric organization, expanded based on the feedback and evaluated in at five other organizations developing software for embedded products. In total we have applied the method at seven large software development companies in Sweden and Denmark: an infrastructure provider company, Volvo AB, Volvo Car Group, Grundfos, Saab Electronic Defense Systems, Sony Mobile and Axis Communications. All of the companies are either market driven or infrastructure providers and all develop embedded software. Due to the confidentiality agreement, we refer to the companies as Company A-G in a randomized order.

From the industrial perspective, our two-year long research project to develop and evaluate MeSRAM started with the intention to develop a tool that would give the companies a graphical result that could be used by all involved parties in the respective company. The graphical result should be easy enough to highlight main metric related areas that (a) are mature or good enough, or (b) need to improve.

Applying the method resulted in in-depth discussions and exchanging of experiences between the participating companies, changing parts of the measurement infrastructure at Company B and exchange of experiences between the first company and the company participating in the pilot project. Each result (i.e. graph) was validated by the interviewees at the respective company (including the metrics person from the metrics research team), i.e. we used qualitative evaluation to judge each outcome. The experiences from the evaluation were that the robustness model can guide the development of a measurement culture and program at any organization – a conclusion from applying MeSRAM to companies with different maturity and measurement culture.

The data collected from the application of MeSRAM allowed us to analyze the differences between the companies to address the research questions RQ2–RQ4. Our results show a number of insights, for example that the companies coming from the waterfall, in-house development use the largest number of metrics, but need improvements in the dissemination and acceptance of them. Another example is the finding that the companies working with outsourcing are generally better in monitoring the usage of metrics but require improvement to widen the scope of the measurement program.

The remaining of the paper is as structured as follows. Section 7.2 describes the previous research related to assessing the quality of measurement programs. Section 7.3 describes measurement programs and their structure in order to provide the foundation for the discussions on the dimensions of the robustness model presented in the forthcoming section. Section 7.4 describes MeSRAM and Sect. 7.5 presents the evaluation of it. Section 7.7 discusses the threats to validity of our study and finally Sect. 7.8 concludes the paper.

7.2 Related Work

Robustness of measurement programs to changes in organizations is an important aspect. Traces of the challenges related to the robustness to change can be found in previous studies of such aspects as longevity of measurement programs. Kilpi et al. [239] presented the experiences of establishing a measurement program at Nokia recognizing the importance of the proper definition of metrics and the infrastructure. However, the experiences presented do not provide a quantifiable set of factors determining the success. MeSRAM addresses this issue by quantifying the concept of robustness and providing the corresponding assessment method.

There are numerous studies describing experiences from establishing measurement programs in industry which usually address the challenges with the initial development and acceptance of the measurement program, but not the challenges related to making the measurement program able to adapt to changes in the environment. One of the studies has been done by Umarji et al. [462], who studied the use of technology adoption theory when implementing metric programs and therefore focusing on the social issues such as management commitment and support. The study is important, but we perceive the technology, infrastructure and the organization of the measurement program as inseparable and therefore all of these need to be included as it is in the case of MeSRAM.

A complement to Umarji et al.'s study is a survey study of 200 participants, conducted by Nessink et al. [336, 337] where the focus was on the organization (employees) and not the management, which resulted in exploring such factors as the roles which are interested in measurement data. Similarly to the study of Umarji et al. we perceive these aspects as inseparable and include them in MeSRAM, thus broadening the view on the factors to both social and technological.

In our previous work [436] we studied the processes of establishing measurement programs in large organizations but we focused on the holistic challenges related to the implementation of the measurement program, not on the robustness to changes. This focus allows to set up widely used measurement programs, but can also lead to the explosion of measurement systems. In a subsequent study of the same organization [432] we found that the measurement infrastructure is equally important as the information needs. The technology behind the infrastructure, however, was not as important as the broad set of metrics. The need to balance the number of measurement systems, their usefulness and the cost to maintain them, are introduced in MeSRAM.

Diaz-Ley et al. [90] developed a framework for small enterprises for assessing the quality of measurement programs. The framework captures the basic attributes of a good measurement program, but needs extensions to scale up the program – which we address in MeSRAM by quantifying the elements of a robust measurement organization.

Jorgensen [220] has studied the longevity of measurement programs from the perspective of the reuse of metrics. As his work shows, this is not an easy task, due to the potentially different definitions of measures. In MeSRAM we expand on this kind of study and propose to explore the metrics from the perspective of organizational change acceptance, which can explain why some metrics are successful and some not (e.g. linking to decisions).

Measurement programs in industry are often associated with introducing or driving the change of organizations. Unterkalmsteiner et al. [463] provide a set of information needs to stakeholders, for successful indicators of software process improvement initiatives. In our work on MeSRAM we complement the set of measures in the category "metrics used" with the aspects related to the design (construction) of the software product – e.g. design stability. In our work we perceive these as capturing the dimension of the "object of change" from the software process improvement literature (e.g. [3]).

Daskalantonakis et al. [84] have developed a method for assessing the measurement technology from the perspective of supporting maturity levels (compatible with the CMMI model). Their work is based on ten themes characterizing measurement processes as part of maturity assessment – e.g. formalization of the measurement process or measurement evolution. We used these themes when designing the categories of MeSRAM, however, we have mostly relied on the theories by Goodman and Dean [157]. The reason for this choice was that Goodman and Dean's theories are more generic and do not link the levels to maturity – something which was explicitly requested by the industrial partners.

In the case of our work we use the theories by Goodman and Dean [157] to describe the introduction of the measurement program as a change in the organization. We follow their recommendations that the effect of change or a single measure should be considered separately in the context of the change. In our work we focus on the ability of the measurement program to be able to support the organizations in conducting the changes – introducing new measures, using the measures in the decision support and providing expert competence to support measurement initiatives at the company.

7.3 Measurement Programs

Measurement programs in industry are socio-technical systems where the technology interacts with stakeholders in order to support certain goals [147, 458]. Even though the term *measurement program* is defined informally in literature, the international standard ISO/IEC 15939:2007 (Systems and Software Engineering: Measurement process) introduces the concept of *measurement management system* which comprises both the measuring systems (e.g. instruments for data collection and visualization), the infrastructure where these operate, the knowledge bases on the use of measures and the stakeholders involved in the measurement process.

In this section we present the view of the measurement program which is derived from ISO/IEC 15939 by applying the standard's concepts in industrial setting. The view was developed based on the workshops and discussions with the companies participating in this study. We structure our description around the methodological aspects of defining and using measures and the implementation aspects of effects the metrics have in organizations.

7.3.1 Defining and Using Measures

The fundamental aspect of measurement is the ability of the measures to correctly capture the measured property. This fundamental aspect is derived from the metrological notion of measurement which is the way in which a given quantity of an object (a measurand) is captured to a numerical property (the measure) [5].

The process of measuring – measurement – is the process of assigning the value to a variable – a metric – in a structured, repeatable and deterministic manner. The measurement process is free from the influence of the goal of measurement and is related to the measured quantity – called base quantity in metrology (c.f. [5, 204]). The process of validation, whether the measure is related to an empirical attribute which is part of an empirical theory, is often referred to as the *empirical measure validation* – also referred to as the usefulness of a metric according to Briand et al. [53].

However, the proper definition of a measure requires that the measure has certain properties, which are often related to the type of measured quantity and the properties of this type. Briand et al. [55] have defined a set of the most common types of measures and a set of their properties. They have defined the following types (characterized only briefly here, for details the readers are referred to the original article [55]):

- Size: capturing the intuitive property of each entity – its size; it has the properties of being non-negative, having null-value (for empty programs) and being additive (capturing concatenation of programs),
- Length: capturing a uni-dimensional view of the size property; it has such properties as non-negativity, null value, non-increasing monotonicity for connected components, non-decreasing monotonicity for non-connected components and disjoint modules.
- Complexity: capturing the difficulty of understanding or using the concept; it has such properties as non-negativity, null value, symmetry, module monotonicity, and disjoint module additivity.
- Cohesion: capturing the "tightness" of how elements are related to each other internally; it has such properties as non-negativity and normalization, null value, monotonicity and cohesive modules.

- Coupling: capturing how tight elements are related to one another externally; it has such properties as non-negativity, null value, monotonicity, merging of modules and disjoint modules additivity.

Although the theoretical (or property-based) measure validation does not address the issue of whether the measure correctly captures the measurand, it provides the fundamental assessment of the correctness of the construction of the measurement method. Briand et al.'s framework was an extension of the work of Weuyker on a method for evaluation of complexity measures [476].

In our work we consider two parts of the theoretical metric validation of higher importance than others – the types of entities measured (e.g. product, project) and the proper definition of the measures, capturing the breadth of the measurement program and its depth. We link these two parts to the robustness model as part of the *metrics used* dimension presented in Sect. 7.4.2.3.

The properties of measures characterize the measures themselves, but not the measurement process. In mathematical terms the measurement process is a mapping of entities from the empirical domain (quantities and their relations) to the mathematical domain (numbers and their relations). Metrology recognizes the notion of limited fidelity of measurement instruments (discussed in the next subsection) and captures that in the notion of uncertainty of a measurement.

The notion of certainty characterizes how well a given measure captures the intended quantity of a measurand. The empirical measure validation is often used to validate that such a mapping is correct [124]. The empirical measure validation is often organized as experiments where the factor levels are often correlated with the measured outputs and the degree to which this correlation is valid (defining its confidence level), is used to assess the validity of the measure. Object-oriented measures were validated in such a manner in multiple research studies (c.f. [166, 444]) and this kind of validation is important to establish the ability of measures to capture abstract properties (e.g. defect-proneness) as well as base quantities (e.g. size).

7.3.2 Implementation of Measurement Programs

Having the measures properly and correctly defined is a prerequisite for a robust measurement program, but is not the guarantee of it. The way in which measures are collected, analyzed and disseminated in the organization is of equal importance. It is referred to as *implementation of a measurement program* which is where the socio-technical theories are used such as [147, 458]. The measurement system combines the social aspects of human perception of measures (e.g. believability of measurement results) with the technology (e.g. the measurement infrastructure used to collect and present measures).

When discussing the effectiveness of the measurement program in its sociological dimension, we choose the organizational change adoption theory by Goodman et al. [157], the later extension by Goodman and Dean [158], and finally its adaptation to the metrics adoption [156]. The theory of change in organization evaluates how well a change is *institutionalized* in the organization – i.e. adopted – and the impact it has on the organization.

The theory of organizational change uses the notion of degree of institutionalization of the change, organized in five facets when conceptualizing the institutionalization:

1. knowledge of the behavior – concerns the extent to which an individual possesses the knowledge of the change in order to be able to perform the new tasks; in terms of the measurement program this relates to how much the organization knows about the measurement program,
2. performance of the behavior (which we rename to "performance of the measurement" in the paper) – concerns the performance of the new tasks; in terms of the measurement program this relates to whether the measurement activities are performed in the organization (for example by a dedicated group of individuals),
3. preferences of the behavior – concerns the attitude to the change; in terms of the measurement program this means that it is perceived as "good" by the organization,
4. normative consensus – concerns the general acceptance of the change – the knowledge that others perform the activity and consensus about the appropriateness of them; in terms of the measurement program this means how well the measurement results from the program are used (for example for making decisions), and
5. values of the behavior – concerns social consensus on the values relevant to the behavior; in terms of measurement systems this means that there is a consensus on what ought to and ought not to be measured and why.

We use these facets when designing the robustness model presented in Sect. 7.4.2. In this paper we focus on the evaluation of the degree of institutionalization of the measurement program. The degree of institutionalization of the change caused by the use of each of the measures requires individual case assessment (as argued by Goodman and Dean [158]). In order to come back to these facets of change in the robustness model we also need to discuss the technological aspects of the measurement programs.

7.3.2.1 Measurement Systems

In this section we discuss the aspects important for the implementation of the measurement systems (the technological dimension of the measurement program). Measurement systems are also instrumental in the "performance of the behavior" facet from Goodman et al.'s organizational change theory.

The concept of a measurement system is not new in engineering in general and in software engineering in particular – measurement instruments and systems are one of the cornerstones of engineering. Measurement instruments (in general) are designed for a single purpose to measure one type of quantity and usually collect one metric (e.g. voltage). Measurement instruments are very fundamental in engineering (e.g. [224, 259, 397, 496]) as they implement the metrological concept of a mapping between an empirical property and the numerical value. The quality of such an implementation is related to the quality of the definition of the mapping and the ability to quantify the measured quantity with a given degree of certainty.

Metric tools are collections of measurement instruments for one entity – the metric tools collect usually a number of metrics at the same time (e.g. length of the program, its complexity). Examples of this kind of metric tools are typical in software engineering (c.f. [481]).

Finally measurement systems are systems which combine a number of measures in order to address an information need of a stakeholder. The measures do not have to come from a single measurement instrument or quantify properties of one type of entity, but can come from multiple measurement instruments. Only the measurement systems make such a combination of multiple measures – called base measures – into more complex ones – called derived measures. They also can add interpretation in form of an analysis model thus providing indicators – c.f. [348, 437].

The notion of a measurement system is closely related to the ISO/IEC 15939 standard and its measurement information model (c.f. [348]). The model recognizes three different types of measures – base measures for quantifying the base quantities like size, derived measures combining the base measures by means of analysis and indicators adding the interpretation to the values of the measures by means of analysis models. Instantiating the measurement information model and the ISO/IEC 15939 standard when designing measurement systems specifies the structure of the measures in measurement systems. There exists a body of research discussing the methods to design measurement systems based on this standard (c.f. [5, 437]).

The ISO/IEC 15939 standard, however, needs extensions towards defining the reference model of measurement (c.f. [5]) in order to define the analysis model consistently over the body-of-knowledge in the given domain (e.g. product complexity). By developing the reference models, the designers of measurement systems codify the best practices and knowledge in the relevant measurement area (relevant to the information need of the stakeholder) thus providing a solid grounding for making decisions based on the values of indicators. This definition addresses another facet of Goodman et al.'s institutionalization of change – normative consensus – it provides the frame of reference for the assessment of how well the measurement is accepted by the community and by the organization [159].

There may be multiple solutions how to realize measurement systems – for example using business intelligence tools and their reporting functionalities or using simplistic MS Excel files. The measurement systems combine the inputs from multiple measurement instruments (either directly of by querying a database) in order to calculate the indicators. The process is specified in the hierarchical measurement information model of the ISO/IEC 15939 standard.

7.3.2.2 Measurement Infrastructure

The measurement infrastructure forms the technological aspect of the measurement program – providing the technical means for realizing the measurement program. Such technical means complement the measurement systems and include the databases for collecting measurement results, execution environment and the dissemination environment. The databases (including knowledge bases as defined by ISO/IEC 15939) are important for the solidity of the storage of measurement results and to provide the possibility to the organization to analyze trends.

In modern software development companies these kind of databases exist as the companies recognize the competitive advantage of storing information and the advantages of business intelligence. Examples of measurement databases that are publicly available are the databases such as ISBSG data repository of product size measurements [283] or the PROMISE data repository of source code and model measurements [43].

7.3.2.3 Measurement Organization

The measurement organization can be seen as a two-fold concept – the organization delivering the measures (e.g. a metric team) and the organization using the metrics (e.g. a software development team). However, both concepts are of sociological nature as they are concerned with the roles, norms and regulations relevant for the measurement program. The norms and roles fall under the facet of performance of the measurement program and under the facet of preferences of the measurement program (and its acceptance).

The measurement program contains the measurement support organization that develops and maintains the measurement program. The support organization can be a dedicated measurement team (a metric team) or a set of roles spread across the company (a virtual metric team). The support organization realizes such tasks as the quality assurance of the measurement program, the functional development of the measurement program, operational and corrective maintenance and supporting the company with measurement competence.

The metric teams can be organized with the roles described in ISO/IEC 15939 standard, e.g. metrics champion, measurement sponsor, measurement analyst, metrics designer, measurement librarian. The metric team should also adhere to professional standards when organizing their way-of-working, e.g. explicit description of their work processes, defining contingency plans. This recognition of the role of the metric team shows the organizational legitimacy of the measurement program support organization – there is a dedicated staff whose job is to develop and maintain the measurement program.

The organization using the measures can also have a varying level of competence of using the measures and indicators. This competence, combined with the measures used and their quality, can determine if the measures are effective – i.e. if they will

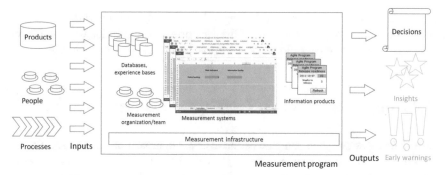

Fig. 7.1 Conceptual model of a measurement program

trigger decision processes [425]. Examples of such decision processes are release planning decisions (c.f. [382]) or software engineering economics (c.f. [42]).

In large organizations it is important that it is clear/transparent who is interested in the results of the measurement and how to interpret them. Only then the measurement results can be used to analyze problems, formulate decisions, monitor implementation of decisions and therefore be effective [425].

7.3.3 Measurement Program Model

Based on the discussion of the elements of the measurement program we can construct a model of an industrial measurement program, conceptually shown in Fig. 7.1.

The central element of the measurement program is the set of measurement systems and information products. The measures and indicators calculated in measurement systems are, together with the analysis models, packaged into information products.

The input to the measurement program is obtained by measuring properties of products, organizations (people) and processes. The output of the measurement program is a set of decisions taken in the organizations, the insights into the organizations' processes, products and projects and the early warnings of the coming problems and challenges. These are usually interconnected – e.g. insights can trigger decisions and decisions can require new insights when being implemented.

7.4 MeSRAM – Measurement System Robustness Assessment Method

MeSRAM is a method for assessing the robustness of measurement programs, consisting of two parts – the robustness model and the assessment method. The robustness model is a set of categories which contain elements which a robust measurement program should have. Grouping the elements into the categories is based on the measurement program model presented in Fig. 7.1 – for example the metric infrastructure of the measurement program is one of the categories. In this section we describe the research that led to the development of the two parts and the parts themselves.

7.4.1 Developing MeSRAM Using Action Research

MeSRAM was designed using an action research approach of Susman and Evered [449] which has been shown to work particularly well when designing and evaluating socio-technical systems [448]. To develop MeSRAM we used two action research cycles – initial development of the robustness model and the assessment method (described as a pilot evaluation results in Sect. 7.5.2) and improvement and application.

7.4.1.1 Action Research Cycle 1: Initial Development

The early version of MeSRAM was designed during a joint workshop with representatives from four companies – Company B, Company C, Company D and Company E. The participants were one line manager, one measurement program leader, one technical specialist (Software Engineering and Management) and one integration leader. All participants were actively involved in both research in software metrics (a number of papers published) and were actively involved in measurement programs in their respective companies. All of them had over 10 years of experience with software process improvement initiatives.

This first version of MeSRAM consisted of three categories (which were not based on a measurement program model) and was used in the pilot study at Company A described in Sect. 7.5.2). It also consisted of a questionnaire to collect the data – an example question was *Do you use Lines of Code metric?* with the following answer alternatives: (i) yes, fully; (ii) partially in some projects; (iii) not at all; (iv) not applicable.

During the evaluation it was found that the categories were insufficient and therefore we conducted the second cycle.

7.4.1.2 Action Research Cycle 2: Improvement and Application

The second cycle of the development of MeSRAM was based on the studies of ISO/IEC 15939:2007 and its definition a measurement program, the IEEE definition of Robustness as a quality attribute [202] and literature studies. The outcome from the first action research cycle was a set of challenges which were not addressed by the initial version of MeSRAM: that the definition of a measurement program (and the corresponding model) was not clear, such as *What infrastructure should support measurement programs?*, *How do we know that the measurement program is accepted in the organization?* or *What competences are needed in the organization to sustain the measurement program?* These challenges were identified as crucial and the companies A – E could provide us with the initial set of experiences on how to define the measurement program, identify roles and what they would expect to see as a sufficient result for this category.

We organized a second workshop with the companies in order to decide how to categorize these questions and how to prioritize the categories for further investigation (using literature studies following the procedure described in Table 7.1). For each of the new categories we (in the second joint workshop with the same participants from companies A – E) decided how we should expand on and we performed review of literature in the area. We followed the relevant parts of the protocol presented by Petersen et al. [359], which we summarize in Table 7.1.

Based on the review we identified relevant metrics in order to show to the practitioners when assessing the robustness. These examples are included as the references in tables in the Sect. 7.4.2. The number of papers mapped to each of the categories of MeSRAM are presented in Table 7.2. The largest number of papers was mapped to the category of *Metrics used* as this category is the broadest one. The fewer number of papers was mapped to the category of *external collaboration*.

When we designed the robustness model we based it on the ISO/IEC model of a measurement program (which we visualize/draw in Fig. 7.1) and we broke down the IEEE definition of robustness into categories which capture:

- the scope/breadth of the measurement program (Metrics used) which captures the inputs of the measurement program (in IEEE robustness definition this means that a broad measurement program is going to operate even if the metrics change)
- the institutionalization/depth of the measurement program (decision support, metrics organization and organizational metric maturity)
- the foundation/infrastructure which executes the measurement program and its solidity (metrics infrastructure, collaboration)

The review and the workshops resulted in the version of MeSRAM presented in this paper. This version was evaluated during the "evaluate" part of the second action research cycle at Company A (to evaluate whether the improved version of MeSRAM captures their measurement program correctly) and Company B (to assure that MeSRAM is not specific to the measurement program of Company A which had provided the improvement feedback for the initial version of MeSRAM).

After the positive feedback on the completeness of MeSRAM from Company A and Company B (learning part of the second action research cycle) we have applied the method at companies C – G. The details of the robustness model and MeSRAM assessment are presented in the following section.

Table 7.1 Application of the systematic mapping procedure of Petersen et al.[359] in the development of MeSRAM

Step of the protocol	Application
Definition of research question	In our study we used the following question *What methods and metrics exist that can be used as examples for the categories of MeSRAM?*
Review scope	The scope of the review was the set of papers in software engineering and software project/product management. In particular we were looking for papers presenting research results based on empirical findings
Conducting the search	We used snowballing to find the relevant articles. We started from the following five papers: • Unterkalmsteiner et al. [464] – to capture the area of software process improvement • Radjenovic et al. [365] and Hall et al. [168] – to capture the area of product performance and quality • Kitchenhamn [246] – to capture the area of software metrics and measurement systems • Ruhe [381] and Staron [425] – to capture the area of decision support • Kaplan et al. [229] – to capture the area of Corporate Performance Measurement and Balanced Scorecard Our starting sample was rather recent except for the work of Kaplan et al. [229]. The criteria for choosing them was that they were a mix of systematic reviews (Hall et al. [168]) and experiences from industry (Unterkalmsteiner et al. [464]). The bootstrapping set covered areas usually recognized as related to measurement programs, such as software process improvement (Unterkalmsteiner et al. [464]), product performance (Hall et al. [168]), product and organization management (e.g. Ruhe [381] and Kaplan et al. [229]), and decision support (Staron [425]) For Kaplan et al. [229] we used forward snowballing to find the updates in the area of Balanced Scorecard since the original work of Kaplan et al. was the most comprehensive work on the topic. For the rest of the papers we used backward snowballing
Database of all papers	Since our goal was to find examples of methods we did not store all papers in a dedicated base, only the papers which were relevant
Screening of papers	We screened the paper based on their context in the original publication and then the title and content. Scanning the content of the papers allowed us to get orientation if there are examples of metrics rather quickly
Relevant papers	The inclusion criteria were: books, papers, technical papers describing methods and metrics used in industry; when several methods or metrics were described in one paper they were treated separately; the papers should include examples; types of papers included – validation research, evaluation research, experience paper The exclusion criteria were: presentations, grey literature describing tools, ideas and toy examples; excluded papers of types – solution proposal, philosophical paper, opinion papers
Keywording using abstracts	We performed snowballing and we used the following keywords: software metric, software measure, measurement, method, experience, case study, action research, empirical study

(continued)

Table 7.1 (continued)

Step of the protocol	Application
Classification scheme	We used MeSRAM's categories as the classification scheme for the found relevant papers
Data extraction and mapping process	For each paper we evaluated whether the method/metric presented was in the scope of MeSRAM and if it was we added it to the auxiliary material for the assessment workshops (as a PDF version of the paper). If needed it was shown to the practitioners. In this paper, however, we provide the reference to the original publication. We continuously verified whether the newly found technique was relevant with the participating practitioners from company B, C, D and E
Systematic map	MeSRAM was used instead of the systematic map

Table 7.2 Number of papers mapped to the categories of MeSRAM

Category	Number of papers mapped to MeSRAM, referenced from Tables 7.4, 7.5, 7.6, 7.7, 7.8, 7.9, 7.10, 7.11, 7.12, 7.13 and 7.14	Number of papers reviewed in full text
Metrics used	30	368
Decision support	2	28
Metrics infrastructure	5	15
Organizational metrics maturity	9	41
Metrics organization	8	29
External collaboration	2	5
Collaboration with academia	2	17

7.4.2 Robustness Model

We base our definition of robustness on two parts – the definition of measurement programs presented in Sect. 7.3, and the definition of robustness as a quality property.

The definition of robustness as a quality attribute – the ability of an algorithm to continue operating despite abnormalities in input, calculations, and environment – is taken from the IEEE Standard Glossary of Software Engineering Terminology [364]. Thus the robust measurement program is a program that continuous to operate despite the changes in the information needs, stakeholders, measurement infrastructure, and measurement support organization.

We define the robustness model for the measurement programs as a set of categories that quantify the above definition. These categories we designed during two workshops and a literature review and they capture a set of elements for each aspect of the measurement program. The model is presented in Fig. 7.2 and each of the categories is linked to the organizational change theory by Goodman et al. [157] or the theoretical and empirical metrics validation by Briand et al. [53]. The link is based on what the category represents – e.g. the category of metrics used requires

the proper definition of a metric and evaluation of its usefulness, which is defined
by the theoretical and empirical metric validation theory.

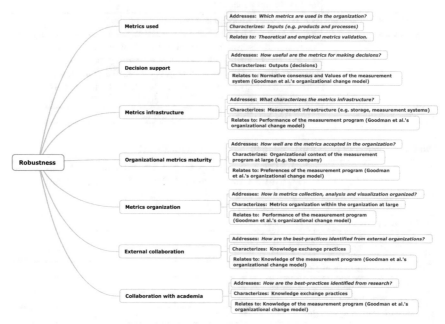

Fig. 7.2 Robustness model of a measurement program

The model's categories map to the measurement program model presented in
Fig. 7.1 as shown in Table 7.3. The last two categories – External collaboration
and Collaboration with academia – map to a subset of experience bases and the
measurement organization/team.

The key elements of each category emphasize the purpose of the category and
finally the facets of the institutionalization of change emphasize their importance in
the organizational change.

Each category groups a set of key elements needed to keep the measurement
program sustainable over a longer period of time:

1. **Metrics organization** – assessing how metrics collection, analysis and visualization is done and by whom.
2. **Metrics infrastructure** – assessing how the measurement program is realized
   technology-wise - e.g. which tools and how they are used.
3. **Metrics used** – assessing which metrics are used in the company, e.g. to assess
   the quality of the product design, measure defects.
4. **Decision support** – evaluating how metrics are used in decision processes at the
   company.
5. **Organizational metrics maturity** – assessing how the organization as a whole
   works with metrics.

Table 7.3 Mapping of MeSRAM's categories to the measurement program model from Fig. 7.1

MeSRAM's category	Mapping to the measurement program model
Metrics used	This category groups the types of valid metrics used in the measurement program. It maps to *Databases* where the metrics are stored, and *Inputs* which describe where the metrics are collected from
Decision support	This category groups the key elements related to normative references in the measurement program and their use in practice for making *Decisions*. It maps to the respective part of the measurement program model
Metrics infrastructure	This category groups the key elements related to the performance of the measurement program. It maps to *Measurement infrastructure* which executes and stores the measurement systems, the *Measurement systems* which describes the measurement systems, and *Information products* which describes how the metrics are disseminated in the organization
Organizational metrics maturity	This category groups the key elements related to the performance of the measurement programs. It maps to the good and poor practices related to measurements, shown as *Experience bases* in the measurement program model
Metrics organization	This category also relates to the performance of the measurement program and its institutionalization. It relates to the *Measurement organization/team* of the measurement program
External collaboration	This category relates to the knowledge of the measurement program and the exchange of experiences. It maps to *Experience bases*, and *Measurement organization/team*
Collaboration with academia	Similar to the external collaboration this category also maps to *Experience bases, Measurement organization/team*

6. **Collaboration with academia** – assessing the status of research-oriented activities at the organization.
7. **External collaboration** – assessing the state of collaboration with other companies - e.g. exchange of experiences.

The categories are designed to be complementary although there can be dependencies between certain key elements of different categories. For example the *metrics used* categories quantifies how many types of metrics are used in the company, but does not discuss how they are used – this is covered by the *decision support* category. Therefore using these two categories together assesses how broad the measurement program is and how well these metrics are used for making the decisions or monitoring the implementation of decisions [425]. These two categories could be seen as different levels of the institutionalization of metrics – using the measures does not distinguish between the "performance of the behavior" and "preferences of the behavior". In the decision support it becomes more evident if the measures are only collected and observed, or if they are actually used in the decision processes (indicating the "normative behavior" level from Goodman and Dean's institutionalization of change theory).

The total number of applied key elements can be used for comparing the robustness of measurement programs and to identify opportunities for cross-learning between the programs, but not to assess the maturity of the program. Some of the key elements form a minimum requirement for a robust measurement program (such elements were either identified in the standards as such or indicated by the companies as such). We indicate the key elements that form the minimum requirement in each of the subsections.

7.4.2.1 Metrics Organization

The metrics organization category groups key elements related to how the measurement program is organized within the company and how known it is. For example, the category assesses whether there is dedicated staff (e.g. metrics team) who manages and maintains the measurement program and whether the team has sufficient resources. Table 7.4 presents all aspects in this category.

One facet of the institutionalization is the recognition of the measurement program as an entity which is maintained by a dedicated organization. A robust measurement program has a solid, professional organization which keeps the program under constant monitoring and has the competence-sharing role at the company. The organization can sustain the measurement program even if the software process improvement initiative which led to the development of metrics in the program finishes. The program is supported by the standards, in an organized manner, with the statements of compliance in place reflecting the "normative behavior" facet of the organizational change theory. Having the organization using standards, prevents the metrics competence from dissolving over time (as individuals change roles and responsibilities in the organization). Using the standards also minimizes the risk of ill-defined metrics and ill-defined measurement processes. The minimum requirements are to keep dedicated roles in the organization and to keep plans for the metrics strategy, and how to manage problems with the execution of the measurement program (contingency plan).

7.4.2.2 Metrics Infrastructure

The performance of the measurement program is an important foundation of its institutionalization. Performing the measurement program can be done in multiple ways, but it should always have elements of security, trustworthiness and visualization. Therefore robust measurement programs are based on a solid measurement infrastructure which includes automation of metrics collection, analysis and visualization as well as secure storage of data – as presented in Table 7.5.

The minimum requirement for the robust infrastructure is establishing the structure which contains the most important metrics, indicators and lesson's learned. This is prescribed by the measurement process standards ISO/IEC 15939. The most robust measurement infrastructure is based on standardized naming conventions, au-

Table 7.4 Key elements in the category of metrics organization

Key element	Aspect of measurement programs
There is a metrics organization (e.g. team)	Professional support, [432]
The organization has sufficient resources	Effective support, [432]
There is metrics org. that maintains existing metrics	Effective cataloguing, [432]
The metrics supports the organization with the competence	Spread of competence, [432]
The metrics org. gives presenations/seminars/courses	Spread of competence, [314]
The metrics organization has good knowledge of the company's products	Embedded in organization, [180]
It is well defined and transparent how the metrics org. prioritizes its assignments	Organization of work, [180]
The metrics organization can handle emergencies	Company goal alignment, [342]
There exists a strategy plan	Company goal alignment, [314]
There exists Metrics champion	Team organization, [314]
There exists Measurement sponsor	Team organization, [314]
There exists Measurement analyst	Team organization, [314]
There exists Metrics designer	Team organization, [314]
There exists Measurement librarian	Team organization, [314]
There exists Metrics team leader	Team organization, [314]
There exists a document that describes how the metrics org. works	Team organization, [314]
There exists a contingency plan	Team organization, [314]
Statement of Compliance for: ISO/IEC/IEEE 15939	Standardization
Statement of Compliance for: ISO/IEC 12207	Standardization
Statement of Compliance for: IEEE Std 1061	Standardization
Statement of Compliance for: ISO/IEC 2502x family	Standardization

tomated information flows, secure storage and solid information quality assessment (automated).

7.4.2.3 Metrics Used

One of the important categories of robustness of the measurement program is the ability to support analysis of data both in the short term (e.g. one software improvement initiative) and the long-term (e.g. over a period of time including multiple changes of software processes/products). Therefore the measurement program should support using metrics in a wide range of areas – e.g. processes, products, businesses.

These metrics should also be **used** and not only **collected**, which leads to spreading the status information and analysis results in the company. The set of metrics used are organized into five sub-categories – business metrics, product metrics, design metrics, organizational performance metrics, and project metrics. The grouping of

Table 7.5 Key elements in the category of metrics infrastructure

Key element	Aspect of measurement program
There exists a structure that contains all/the most important metrics	Completeness of measurement systems, [434]
The infrastructure is secure	Controlled access to information, [474]
The infrastructure is built up so that is supports automation	Efficiency of data collection, [437]
All measurement systems include Information Quality	Reliability and trustworthiness of data, [431]
The infrastructure supports/enables dissemination of information products	Visualization and communication, [352]
There exist naming rules for folders and files	Standardized storage, [437]

Table 7.6 Key elements of business metrics

Key element	Aspect of measurement programs
Customer	Balanced scorecard, [339]
Value	Delivering business value, [170]
Financial perspective	Cashflow and return on investment, [268, 339]
Product delivery	Delivery efficiency, [6]
Defects in products	Perceived product quality, [488]

the metrics in these categories is a result of the workshop with the collaborating companies, reflecting their best practices.

Business: The business metrics quantify such aspects of company operations as customer strategies, value measurements, financial performance, product delivery efficiency and defects in products – as presented in Table 7.6. This category of measurement is related to how well the company monitors its operations and has quantified strategies related to the metrics and indicators.

Robust measurement programs have stakeholders in the management team of the measured company. The Balanced Scorecard postulates using multiple perspectives covered by the program, e.g. customer, financial (covered in this category). The categories of the Balanced Scorecard approach of product and internal business perspective are covered under the "product" category in MeSRAM and in "Organizational performance".

Product: The business area quantifies the operation of the company and its business performance, but has to be complemented with the perspective of product performance. This area quantifies how good the product is, what the potential is (e.g. product feature backlog) or how ready the product is for being released – as presented in Table 7.7.

Design: Design measures are different from the product measures as they capture the internal quality of software [222]. Robust measurement programs distinguish between these two in order to provide a more complete coverage of the measured areas – as presented in Table 7.8.

Table 7.7 Key elements of product metrics

Key element	Aspect of measurement programs
Product backlog	Speed in product development, [236]
Readiness/Running tested features (RTF)	Product release readiness, [438]
Defects	Product quality, [354]
Product properties	Product monitoring, [96]
Product performance	Continuous product improvement
Product management	Efficient product decisions
Maintenance	Cost-effective product maintenance

Table 7.8 Key elements of design metrics

Key element	Aspects of measurement programs
Design stability	Design measures, [11]
Product/code stability	Code stability, [428]
Design debt	Technical debt, [173]
Defects	Quality and motivation, [267]
Size	Size vs. quality, [56]

Table 7.9 Key elements of organizational performance metrics

Key element	Aspects of measurement programs
Velocity	Speed of the organization, [174]
Throughput/Efficiency	Organization performance, [163]
Customer perspective	Linking to company goals, [268]
Financial perspective	Linking to company goals, [268]
Internal business process perspective	Performance indicators, [358]
Delivery precision	Predictability, [77]
Innovation and learning growth	Long-term perspective, [268]
Employee assets	Skill levels, [87, 125]
Ways of working	Continuous process improvement, [174]

The robust measurement program should capture at least the elements of stability of the design, the size of the product, design debt and defects. Depending on the purpose of the software the measurement program can build on domain specific standards.

Organizational performance: Measuring organizational performance is a part of every mature, long-term measurement program. The measurement program should support the organization in measuring how good it is and how well it develops. This is important for the long-term evolution of the organization. Aspects which are measured are presented in Table 7.9.

Table 7.10 Key elements of project metrics

Key element	Aspect of measurement programs
Status	Controllability of projects, [125]
Progress	Controllability of projects [393]
Release readiness	Project ability to deliver, [403, 438]
Quality	Quality of products
System management	Standards e.g. ISO/IEC 12207
Design	Standards e.g. ISO/IEC 25000
Integration	Velocity of product integration, [99]
Test	Test effectiveness and efficiency, [309]
Prediction	Predictability, [67]
Team	Team properties, [41]
Legacy	Carry-over between projects, [170]

The set of measures shows how fast the organization is (velocity), what the efficiency of the organization is (throughput/efficiency) and how well the organization responds to customer requests (customer perspective).

Project: A robust measurement program includes measures and indicators for project managers for the monitoring of project progress. There should be at least one measure for each of the categories in Table 7.10. This category is one of the most mature fields of measuring and in the table we only give examples related to new trends in software engineering which contain modern metrics – e.g. metrics for Lean software development enterprises.

7.4.2.4 Decision Support

The institutionalized robust measurement programs must support decision processes in the company – using of metrics should trigger decisions formulations and the decision executions should be supported by measuring, as it is shown in Table 7.11.

Along with the use of metrics for decision support comes the trust in the measurement program. The prerequisite for the use of metrics in decision processes is to clarify who and why is interested in the metrics data. The next key elements are the ability to clearly interpret the values of the metrics – e.g. what does it mean to have a certain degree of complexity and how to interpret a number. The ability to interpret the results is linked to the ability to react upon them (being able to take concrete actions to make the change required to improve the value of the metric).

It should also be clear whether the metrics are designed to trigger the decisions or to monitor the implementation of the decisions. Indicators and KPIs (Key Performance Indicators) are often used to monitor entities and trigger the decisions and they are visualized with the decision criteria. However, once the decision is formulated indicators are complemented with more detailed metrics to monitor that the decision's implementation is in the right direction. For example, product quality

Table 7.11 Key elements of the decision support category

Key element	Aspect of decision support
It is clear/transparent who is interested in the metrics data	Defining measurement systems, [436]
Meaning/interpretations of metrics are defined	Defining measurement systems, [436]
Metrics are used for analyses of problems/root causes	Critical role of measures, [425]
Metrics and indicators are used to formulate decisions (trigger)	Critical role of measures, [425]
Metrics and indicators are used to monitor implementation of decisions (pull)	Critical role of measures, [425]
It is clear which metrics and indicators are used for technical and managerial areas respectively	Critical role of measures, [425]

is often calculated as the number of defects and visualized with the decision criteria that it should not exceed a specific level. However, when there is a need to improve the quality, metrics such as test progress, product complexity, design stability are used to monitor that the reduction of the number of defects (quality) indeed leads to the increased quality of the product.

Finally it is important in which domain the decisions are taken – the managerial domain (e.g. project or line) or the technical (e.g. product) domain. In modern organizations the project and product are often orthogonal to each other and the parameters of both need to be balanced to find the optimal set-up for the project and product. For example by balancing the functionality of the product with the release time requirements of the project.

7.4.2.5 Organizational Metrics Maturity

Organizational metrics maturity is required for robust measurement programs as it reflects the depth of the acceptance of the measurement program. The organization understands the importance of such basic measurements as the number of defects and can prioritize them, which is important to spread the understanding for the quantitative data (metrics) and to be able to set processes to collect such data. The processes can be automated if the measurements are repeatable, which indicates that the organization has the stability required to collect such data. The manual collection is used as a complement for those measures/indicators which require manual intervention (e.g. asking) or is done sporadically and the automation is too difficult/costly in this context.

As presented in Table 7.12, it is also important that the metrics and indicators available in standard tools are understood by the organization (e.g. which level McCabe cyclomatic complexity of a module is acceptable).

Table 7.12 Key elements of the organizational metrics maturity category

Key element	Aspect of maturity
There is a prioritized list of defects per product	Basic measurements, [197]
There is a list over the most complex SW modules	Basic product insight, [197]
Metrics and indicators are collected/calculated using documents and repeatable algorithms	Standardization, [211]
Metrics and indicators are collected/calculated manually	Wide collection of metrics, [218]
Metrics and indicators are collected/calculated automatically	Project measurement, [183, 217]
Metrics and indicators are visualized with decision criteria	Visualization, e.g. [352]
Metrics and indicators are accompanied with information quality/reliability evaluation	Information quality, e.g. [17, 431]
Metrics and indicators available in standard tools (e.g. Eclipse, MS Excel) are used and understood in the organization	Integration of technology, e.g. [464]

Table 7.13 Key elements of collaboration with academia

Key element	Aspect of collaboration
The metrics org. has collaboration with academia	Effective collaboration model, [388, 482]
The metrics org. executes metrics research projects	Effective collaboration model, [388, 482]
The metrics org. publishes papers	Effective collaboration model, [388, 482]
The metrics org. has students on site	Effective collaboration model, [388, 482]
The metrics org. supervises bachelor/master theses	Effective collaboration model, [388, 482]

7.4.2.6 Collaboration with Academia

There are constantly new methods, tools and techniques published in the area of metrics. Almost every new software engineering technique comes with a set of measures related to the technique. In order to be constantly up-to-date with the techniques and to be able to operationalize these techniques, companies need to collaborate with academia. To operationalize metrics developed in another context often requires to re-design part of the metrics or their adaptation to another context. This process can be efficient if the industrial partners contribute with the in-depth knowledge of the context and the academic partners contribute with the competence of re-designing the metrics. An example of such collaboration can be found in [388, 482]. We present the key elements in Table 7.13.

7.4.2.7 External Collaborations

Equally important to the collaboration with academia is the collaboration with peers, i.e. other units within the same company and with other companies. The collaboration with peers stimulates exchange of good practices and practical experience with

Table 7.14 Key elements of external collaboration

Key elements	Aspect of collaboration
The metrics org. has collaboration with other units of the company	Exchange models [367]
The metrics org. has collaboration with other companies	Learning [160]

metrics, measurement processes and organizational aspects. Since measurement is usually not the core business for software development organizations, the collaborations with peers open up for free discussions on which metrics have been proven to be useful and in which situations. The key elements of the external collaboration are presented in Table 7.14.

Successful collaborations can stimulate building centres of excellence which attract world-class research and development in the area of interest. Such centers are often a cost-efficient way of long-term cost share of non core business initiatives (e.g. measurement programs).

7.4.3 Assessment Method

The second part of MeSRAM is the assessment questionnaire. The questionnaire consists of questions which are to be asked to company representatives. The representatives should be members of the metrics organization (if it exists) or members of an appropriate part of the organization, such as quality management, line management, or project management. These roles in the organization are the usual roles which work with measurement programs (either as providers of measurement systems or as stakeholders):

- line and project managers take decisions and therefore can answer the questions about the decision support
- metrics organization can answer the questions regarding the measurement infrastructure and the metrics collected
- product managers can answer the questions regarding product, customer and financial metrics
- quality managers and designers/architects can answer the questions about team, design and quality measures
- collectively these roles can answer questions about the organizational maturity and collaborations.

An excerpt from the evaluation question for the metric organization category is presented in Fig. 7.3, which illustrates that assessment questions are constructed by transforming the key elements into questions. Follow-up questions can be added to investigate further aspects – e.g. how the collaboration is organized or how the metrics are used. The questions that are asked are related directly to the aspects of the measurement program, for example: *Is there a metric organization in the company?* and the possible answers should be: *yes*, *no* and *I don't know*. If the answer is *yes* then there should be a follow up question about examples – to ensure that the answer is correct. If the answer is *I do not know* then there should be a follow up question about who can be asked to obtain the answer.

Is there a metrics organization (e.g. team) at your company?

❑ *Yes*
❑ *No*
    ❑ *If "No", why not?*
❑ *Don't know*
    ❑ *If "Don't know" – who may know the answer?*

Fig. 7.3 An example of a question from the category "Metric organization"

    When presenting the results of the assessment a radar chart should be used with each category in a separate axis, as exemplified in Sect. 7.6.1.1 in Fig. 7.5. To create the chart each axis should be scaled to 100%– 00% corresponding to the number of all key elements for the category which is represented by the axis. The value of the data point for the axis should be the percentage of the *yes* answers.

7.5 Evaluation of MeSRAM in Industry

In order to evaluate MeSRAM we applied the method in seven companies and after the application we discussed the completeness and correctness of the method with the participants. In this section we describe how we designed the evaluation and provide the rationale for this design. We also present the results of the evaluation.

7.5.1 Design of the Evaluation

This was done in assessment workshops (one per company) with the goals to:

- make the assessment of the robustness of the company's measurement program
- discuss the completeness of the categories in the robustness model
- find best practices in measurement programs at the companies,
- identify improvement opportunities, and
- identify the dependencies between the categories of the robustness model.

    These workshops were organized per company and conducted at company's premises. For some of the companies (Company B, Company C, Company D) we conducted two workshops in order to compare how different levels of the company worked with measurements (e.g. software vs. product development). We describe the design of these workshops and their outcome in more detail in the following subsection.

We conducted three types of workshops in order to evaluate MeSRAM from different perspectives:

- pilot workshop – at company A we conducted an assessment workshop with the initial version, with a long open-discussion session with the objective to discuss how well MeSRAM covers the company's measurement program.
- evaluation workshop – at companies B–F we had two hours assessment sessions with quality managers, lead designers, architects and project managers. The focus of these workshops was to collect the data and to discuss its completeness.
- remote workshop – at company G we trained one industry representative who conducted the workshop at the company with the goal to check if the method can be applied without the involvement of the authors of the method (to assess the generalizability of the method).

For the pilot study we designed and conducted a workshop with a focus group at Company A. The focus group included quality managers, software architects, method specialists and product managers. All subjects had a number of years of experience at the company and its products. The company had a documented track record of working with measurements and had a well-developed quality organization working with both internal quality metrics and the advanced customer satisfaction and market analysis. However the company was not involved in the design of MeSRAM and therefore was the best candidate to initially evaluate MeSRAM.

After the study at Company A the improved MeSRAM was applied at Company B and Company D in order to validate the improvements. It was applied in the same unit which was involved in designing the method.

After the assessment at Company A, Company B, and Company D we continued the evaluation by conducing the assessment at Company C, E, F, and finally Company G. After each assessment we presented the results to each company and discussed whether the radar diagram correctly captures the subjects' perceptions of the robustness of their measurement programs.

The study concluded by the common reporting workshop with all involved companies where we presented the results, obtained feedback about MeSRAM as a method and identified improvement opportunities for the companies. During this reporting workshop we discussed whether MeSRAM "quantifies" the robustness of measurement programs correctly, whether the results of the assessment of the companies' measurement program correspond to their perception of the robustness of their measurement programs, and whether the radar chart provides the right visualization of the robustness of the measurement programs.

7.5.2 Results of the Pilot Study at Company A

SW Development at Company A is performed in a distributed, multi-site, environment and executed according to the principles of Agile software development through empowered software development teams and frequent SW releases to the market and consumer. The version of MeSRAM presented at Company A was minimum viable method, which was devised in order to assess the feasibility of the approach in another setting (than Company B where the method was designed). The discussions with the focus group resulted in the radar diagram of the first version of MeSRAM as presented in Fig. 7.4.

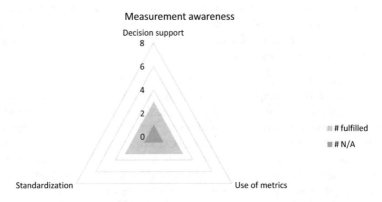

Fig. 7.4 First version of MeSRAM: Visualization of the robustness of the measurement program at Company A

Based on the discussions after the assessment interview during the pilot study we found a number of improvement areas for MeSRAM:

- The categories of MeSRAM were too few and did not reflect the measurement program of Company A. Company A's quality organization was responsible for the measures and therefore their measurement program reflected the focus on quality and customer-related measurement.
- For each key element of each category it was good to have an example to explain (if necessary) what is meant by the key element.
- The number of key elements in each each category should be expanded to capture the diversity of the measurement programs studied.

As a consequence of this feedback we asked Company A to give us a quick overview of what is missing and then we used that (together with ISO/IEC 15939 and ISO/IEC 25000) to make the model of the measurement program (Fig. 7.1). We validated the measurement program model with the Companies B-G and when the model was complete we defined the robustness model using literature review and workshops with the companies (Fig. 7.2) and then the new version of MeSRAM, based on the measurement program model and the robustness model.

7.5.3 Results of Assessment

In Table 7.15 we present the results of which measures that are used in each of the companies. The metrics which are used by all companies are: Defects in product (MU-5), Defects in design (MU-8), Status (MU-27), Progress (MU-28), Integration (MU-33), Test (MU-34), Product delivery* (MU-4), Readiness/RTF* (MU-7), Velocity* (MU-18), Delivery precision*(MU-23), Release readiness* (MU-29), Quality* (MU-30), and Prediction* (MU-35). The metrics designated with an asterix (*) were used only in some parts of an organization in case we collected the data from two sources – e.g. Company B-1 and B-2.

We could notice that the metrics which are used more often than others relate to the productivity of the organizations, the quality of the products and the status of the development – therefore these are often prioritized. On the other hand the metrics which are used least often is the "Design stability" (MU-13) metrics in the sub-category of design. This was explained by our interviewees by these types of metrics requiring a long-term and systematic work as well as significantly more effort than the common "straightforward" measures.

In Table 7.16 we show how the measurement program supports decision making at the companies. It shows that three aspects – DS-3, DS-4 and DS-6 – are used more often than others (in all studied companies, but not in all their departments).

Table 7.17 shows the perceived organizational metrics maturity. In this category there are many aspects which are used by all studied companies – OM-1, OM-3, OM-4, OM-5, OM-6 and OM-7.

The first of these aspects indicates that basic measures present in all companies which have been discussed in Table 7.15 (MU-5) are known and visible in the organizations. For example the defects are prioritized and worked on (OM-1). Another aspect (OM-3) shows that in all cases the measurement is done manually (either as a complement to the automatic process – in 9 out of 10 cases – or as the only measurement process – in 1 case). This combination of automated and manual collection allows flexibility in adjusting to different information needs for different decisions.

Table 7.18 shows the results in the category of metrics organization. The results show that only two companies have a dedicated metrics organization, but that there are four companies which have the roles specified in the measurement standard – e.g. metrics champions (MO-8). We have found that this is caused by the fact that in large, agile organizations the metrics competence is usually spread over multiple places.

Table 7.19 presents the results from the category of metrics infrastructure. None of the companies gave a positive answer to the question whether information quality in all measurement systems is available (MI-4). Some companies had this mechanism present in the majority of measurement systems. However, it is important that

Table 7.15 Results: metrics used (Y - metrics are used; N - no metrics are used; ? - don't know

ID		A	B-1	B-2	C-1	C-2	D-1	D-2	E	F	G
	Business										
MU-1	Customer	Y	Y	Y	?	N	N	Y	Y	Y	Y
MU-2	Value	Y	N	N	Y	Y	Y	Y	Y	?	Y
MU-3	Financial perspective	Y	N	N	Y	Y	Y	?	Y	?	Y
MU-4	Product delivery	Y	Y	?	Y	Y	Y	Y	Y	Y	Y
MU-5	Defects in products	Y	Y	Y	Y	Y	Y	Y	Y	Y	Y
	Product										
MU-6	Product backlog	Y	Y	?	Y	Y	Y	?	Y	Y	?
MU-7	Readiness/RTF	Y	Y	Y	N	Y	Y	Y	Y	Y	Y
MU-8	Defects	Y	Y	Y	Y	Y	Y	Y	Y	Y	Y
MU-9	Product properties	Y	N	N	Y	Y	Y	Y	Y	Y	Y
MU-10	Product performance	Y	N	N	Y	Y	Y	Y	Y	Y	Y
MU-11	Product management	Y	N	N	Y	Y	Y	?	N	?	?
MU-12	Maintenance	Y	Y	Y	Y	N	Y	Y	Y	Y	?
	Design										
MU-13	Design stability	Y	N	N	N	Y	N		N	?	N
MU-14	Product/code stability	Y	?	?	Y	Y	N	N	Y	?	N
MU-15	Design debt	?	Y	Y	Y	Y	N	N	Y	Y	N
MU-16	Defects	Y	Y	Y	Y	Y	Y	N	Y	?	Y
MU-17	Size	Y	?	?	Y	Y	N	Y	Y	Y	Y
	Organizational performance										
MU-18	Velocity	Y	Y	Y	Y	Y	Y	N	Y	Y	Y
MU-19	Throughput/Efficiency	Y	Y	Y	Y	Y	Y	Y	Y	?	Y
MU-20	Customer perspective	Y	N	N	?	N	Y	N	Y	N	?
MU-21	Financial perspective	Y	Y	Y	Y	Y	Y	?	N	N	Y
MU-22	Internal bus. process perspective	?	Y	Y	Y	Y	Y	N	N	N	?
MU-23	Delivery precision	Y	Y	Y	Y	Y	Y	?	Y	Y	Y
MU-24	Innovation and learning growth	Y	Y	Y	Y	Y	Y	N	N	N	?
MU-25	Employee assets	N	Y	Y	Y	Y	Y	Y	Y	Y	?
MU-26	Ways of working	N	Y	Y	Y	Y	Y	Y	N	Y	?
	Project										
MU-27	Status	Y	Y	Y	Y	Y	Y	Y	Y	Y	Y
MU-28	Progress	Y	Y	Y	Y	Y	Y	Y	Y	Y	Y
MU-29	Release readiness	Y	Y	Y	N	Y	Y	Y	Y	Y	Y
MU-30	Quality	Y	Y	Y	Y	Y	Y	?	Y	Y	Y
MU-31	System management	Y	Y	Y	Y	Y	Y	Y	Y	?	?
MU-32	Design	Y	?	?	Y	Y	N	Y	Y	?	?
MU-33	Integration	Y	Y	Y	Y	Y	Y	Y	Y	Y	Y
MU-34	Test	Y	Y	Y	Y	Y	Y	Y	Y	Y	Y
MU-35	Prediction	Y	Y	Y	N	Y	Y	Y	Y	Y	Y
MU-36	Team	?	Y	Y	Y	Y	Y	?	N	?	Y
MU-37	Legacy	Y	Y	Y	N	Y	Y	N	Y	N	?

Table 7.16 Results: Decision support

ID		A	B-1	B-2	C-1	C-2	D-1	D-2	E	F	G
DS-1	It is clear/transparent who is interested in the metrics data	Y	Y	Y	Y	Y	N	N	Y	N	Y
DS-2	Meaning/interpretations of metrics are defined	Y	Y	Y	Y	N	Y	N	Y	N	Y
DS-3	Metrics are used for analyses of problems/root causes	Y	Y	Y	Y	N	N	Y	Y	Y	Y
DS-4	Metrics and indicators are used to formulate decisions (trigger)	Y	Y	Y	Y	Y	N	N	Y	Y	N
DS-5	Metrics and indicators are used to monitor implementation of decisions (pull)	Y	Y	Y	Y	Y	N	N	N	N	N
DS-6	It is clear which metrics and indicators are used for technical and managerial areas respectively	Y	Y	Y	N	Y	N	Y	?	Y	N

all measurement systems are equipped with this mechanism as, for example, the problems in one measurement system can propagate to other measurement systems.

Finally, Table 7.20 summarizes the results in collaboration both with academia and with external partners. The results show that the companies prioritize the internal collaboration higher than the external one. During our workshops it was found that there are two reasons for it: the common organizational goals of organizations within one company and the ability to be fully transparent within own company.

Table 7.17 Results: Organizational metrics maturity

ID		A	B-1	B-2	C-1	C-2	D-1	D-2	E	F	G
OM-1	There is a prioritized list of defects per product	Y	Y	Y	Y	Y	Y	Y	Y	Y	Y
OM-2	There is a list over the most complex SW modules	Y	Y	Y	Y	Y	N	?	Y	?	Y
OM-3	Metrics and indicators are collected/calculated using documents and repeatable algorithms	Y	Y	Y	N	Y	Y	Y	Y	Y	Y
OM-4	Metrics and indicators are collected/calculated manually	Y	Y	Y	Y	Y	Y	Y	Y	Y	Y
OM-5	Metrics and indicators are collected/calculated automatically	Y	Y	Y	Y	Y	N	Y	Y	Y	Y
OM-6	Metrics and indicators are visualized with decision criteria	Y	Y	Y	Y	Y	N	Y	Y	Y	Y
OM-7	Metrics and indicators are accompanied with information quality/reliability evaluation	Y	?	N	N	N	N	N	N	N	N
OM-8	Metrics and indicators available in standard tools (eg Eclipse, MS Excel) are used and understood in the organization	Y	Y	Y	Y	Y	N	Y	Y	Y	Y

Table 7.18 Results: Metrics organization

ID		A	B-1	B-2	C-1	C-2	D-1	D-2	E	F	G
MO-1	There is a metrics organization (role, team, group,)	N	Y	Y	N	N	N	N	Y	N	N
MO-2	The metrics organization has sufficient resources	N	N	N	N	N		N	Y	N	N
MO-3	There is metrics org that maintains existing metrics	Y	Y	Y	Y	N	Y	N	Y	Y	N
MO-4	There is a metrics org that supports the organization with metrics related issues (eg what to measure, how to measure)	Y	Y	Y	Y	N	Y	N	Y	N	N
MO-5	The metrics organization has good knowledge of the company's products	Y	N	Y	Y	N	Y	?	Y	?	N
MO-6	It is well defined and transparent how the metrics org prioritizes its assignments	Y	N	?	N	N	N	?	Y	N	N
MO-7	The metrics organization can handle emergencies	Y	N	?	N	N	Y	?	Y	N	N
MO-8	There exists a role: Metrics champion	N	Y	?	Y	N	Y	N	N	N	Y
MO-9	There exists a role: Measurement sponsor	N	Y	Y	Y	N	N	N	Y	N	N
MO-10	There exists a role: Measurement analyst	N	Y	Y	Y	N	Y	N	?	N	Y
MO-11	There exists a role: Metrics designer	N	Y	Y	Y	N	Y	N	N	N	Y
MO-12	There exists a role: Measurement librarian	N	N	N	N	N	Y	N	N	N	N
MO-13	There exists a role: Metrics team leader	N	Y	Y	N	N	N	N	N	N	N
MO-14	There exists a document describing how the metrics org. works	N	Y	Y	N	N	?	N	N	Y	N
MO-15	There exists a strategy plan	Y	Y	Y	N	N	Y	N	?	N	N
MO-16	There exists a contingency plan	N	Y	N	N	N	Y	N	N	?	N
MO-17	The metrics org gives presenations/seminars/courses	N	N	N	Y	N	?	N	N	N	N
MO-18	There exists a Statement of Compliance for: ISO/IEC/IEEE 15939	?	Y	Y	N	N	?	N	Y	N	N
MO-19	There exists a Statement of Compliance for: ISO/IEC/IEEE 12207	?	Y	Y	N	N	?	N	?	N	N
MO-20	There exists a Statement of Compliance for: IEEE Std 1061	?	Y	Y	N	N	?	N	?	N	N
MO-21	There exists a Statement of Compliance for: ISO/IEC 2502x family	?	Y	Y	N	N	?	N	Y	N	N

Table 7.19 Results: Metrics infrastructure

ID		A	B-1	B-2	C-1	C-2	D-1	D-2	E	F	G
MI-1	There exists a structure that contains all/the most important metrics	Y	Y	Y	N	N	Y	N	Y	Y	Y
MI-2	The infrastructure is secure	Y	Y	Y	N	Y	Y	N	Y	Y	Y
MI-3	The infrastructure is built up so that is supports automation	N	N	N	N	?	N	Y	Y	Y	Y
MI-4	All measurement systems include Information Quality	?	N	N	N	N	N	N	N	?	N
MI-5	The infrastructure supports/enables dissemination of information products	?	Y	Y	Y	?	Y	N	N	Y	Y
MI-6	There exist naming rules for folders and files	?	Y	?	N	N	N	N	N	?	N

Table 7.20 Results: External collaboration and collaboration with academia (MO - metrics organization)

ID		A	B-1	B-2	C-1	C-2	D-1	D-2	E	F	G
	Collaboration with academia										
AC-1	MO has collab. with academia	N	Y	N	Y	Y	Y	Y	Y	N	N
AC-2	MO executes research projects	Y	Y	N	Y	Y	Y	Y	Y	N	N
AC-3	MO publishes papers	N	Y	N	Y	Y	Y	Y	Y	N	N
AC-4	MO has students on site	N	Y	Y	Y	Y	Y	N	Y	N	N
AC-5	MO supervises BSc/MSc theses	N	Y	N	Y	Y	Y	N	N	N	N
	External collaboration										
EC-1	MO has collab. within company	Y	Y	Y	Y	Y	Y	Y	N	Y	N
EC-2	MO has collab. with other companies	N	Y	N	Y	Y	Y	N	Y	N	N

7.5.4 Feedback from the Companies

After each of the assessment sessions where we collected the data for MeSRAM we discussed the results from the assessment with the companies. We showed the results from the previous assessments and compared the measurement programs.

During the reporting workshop in the end of the study, we presented the results (the radar diagrams presented in Figs. 7.4, 7.5, 7.6, 7.7, 7.8, 7.9, 7.10 and 7.11 and the corresponding data from Tables 7.15, 7.16, 7.17, 7.18, 7.19 and 7.20) to representatives from all participating companies (including the participants of the assessment sessions).

The feedback was that the results of the evaluation correspond to the participants' perception of their measurement program. Companies where the measurement program was "older" were ranked higher on the scales and the companies where the measurement programs were "newer" (e.g. F and G) were ranked lower. This difference in ranking is caused by the fact that the "older" measurement programs have already been subjected to changes in the organization, showing that their construction is robust to changes.

The visualization using the radar diagram was found to be an effective way of showing how robust the measurement programs are. During the discussions a number of alternatives were discussed such as using a "robustness index" which would provide a single number to allow for comparisons. However, the idea of a single index was rejected as the companies were interested in assessment of the status and finding improvements – goals for which the radar chart visualization provided the required details.

The feedback from the participants of the assessment sessions and of the reporting workshop was that the robustness model is complete and captures the aspects which are relevant for the measurement programs – technology and infrastructure, organization, acceptance of the measurement program, decision support and learning/collaboration. Their feedback was that the method can be used to drive concrete improvements of the measurement program implementations in their respective organizations. A number of such improvements were identified immediately.

7.5.5 Identified Improvements of the Measurement Programs

After the performed assessment at companies A–G we could observe direct improvement initiatives at these companies. The direct improvement initiatives observed were:

- Evaluation of the quality of indicators at company D. The stakeholders of the studied measurement programs designed a quality model for indicators based on the Goodman and Dean's model [158]. This evaluation resulted in the reduction of the number of indicators.
- Initiated work on the development of information radiators and dashboards at companies D, E and F. The companies identified a common need for improvement of the dissemination of development status and decided to start a joint software improvement project.
- Joined seminars between companies B, C, and D. The companies exchanged the best practices and based on that improved their measurement infrastructures.
- A survey of the most commonly used metrics in companies B – G which helped the companies to identify new information needs and to prioritize improvement opportunities for their measurement programs.
- Initiated the development of a metric portfolio (a catalogue of metrics which have been found to work well, e.g. from published empirical experience or experience from the companies)
- Initiated the development of common infrastructure to exchange the knowledge about metrics (web portal with the links to the measurement tools used and to a description of measurement procedures of interest for the companies) – a inter-company knowledge-base.

In our further work we plan a longitudinal study on the long-term effects of the assessment at the companies.

7.6 Analysis and Interpretation

In Sect. 7.5 we collected the data about the measurement programs, and we can analyze it from a number of perspectives. We can analyze the data to address research questions related to the characteristics of the companies and whether these characteristics affect the measurement programs. We first analyze the results per company and then address the following research questions:

1. To what extent do the measurement programs differ depending on the process model?
2. To what extent do the measurement programs differ depending on the product type?
3. To what extent do the measurement programs differ depending on whether the development includes outsourcing or is fully in-house?

In order to analyze the results from Tables 7.15, 7.16, 7.17, 7.18, 7.19 and 7.20 where some of the companies participated in two sessions (e.g. B-1 and B-2) we consolidated the results from two sessions into one series in the following way – if the answer was "Y(es)" in one of the sessions we used "Y" for the company, otherwise we used "N(o)" if the answers were both "N" or "N" and "? (Don't know)".

For the first research question regarding the differences per process model we investigated which process models are adopted in each of the organizations. All organizations considered themselves as being agile when developing software, but their agile software development was usually a part of a bigger, overarching, process of product development. These overarching processes were Lean and Agile (Company A, B, and G), V-model (Company D, E, and F), Waterfall (Company C).

For the second research question regarding the differences per product type we organized the companies based on two product types – consumer products (Company A, D, F and G) and infrastructure products (Company B, C and E). As consumer products we considered devices bought by individuals (e.g. a mobile phone) whereas as an infrastructure product we considered devices being bought as a corporate/government customers.

Finally, the third research question which we investigated is the difference between the measurement programs depending whether the company works with external suppliers of software (outsourced software development, company D and E) or whether they work with in-house software development (Company A, B, C, F, and G).

7.6.1 Analysis per Company

To analyze the results per company we used the radar diagrams for visualization and we used the tables presented in Sect. 7.5 to discover the differences. Each radar chart was created by counting the number of *yes* answers and scaling it to 100% – 100% corresponding to the number of all key elements for the category which is represented by the axis.

7.6.1.1 Company A

The pattern presented in Fig. 7.5 shows a situation of a company which is mature in metrics collection with an outspoken strategy for using metrics, but without the dedicated metrics team/organization. In the case of Company A metrics were collected as part of market analyses and quality management. The metrics were carefully selected and were provided for decision support for managers (with outspoken decisions to be taken based on the metrics) and were spread to the organization (e.g. as part of market analysis surveys). The types of metrics collected indicate the company's tradition in end user, market-oriented software development, e.g.: trends in social media (number of persons with particular opinion) or brand quality (e.g. problems with specific functions discovered before the release).

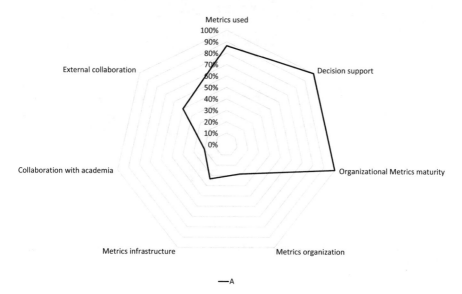

Fig. 7.5 Visualization of the robustness of the measurement program at Company A

7.6.1.2 Company B

The size of the organization at the time of the study amounted to several hundred engineers; projects were staffed with up to a few hundred engineers. Projects were increasingly often executed according to the principles of Agile software development and Lean software development. In this environment, various teams were responsible for larger parts of the process compared to traditional processes: design teams (cross-functional teams responsible for complete analysis, design, implementation, and testing of particular features of the product), product verification and integration testing, etc. The organization used a number of measurement systems for controlling the software development project (per project), a number of measurement systems to control the quality of products in field (per product) and a measurement system for monitoring the status of the organization at the top level.

At Company B we studied the measurement program established in one of the product development organizations responsible for more than 5 products. The measurement program included both the metric team and a set of automated measurement systems.

Figure 7.6 shows a pattern for the organization with a dedicated metrics team (denoted as B-1 in the figure). The management of the measurement program and

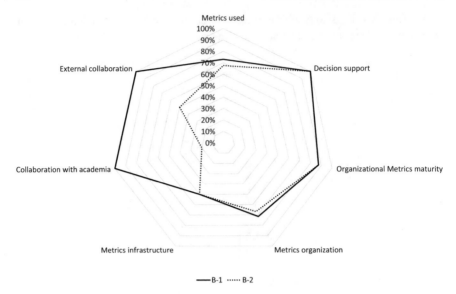

Fig. 7.6 Visualization of the robustness of the measurement program at Company B – two organizations are studied B-1 and B-2

its underlying infrastructure were organized, documented and provided with a clear mandate from the organization (which is shown in a high score on the metrics organization category). However, the use of the provided measures in the decision processes was not at the maximum. This was caused by centralization of the responsibility for the measurement program – the metric team provided the reliable measurement systems but was not in control of how the results were used in the company.

To further understand how MeSRAM captures breadth of a large organization we conducted another interview with a senior line manager responsible for a large organization at another continent (denoted B-2).

The chart shows that the organizational metrics maturity and the measurement infrastructure differed between B-1 and B-2 even though they were part of the same company. The differences were caused by the way in which measurement programs are maintained. One of the aspects which was interesting was the difference in the decision support and metrics used categories. Even though the metrics were equally used in the decision support, in the case of B-2 the number of categories covered was smaller than in the case of B-1 – indicating the two organizations shared the same principles, but they mostly focused on their specific measurement areas.

7.6.1.3 Company C

The studied organizational unit within Company C developed embedded software and graphical user interfaces for a large product. The specific product we worked on was part of a larger product developed by several hundred developers, designers, testers, analysts etc. The historic project developing the product was driven in increments and did not utilize cross functional teams. The project management did some manual metrics on trouble reports. The organization evolved into using more agile processes and cross functional teams. A lot of improvements and optimizations were done regarding software build and delivery times. Also to improve customer value, market competitiveness and profit, the studied organization at Company C was going through a Lean transformation.

The results from the evaluation of one project are presented in Fig. 7.7 as C-1 and shows a pattern with the emphasis on the decision support.

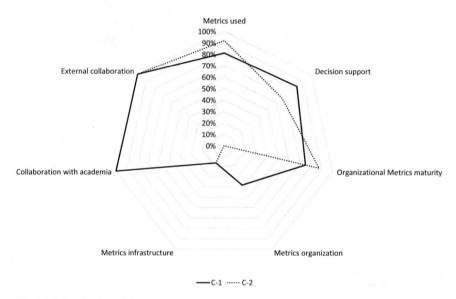

Fig. 7.7 Visualization of the robustness of the measurement program at Company C as a whole

The study was also conducted at the entire development organization at Company C (i.e. responsible for multiple projects), with the results presented as C-2. This pattern shows a company with good pioneer projects in certain categories of MeSRAM. The project assessed in Fig. 7.7 was rather new, where the organization introduced new techniques. However, the entire organization was large and required more time to change, which is shown as the lower robustness of measurement programs in general on the company level.

7.6.1.4 Company D

Company D developed embedded software for a large and distributed product and it also outsourced some of the development to its suppliers. The software development processes at the company were a variation of a V-model and usually consisted of few hundred engineers. At Company D we studied processes of using measurement data, concentrated around a company-wide reporting system for project status. In this set up the software development was only one of several parts of the reporting. Studying the company-wide system provided us with the possibility of observing and exploring the interface between software development and other branches of product development projects – e.g. mechanical engineering. The results from the evaluation at one part of the R&D organization are presented in Fig. 7.8 as D-1.

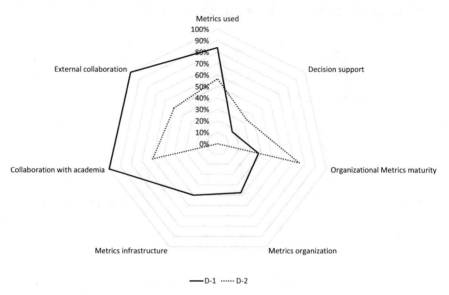

Fig. 7.8 Visualization of the robustness of the measurement program at Company D – the entire R&D perspective

It is worth to note that the decision support at the company was often done based on measures (decisions are triggered), but the monitoring of decisions was often done based on the strategy of task-forces. The task-forces were given the responsibility for quick delivery of high quality solution and had local measures to support that goal.

The results from the evaluation at another (smaller) part of the R&D department are presented as D-2. The difference in these diagrams shows a typical measurement program spread over two departments of R&D – the departments which complement each other.

The results from Company D show also a pattern of the measurement program in a highly-competitive, market-driven organization. The company had an outspoken strategy for product measurements with the holistic view on the product. The customer experience was of top importance and therefore there were outspoken units monitoring company's attainment of goals in such strategic directions. The lower levels of the organization were often given freedom to define own measurement programs, which relate to the company's strategy.

Company D used the largest number of metrics from the companies in our study. However, Company D collected them in a distributed way (no metric organization) and in a manual way. As a result this company identified improvement potential for their measurement program – introducing standardization, establishment of a metric organization (team) and increasing the level of automation. Company D noticed that they collect many metrics, but they spent too much manual effort for that and they could benefit from automation of their measurement processes and prioritization of which metrics to use and when.

7.6.1.5 Company E

The organization which we worked with at Company E developed embedded software which was part of a larger product. The collaborating unit consisted of designers, business analysts and testers at different levels. The process was iterative, agile and involved cross functional teams.

The company used measurements to control the progress of its projects, to monitor quality of the products and to collect data semi-automatically, i.e. automatically gathering of data from tools but with manual analysis of the data. The metrics collected at the studied unit fell into the categories of contract management, quality monitoring and control, predictions and project planning. The intention of the unit was to build a dashboard to provide stakeholders (like project leaders, product and line managers or the team) with the information about the current and predicted status of their products. The results are presented in Fig. 7.9.

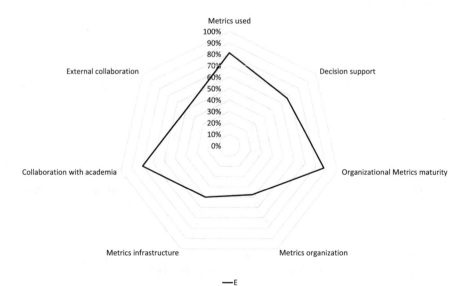

Fig. 7.9 Visualization of the robustness of the measurement program at Company E

This organization could show a number of good examples of how measures were defined with the decision criteria and the link to the decisions. The measures were documented and stored in a central repository accessible to anyone within the development unit. The management used these measures when assessing the organization's performance and when assessing the performance of the organization's products.

7.6.1.6 Company F

Software development at Company F was moving into a platform based way of working where the processes are based on the agile principles with frequent deliveries and empowered software development teams. The teams were multidisciplinary and comprised designers, architects and testers who deliverwed new features across the product range. To facilitate the transformation, a runway team was established to take of e.g. the architectures and tooling part of the work. The size of the software at this company was an order of magnitude smaller than at the other companies.

The results from the evaluation are shown in Fig. 7.10 and show an organization which was at the starting point for building a robust measurement program. The category which seems to be the most advanced is the infrastructure, which is in this case an internal portal with the metrics information.

The company had measurement initiatives before which indicates the fact the some elements of the metrics organization existed, but the company did not manage to build a wide measurement organization – a goal left aside during the current re-organization.

Fig. 7.10 Visualization of the robustness of the measurement program at Company F

The chart shows that there was an awareness in the organization about the role of software metrics and the associated measurement programs. There were also metrics which were used in the organization and decisions are often based on results of measurements. However, there was no outspoken metric organization which made the program susceptible to changes in staffing on an individual level – the success of the measurement program was often dependent on the right individual taking the responsibility at the right moment.

7.6.1.7 Company G

Software development processes at Company G were based on the agile principles with frequent deliveries to the main branch and empowered software development teams. The teams at the company were multidisciplinary and comprised designers, architects and testers. The data was collected by the collaborating partner at the company who had a number of years of experience working with company products and processes. The respondent had a large network within the company which minimized the risk of subject bias.

The results are presented in Fig. 7.11 and show that the company was in a process of building a robust measurement program. The infrastructure and the measurement program were similar to company F (although different measures are used and collected).

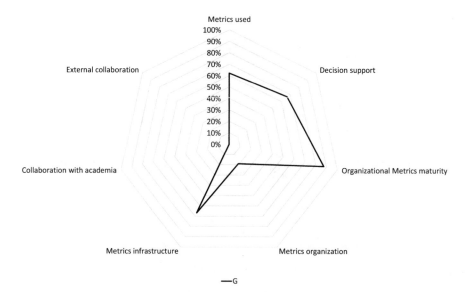

Fig. 7.11 Visualization of the robustness of the measurement program at Company F

7.6.1.8 Summary

To summarize the results from all companies, we can conclude that each company in the study showed good practices and showed some improvement potential. We can observe that the companies which are only starting with the measurement program show a trend which is logical – organization maturity (and its needs for measurement) drive the development of the measurement program. The companies which were more advanced in the implementation of the measurement program also showed the pattern that there are items to improve – e.g. dissemination of measures and the metrics infrastructure. We could also observe that MeSRAM captured the diversity of the organization of measurement programs – from a dedicated metric team in company B to the distributed organization in companies A and C.

7.6.2 Differences per Process Model

In this analysis we were interested in exploring whether the measurement programs of the companies which consider themselves to be lean and agile and the companies where their agility is a part of the development process. The differences are visualized in Fig. 7.12.

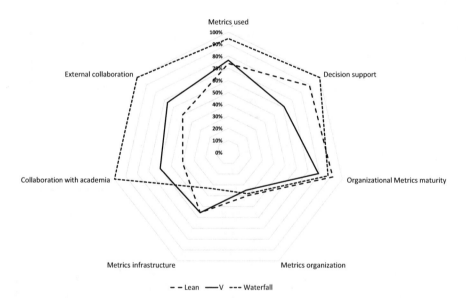

Fig. 7.12 Measurement programs per process model

We have found that the company which has the tradition in the waterfall model (Company C) used more metrics than the other companies and its metric organization was more distributed than in the other companies. Exploring which metrics were used by the waterfall company and not by all other companies show that the following metrics are used more often: Value, Financial perspective, Product backlog, Product management, Design stability, Product/code stability, Design debt, Defects, Internal business process perspective, Innovation and learning growth, System management, Design, Team Legacy.

The metrics which are not collected were the customer-related metrics, but the reason was not the process itself, but the developed product does not have a customer such as the mass market companies.

The waterfall company seems to be also better than the companies with the other processes in the category of decision support, which can be explained by the traditional separation of product management from the software development and the need to use metrics to make decisions about products in a more formal way (than the companies working in a Lean/Agile environment where the product management and software development are closer to/integrated with each other).

The comparison between the V-model companies and the Lean companies show that the V-model companies are better in collaboration, whereas the Lean companies are better in organizational metrics maturity.

7.6.3 Differences per Product Type

In this analysis we were interested in exploring whether the measurement programs of the companies which develop products for the mass market (consumer products) are generally different from the measurement programs of the companies which develop infrastructure products. The infrastructure product development companies are generally governed by contracts with their customers and therefore we wanted to explore if that contractual relation to their customers affects the metrics they use or how they work with the metrics. Figure 7.13 shows the summary of the differences.

The diagram shows that the measurement programs in the infrastructure companies are more advanced than in the mass market companies. As the large products usually entail larger projects and these entail more need to monitor/control, this conclusion is aligned with the expectations. We could also observe that the metrics are generally used to a larger extent in the decision support. The diagram also shows that the metrics infrastructure and collaboration are more developed in the measurement programs in the infrastructure development companies.

The metrics which are used more often by the consumer-product development companies are: Customer, Value, Financial perspective, Product management. The metrics used more often by the infrastructure companies are: Design stability, Product/code stability, Product backlog, Maintenance metrics, Design debt, Design defects, Throughput/efficiency, Employee assets metrics, System management metrics, Legacy metrics, Internal business process perspective metrics, Innovation and learning growth metrics, ways of working metrics, Design metrics, and team metrics.

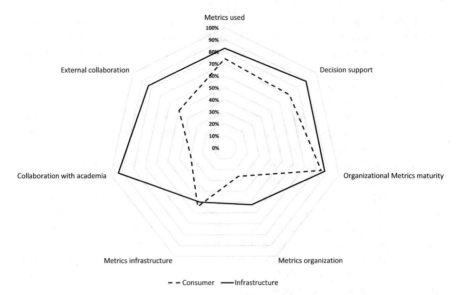

Fig. 7.13 Measurement programs per product type

7.6.4 Differences per Development Type

In this analysis we were interested in exploring whether the measurement programs
of the companies, which have external suppliers are generally different from the
measurement programs of the companies which develop their software in-house.
Since working with external suppliers implies having a contract and generally a
limited insight into the status of the development we wanted to explore whether this
affects the way in which the companies work with the measurement programs (e.g.
whether they compensate the lack of insight by measures of a specific kind).

Figure 7.14 shows the summary of the differences. The companies which work
with suppliers and outsourcing seem to use more metrics than the companies working with in-house software development. This indicates that having this kind of
relationship regulated by the contract can indeed influence the measurement program positively. The exceptions are such metrics as design debt or design stability,
which are used more by the in-house companies. It seems to be natural since these
metrics require the access to the detailed design or source code, which is not possible
for the companies working with outsourcing.

Another interesting observation is the fact that the metric organizations in the
outsourcing companies are generally more advanced that in the in-house companies.
Such aspects as: "There is metrics org. that maintains existing metrics", "There is a
metrics org that supports the organization with metrics related issues (e.g. what to
measure, how to measure)", "The metrics organization has good knowledge of the
company's products", and "The metrics organization can handle emergencies" are
used by all outsourcing companies.

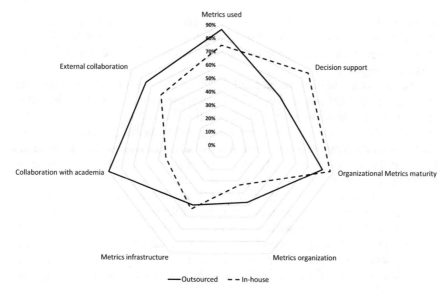

Fig. 7.14 Measurement programs per development type

The outsourcing companies seem also to be generally better in terms of collaboration with academia and with other companies, which again can be caused by the fact that they, somewhat per definition, work with their contractors and need to exchange the metric information.

Finally, we can observe that the companies working with the in-house software development are better (generally) in managing their metric infrastructure, although only with a small difference. The difference is caused by the fact that none of the outsourcing companies uses a consistent naming for their measurement-related files and folders (which again can be caused by supplier-specific set-up of the measurement program).

7.7 Threats to Validity

The construction of the method and its evaluation is based on a collaborative research project described by Sandberg et al. [388] which is a specific kind of an empirical study where practitioners and researchers work together. In this research design we use the framework by Runeson et al. [385] to evaluate and minimize the threats to validity of the study.

The main threats to *external validity* are related to the generalizability of the results. We focused on minimizing this threat by conducting the study at multiple companies. The companies were located at different geographical sites and two interviews were done without the involvement of the researchers (second interview at Company C and in the interview at Company G). Since the practices of each of the companies were different and had evolved independently, the ability of MeSRAM to quantify the robustness shows that the method is not specific to the context in which it was developed.

The main threat to the *construct validity* of this study is the development of the method. The method was developed based on literature studies and the workshop with the practitioners. In order to minimize the risk that the construction of the method was flawed, we conducted a pilot study, which resulted in redesigning of the method – including more categories and topics in the categories. The usage of the improved method at the same pilot-study company with the correct quantification showed that the improvement was indeed sufficient.

Another threat to validity is the use of "Don't know" in the assessment method and the ability to draw conclusions in the presence of multiple "Don't know" answers. There is no pre-defined threshold of how many (percentage-wise) of these answers should stop from drawing the conclusions. In MeSRAM we recommend to use this type of answers to guide further investigation – i.e. asking who may know the answer and follow up on it. If there is no such person then the answer should be interpreted as "No" instead.

The main threat to the *internal validity* is the researcher bias. In order to minimize it we conducted two interviews without the involvement of the researchers (second interview at Company C and in Company G). After the interviews we have asked the interviewers at Company C and G about the difficulties in interpreting the questions or the answers – the response was that there was no ambiguity and the respondents could effectively discuss the questions.

Finally, the main threat to the *reliability* of our results is the risk that the analyses performed by different researchers would lead to different results. This risk is minimized by the fact that we provide full results in the tables which can be analyzed by other researchers.

7.8 Conclusions

Measurement programs in large software development organizations are subject to constant changes since as the software market changes, so do the software development organizations and their information needs. The evolution of measurement programs is natural and should be monitored and managed in order for the measurement program to remain effective and efficient for the organization. From the perspective of the measurement programs, these changes in the organization can cause its decay and in the end its failure if not institutionalized properly.

In this paper we explored the notion of robustness of the measurement program from the perspective of the properties of measures used (e.g. how well they measure the empirical properties they are defined to measure) and from the perspective of institutionalization of the measurement program (e.g. how well the measurement program is established in its context – the company or the internal organization).

We developed a method – MeSRAM – for assessing the robustness of measurement programs. The method consists of two parts – the robustness model for measurement programs and the assessment method.

Our evaluation of the method showed that it captures the differences in the measurement programs in industry. The seven companies which were part of the evaluation had different programs and these differences show after the assessment. After the assessment itself, the companies also identified a number of improvements in their measurement program based on the experiences from other companies.

In our further work we plan to conduct a longitudinal study of the improvement of the measurement programs at the studied companies in order to evaluate the depth of the impact of such an assessment as MeSRAM did. We also intend to conduct a deeper study on the *best-in-class* measurement experiences in the studied companies.

Chapter 8
Recognizing Lines of Code Violating Company-Specific Coding Guidelines Using Machine Learning

Miroslaw Ochodek, Regina Hebig, Wilhelm Meding, Gert Frost, and Miroslaw Staron

Abstract Software developers in big and medium-size companies are working with millions of lines of code in their codebases. Assuring the quality of this code has shifted from simple defect management to proactive assurance of internal code quality. Although static code analysis and code reviews have been at the forefront of research and practice in this area, code reviews are still an effort-intensive and interpretation-prone activity. The aim of this research is to support code reviews by automatically recognizing company-specific code guidelines violations in large-scale, industrial source code. In our action research project, we constructed a machine-learning-based tool for code analysis where software developers and architects in big and medium-sized companies can use a few examples of source code lines violating code/design guidelines (up to 700 lines of code) to train decision-tree classifiers to find similar violations in their codebases (up to 3 million lines of code). Our action research project consisted of (i) understanding the challenges of two large software development companies, (ii) applying the machine-learning-based tool to detect violations of Sun's and Google's coding conventions in the code of three large open source projects implemented in Java, (iii) evaluating the tool on evolving industrial codebase, and (iv) finding the best learning strategies to reduce the cost of training the classifiers. We were able to achieve the average accuracy of over 99% and the average F-score of 0.80 for open source projects when using ca. 40K lines for training the tool. We obtained a similar average F-score of 0.78 for the industrial code but this time using only up to 700 lines of code as a training dataset. Finally, we observed the tool performed visibly better for the rules requiring to understand a single line of code or the context of a few lines (often allowing to reach the F-score of 0.90 or higher). Based on these results, we could observe that this approach can provide modern software development companies with the ability to use examples to teach an algorithm to recognize violations of code/design guidelines and thus

Reprinted with permission from the copyright holder. Originally published in Empirical Software Engineering 25.1 (2020): 220–265. DOI: https://doi.org/10.1007/s10664-019-09769-8

increase the number of reviews conducted before the product release. This, in turn, leads to the increased quality of the final software.

8.1 Introduction

Software developers in big and medium-size software development companies and organizations are working with codebases that are usually of several millions of lines of code. To cope with this code size and at the same time comply with the agile and lean paradigms, e.g. continuous delivery, developers have access to tools that help them with the code review management. Code reviews tools (e.g. static, dynamic, automatic, manual, purchased/own developed review tools) are important for maximizing the quality of the software product that is under development.

Violations in coding guidelines lead to a double negative effect. On the one hand, having to check for inconsistent styles and violated guidelines requires time and slows down the reviewers—taking away time for finding serious mistakes or bad smells. On the other hand, it is known that inconsistent styles make it harder for reviewers to read and understand the code [304, 414].

Many companies adopted fast-feedback loops where the source code is reviewed per commit, in small chunks and often outside of the compiler environment [315]. Tools like Gerrit are used for managing these reviews, but they need integration with tools checking for violations of code/design guidelines.

These code analysis tools and style checkers have the potential to support code reviews. These techniques have advanced significantly during the recent years and can provide over 90% accuracy in finding potential code guideline violations for pre-defined rules. Also, they have been shown to trigger the right discussions during the code review. [412] showed that 73% of the suggestions from the static analysis led to discussions and, in turn, improvements of the source code quality.

However, continuous integration with its fast-feedback loops poses a challenge for the adoption of these tools in the industry. Source code is often too large to be compiled completely for each commit, and tools like Gerrit even promote the review at the level of code commit differences. In addition, coding styles, and thus code/design guidelines, are often company or even project-specific [456], and evolve as the product matures. For example, some conventions used by our industry partners can be found in widely accepted standards or coding conventions, such as camel case variable naming. Others can become very specific to the companies programming environment, concerning aspects such as build time variants. Thus, static code analysis tools and style checkers need to be constantly extended to capture the new rules[1] and the evolution of the existing rules. Both the need for analyzing incomplete code and flexibility in evolution are not well supported by existing tools. This construction can require significant effort as it requires practitioners to learn

---

[1] We will use the term "rule" interchangeably with the term "guideline" since the guidebooks of our industrial partners and most of the commonly adhered coding conventions are composed as sets of rules.

specific APIs [341]. Finally, our industrial partners develop and use their custom Domain Specific Languages (DSLs) for which static code analysis tools do not exist and since they are mostly proprietary and company-specific there are not enough resources to develop and maintain dedicated static code analysis tools.

In this paper, we address the problem of *How to support new ways of reviewing code in continuous integration in large and medium-size software companies?* We present an action research study [26, 447] that aimed at investigating the possibilities of supporting code reviews by automatically recognizing company-specific code guidelines violations in large and medium scale, industrial source code, without the need to learn new ways of specifying the rules – i.e. by example.

Our action research study was designed in four cycles, which gradually progressed from theoretical studies and theory-building into industrial practice and action-taking, following the organizational change model by [157]. In the first cycles, we follow the "research as action" principle and we gradually shift to "change as action" in the last cycles, as practiced often in collaborative action research as prescribed by [305]. We worked with two companies which develop embedded software in Scandinavia: a large infrastructure provider and provider of consumer products in the embedded software domain. Both companies allowed us to analyze the source code of their products and provided access to architects and designers—all with over 10 years (partially over 20 years) of experience in the domains.

As a result, we developed a method and implemented a machine learning-based (ML-based) tool to recognize violations of code/design guidelines that is trained on a small number of examples, is language-agnostic, and does not require the code being analyzed to compile. In the method developed together with our industrial partners, instead of defining and developing rules, the software architects recognize violations in the code, mark the code and teach the tool to recognize similar patterns. Over time, the examples evolve as the codebase evolves, which reduces the need for manual management of rules, and in the end, leads to automation of code reviews using company-specific coding guidelines. The opinion of the practitioners from the cooperating companies is the tool in its current version can complement static code analysis tools they use (e.g., to perform quick or partial codebase quality checks before the complex static code analysis tools are run to analyze the whole codebases) or fill the existing gap by enabling analyzing code written in programming language for which such static code analyzers do not exist or code that does not compile. Ultimately, the example-based approach could potentially evolve to automatically learn to recognize poor quality code from the automatic code reviews. However, at this stage, we focus on training the tool to detect violations of existing company-specific guidelines.

The contributions from the study are:

- we found that by using machine learning (ML) to perform a line-level code analysis it is possible to match the accuracy of static code analysis when identifying violations of guidelines requiring to understand a limited code context (i.e., a single line or a few lines of code),
- we show that using active learning for sampling training data provides the most accurate results in recognizing violations of company-specific coding guidelines

and allows reducing the effort required to train the ML-based tool (a smaller number of training examples was needed to achieve the same (or higher) prediction quality as in the case of manual selection of examples),

- we show that the frequencies of tokens are a valuable source of information while recognizing code violations and allow to perform this task without the need for parsing or compiling the code,
- we show that the approach works both on industry-wide standards applied to open source and on the company-specific, proprietary guidelines applied to professionally developed code from two large companies. Therefore, using the ML-based tool can help to reduce the effort of manual code review, and
- we report observations from the *in situ* application of ML to analyze code in industrial environments that could help practitioners to adopt ML-based approaches in their companies (i.e., the strategies to minimize the effort of labeling data, the effect that the guidelines and code evolution can have on the accuracy of an ML-based tool).

The rest of the paper is structured as follows. Section 8.2 outlines the most important related research in the area of code reviews and applying machine learning for this task. In Sect. 8.3, we present a machine-learning based code analyzer. Section 8.4 describes the research methodology applied and our research design. The results of each of the four action-research cycles are presented in Sect. 8.5. Section 8.6 discusses threats to validity of our study. Finally, we summarize the findings in Sect. 8.7.

8.2 Related Work

Code reviews have been studied extensively and we started first with the overview of the existing works in this area. We review the related work from two perspectives—comparison between static code analysis/style checker tools and from the perspective of academic and using machine learning for static code analysis.

8.2.1 Comparison Between Tools

Static code analysis tools and style checkers are widely used development tools with over hundreds of tools listed alone in Wikipedia. The compare a sample of these tools for this paper, we decided on a set of comparison criteria inspired by the taxonomy of [340]:

Supported Languages: Due to the needs of our industry partners, we will focus on tools for C and C++.
Compilation Requirements: This criterion is inspired by Novak's *technology* and *input* dimensions. The focus is on the tool's requirements on the syntactic correct-

ness and completeness of the code. Possible values are: "parsing" (code needs to be syntactically correct)", "linking" (code needs to be complete to run the analysis), and "robust" (robust against most syntactical errors, no linking required).

Extensibility: The criterion is a refined dimension from [340] and describes whether the tool can be extended with additional rules/checks. Possible values are: "no" (extensible only by feature request), "imperative" (extensible by writing imperative code, e.g. in plug-ins), "declarative by rule" (extensible by declarative specification of rules), and "declarative by example" (extensible by declaration of valid and invalid code examples).

Configurability: The category refines Novak's dimension with the focus on the subject of the configuration. Possible values are: "no" (rules cannot be configured), "rules by parameter" (single rules can be configured via parameters), "rules by example" (single rules can be configured via examples), "ruleset" (Selection of what rules should be applied - single rules or sets of rules), and "other" (other configuration options).

Interoperability: The category is inspired by Novak's *user experience* dimension and focuses on how the tool can be used in a tool environment. Possible values are: "stand-alone" (the tool has a stand-alone version), "IDE" (there are IDE/Editor plug-ins available), and "collab. tools" (Integration to collaborative development tools, such as Github and Gerrit is available).

Access to Results: The category captures, inspired by Novak's *output* dimension, whether the tool's results can be accessed externally or exported. Possible values are: "no external" (the results cannot be exported easily), "API" (the results can be accessed via an API, e.g. via web services), and "file-export" (Results can be exported to file formats such as HTML or text).

Static Code Analysis Tools for C/C++

In the following paragraphs, we discuss a sample of static code analysis tools for C and C++ with regards to the criteria above (see Table 8.1). We selected the sample by starting with the tools that are discussed in known comparative studies on static code analysis tools, namely the works of [51, 109, 121, 291, 405].

In the end we chose to select the 6 tools addressed by most of these studies: Coverity Scan,[2] KlocWork,[3] PolySpace,[4] Splint,[5] CPPcheck[6] and Flawfinder.[7] All of these tools are mostly targeting the detection of errors and security issues in the code.

---

[2] Coverity Scan https://scan.coverity.com/users/sign_in

[3] KlocWork https://support.roguewave.com/documentation/klocwork/en/10-x/whichtypeofchecker tocreatekastorpath/

[4] PolySpace https://se.mathworks.com/discovery/static-code-analysis.html

[5] Splint http://www.splint.org/

[6] CPPcheck http://cppcheck.sourceforge.net/

[7] Flawfinder https://www.dwheeler.com/flawfinder/

Table 8.1 Comparison between popular static analysis tools and code style checkers.

Tool	Supported Languages	Compilation Requirements	Extensibility	Configurability	Interoperability	Access to Results
Static Code Analysis Tools						
Coverity Scan	C/C++	parsing/ (linking)	imperative	N/A	stand-alone/ IDE/ collab. tools	API
KlocWork	C/C++	parsing/ (linking)	imperative	rules by parameter/ ruleset	stand-alone/ IDE/ collab. tools	API
PolySpace	C/C++	parsing/ (linking)	N/A	ruleset	stand-alone/ IDE	N/A
Splint	C	parsing/linking	declarative by rule	N/A	stand-alone	no external
CPPcheck	C/C++	parsing/linking	declarative by rule	other	stand-alone/ IDE/ collab. tools	file-export
Flawfinder	C/C++	robust	declarative by rule	other	stand-alone/ IDE	file-export
Style Checkers						
CodeCheck	C/C++	parsing	imperative	N/A	stand-alone	file-export
Uncrustify	C/C++	parsing	no	rules by parameter	stand-alone/ IDE	file-export (config.)
KWStyle	C/C++	parsing/linking	no	rules by parameter	stand-alone/ collab. tool	N/A
C++ Style Checker	C++	parsing/linking	N/A	ruleset	stand-alone	file-export
Learning/Example-Based Approaches						
Naturalize	C/C++	parsing/linking	no	rules by example	stand-alone/ IDE/ collab. tools	N/A
Code Style Analytics	N/A	parsing/linking	no	rules by example	N/A	N/A
CCFlex	C/C++	robust	declarative by example	ruleset	stand-alone / collab. tools	file-export

Most of the static code analysis tools require the code to parse and link, due to their analysis methods: Coverity Scan and KlocWork perform data-flow analysis, PolySpace uses formal methods, and Splint uses theorem proving. Some of these tools can run on a single source file but perform a shallow analysis, based on assumptions on the missing code, only. The exception is Flawfinder, which can handle code that is incomplete and does not necessarily parse, due to the token-based analysis.

Coverity Scan (according to [109]) and KlocWork can both be extended with new checkers imperatively. Splint, CPPCheck, and Flawfinder can be extended as well by the declaration of new rules. This happens in the form of regular expressions in CPPCheck, which is not easy as internal variables need to be known. Flawfinder allows exchanging the database with new pattern specifying invalid situations. None of these extension mechanisms is trivial to use.

KlocWork allows to configure single rules, e.g. by defining metric thresholds, and to define rulesets (called "taxonomies") and PolySpace allows a selection of the rules to be applied. CPPcheck allows to configure the used language version and Flawfinder allows to exclude code-lines from the analysis.

With the exception of Splint, each tool can be integrated into at least one IDE or code editor, such as Eclipse, Rhapsody UML, VIM or emacs, or offer integration to collaboration tools, such as Hudson or Jenkins. CPPcheck and Flawfinder allow a. export of results to HTML and Coverity Scan and KlocWork provide APIs.

Style Checkers for C/C++

In contrast to static code analysis tools, style checkers mainly focus on aspects of the code that do not directly impact the behavior of the system. Nonetheless, having a consistent style can significantly improve readability of the code and with that maintainability and quality. In the following, we discuss for well known examples for Style Checkers that target C or C++: CodeCheck,[8] Uncrustify,[9] KWStyle,[10] and C++ Style Checker Tool.[11]

CodeCheck and Uncrustify both parse the code, while KWStyle and C++ Style Checker Tool also require the code to be linked. Only CodeCheck can be extended by writing new checkers. The checks of Uncrustify and KWstyle cannot be extended without extending the tools themselves. However, both tools allow configuring single rules, e.g. by specifying the allowed length of a code line. The C++ Style Checker Tool enables a selection of rules/rule-sets to be applied.

Uncrustify has a plug-in for the UniversalIndentGUI and exports rule configurations. KWStyle can be integrated into Git. Finally, CodeCheck and C++ Style Checker Tool both allow to export results, e.g. into HTML or XML.

---

[8] CodeCheck http://www.abxsoft.com/

[9] Uncrustify http://uncrustify.sourceforge.net/

[10] KWStyle https://kitware.github.io/KWStyle/

[11] C++ Style Checker Tool http://www.semdesigns.com/Products/StyleChecker/CppStyleChecker. html?Home=StyleChecker

8.2.2 Machine Learning for Static Code Analysis

There are numerous studies applying ML algorithms to evaluate code quality. However, according to our best knowledge, none of them solely focus on recognizing company-specific code guidelines violations in code using examples. Also, most of these tools are at the early stages of development and are not ready to be integrated into industrial code-review pipelines.

Among these studies, there are some that localize defects at the level of code lines or statements. For instance, [59] proposed a fault invariant classifier that uses a dynamic (runtime) analysis to extract semantic properties of the program's computation as features describing the code.

[21] proposed to use Normalised Compression Distance to find potential string overflows, null pointer references, memory leaks, and incorrect API usage. [68] reported findings on using machine learning techniques to detect defects in C programs at Oracle. They used neural networks and a large corpus of programs to compare the prediction quality of ML-based classifier against four static program analysis tools, including Parfait used internally at Oracle. Their conclusion was that the ML-based tools were not suitable replacements for static program analysis tools due to the low precision of the results.

[10] and [456], present with Naturalize[12] and a code style analytics tool, two approaches that adapt style checking to a code-base by configuring rules according to what is typical for that codebase.

[456] bases the configuration on an assessment of metrics, such as method lengths, number of CamelCase variables, or number of opening braces on the same line for loops.

Recently, Qing Mi et al. [322] studied the possibility of classifying source code depending on its readability. They used three Convolution Neural Networks operating on different levels of granularity (character-level, token-level, and AST-Tree nodes level). The accuracy of the proposed DeepCRM+ConvNets method was evaluated on the open source code since training the networks required large amounts of labeled data.

Finally, the tool we use in this study is called Flexible Code Counter/Classifier (CCFlex). It was developed by the authors of this paper and used to perform software size measurement in one of the previous studies ([341]). However, since the tool is a general-purpose code classifier, it could be adapted to detect violations of coding-style guidelines.

8.2.3 Machine Learning for Code-Smell Detection

[131, 133] presented an experiment to compare how good different machine learning algorithms would be in learning to detect code smells. While Fontana et.

---

[12] Naturalize http://groups.inf.ed.ac.uk/naturalize/

al. report on reaching an accuracy of 95%, [89] challenged these results with a replication study. The replication shows that the selection of the dataset including the balance of violations with none-violations as well as an unrealistic characteristic of violation cases can lead to an up to 90% too high precision.

Although the aforementioned studies use the same classification algorithms as we do in our study (e.g., decision trees, random forest), they differ in the approach to feature extraction. The studies on code-smell detection use code metrics to describing units of code (e.g., metrics of size, complexity, cohesion, coupling, encapsulation, or inheritance), while in this study, we extract linguistic features (e.g. number of "if" statements, which words/variables/statements were used in a line) directly from the source code in a similar way as it is done in the field of natural language processing (e.g., by using the bag-of-words model).

Also, code smells are typically concerning architectural aspects and larger chunks of code than coding guideline violations. However, it is nonetheless interesting to compare progress in applying machine learning in the two fields. We especially expect the relevance of realistic data in training and evaluation to be valid for machine learning of coding guideline violations.

8.2.4 Summary

As shown in Table 8.1, most existing static code analysis tools and style checkers need to parse the code and often even link it to fully apply their analysis. This also holds for most of the ML-based approaches. The only exceptions are Flawfinder and *CCFlex*, which are both robust, due to token- or text-based analysis.

Extensibility is never trivial. Even when a declaration of rules is allowed, there is a steep learning curve to understand the declaration languages. CCFlex and Deep-CRM+ConvNets provide an alternative approach, allowing developers to define extensions, by listing examples in the language they usually work in.

The other ML-based approaches are limited with regards to the type of violations that can be found. This is something that also holds for Flawfinder for which the specialization on security seems to limit the type of extensions possible.

Finally, most of the ML-based tools (e.g., DeepCRM+ConvNets) are experimental/research tools at the early stages of development. Therefore, they lack documentation and usability features what makes them hard to use by practitioners.

8.3 The CCFlex Tool

The CCFlex tool (Flexible Code Counter/Classifier) was initially designed to perform software size measurement [341]. In this study, we adapted the tool to detect code guidelines violations in the code. Since the tool evolved over the course of the study, here, we describe its final design to give the reader a complete overview of how the tool operates. The tool is distributed as Open Source and available on GitHub.[13]

8.3.1 Architecture

The version of CCFlex used in the previous study was implemented as a monolithic Java application. In the course of this study, we decided to redesign the tool so it is possible to change the processing pipeline without the need for recompiling or redeploying the tool. We used the pipes-and-filters architecture style, where we use a number of independent components (filters) that could be organized into processing pipelines. We also switched to the Python ML technological stack to implement the tool. However, filters can be implemented in any programming languages as long as they accept input and produce output in the agreed format. The total size of the Python code is around 5K source lines of code (SLOC) with the average size of a filter of ca. 140 SLOC. The full documentation of the filters is available on the project's GitHub page.

A typical processing pipeline used in this study is presented in Fig. 8.1. Before the training begins, we need to prepare a training codebase with labels. The lines violating coding guidelines are labeled by adding a configurable prefix to each of them. For instance, if we configured the prefix to be "@!", then the line "@! int MyVAR = 10;" would be recognized as a line violating the coding guideline.

The first filter used in the pipeline presented in the figure is called *lines extractor*. It traverses through a codebase, extracts each line, its class label, and stores the results in a CSV file. The output file can be passed any of the available feature extractors. Each extractor adds column(s) (extracted features describing each of the lines) to the CSV file. The output files produced by feature extractors can be merged using specialized filters (they are omitted in Fig. 8.1 for the sake of brevity). On top of that, we can use *feature selection* filters to reduce the dimensionality of the feature space using the algorithms available in Python sklearn library. Features selection is performed on training codebase and then also applied to code that is going to be evaluated by dropping rejected features. Finally, the produced CSV file can be loaded by one of the filters that *train a classifier* and use it to classify the new lines. The results are stored in an output CSV file and can be passed to one of the report-generation filters.

In addition to the filters, CCFlex provides a suite of standalone tools allowing to perform independent tasks, like the selection of lines to label using Active Learning (AL) [142] or checking the consistency of line labels provided by a human (i.e., identifying lines having similar representation in the feature space but different labels).

---

[13] CCFlex https://github.com/mochodek/py-ccflex

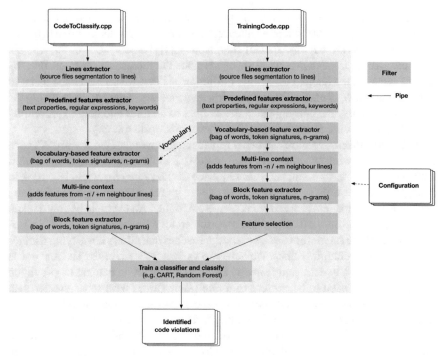

Fig. 8.1 An example of a typical CCFlex processing pipeline

8.3.2 Feature-Extraction Filters

The feature extractors implemented in CCFlex can be divided into three categories: predefined features extractors, vocabulary-based extractor, and block-feature extractors.

Predefined features extractors process lines of code and extract the features defined by the user, e.g., counts occurrences of a given substring in a line or number of characters or words. For instance, one could configure a filter to count the number of string "for" in a line and extract it as a feature.

Vocabulary-based extractors use the bag-of-words (BOW) model to extract features. Bag-of-words uses a vocabulary that can be either automatically extracted from the training examples or predefined (CCFlex supports both approaches). When the vocabulary is extracted from the training code it has to be passed as an input to the filter extracting features using BOW on the code to be evaluated (see Fig. 8.1). BOW counts the occurrences of tokens in the code that are in the vocabulary (the code is tokenized). Also, it can count occurrences of sequences of tokens called n-grams (e.g., bi-gram or tri-grams). N-grams are a valuable source of information for finding code guidelines violations since it is often important to understand the context in which a given token appears (e.g., `int a` vs. `class a`).

We introduced several modifications to a commonly used bag-of-words extraction algorithm. Firstly, we introduced an alternative tokenizer that split each line to tokens using not only white but also special characters: ()[]{}!@#$%^&*-=;:'"\|'~,.<>/?. The split strings are also preserved as tokens since the represent constructs used by many programming languages. Another difference is that we convert each token to what we call *token signature* before creating a vocabulary. This allows reducing the size of vocabulary, and consequently, the number of features and help in preventing overfitting to specific names of variables or methods while training.

To create a token signature, we firstly replace each uppercase letter with "A", each lowercase letter with "a", and each digit with "0", while special characters are left unchanged (e.g., "_"). Then, each subsequence of the same characters is shrunk to a single character only (e.g., *aaa* to *a* or __ to _). The same is repeated for pairs and triples of characters (e.g., *AaAa* is converted to *Aa*). An example of how a token signature and bag-of-words model are constructed for a line is presented in Fig. 8.2.

Block-feature extractors use heuristic approaches that allows identifying features spanning through multiple lines. We have two variants of such tools. The first one is based on the already extracted features. Each block feature is defined by providing the features that need to be present in a line (their values have to be greater than zero) to treat the line as *start* or *end* of the block. Similarly, it is possible to define forbidding features. If any of the forbidding features are present in a line (its value is greater than zero) the line cannot be considered as a start or end of the block. All the lines between the start and end of a block belong to that block (the value of the block feature is set to one). An example of extracting a block-comment feature is presented in Fig. 8.2. The second variant of block-feature extraction is based on training and using a separate classifier to identify the starts and ends of block features.

8.3.3 Classification Algorithms

While designing ML-based filters, we took into account two observations made while analyzing the coding guidelines and discussing them with our partners. Firstly, we had to accept the fact that the size of a training sample would be very small since the code guidelines used by our industrial partners included only a limited number of examples (additional examples would have to be provided by the users). Secondly, the traceability of the decision made would be welcomed. Therefore, we preferred to use ML-algorithms that provide explanations of how the decision is made. We decided to use decision trees since they are commonly considered as interpretable models ([139]). Consequently, we have integrated into CCFlex and used in this study a set of decision-tree-based algorithms, such as CART, C5.0 Decision Trees, and Random Forest.

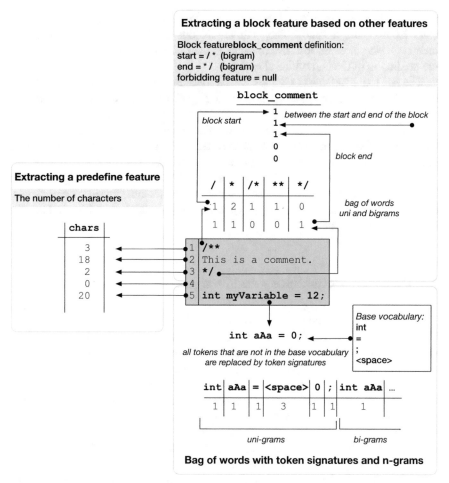

Fig. 8.2 An example of extracting bag-of-words (with an example of generating token signature), block feature, and a predefined feature for a fragment of code

8.3.4 Active Learning

Active learning (AL) aims at training an accurate prediction model with minimum cost by labeling most informative instances [142]. In essence, AL is an iterative and interactive process of performing two steps: *measuring the uncertainty of classification* and using this information to *query* unlabeled instances.

There are many ways to measure uncertainty and strategies to query for labels. In our study, we use the query by committee (QBC) strategy (the implementation available in the modAL[14] Python library) using committee of decision trees (CART), K-Nearest Neighbours (KNN), and Random Forests as base learners. In the QBC

---

[14] modAL https://github.com/cosmic-cortex/modAL.

strategy, when an instance is queried, each member of the committee votes on the class label of the instance. The final predictions are the majority voting of the members. The most informative instance is the one with the most disagreement in the prediction of the committee classifiers.

The AL tool available in CCFlex allows for interactive labeling of code with the use of the selected querying strategy (either QBC or single classifier uncertainty sampling). The user is presented with a line of code in its context (a few proceeding and following lines) and asked to label the line (decide whether the line violates a coding guideline or not). Then, the line is added to the training codebase and another query is performed to select the next line to be labeled.

When using this tool in our study, we always started from creating an initial training dataset by adding positive and negative examples available in the companies' coding guidebooks and then used the QBC querying strategy to poll more lines for labeling from the codebase.

8.4 Research Methodology and Design

The study of the violations of the coding guidelines needs to be conducted in the industrial context, where the interaction between the researchers and the studied organization stimulates learning for both sides. For the theory development (research), the learning of the practical side of constructing coding/design guidelines, recognizing the violations and the acceptance of accuracy are important. For the application (industry), the learning of how the limitations and their impact on how to check guidelines automatically are important. For this kind of context, action research is the most suitable research methodology, as it emphasizes the learning and theory development from empirical observations in the industrial context [26].

We use the opportunity to work closely with two industrial partners, which provided the context of our research and allowed us to work on their premises, with their codebase and software engineers. Both companies were present in discussing the results of all action-research cycles and deeply involved in the cycles when the researchers worked on their premises.

Company A is a leading provider of consumer products in the embedded software domain. The company has a tradition of collaboration with software engineering researchers and being part of action research projects. The company allowed us to analyze their platform code used in a large number of their products and provided access to a software architect, and three designers which have formulated the rules which have been as learning input—all with over 10 years experience in the domain.

Company B is a leading provider of infrastructure products in the embedded software domain. The company has a long tradition of collaborating with software engineering researchers and over ten years of experience in running action research projects. The company provided us with the access to their source code and collaboration with two architects with over 20 years of experience with the company's products and with design/code quality.

Both companies are involved in the development of the tool as their operations moved towards continuous deployment and their intention is to increase the automation of software development by increasing the use of machine learning and autonomous computing techniques for software engineering tasks. The intention is to find methods to identify violations of their proprietary guidelines with as little manual work as possible.

In Table 8.2, we summarize each of the action research cycles. The details of the results are presented in Sect. 8.5.

As the essence of action research projects is that they combine the learning with the design of the study, thus being a flexible research design [376], we detail the choices we made for each cycle in the following section, including the results from each of the action research steps.

8.5 Execution and Results

In this section, we present the evaluating and learning activities from the action research cycles.

8.5.1 Action Research Cycle 1 – What Coding Guidelines Are Used by Our Industrial Partners?

8.5.1.1 Cycle Goal and Research Procedure

The goal of the cycle was to investigate the coding guidelines of our industrial partners. In particular, we wanted to:

- understand the types of rules that are in the companies' guidebooks,
- check the quality of the rules (whether they are unambiguous and their violations can be found by analyzing code).

We investigated rules in the Company A and B guidebooks and categorize them based on the information required to identify their violations. We assessed the quality of the rules and consulted our findings with software engineers from both companies.

8.5.1.2 Cycle Execution and Results

After reviewing the literature, we learned that there is no agreed taxonomy that could be used to categorize coding guidelines (and their violations). For instance, [340] compared four static code analysis tools and showed that each of the tools uses a different set of categories, and even within a single taxonomy multiple criteria are often used to define these categories. For instance, some categories refer to syntax and

Table 8.2 Summary of action research cycles

Cycle	Diagnosing	Action planning	Action taking/Executing	Evaluating	Learning
1	What coding guidelines are used in the industry?	We planned to conduct a document analysis at partner companies to understand how they design their coding guidelines and the content of these guidelines.	We changed the way of grouping of guidelines—from thematic to scope-based; we analyzed 45 and 66 guidelines and classified them according to this new grouping.	We found that some guidelines need quality improvement because of their ambiguity or difficulty to make the assessment.	Most of the coding guidelines are different between the companies, which means that the potential tool has to be adapted and tuned on a per-company basis.
2	Which of available tools can be adapted to recognize violations of code guidelines assuming that code might not parse or compile?	We planned to review the most popular tools for C/C++ code analysis and compare extendability, readability and usability of the tools to find a tool that is easy to extend, does not require parsing or compiling the code, and can recognize code guidelines violations in code.	We reviewed 13 tools for C/C++ code analysis. We refactored CCFlex (a machine-learning-based tool) and performed a benchmark study on a problem of finding violations of popular Sun and Google coding conventions for Java by comparing on 3 open source projects.	CCFlex could recognize 98.98%–99.93% of lines violating any of the Java Sun's and Google's coding style guidelines	Since we could recognize almost all of the lines with violations, we set off to check the guidelines from the industrial partners.
3	What is the accuracy of the recognition of the violations of guidelines in the industrial settings and how it depends on coding style?	We planned to assess different situations: old/legacy codebase (before the guidelines), modern codebase (currently under development) and in-between (code which was developed alongside the development of the guidelines).	We analyzed three codebases of Company A: we assessed 3 out of 45 guidelines; using different configurations of CCFlex and a limited number of iterations.	We could achieve satisfactory results of up to 87% Recall for the evaluated guidelines.	We needed to conduct a formal evaluation with Company B to first evaluate the generalizability of the findings and secondly investigate if we are able to reduce the number of false-positives.
4	How much training of CCFlex is needed to minimize the percentage of false-positives?	We selected one or two guidelines per type of rule (taxonomy) and defined a procedure on how to sample code for training.	We conducted the assessment of seven rules at Company A and used two different strategies for selecting lines in the training set—manual selection and Active Learning; we assessed the code quality of a product. We evaluated the approach on a large codebase of over three million SLOC. The number of trials varied from three to seven and the F-score varied from 0.04 to 1.00	We found that the identified violations were accurate and the architects used them in their quality improvement after the study.	Active learning allows to achieve higher F-score in fewer iterations and provides higher F-score for the entire codebase.

programming concepts (e.g., naming conventions, code layout, exceptions handling) while others are defined by referring to quality attributes of software products that could be affected by certain violations (e.g., maintainability, security, or performance problems).

Since we wanted to automatically identify lines of code violating coding guidelines, we proposed a different taxonomy that categorizes violations based on the information that is required to recognize them in the code. The taxonomy is presented in Fig. 8.3. It groups guidelines into three main categories.

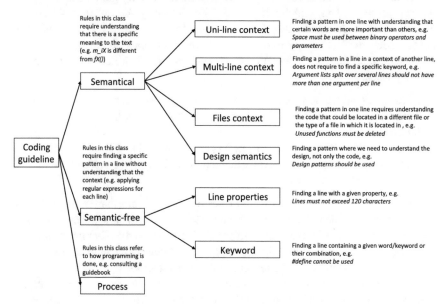

Fig. 8.3 Taxonomy of code guidelines violations.

The first root category groups "semantical" coding guidelines. Finding violations of such rules requires understanding the meaning of a text in its context. Depending on the size of the context, we distinguish four sub-categories: a uni-line context—we need to understand the meaning of the tokens/words in a single line (e.g., the rule stating that there can be only one statement in a line), multi-line context—we need to understand the meaning of words/tokens in a sequence of lines (e.g., braces must be used for all compound statements), files context—we need to be able to relate the code in different files or understand file properties (e.g., unused functions must be deleted), and design context which goes beyond understanding code constructs and requiring recognizing the design intent (e.g., design patterns should be used). For uni-line context we do not take into account the possibility of intentionally breaking the line in the middle of statement.

The second root category groups "semantic-free" coding guidelines. Finding violations of such rules requires recognizing the presence of some patterns in a line of code (without the need for understanding the role or meaning of particular tokens or words). We distinguish two sub-categories: line properties—a guideline refers to a quantifiable property of text (e.g., the number of characters in a line shall not exceed 120 characters) and keyword-based guidelines—we need to find a keyword or combination of keywords (or lack of such) in the text (e.g., union types shall not be used—we need to find the keyword `union`).

The remaining root category is called "process" coding guidelines. The guidelines belonging to this category regards the development process (e.g., the necessity of consulting a guidebook).

We used the proposed taxonomy to categorize the coding guidelines of our industrial partners. The guidebook provided by Company A contained 45 coding guidelines while the one used by Company B included 66 rules. The distribution of the rules between the categories of our taxonomy is presented in Fig. 8.4.

When classifying the rules into the categories, we identified three groups of outlying rules:

- *rules as documentation*: no style-related coding guidelines, but rather hints about what libraries or interfaces to use or what protocols to follow when calling an interface,
- *optional rules*: either a whole rule or its part is optional to follow,
- *rules on external information*: rules that require information outside of the studied code, e.g. user requirements.

Rules that serve as documentation and rules on external information might be extremely difficult to identify and certainly have special needs to the static code analysis approach, such as consideration of multiple files at once. On the other hand, optional rules might as well be ignored by any approach. Therefore, we defined these three types of rules to be out of scope for the further investigation.

We also observed that some rules were imprecise and could have different interpretations. We consulted each of such rules with the companies, and as a consequence, some rules were indicated as to be improved.

The performed analysis resulted in narrowing our study to rules belonging to four categories: semantical uni-/multi-line context and semantic-free line properties and keywords. We observed that the rules belonging to the three remaining categories were either not related to code (process rules), violations could not be mapped to particular lines (design semantics, e.g., usage of design patterns), examples were not available in the guidebook and would be very difficult to get (design semantics) or span through multiple source files (semantical files context, e.g., unused functions should be deleted).

a)   b)

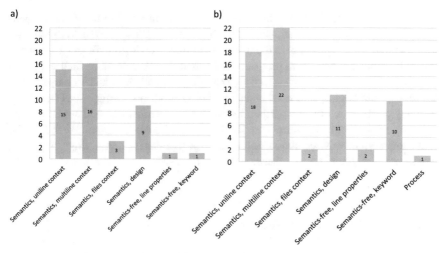

Fig. 8.4 The number of coding-guideline rules identified for (**a**) Company A and (**b**) Company B

8.5.2 Action Research Cycle 2 – Selecting a Tool Capable of Recognizing Code Guidelines Violations of Our Partners

8.5.2.1 Cycle Goal and Research Procedure

The goal of the second cycle of our action research study was to find a tool capable of recognizing violations of our partners' coding guidelines while also meeting the quality attribute requirements they perceived as important, namely:

- the proposed solution needs to be easy to extend or modify without the need of learning any API or having a deep understanding of static code analysis techniques,
- running the code analysis should not require parsing or compiling the code.

The rationale behind the first requirement is that the code guidelines are specific to each company and can evolve or change in time. Therefore, the tool needs to be easy and cost-effective to maintain. The second requirement is motivated by the fact that some of the code of our partners might not compile when taken outside of the runtime environment. Also, at some stage, it is expected that the tool could be integrated into code-reviewing tools such as Gerrit and be able to recognize the violations in fragments of code being reviewed that might not parse as well (e.g., in form of Git diffs).

We planned to review the tools for C/C++ code analysis and ML-based tools. Based on the results of the analysis we wanted to select a tool to be used in the next cycles of the study.

We then planned to perform a simulation study to preliminarily evaluate the accuracy of the tool in finding lines violating two well-known coding standards—

Google Java Style Guide[15] and Sun Java Code Conventions[16] in the code of open-source projects. Since it was supposed to be a feasibility study, we wanted to consider a simpler but similar problem to the one of recognizing code guidelines violations in the code of our partners. Java programs are generally easier to parse than programs written in C++, which is considered an extremely difficult language to parse [205]. Secondly, both coding standards focus on coding style/formatting issues (similarly to many of the rules of our partners) and cover all semantical and semantic-free subcategories of our taxonomy (see Tables 8.3 and 8.4). We assumed that if the tool cannot effectively recognize violations of guidelines in such settings, its tuning would not likely lead us to achieve satisfactory results for our partners' code and rules.

8.5.2.2 Cycle Execution and Results

Our comparison of the existing tools in Sect. 7.2 showed, that there are only two tools that are robust with regards to the defined quality requirements, i.e., Flawfinder and CCFlex. However, Flawfinder's is specialized to recognize security-related problems and its extensibility is limited to similar types of issues (still, extending the tool requires understanding and modifying a built-in database of patterns). On contrary, CCFlex allows extending the tool to support a new rule by providing examples of lines following and violating the rule. Therefore, it does not require learning any API or implementing any algorithms. However, the original tool was designed to solve a different problem of recognizing lines to be counted while measuring the physical size of software products. Therefore, we decided to first investigate if the CCFlex tool can be effectively used to recognize code guidelines violations before making the final decision of presenting it to industrial partners and adapting it to recognize violations of their coding guidelines.

As a feasibility study, we investigated how effective the CCFlex tool in recognizing lines of code violating coding guidelines depending on the number of labeled lines used for training. We assumed that when using an ML-based tool, such as CCFlex, instead of a static code analysis tools there could be a trade-off between the accuracy of the tool and its extensibility. We took the CCFlex tool and used Checkstyle[17] to find lines violating Google Java Style Guide and Sun Java Code Conventions.

We performed validation on a dataset containing samples of code from three Java open-source projects: Eclipse Platform, Jasper Reports, and Spring Framework. For each project, we randomly sampled source code files that in total consisted of around 15K SLOC (Eclipse Platform 15,588 SLOC, Jasper Reports 14,845, and Spring Framework 14,869 SLOC). The whole datasets contained 45,302 SLOC. We perceived the code of Eclipse Platform and Spring Framework as being well

---

[15] Google Java Style Guide http://checkstyle.sourceforge.net/reports/google-java-style-20170228.html

[16] Code Conventions for the Java Programming Language: Contents http://www.oracle.com/technetwork/java/javase/documentation/codeconvtoc-136057.html

[17] Checkstyle: http://checkstyle.sourceforge.net.

documented and convergent with the coding standards for Java. Contrary, the code of Jasper Reports seemed to violate the basic rules of the conventions (e.g., placing an opening curly bracket of a compound statement in a new line).

The Checkstyle tool was used as an oracle to automatically label the lines that were violating code-style *any* of the rules proposed by each of these standards. As a result, we initially constructed eight datasets:

- All–Sun (Count: 10,821, Ignore: 34,481)
- Eclipse-Sun (Count: 3,003, Ignore: 12,585)
- Jasper-Sun (Count: 5,046, Ignore: 9,799)
- Spring-Sun (Count: 2,772, Ignore: 12,097)
- All–Google (Count: 30,727, Ignore: 14,575)
- Eclipse-Google (Count: 11,157, Ignore: 4,431)
- Jasper-Google (Count: 10,546, Ignore: 4,299)
- Spring-Google (Count: 9,024, Ignore: 5,845)

All the datasets seemed unbalanced with respect to the number of lines belonging to the considered decision classes (violation and non-violation). The percentage of lines violating certain rules of both standards are presented in Table 8.3 and 8.4. The data presented in the latter table shows that nearly all the lines violated the Google's rule stating that developers shall avoid using tabular characters (97.91–99.42%) and more than half of the lines used wrong indentation levels (53.82–69.01%). The frequency of the other rules violations was visibly lower. Therefore, we decided to introduce another variant of each data set by excluding the two over-represented types of violations to avoid making the problem too trivial (we denoted this sets as Google'):

- All–Google' (Count: 4,423, Ignore: 40,879)
- Eclipse-Google' (Count: 1,066, Ignore: 14,522)
- Jasper-Google' (Count: 2,365, Ignore: 12,480)
- Spring-Google' (Count: 992, Ignore: 13,877)

We performed ten runs of 10-fold cross-validation procedure. We evaluated the prediction quality of the classifier based on a set of commonly used measures, such as Accuracy, Precision, Recall, and F-score.

The results of the cross-validation are presented in Table 8.5. The accuracy for the Sun's coding standard ranged between 99.05% and 99.55%. For the Google and Google' coding standards, the accuracy ranged between 99.70–99.93% and 98.91–99.26%, respectively. The observed accuracy seemed stable between the runs of the cross-validation procedure (the maximum standard deviation for accuracy was equal to 0.29%). We also did not observe any visible differences between Precision and Recall, which ranged between 0.99 and 1.00.

The learning curves for the accuracy are presented in Fig. 8.5. We observed that even for a small dataset consisting of 2% of the whole dataset, the observed Accuracy was high—95.64% for Sun Java Coding Conventions, and 99.22% / 95.05% for the Google / Google' Java Style Guides. We also noticed that the variability the results was visibly higher for the smaller datasets.

Table 8.3 The percentage of lines violating Sun Java Coding Conventions (Checkstyle)

Violation of the Sun's guidelines	All%	Eclipse%	Jasper%	Spring%
Line is longer than 80 characters (Line properties)	40.70	55.04	20.13	62.59
Parameter should be final (Uni-line context)	19.41	26.37	11.79	25.72
'{' should be on the previous line (Multi-line context)	13.67		29.31	
Missing a Javadoc comment (Multi-line context)	10.67	12.52	9.77	10.32
Class designed for extension without Javadoc (Design semantics)	9.03	6.93	12.88	4.29
Line has trailing spaces (Uni-line context)	8.78		18.83	
Expected @param tag (Multi-line context)	5.73	9.26	2.93	7.00
Hidden field (Files context)	3.90	2.73	3.03	6.75
Variable must be private and have accessor methods (Multi-line context)	2.73	1.76	4.68	0.22
Symbol is not followed by whitespace (Uni-line context)	2.50	2.30	3.94	0.07
File contains tab characters (this is the first instance) (Keyword)	2.40	3.40	1.35	3.25
Expected an @return tag (Multi-line context)	2.27	0.07	1.45	6.17
'}' should be on the same line as the next part of a multi-block statement (Multi-line context)	1.72	0.33	1.01	4.51
Avoid inline conditionals (Uni-line context)	1.45	2.36	0.55	2.09
'if' construct must use '{}'s (Multi-line context)	0.85	3.06		
Expected @throws tag (Multi-line context)	0.69		0.87	1.12
First sentence should end with a period (Multi-line context)	0.61	1.20	0.02	1.05
Symbol should be on a new line (Multi-line context)	0.52		0.10	1.84
Symbol is followed by whitespace (Uni-line context)	0.50	0.87	0.55	
Name must match pattern '^[A-Z][A-Z0-9]*(_[A-Z0-9]+)*$' (Uni-line context)	0.46	0.67	0.42	0.32
Redundant 'final' modifier (Multi-line context)	0.34	1.23		
Symbol is not preceded with whitespace (Uni-line context)	0.34	0.77	0.26	0.04
Unused import (Multi-line context)	0.34	0.20	0.10	0.94
Redundant 'public' modifier (Multi-line context)	0.30	0.60	0.18	0.18
Symbol is preceded with whitespace (Uni-line context)	0.29	0.03	0.57	0.04
Magic number (Uni-line context)	0.20	0.47	0.06	0.18
'for' construct must use '{}'s (Multi-line context)	0.14	0.50		
'static' modifier out of order with the JLS suggestions (Uni-line context)	0.10	0.27	0.04	0.04
File does not end with a newline (Uni-line context)	0.10	0.30	0.04	
Class should be declared as final (Uni-line context)	0.08	0.30		
Avoid nested blocks (Multi-line context)	0.07	0.03	0.14	
Extra HTML tag found (Multi-line context)	0.06	0.17		0.07
Utility classes should not have a public or default constructor (Design semantics)	0.05	0.17		
Unused @param tag (Multi-line context)	0.04	0.13		
Inner assignments should be avoided (Multi-line context)	0.03	0.10		
Unclosed HTML tag found (Multi-line context)	0.03	0.03		0.07
Unknown tag (Uni-line context)	0.03	0.10		
'else' construct must use '{}'s (Multi-line context)	0.02	0.07		
Expression can be simplified (Multi-line context)	0.02	0.07		
Method length greater than 150 (Multi-line context)	0.02	0.07		
Unable to get class information for @throws tag (Checkstyle error)	0.02			0.07
'protected' modifier out of order with the JLS suggestions (Uni-line context)	0.01	0.03		
'public' modifier out of order with the JLS suggestions (Uni-line context)	0.01	0.03		
Array brackets at illegal position (Uni-line context)	0.01	0.03		
Comment matches to-do format 'TODO:' (Multi-line context)	0.01	0.03		
Redundant 'private' modifier (Multi-line context)	0.01		0.02	
Switch without "default" clause (Multi-line context)	0.01		0.02	

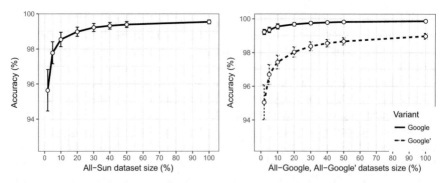

Fig. 8.5 Learning curves showing impact of the dataset size on Accuracy

Table 8.4 The percentage of the lines violating Google Java Style Guide (Checkstyle)

Violation of the Google Java style	All%	Eclipse%	Jasper%	Spring%
Line contains a tab character (Keyword)	98.83	99.42	97.91	99.16
Incorrect indentation level (Multi-line context)	59.48	55.05	69.01	53.82
'{' should be on the previous line (Multi-line context)	4.81		14.02	
Line is longer than 100 characters (Line properties)	3.83	3.47	2.66	5.66
First sentence of Javadoc is incomplete (period is missing) or not present (Multi-line context)	1.36	1.18	2.36	0.40
At-clause should have a non-empty description (Uni-line context)	1.03	2.43	0.41	0.01
<p> tag should be preceded with an empty line (Multi-line context)	0.75	0.18	0.08	2.24
'}' should be on the same line as the next part of a multi-block statement (Multi-line context)	0.61	0.09	0.48	1.39
'package' should be separated from previous statement (Uni-line context)	0.31	0.25	0.63	0.01
'if' construct must use '{}'s (Multi-line context)	0.30	0.82		
Whitespace around a symbol is not followed by whitespace (Uni-line context)	0.28	0.46	0.33	
Abbreviation in name must contain no more than '2' consecutive capital letters (Uni-line context)	0.22	0.04	0.60	
Missing a Javadoc comment (Multi-line context)	0.18	0.11	0.40	0.02
Symbol should be on a new line (Uni-line context)	0.18		0.05	0.55
Wrong lexicographical order for import (Uni-line context)	0.16	0.14	0.22	0.11
Whitespace around a symbol is not preceded by whitespace (Uni-line context)	0.12	0.21	0.12	0.01
Member name must match pattern '$^\wedge$[a-z] [a-z0-9] [a-zA-Z0-9]*\$' (Uni-line context)	0.11	0.12	0.19	
<p> tag should be placed immediately before the first word. with no space after (Uni-line context)	0.10	0.20	0.09	
')' is preceded with whitespace (Uni-line context)	0.10	0.01	0.27	
'(' is followed by whitespace (Uni-line context)	0.09	0.01	0.27	
'for' construct must use ''s (Multi-line context)	0.05	0.13		
'static' modifier out of order with the JLS suggestions (Uni-line context)	0.04	0.07	0.02	0.01
Empty line should be followed by <p> tag on the next line (Uni-line context)	0.04	0.04	0.04	0.03
Overload methods should not be split (Multi-line context)	0.04	0.01	0.08	0.02
Empty catch block (Multi-line context)	0.03	0.07	0.01	
Javadoc comment has parse error (Multi-line context)	0.02	0.04		0.03
At-clauses have to appear in the order '[@param. @return. @throws. @deprecated]' (Multi-line context)	0.02	0.04		0.01
Distance between variable declaration and its first usage is more than '3' (Multi-line context)	0.02	0.04		
'METHOD_DEF' should be separated from previous statement (Multi-line context)	0.01			0.04
Single-line Javadoc comment should be multi-line (Uni-line context)	0.01			0.04
Local variable name must match pattern '$^\wedge$[a-z]([a-z0-9] [a-zA-Z0-9]*)?\$' (Multi-line context)	0.01	0.03		
'else' construct must use '{}'s (Multi-line context)	0.01	0.02		
Each variable declaration must be in its own statement (Uni-line context)	0.01	0.02		
Parameter must match pattern '$^\wedge$[a-z]([a-z0-9] [a-zA-Z0-9]*)?\$' (Uni-line context)	0.01	0.02		
'CTOR_DEF' should be separated from previous statement (Multi-line context)	0.00	0.01		
'protected' modifier out of order with the JLS suggestions (Uni-line context)	0.00	0.01		
'public' modifier out of order with the JLS suggestions (Uni-line context)	0.00	0.01		
Array brackets at illegal position (Uni-line context)	0.00	0.01		
Catch parameter name must match pattern '$^\wedge$[a-z]([a-z0-9] [a-zA-Z0-9]*)?\$' (Uni-line context)	0.00	0.01		
GenericWhitespace '>' is followed by whitespace (Uni-line context)	0.00	0.01		
Redundant <p> tag (Multi-line context)	0.00			0.01
Top-level class BookmarkStack has to reside in its own source file (Files context)	0.00		0.01	
Switch without "default" clause (Multi-line context)	0.00		0.01	

Table 8.5 The results of the prediction quality evaluation — lines violating any of the coding convention's rules (averages and standard deviations)

Guidelines	Dataset	Accuracy %	Precision	Recall	F-score
Sun	All	99.54±0.11	1.00±0.00	1.00±0.00	1.00±0.00
Sun	Eclipse	99.05±0.27	0.99±0.00	0.99±0.00	0.99±0.00
Sun	Jasper	99.55±0.20	1.00±0.00	1.00±0.00	1.00±0.00
Sun	Spring	99.15±0.22	0.99±0.00	0.99±0.00	0.99±0.00
Google	All	99.87±0.06	1.00±0.00	1.00±0.00	1.00±0.00
Google	Eclipse	99.93±0.06	1.00±0.00	1.00±0.00	1.00±0.00
Google	Jasper	99.70±0.14	1.00±0.00	1.00±0.00	1.00±0.00
Google	Spring	99.88±0.11	1.00±0.00	1.00±0.00	1.00±0.00
Google'	All	98.98±0.17	0.99±0.00	0.99±0.00	0.99±0.00
Google'	Eclipse	99.26±0.29	0.99±0.00	0.99±0.00	0.99±0.00
Google'	Jasper	99.03±0.26	0.99±0.00	0.99±0.00	0.99±0.00
Google'	Spring	98.91±0.29	0.99±0.00	0.99±0.00	0.99±0.00

After finishing the last cycle of our study, we decided to revisit this analysis and extend it to learn more about the accuracy of CCFlex when detecting violations of different types of coding rules.[18] This time, we trained separate binary classifiers (decision trees) for each of the rules in the Sun's and Google's coding conventions and evaluated their accuracy by performing 10-runs of 10-fold cross-validation. We used stratified sampling to create folds to avoid the situation when some of the training datasets would not contain any violations. Since this part of the analysis was performed after the last cycle of our study, we used the final version of the CCFlex tool with all the features presented in Sect. 8.3.

The prediction quality for the rules that have at least 10 violations in the dataset are presented in the Table 8.6 (Sun Java Coding Conventions) and Table 8.7 (Google Java Style Guide). The observed prediction quality was high with the average F-score around 0.80 (for 50% of the rules, F-score was 0.90 or higher). It seems that the easiest to detect were violations of the rule belonging to the keyword category. Also, a high prediction quality was observed for the rules belonging to the line-properties category (F-score equal to 0.947 and 0.996). These rules regarded the maximum number of characters in a line. The tool was not able to achieve the perfect F-score although there was a feature 'number of characters' that was solely sufficient to recognize violations of these rules. However, after further investigation, we have learned that Checkstyle ignores lines with package and import statements while recognizing violations of these rules what increases the complexity of the rules and explains the difficulties in learning to recognize violations of these rules.

---

[18] The replication package for this analysis is available at https://github.com/mochodek/py-ccflex-java-sun-google.

For the multi-line-context rules, we observed that the tool was effective in recognizing their violations as long as the rules required to "understand" the context of a few lines (e.g. '{' should be on the previous line, 'for' construct must use '{}'s, 'Missing a Javadoc comment'). At the same time, it had difficulties in learning to recognize violations of multi-line rules that required capturing relationships between the lines in larger chunks of code (e.g., 'Expected @param tag', or 'Expected an @return tag'). The worst accuracy was observed for the rule requiring to recognize "unused imports" (F-score = 0.03) and the rule stating that the overloaded methods should be kept together (F-score = 0.00). However, this was not a surprising result taking into account that CCFlex does not extract features allowing to capture such dependencies in the code.

For the uni-line-context rules, one of the two rules that were most difficult to learn was the rule disallowing using so-called 'magic numbers' (F-score = 0.32). Magic numbers are numeric literals that are not defined as constants, however, Checkstyle does not consider the numbers $-1, 0, 1$, and 2 to be magic numbers. Unfortunately, since we used token signatures in our analysis, all of the numbers in the code were simplified to '0' making it difficult to learn the rule.

There was only one rule belonging to the design-semantics category in the considered coding conventions ('Class designed for extension without Javadoc'). We observed a high prediction quality for this rule (F-score = 0.95), however, this could be caused by the fact that it is a specific case of the 'Missing a Javadoc comment' rule.

We observed a moderately high prediction quality for the rule 'Hidden field' that belongs to the files-context category (F-score = 0.75). The rule states that a local variable or a parameter shall not shadow a field that is defined in the same class. Achieving such a high accuracy was a surprising result since we were not able to find any features extracted by CCFlex that could allow us to detect shadowing of fields. However, there might some correlations or coexistence of code structures in the considered source code that allowed the tool to indirectly learn to recognize lines violating this rule.

Finally, we repeated the analysis for different sub-samples of the original dataset to observe how the size of the training dataset affects the prediction quality of the classifiers. We used stratified sampling to create sub-samples containing 5% (2,265 SLOC), 10% (4,530 SLOC), 20% (9,060 SLOC), 30% (13,591 SLOC), 40% (18,121 SLOC), and 50% (22,651 SLOC) of the lines from the original dataset. The obtained learning curves for different categories of coding guidelines are presented in Fig. 8.6.[19] The observations are similar to those from the previous analysis. In most cases, the accuracy increases while variance decreases with the increase of the dataset size.

---

[19] To have at least two violations of the rules in each of the smallest 5% datasets (one line for training and the second one for the validation), we included only the rules that had at least 40 violations in the code.

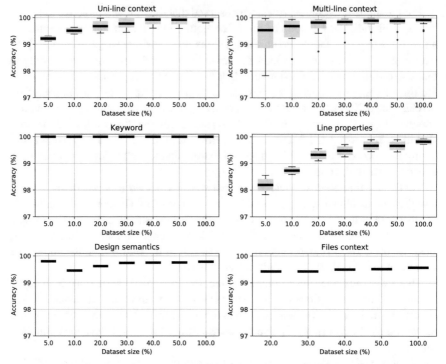

Fig. 8.6 Learning curves showing impact of the dataset size on Accuracy of predicting certain violations types (only the rules having at least 40 violations are presented)

Based on the results of this analysis we made the following observations:

- CCFlex was able to achieve high accuracy of identifying lines violating the coding guidelines for the simplified problem of recognizing lines violating *any* of the rules and for the problem of identifying violations of particular rules. However, for the latter problem, we observed rules for which the tool failed to learn to recognize their violations.
- CCFlex was able to achieve high accuracy even for the smallest datasets. Therefore, it seemed that the CCFlex could also be used to identify lines violating similar coding standards even if the lines had to be labeled manually.
- Sun's and Google's guidelines could be mapped to the proposed taxonomy. However, by comparing these guidelines and Java Open Source code to guidelines and C/C++ code of our industrial partners, the latter seemed to be more complicated and richer when it comes to syntax and language constructs being used. Therefore, we perceived the accuracy observed in this study as an upper bound of what we could expect for the study on the code of our partners.

Table 8.6 The results of the prediction quality evaluation for lines violating particular Sun Java Coding Conventions rules (45,302 SLOC; rules with at least 10 violations)

Rule	N	Accuracy %	Precision	Recall	F-score
'{' should be on the previous line. (Multi-line)	1,479	99.98	0.998	0.997	0.997
Line is longer than 80 characters (Line properties)	4,404	99.93	0.997	0.996	0.996
Avoid inline conditionals. (Uni-line)	153	100.00	0.997	0.991	0.994
'for' construct must use '{}'s. (Multi-line)	15	100.00	1.000	0.987	0.993
Parameter should be final (Uni-line)	1,597	99.90	0.983	0.990	0.987
Missing a Javadoc comment. (Multi-line)	1,153	99.88	0.979	0.975	0.977
Variable must be private and have accessor methods (Multi-line)	295	99.95	0.971	0.949	0.960
Line has trailing spaces. (Uni-line)	950	99.82	0.958	0.954	0.956
'static' modifier out of order with the JLS suggestions. (Uni-line)	11	100.00	1.000	0.909	0.952
Class designed for extension without Javadoc (Design semantics)	977	99.79	0.938	0.965	0.951
'if' construct must use '{}'s. (Multi-line)	92	99.98	0.906	0.983	0.943
Symbol is preceded with whitespace. (Uni-line)	31	99.99	0.966	0.919	0.942
'}' should be on the same line as the next part of a multi-block statement (Multi-line)	186	99.93	0.884	0.949	0.915
Name must match pattern '^[A-Z] [A-Z0-9]*(_[A-Z0-9]+)*$' (Uni-line)	50	99.97	0.810	0.922	0.862
Expected @throws tag (Multi-line)	74	99.95	0.838	0.866	0.852
Symbol is followed by whitespace. (Uni-line)	48	99.97	0.822	0.871	0.845
Symbol is not followed by whitespace. (Uni-line)	253	99.81	0.823	0.831	0.827
Expected an @return tag. (Multi-line)	246	99.79	0.814	0.802	0.808
Expected @param tag (Multi-line)	508	99.55	0.796	0.801	0.799
Redundant 'final' modifier. (Multi-line)	37	99.96	0.760	0.805	0.781
Hidden field (Files context)	388	99.57	0.752	0.744	0.748
Symbol should be on a new line. (Multi-line)	56	99.94	0.782	0.709	0.743
Symbol is not preceded with whitespace. (Uni-line)	35	99.95	0.699	0.683	0.690
First sentence should end with a period. (Multi-line)	66	99.91	0.686	0.679	0.682
Redundant 'public' modifier. (Multi-line)	32	99.95	0.623	0.606	0.614
Magic number (Uni-line)	22	99.92	0.268	0.382	0.315
Unused import (Multi-line)	37	99.85	0.034	0.032	0.033

8.5.3 Action Research Cycle 3 – How Can We Recognize the Violations Provided by the Industrial Partners?

8.5.3.1 Cycle Goal and Research Procedure

When **diagnosing** the problem of how to recognize the violations provided by industrial partners, we studied their coding/design guidelines.

Table 8.7 The results of the prediction quality evaluation for lines violating particular Google Java Style Guides rules (45,302 SLOC; rules with at least 10 violations)

Rule	N	Accuracy %	Precision	Recall	F-score
Line contains a tab character. (Keyword)	30,366	100.00	1.000	1.000	1.000
'(' is followed by whitespace. (Uni-line)	29	100.00	1.000	1.000	1.000
'{' should be on the previous line (Multi-line)	1,479	99.98	0.997	0.998	0.997
Incorrect indentation level (Multi-line)	18,277	99.51	0.993	0.995	0.994
At-clause should have a non-empty description. (Uni-line)	315	99.99	0.990	0.995	0.992
'package' should be separated from previous statement. (Uni-line)	95	99.99	0.979	0.989	0.984
'for' construct must use '{ }'s. (Multi-line)	15	100.00	1.000	0.940	0.969
')' is preceded with whitespace. (Uni-line)	30	100.00	0.967	0.963	0.965
'if' construct must use '{ }'s. (Multi-line)	92	99.98	0.929	0.977	0.952
Line is longer than 100 characters (Line properties)	1,178	99.73	0.954	0.940	0.947
First sentence of Javadoc is incomplete (period is missing) or not present. (Multi-line)	417	99.88	0.909	0.963	0.935
'}' should be on the same line as the next part of a multi-block statement (Multi-line)	186	99.92	0.867	0.957	0.910
<p> tag should be preceded with an empty line. (Multi-line)	230	99.91	0.918	0.900	0.909
'static' modifier out of order with the JLS suggestions. (Uni-line)	11	100.00	1.000	0.818	0.900
<p> tag should be placed immediately before the first word, with no space after. (Uni-line)	31	99.97	0.791	0.790	0.790
Abbreviation in name must contain no more than '2' consecutive capital letters (Uni-line)	68	99.93	0.769	0.794	0.782
Member name must match pattern '^[a-z] [a-z0-9] [a-zA-Z0-9]*$' (Uni-line)	33	99.97	0.775	0.758	0.766
Missing a Javadoc comment. (Multi-line)	56	99.93	0.718	0.721	0.719
Symbol should be on a new line (Uni-line)	55	99.92	0.702	0.658	0.679
Whitespace around a symbol is not followed by whitespace (Uni-line)	73	99.88	0.632	0.641	0.636
Whitespace around a symbol is not preceded by whitespace (Uni-line)	35	99.94	0.620	0.643	0.631
Empty line should be followed by <p> tag on the next line. (Multi-line)	11	99.98	0.651	0.545	0.592
Wrong lexicographical order for import (Uni-line)	49	99.85	0.310	0.306	0.308
Overload methods should not be split (Multi-line)	11	99.96	0.000	0.000	0.000

Once we understood that we can recognize the same violations as a popular style checking tool, we set off to recognize the violations of the coding/design guidelines at Company A. Company A has 45 coding guidelines and a codebase distributed over several source code repositories. Each of the repositories contains a dedicated part of the product and is ca. 50,000 SLOC in size. The code is written in C. The goal of this cycle was to explore whether it is possible to recognize violations of different types of rules in the industrial context. In particular, we were interested in studying how different coding styles can influence the accuracy of the ML-based tool. Our constraints were that we set off to spend two working days at the company site. We obtained coding guidelines beforehand, but we were not able to obtain access to the source code until we arrived at the company site.

In Company A, we **planned** the evaluation of three coding guidelines belonging to different categories of our taxonomy. The company provided us with the unique possibility to study designated codebases developed at three different time periods — (i) long before the guidelines were defined, (ii) in the same period when guidelines were being defined, and (iii) long after the guidelines were defined. This provided us with the opportunity to study the question: *What is the influence of the difference between programming styles of the training and classified codebase?* In particular, we wanted to understand whether the evolution of the codebase requires the evolution of the examples used to train our machine learning and which configurations of CCFlex parameters provide best results in terms of finding violations.

In our plan, we decided to recognize the following guidelines:

- Pre-processor directives must be placed at the beginning of an empty line, and must never be indented (semantics, uni-line context). We chose this rule because it requires understanding the position of specific tokens in a line.
- For public enumerations, the members of enum should follow the pattern, i.e., the name of the component, underscore, and the value name, for example `ComponentName_ValueOne = 0` (semantics, multi-line context). We chose this rule because it requires to understand the context, i.e. recognition of the lines within "enum" blocks. We expected that this type of recognition could be difficult for CCFlex as it is primarily designed for one-line rules.
- Names of the variables should follow the so-called camel case format — each word or abbreviation in the middle of the name begins with a capital letter (semantics, uni-line context). We expected that this type of recognition could be difficult for CCFlex as it requires to understand the concept of lower and upper cases and the fact that the token represents the variable name.

We planned to conduct as many exploratory trials as possible within the two days company visit. We planned to experiment with the following configurations of CCFlex (and their combinations):

- Bag of words — to explore whether this way of providing meaning to the constructs allows teaching the tool quicker.
- Active Learning — to explore the ease-of-use of providing examples line-by-line (suggested by active learning) rather than manually.

- Adding new features — to explore how important it is to have the right set of features for the decision tree (CART) algorithm used in CCFlex; in particular whether it is better to rely on bag-of-words or on adding the ability to recognize specific keywords.

During each trial we took three measurements: (i) number of lines in the training file, (ii) number of lines found as violations (true-positives + false-positives) and (iii) number of correct violations (true-positives).

Based on these trials, we wanted to learn how to prepare the evaluation strategy for the next cycle at Company B. We wanted to explore which strategies work best, what Recall we can achieve and differences between these parameters, types or guidelines and the Recall measure.

Since we intended to use this action research cycle to learn the practical challenges of recognizing violations in the real product source code, we did not have an oracle in terms of tools to recognize these violations. The company used manual reviews as one of the quality assurance techniques, and therefore we followed the same principle—we studied the identified violations and focused on the ratio between the true-positives and false-positives since we would not be able to manually verify all the negatives.

8.5.3.2 Cycle Execution and Results

Execution: Pre-processor Macros

The results from the evaluation are presented in Fig. 8.7. It shows that the first trial resulted in the highest number of violations found and the highest number of correct violations (true-positives). The legacy code was developed before the coding guidelines were in place and designers could not follow them; the size of the legacy code during this evaluation was 40,010 LOC. For this trial, we used a sample from the legacy codebase for training. We classified 291 lines of code as the training set (based on one file from the legacy codebase, example of code from the coding guidelines, and variations of these).

In the second trial, we used the same training set and we applied the classifier to a new codebase, which was developed after the guidelines were in place; therefore the guidelines should be followed. The size of that code was 41,704 LOC. As Fig. 8.7 shows, the number of correctly classified violations was significantly lower. However, there were multiple cases where the classifier found violations incorrectly (false-positives). The incorrectly classified violations were caused by the change in the company's style for writing constants as preprocessor directives. In the legacy codebase, the preprocessor constants were often defined using small letters, while the enum values were defined using capital letters. In the new codebase, the preprocessor constants were defined using capital letters, which introduced false-positives in the evaluation. CCFlex recognized these pre-processor constants as violations of the rule since their name did not have the corresponding context, e.g. no corresponding module name was present in the succeeding lines.

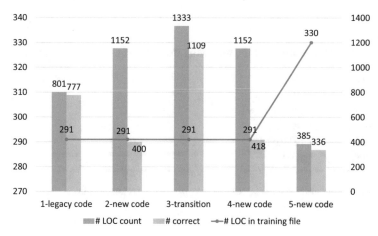

Fig. 8.7 Size of the training set for each trial at Company A – recognizing preprocessor macros

In the third trial, we used the same training set and applied the classifier to the transition codebase. It was the codebase which was developed at the same time when coding guidelines were defined, so it could contain violations. The size of this codebase was 55,026 LOC. The industrial partners provided us with this codebase with the motivation that "it resembles a situation when someone did not always follow the guidelines." As Fig. 8.7 shows, there were more violations and the classifier was more correct in finding the violations.

In the fourth trial, we used the same training set, but included the statistics of the most commonly used words as features (bag-of-words). When applied to the same new codebase as in trail 2, this decreased the number of false-positives.

In the fifth trial, we added 40 lines as examples from the new codebase, which resulted in a visible decrease in the number of false-positives. The percentage of correctly identified violations was 87%.

For the **evaluation** part, we conducted a workshop with four representatives at the company site, who are architects, designers, and managers. We presented them with the identified violations and noted their reflections. During the discussion with the architects from Company A, they assessed these results as valuable from the practical perspective.

From these five trials, we could **learn** that it is important to use the same programming style for the training and the validation set. We learned that, although from the same company, the coding style evolves significantly over time and this has an impact on the correctness of the identification (if the training set does not evolve together with the coding style). We have also learned that the size of the training set can be small: 291–331 SLOC to achieve a satisfactory prediction quality for a basic semantic, uni-line context guideline.

Execution: Enums

For this guideline, we were provided the following example of a code that follows it.

```
typedef enum
{
  ComponentName_ValueOne = 0,
  ComponentName_ValueTwo,
  ComponentName_ValueThree
} ComponentName_MyEnum;
```

Based on this guideline we could provide the following example of a violation to bootstrap the training of CCFlex.

```
typedef enum
{
  ValueOne = 0,
  VALUETWO,
  three
} ComponentName_MyEnum;
```

These guidelines require to understand the multi-line context of the line, i.e. that the guideline applies to the content of an enum and is not just a standard variable declaration. Therefore, in this trial, we tested the ability of CCFlex to recognize violations requiring to understand the context, both in terms of the name of the component (name of the enum) and the name of the enum constant.

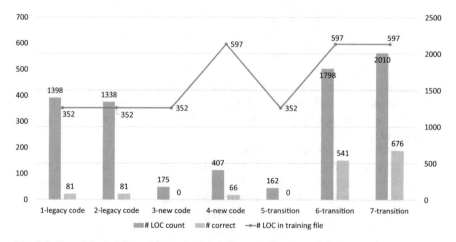

Fig. 8.8 Size of the training set for each trial at Company A – recognizing enums

The results from recognizing violations of naming of enums is presented in Fig. 8.8. We use the same measurements as previously—the number of lines in the training set, the number of lines classified as violations and the number of lines correctly classified as violations.

For the first trial, we used the same training set as for the first trial of the recognizing pre-processor macros, removed the previous labeling and added the example and counterexample of the guideline for enums. The training set contained 352 lines. We used the bag-of-words parameter in the first trial and no bag-of-words in the second trial. The number of lines violating the guideline was 1398 and 1338 respectively, with 81 correct instances in both cases.

For the third trial, we changed the codebase for validation and the number of correctly identified dropped to 0, which was caused by the same issue as for pre-processor macros—the company changed the naming conventions. In order to reduce that problem, we used active learning, which resulted in adding 245 lines in the training set. The number of correctly identified violations increased to 66, and the number of all instances classified as violations increased to 407 lines.

For the fifth trial, we repeated the set-up of the third trial but changed the codebase to transition code. We did not capture any violations correctly, and 162 lines were falsely identified as violations. Using the same training set in the sixth trial as for the fourth trial, i.e. 597 lines mixed from the legacy code and the new code, we correctly identified 541 violations and 1798 lines in total as violations. For the last, the eight trial, we started with the 352 lines of the training set and used active learning to complement with 245 lines, we increased the number of identified violations to 2010 and the correctly identified violations to 676.

Execution: Camel Cases

For the last guideline, we used the same base training set and complemented it with 16 examples of correctly and incorrectly used camel cases. Also, we labeled the lines in the base training set where the rules were not followed.

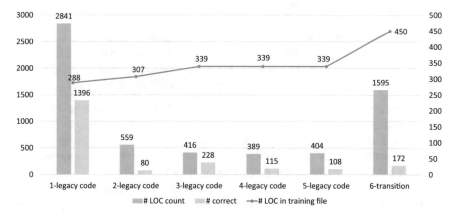

Fig. 8.9 Size of the training set for each trial at Company A – recognizing camel cases

The results are presented in Fig. 8.9, with the same measurements as for the previous two guidelines.

For the first trial, with 288 lines in the training set, we identified 2841 lines as violations, with 1396 correct instances. Increasing the number of lines in the training set decreased the number of correctly identified instances and the total number of instances to 80 and 559, respectively. This was a deterioration, as we had established that there are 1396 violations in the first trial. Therefore, in the third trial, we applied active learning and increased the number of lines in the training set to 339 from the original 288. This resulted in the increase of the correctly identified instances, but only to 228. In the fourth trial, we used the bag-of-words, which decreased the number of instances found, consistent with our previous observations for recognizing enum naming violations. In the fifth trial, we increased the number of lines in the training set, providing more examples from the false-positives found in the fourth trial. However, there was even a decrease in the number of instances classified correctly.

Finally, we applied the algorithm trained on the old code, with active learning using lines from the transitional code, on the transitional code. The training set contained 450 lines and we found 1595 violations, out of which 172 were correctly recognized as violations, the rest was false-positives. Due to the fact that the company visit was limited in time, that was the last trial we could perform.

We **learned** that the original set-up of CCFlex at that time did not allow to find violations of camel case guideline with a satisfactory Recall. We identified the need to use bi-grams, block features, and token signatures in the next version of CCFlex and applying it to the next company.

8.5.4 Action Research Cycle 4 – How Much Training of CCFlex Is Required to Reduce the Percentage of False-Positives?

8.5.4.1 Cycle Goal and Research Procedure

In the last cycle of our action research, we used Company B as the case, where we had the opportunity to study 66 coding guidelines. We focused on the understanding of how much training data and iterations are needed to train a classifier for different types of rules from our taxonomy. We chose seven guidelines to evaluate:

- 120 characters—line length must not exceed 120 characters (semantics-free, line properties).
- Braces in compound statements—braces must be used for all compound statements (semantics, multi-line context)—this rule helps to control the readability of the code and thus minimize programming mistakes.
- Do not use variants—software units must not have variants at build-time (semantics-free, keyword)—this rule helps to assure that #ifdef pre-processor statements are used scarcely to minimize the need for understanding which code is compiled during each build.

- Named constants—named constants must be used (semantics, uni-line context)—instead of using untyped #define pre-processor directive, this rule helps to enforce usage of constants, which are typed.
- One statement per line—only one statement per line of code is allowed (semantics, uni-line context)—this rule helps to enforce the simplicity of the code and reduce the cognitive burden when reading the code.
- Use Enum classes—C++11 Enum classes must be used instead of traditional enum types (semantics-free, keyword)—instead of enum types, the code should use enum classes, which can enforce constructors, typing, and destructors.
- Use constants instead of macros—C++ constructs must be used instead of pre-processor macros (semantics-free, keyword).

Based on the observations from the previous action-research cycle, we made two modifications to the research procedure. Firstly, we designed oracles for the research purposes, i.e. dedicated, heuristic scripts implemented to recognize violations of specific rules. We needed that script in order to be able to calculate the Precision, Recall and F-score measures. Secondly, we found a source codebase without the gradual progression of quality like it was in the case of Company A; all code in the codebase should follow the coding guidelines.

We set the following stop criteria for each trial: 90% in Precision or Recall (on the module from which we polled the training examples) or seven training iterations (but a minimum of three trials to verify that the observed prediction quality is stable). The second criterion was important as we wanted to limit our training set to less than 800 LOC in order to assure that it is not very time consuming for practitioners to classify the code.

8.5.4.2 Cycle Execution and Results

The summary of the Precision, Recall, and F-score for all rules for Company B is presented in Fig. 8.10.

The summary shows that for simple coding guidelines, like the guideline "Line length must not exceed 120 characters", the training took only three iterations. However, for the most complex guidelines, like "Braces must be used for all compound statements", even seven iterations did not result in high Precision, Recall and F-score.

The summary for the F-score, per rule and per training trial is presented in Fig. 8.11. Each line represents one rule and the number of trials differs per rule because not all rules required the same number of lines in the training set to reach the stop criteria. Although the goal was to add 100 lines to the training set for each trial, some rules required context and therefore we needed to add extra lines to close blocks (for example for enum or comment).

The figure shows that there is a big difference between the achieved F-score per rule, which is consistent with the results presented in Fig. 8.10. The F-score for the entire codebase (ca. 3M SLOC) is usually lower than the F-score for the last training trial on the module from which we polled the examples to the training set. The reason

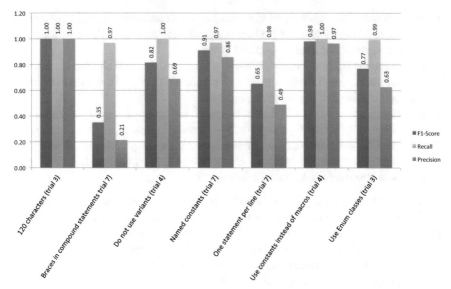

Fig. 8.10 Precision, Recall and F-score for all trials at Company B

is that the code in the module used for training trials did not contain all possible language constructs which were present in the entire codebase.

In order to understand the impact of using active learning, we performed the same trials, adding the lines to the training set using pool-based active learning. We tried two querying strategies (i) uncertainty sampling and (ii) committee-based vote entropy sampling [81] (a committee of random forest, CART, and k-nearest neighbors classifiers). However, the latter strategy turned out to be superior. The results for committee-based sampling are presented in Fig. 8.11.

Figure 8.11 shows that the F-score is higher if we use active learning. Therefore, we recommend this strategy as the main strategy compared to the manual selection of lines for the training set.

The rule with the lowest F-score, "Brackets must be used for all compound statements," was the most difficult one for CCFlex. The lowest score is based on low Recall, which means that CCFlex provided too many false-positives. However, when developing the oracle for this rule, we also noticed that it was difficult to assess which line is indeed a false-positive and which is not even when writing a dedicated tool for this purpose—simply because of the way the code was written at Company B (e.g., using many of the advanced features of C++ 11 and local code optimizations).

8.5.5 *Summary of the Results*

The outcomes of each of four action-research cycles provided us with valuable insights into using an ML-based tool to recognize company-specific code guidelines violations in code.

From the second cycle, we have learned that the ML-based tool, such as CCFlex, can achieve a high prediction quality for Java coding-style/formatting guidelines when enough examples are provided (CCFlex was able to detect lines violating Sun Coding Conventions and Google Java Style Guide, without determining the type of violation, with the Accuracy around 99% and with Recall and Precision ranging between 0.99 and 1.00).

The following third and fourth cycles revealed some pros and cons of using such a tool in an industrial environment. We trained the CCFlex tool to recognize violations of ten guidelines from the guidebooks of our partners and were able to achieve 0.97 and higher Recall for all the rules we were able to calculate the measure for (Company B). Unfortunately, for some of the guidelines, high Recall was achieved by sacrificing Precision, which ranged from 0.35 to 1.00 depending on the rule.

When combining the results from the cycles two to four, we can state that a pleasant property of ML-based tools for recognizing code violations is that a single tool can be used to detect violations for different programming languages without the need of modifying the code of the tool (of course, it has to be trained for each of the applications).

When it comes to training strategies, we have observed that for most of the rules, we were able to achieve a high Recall even if the training dataset contained only around 300 SLOC. We initially tried to compose training sets by selecting examples from guidebooks and manually adding positive and negative examples from a sample of the codebase, however, we observed that using Active Learning resulted in better accuracy. The general observation was that the rules requiring understanding multi-line context were more difficult to train, while the rules based on text properties or keywords tend to be easier to tackle with. Although we were able to achieve a high Recall (0.97 and more) for all types of rules, Precision was visibly lower for the multi-line context rules (0.21 and 0.33). The rule regarding line properties was the easiest to train (even with a small training dataset of ca. 100 lines). However, this seems possible only when the property in question is used as a feature (in this case the number of characters in the line). Finally, we experienced that the difficulty of training a classifier can also be determined by other factors such as the inherent complexity of the code, i.e., the richness of the programming-language syntax, overloaded operators, local code optimizations, etc.

Finally, we made some observations regarding the maintainability of ML-based tools for code analysis. Firstly, we have learned that designing custom, specialized features can help in recognizing violations when the considered training sample is small. For instance, we were successful in using our token signatures or predefined, keyword or short-pattern based features. We have also learned that the coding style can evolve over time and this could have an impact on the correctness of the violations recognition (if the training set does not evolve together with the coding style).

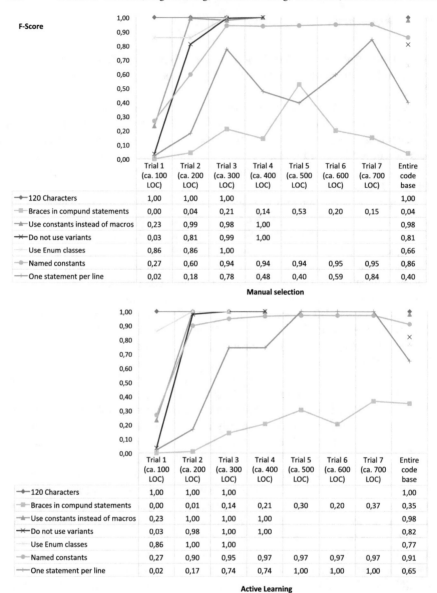

	Trial 1 (ca. 100 LOC)	Trial 2 (ca. 200 LOC)	Trial 3 (ca. 300 LOC)	Trial 4 (ca. 400 LOC)	Trial 5 (ca. 500 LOC)	Trial 6 (ca. 600 LOC)	Trial 7 (ca. 700 LOC)	Entire code base
120 Characters	1,00	1,00	1,00					1,00
Braces in compund statements	0,00	0,04	0,21	0,14	0,53	0,20	0,15	0,04
Use constants instead of macros	0,23	0,99	0,98	1,00				0,98
Do not use variants	0,03	0,81	0,99	1,00				0,81
Use Enum classes	0,86	0,86	1,00					0,66
Named constants	0,27	0,60	0,94	0,94	0,94	0,95	0,95	0,86
One statement per line	0,02	0,18	0,78	0,48	0,40	0,59	0,84	0,40

Manual selection

	Trial 1 (ca. 100 LOC)	Trial 2 (ca. 200 LOC)	Trial 3 (ca. 300 LOC)	Trial 4 (ca. 400 LOC)	Trial 5 (ca. 500 LOC)	Trial 6 (ca. 600 LOC)	Trial 7 (ca. 700 LOC)	Entire code base
120 Characters	1,00	1,00	1,00					1,00
Braces in compund statements	0,00	0,01	0,14	0,21	0,30	0,20	0,37	0,35
Use constants instead of macros	0,23	1,00	1,00	1,00				0,98
Do not use variants	0,03	0,98	1,00	1,00				0,82
Use Enum classes	0,86	1,00	1,00					0,77
Named constants	0,27	0,90	0,95	0,97	0,97	0,97	0,97	0,91
One statement per line	0,02	0,17	0,74	0,74	1,00	1,00	1,00	0,65

Active Learning

Fig. 8.11 F-score per trial when selecting the lines to the training set manually and with active learning for a module from which training samples were polled and for entire codebase

Therefore, when maintaining an ML-based code detector, one has to maintain a list of examples and re-train the tool over time instead of maintaining the source code of the detector, as it is in the case of static-code-analysis tools.

8.6 Validity Evaluation

In our action research study, we evaluated a number of validity threats, based on the framework provided by [483].

The main *construct validity* threats which we identified are related to the choice of coding/design rules and the stop criteria. To mitigate the risk that we bias the evaluation by selecting a very similar, narrow group of coding guidelines to train CCFlex, we based our choices on the taxonomy of coding guidelines that group guidelines based on the context that need be understood to find violations of guidelines. We covered four categories of coding guidelines: semantic uni-/multi-line context and semantic-free line properties and keywords. The remaining three categories were either outside of our interests for this study (process-level rules) or we were not able to describe the contextual information at the level of a single line of code (multiple files context or design decisions). The choice of the stop criteria was arbitrary in cycle 4, which was a deliberate choice as we wanted to understand whether it is possible to achieve satisfactory results with a low number of training instances (lines of code). The alternative would be to continue the Active Learning trials beyond the seven trials to achieve 90% F-score, but we left this as an open issue for our further work aimed at studying the minimum sufficient set of training examples balanced with the size of the feature set.

Also, it is important to emphasize that the coding style violations do not have to strongly correlate with code faults or product quality. When analyzing the coding guidelines of our industrial partners, we observed that most of the rules in their guidebooks were there to improve code readability and communication between software developers. However, there were also examples of guidelines that forced (or forbade) using some code constructs that could affect the performance of the systems or cause memory management problems (and consequently lead to defects).

The main *internal validity* threat is the fact that in many cases it was not obvious whether a violation found by CCFlex was indeed a violation. For example, for recognizing camel case styled functions, it was not easy to find which of the following two is correct: (i) `isECUPresent()` or (ii) `isEcuPresent()`. Consulting the practitioners led to diverse opinions. For these cases, we chose to include the second version as correct. For all cases like this, we consulted the practitioners and discussed them in our research team to minimize the researcher bias.

The main *conclusion validity* threat is the fact that for we created the oracles in cycle 4 ourselves. The oracles are mainly based on pattern matching and simple parsers. Therefore, they should be treated as heuristics (the scripts are available in CCFlex Github repository). Although we tested the tools manually, we did not provide validation against any industrial tool, this is a threat we need to accept. However, based on the cycle 2, where we evaluated the ability of CCFlex to find violations similar to industry-grade tools, we believe that this threat does not bias our conclusions. Since CCFlex's ability to "mimic" another tool was above 95%, we believe that the accuracy differs by as much as 5% and therefore can be neglected.

Finally, in order to minimize *external validity* threats of being unrepresentative, we diversified our study by including both open source and proprietary codebases.

We chose to use oracles that are used in industry (Checkstyle) and own oracles. We evaluated the tool at two different companies, with different coding/design guidelines and different contexts.

Although the results found in the initial study on open source Java projects were slightly better than those in the industrial C/C++ projects, this cannot be taken as a prove that there is a difference in the accuracy of the tool between programming languages because of the visible differences in the study setup, e.g., such as the size of the datasets, the set of guidelines used, detecting lines violating the rules vs. determining the types of violations, or differences in the character of open source and closed source systems.

Finally, we compared various static analysis and style checkers to CCFlex. The observed promising results for C, C++, and Java indicate that similar results might be expected for other imperative languages as well as other companies and other codebases.

8.7 Conclusions

In this paper, we presented the results of an action research study that aimed to support code reviews by automatically recognizing company-specific code guidelines violations in large-scale, industrial source code. The study was performed in the collaboration with two large companies located in Scandinavia developing software-intensive products where we worked on premises of these companies to analyze their code and code/design guidelines.

The study was divided into four action-research-study cycles. In the first cycle, we analyzed the coding guidelines of our partners and proposed a taxonomy to categorize coding rules depending on the information required to automatically recognize their violations in code. We also identified some requirements and constraints for violation-detecting software tools, which were the ease of adapting the tool to handle new or altered rules, as well as the possibility of processing the code without the need of parsing or compiling it. Based on the conducted literature review study, we learned that nearly all of the existing tools do not meet these requirements. The most promising tools were machine-learning-based ones as they allow for flexible evolution as requested by our industrial partners.

In the second cycle, we performed a preliminary validation of one of the machine-learning-based tools called CCFlex on the codebase of three Java open source products. We looked for violations of Google Java Style Guide and Sun Java Code Conventions, which are two widely accepted coding style/formatting guidelines for Java to learn that the tool was able to detect the lines violating *any* of the guidelines as well as the lines violating *specific* rules with the average accuracy of ca. 99% and the average F-score of ca. 0.80. Although the overall accuracy was high, we observed that the tool had difficulties in detecting violations of the rules that required to understand the context of multiple lines (e.g., finding unused imports).

In the following two cycles, we investigated the possibility of training the tool to recognize lines violating 10 rules from our industrial partners' coding guidebooks. As a result of these studies, we found that:

- we were able to train the ML-based tool by using the maximum of around 700 SLOC to achieve the average F-score of 0.78. Although we obtained a high Recall (0.97 or higher) for all of the rules (often by using only 300 SLOC), it was usually at the cost of high false-positive rates (Precision ranged from 0.21 to 1.00 depending on the rule). The best results were obtained for the rules requiring understanding the context of a single line (semantical uni-line context, semantic-free line properties, and keywords) while the rules requiring to understand the context of multiple lines were far more difficult to train.
- the ML-based tool was able to recognize code guidelines violations by using features extracted directly from the text (e.g., frequencies of tokens) without the need for parsing or compiling the code,
- we observed that the best strategy for training the tool to recognize violations of company-specific guidelines was to start with the examples provided in the companies' code guidebook and then use Active Learning to poll lines from a sample of the codebase to label.
- we have learned that using ML-based code analysis tools bring new challenges when it comes to maintenance in comparison to static-code-analysis tools (that require source code modification) which is maintaining examples in training codebase.

Finally, our study showed that the same ML-based tool can be trained to recognize violations of different coding guidelines and even for different programming languages (C, C++, and Java).

Future Work

Our further work includes the integration of our tool with Gerrit—a modern code review tool used in industry (and train the tool on the commit-level) and further studies of industry-wide standard rules like MISRA C++.

We also want to further investigate how *rules that serve as documentation*, *rules on external information*, and *optional rules* (see Sect. 8.5.1) can be captured with our approach in future.

Furthermore, many static code analysis tools, e.g. Splint and CPPCheck, style checkers, e.g. CodeCheck, and approaches for code smell detection, e.g. DECOR by [327] and BOA by [101], offer the option to formulate new rules, often using their own languages. What motivated the use of machine learning in this paper is that it enables the industrial users to formulate new rules without having to learn a new language and not having to verify whether the newly written rules are doing what they are supposed to do. In future work, we plan to further investigate whether specifying rules with our approach is really easier and/or less time consuming for practitioners than writing rules with DECOR, BOA, Splint, or CodeCheck.

Chapter 9
SimSAX: A Measure of Project Similarity Based on Symbolic Approximation Method and Software Defect Inflow

Miroslaw Ochodek, Miroslaw Staron, and Wilhelm Meding

Abstract

Background: Profiling software development projects, in order to compare them, find similar sub-projects or sets of activities, helps to monitor changes in software processes. Since we lack objective measures for profiling or hashing, researchers often fall back on manual assessments.

Objective: The goal of our study is to define an objective and intuitive measure of similarity between software development projects based on software defect-inflow profiles.

Method: We defined a measure of project similarity called SimSAX which is based on segmentation of defect-inflow profiles, coding them into strings (sequences of symbols) and comparing these strings to find so-called motifs. We use simulations to find and calibrate the parameters of the measure. The objects in the simulations are two different large industry projects for which we know the similarity a priori, based on the input from industry experts. Finally, we apply the measure to find similarities between five industrial and six open source projects.

Results: Our results show that the measure provides the most accurate simulated results when the compared motifs are long (32 or more weeks) and we use an alphabet of 5 or more symbols. The measure provides the possibility to calibrate for each industrial case, thus allowing to optimize the method for finding specific patterns in project similarity.

Conclusions: We conclude that our proposed measure provides a good approximation for project similarity. The industrial evaluation showed that it can provide a good starting point for finding similar periods in software development projects.

Reprinted with permission from the copyright holder. Originally published in Information and Software Technology 115 (2019): 131–147. DOI: https://doi.org/10.1016/j.infsof.2019.06.003

253

9.1 Introduction

Understanding similarity between software development projects is important when predicting defect inflow based on history, predicting development effort, benchmarking productivity of project teams, or evaluating whether the practices of one project apply to another one.

All the existing approaches to assess similarities between projects known by the authors focus on *cross-sectional* evaluation. For instance, there are studies on effort estimation where each project is described by a set of attributes (e.g., size of the product, business domain, technology) and where unsupervised methods such as clustering are often used to construct homogeneous training data sets (e.g., [24, 282, 319, 320, 411]). Similarity evaluation is also one of the common steps of analogy-based effort estimation methods [200]. In the studies on productivity benchmarking, software projects are also described by similar sets of attributes as in the studies on effort estimation (e.g., [283, 311]). Finally, similar approaches to measurement are also used in studies on software development process transformations. Although monitoring of such transformations naturally involves time, the measurement and assessment of the impact of changes being made are typically performed in a cross-sectional manner—by taking snapshots of and comparing values of Key Performance Indicators (KPIs) [174, 347]. All of these approaches ignore the dynamics of attributes' changes over time when assessing similarity. Considering such information is especially important when quantifying similarity based on measurement in the form of *time series*, such as defect-backlog profiles (the number of defects that were submitted or resolved over time) or commits of source code churns. Defect-backlog profiles seem especially useful for comparing software development projects as the way the defects are managed by a project team provides valuable insights about the employed software development processes [369].

In the literature, we find a number of measures and methods that can be used for measuring distance (similarity) between time series, for example calculating the Euclidean distance or Dynamic Time Warping (DTW). Although they are useful for tasks performed by computers such as sequence classification or clustering [141], they might not be that easily interpreted by human decision makers. Let us consider, for instance, the distance measures calculated for two defect-inflow profiles presented in Fig. 9.1. It is hard for a decision maker to state whether they are similar or not by calculating the Euclidean distance or DTW, because the distance is expressed in absolute terms (e.g., 194 or 73 points). Therefore, to make such measures useful for software engineers, the similarity should be expressed in an easy to interpret way, as a percentage, e.g. 80% similar or 20% different.

To address this shortcoming of the Euclidean distance and DTW, in this study, we define a new measure of project similarity called SimSAX. It is inspired by DNA-sequences analysis methods. It processes time series, in particular sequences of defect inflows, coding them into strings of symbols and compare these strings. It allows quantifying the similarity as a percentage, and it can help to find particular segments of defect inflow profiles that are similar and thus the similar corresponding projects' activities. We also show that such similarities can have practical meaning and it can

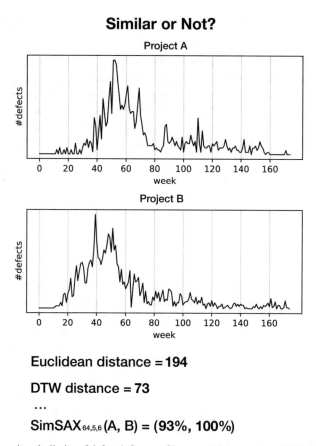

Fig. 9.1 Measuring similarity of defect-inflow profiles—available metrics and SimSAX

reflect the similarities between the ways of working by software development project teams. Therefore, our contributions in this paper are as follows:

- we propose a new similarity metric called SimSAX that can be used to evaluate similarity of projects based on defect-inflow profiles,
- we perform a simulation study on two large commercial projects to study the metric capabilities of finding similarities in defect-inflow profiles depending on the configuration parameters of the measurement method,
- we validate the capabilities of the measure to capture similarities of defect-inflow profiles and the ways of working of project teams by interviewing the projects' team members,
- we scale-up research by applying the measure to identify similarities between five agile and six open source projects,
- we present the practical recommendations on applying the SimSAX measurement in software projects that can be useful to monitor process transformation or

supporting creating homogeneous training data set when building prediction models.

The paper is organized as follows. Section 9.2 discusses the related work regarding measuring similarity of software projects. In the following Sect. 9.3, we explain the relationship between defect inflows and ways of working in software projects. Then, we introduce the SimSAX measure in Sect. 9.4. Section 9.5 presents the design of the simulation and interview studies conducted to validate the proposed measure. The results of the studies are presented and discussed in Sect. 9.6. We conclude our findings in Sect. 9.7.

9.2 Related Work

The evaluation of the similarity between software projects has been studied in multiple contexts.

A mapping study conducted by Ali Idri et al. [200] investigated 65 studies on Analogy-based Software Effort Estimation (ASEE) methods to learn that similarity evaluation is one of the common steps of these methods. It aims at retrieving cases that are the most similar to the project under development using similarity measures. According to the authors of the mapping study, most of the ASEE methods describe projects with the use of both numerical and categorical features and most of them employ Euclidean distance to measure similarity between projects. They also found a few studies that used fuzzy logic to evaluate similarity, i.e., F_ANGEL [199, 201], or proposed a custom similarity measure [38]. However, all of these studies focused on cross-sectional assessment of the similarity between projects without taking into account changes in the projects over time.

Similarity measures were also employed in the studies using clustering to support existing effort estimation methods or to study them. For instance, Menzies et al. [320] used clustering and Euclidean distance to investigate whether project managers should rely on global or local lessons learned when they plan to make changes in their projects to minimize the development effort or the rate of defects. Silhavy et al. [411] and Bardsiri et al. [24] used clustering to support algorithmic effort estimation methods by finding homogeneous sets of projects for training. Both studies used standard distance measures, i.e., Euclidean, Manhattan, or Cosine distance. Again, none of the studies considered the change of projects characteristics in time.

Evaluating (dis)similarity between the projects is also in the scope of studies on monitoring the organizational transformations (e.g., agile transformations). In this context, the task is not about finding similar projects but it aims at verifying whether the changes introduced to the organization have the expected impact on the ways of working. Studies by Olszewska et al. [347] and Heidenberg et al. [174] proposed sets of KPIs that should be monitored in large-scale agile transformations. Although such monitoring naturally involves time, none of the studies considered measurements to be represented and analyzed in the form of time series. Instead, they proposed to analyze and compare snapshots of the KPIs over time.

The problem of evaluating similarity between time series has been broadly studied outside of the software engineering context. Numerous similarity measures have been proposed over the years. Esling and Agon [111] performed an exhaustive review of twenty-eight popular similarity measures. They grouped them into four main categories: shape-based, edit-based, feature-based, and structure-based. According to their study, the choice of a similarity measure highly depends on the nature of the data to analyze as well as application-specific properties that could be required. However, they did not evaluate the measures from the perspective of ease of interpretation by human decision makers. Nevertheless, we could learn from their study that the shape-based measures (e.g., Euclidean distance, DTW) are a plausible choice when time series are relatively short and visual perception is a meaningful description, but on the other hand, it is worth considering structured-based measures (in particular, compression-based ones) when sequences are longer. The proposed SimSAX measure combines these two approaches since it firstly applies compression and then evaluates the similarity of shapes.

We base the SimSAX measure on the studies on motif identification in time series. The task of motif identification is to find recurring sub-sequences of values within a single time series [274, 329, 398]. In this study, we use similar techniques to discover motifs (similarities) between different time series. In particular, we use the method called Symbolic Aggregate approXimation (SAX) [273] that allows compressing and transforming a time series into a sequence of symbols. Also, according to our best knowledge, these techniques have not been used to identify similarities between defect-inflow profiles.

Finally, the process of finding similarities between time series can be supported by clustering methods. These methods use (dis) similarity measures or models to automatically group objects (e.g., k-Means, k-Medoids, hierarchical clustering [8], Spectral Clustering [410], regression clustering [409]). However, there are at least two limitations of these methods from the perspective of applying them to identify similarities between ways of working in software development projects reflected in defect-inflow profiles. Firstly, we need to perform a subsequence time-series clustering (e.g., by using moving windows) because similarities might span through different parts of the compared defect-inflow profiles. Unfortunately, as it has been shown by Keogh and Lin [234], when the subsequence time-series clustering is performed on a single time-series, it produces meaningless clusters. Therefore, clustering methods cannot be used to find meaningful, repeating patterns within a single defect-inflow profile. Secondly, when applying clustering methods, every object has to be assigned to one of the clusters. Therefore, the only thing we know about the members of a cluster is that they are more similar to each other than to the objects belonging to other clusters. Thus, we need to be able to interpret the distance measures to evaluate the similarity of the members of each cluster.

9.3 Defect Backlogs and Ways of Working

Software development methodologies prescribe different practices and sequences of activities for design, implementation, and testing. These different sequences result in different ways of how software engineers identify and report defects.

The collection of all known defects which remain to be resolved in the project is called *defect backlog* [439]. The number of defects reported in a given time frame is called *defect inflow*. The most commonly used time frame is one week. If software engineers focus more on testing than the implementation of new functionality, they discover and report more defects compared to when they focus on implementation rather than testing.

As an example, we can compare ways of working in waterfall and agile software development projects of our industrial partner, shown in Fig. 9.2. In the waterfall ways of working, the functionality of an entire product is implemented before the testing begins. Consequently, not many defects are reported during the implementation. Once the testing starts, the number of reported defects spikes. In agile software development, the implementation and testing are intertwined—each small functionality increment is tested directly after the implementation of that increment is committed to the main code branch. This means that in a model agile software development project the defect inflow is more-or-less constant.

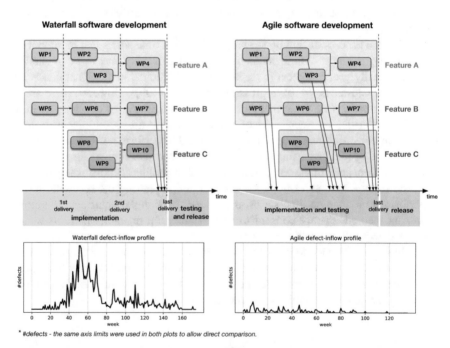

Fig. 9.2 The influence of integration and testing at our industrial partner on defect-inflow profiles (at the bottom: examples of defect-inflow profiles for the same product when it was developed using waterfall and agile ways of working)

Figure 9.2 shows that there is an empirical relationship between the ways of working and the defect inflow, via testing practices. As we can see, Continuous Integration (CI) in agile software development reduces the amplitude of the defect inflow per week. The existence of local increasing trends in defect inflow shows that more code has been tested and therefore more defects were found; the decreasing trend means that less testing is done and therefore fewer defects are discovered and reported. Ultimately, if all code is delivered at once and then tested, the trend resembles the one on the left in Fig. 9.2. However, the majority of industrial projects are somewhere in the spectrum between being fully waterfall and fully continuous implementation/testing.

As we could observe this kind of dependency in other studies and in other companies [369], we identified an opportunity to use the defect inflow as an indicator of ways of working adopted by a software development project team.

9.4 Definition of SimSAX

SimSAX (Similarity-based on Symbolic Aggregate approXimation) is inspired by the research in bioinformatics where computer techniques are used to compare and assemble DNA sequences. The basis for these techniques is the segmentation of DNA into a sequence of letters (A, C, G, T) corresponding to the names of nucleotides forming a DNA chain. Our proposed method transforms a time series (i.e., defect inflow) into a sequence of symbols (*words*). This allows using similar techniques to the ones used to analyze DNA sequences, e.g., for sequence alignment. Since the symbols correspond to levels of the original variable, we obtain a coarse-grain representation of the original time series. The granularity can be controlled by the transformation parameters.

The definition of SimSAX is presented in Table 9.1, using the format proposed by ISO/IEC 15939:2017 standard for specifying Quality Measure Elements (QME) [348], [433]. The process of extracting and transforming a list of defect reports into a time series—a defect inflow profile, and further into sequences of symbols (words) is presented in Fig. 9.3. Also, the figure shows how words are compared to find so-called *motifs*.

According to the terminology used in the studies on time-series analysis, *motif* is recurring subsequence in a time series. In genetics, sequence *motifs* are short, recurring patterns in DNA that are presumed to have a biological function [88]. In this study, we define *motif* as recurring *word* that occurs in both compared defect-inflow profiles.

$SimSAX_{n,w,a}$ defines a family of similarity measures over the combinations of three parameters: window length (n), word length (w), and alphabet size (a). A particular combination is called *configuration*. For instance, $SimSAX_{64,5,4}$ uses the configuration of $n = 64$, $w = 5$, and $a = 4$. Later in this paper, we will use the name $SimSAX_{n,w,a}$ to refer to the proposed measure.

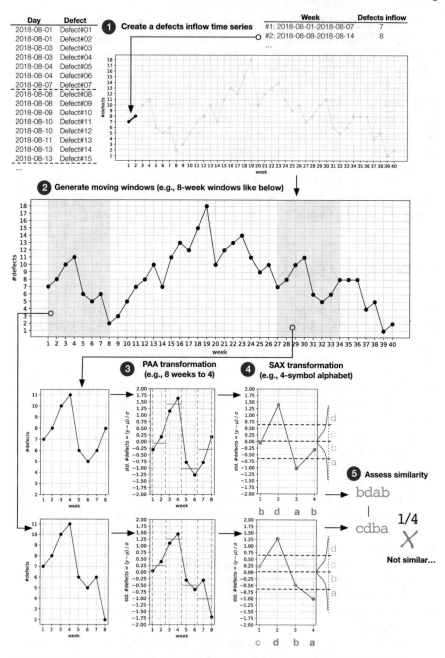

Fig. 9.3 Transforming defect inflow into sequence of symbols and assessing similarities between two windows

Table 9.1 Measurement construct for SimSAX$_{n,w,a}$ according to ISO/IEC 15939:2017

QME Attribute	Definition
Measurable Concept	Similarity between defect-inflow profiles
Relevant Entities	1. Projects P_A and P_B 2. Defect reports in projects P_A and P_B
Attributes	1. Defect report submission time stamp 2. Considered project period (start and end time stamps)
Base Measures	Number of defect reports submitted in each week (so-called defect-inflow profile), separately for projects P_A and P_B, denoted as A and B, respectively
Measurement Method	1. Collect all defect reports for projects P_A and P_B 2. Filter defect reports, separately for each project, so their submission date is within the considered project's period start and end time stamps. 3. Calculate start and end time stamps for each week within the projects' periods. 4. Filter and count the number of submitted defect reports for each week in a project to create a defect-inflow profile (A and B).
Type of Measurement Method	Objective
Type of Scale	Ratio
Unit of Measurement	Defect reports / Week (sequence of)
Derived Measure	**SimSAX$_{n,w,a}$(A,B)** is a tuple (X, Y), where X is the percentage of weeks in the defect inflow A covered by at least one motif of length n found in both defect inflows A and B (similarly, Y is the percentage of weeks in the defect inflow B covered by any of the motifs).
Measurement Function	1. Generate moving windows of length n for A and B (*window*) 2. Reduce the dimensionality of each *window* to w with the use of PAA (*window'*) 3. Discretize each *window'* with SAX (use the alphabet of size a) to convert it into a *word* 4. Find all equal pairs of *words* occurring in both A and B (call them *motifs*) 5. Divide the number of weeks in A covered by at least one *motif* by the number of weeks in project P_A and multiple it by 100%; repeat this step for project P_B.

The measurement procedure and calculation of SimSAX$_{n,w,a}$ consists of the following steps:

Step 1: Create a time series. Since the method operates on time series, we need to transform our data into a time series by counting occurrences of events in time (i.e., submissions of defect reports). In this paper, we focus on defect-inflow profiles, which is created by counting the number of defect reports submitted in a given week (*#defects*).

Step 2: Generate moving windows. The method determines the similarity between time series by comparing constant-length subsequences, called windows. The length of window (n) determines the resolution of the method. We generate windows by moving through the original time series with the stride of one week. In the example shown in Fig. 9.3, we generate 8-week windows.

Step 3: Reduce dimensionality with PAA. Piecewise Aggregate Approximation (PAA) [275] can be used to reduce the dimensionality of each window from n to w ($w < n$, typically $w << n$).

Before we apply PAA, we firstly standardize each window to have zero mean and unit variance:

$$y_i' = \frac{y_i - \mu}{\sigma} \tag{9.1}$$

where: y_i' is the i-th element of the standardized window, y_i is the i-th element of the original window, and μ is the mean value of the window.

The window is then divided into w equal sized segments. The mean value of the data falling within a segment is calculated and a vector of these values becomes the data-reduced representation. Formally, the i-th element y_i'' of the transformed window is calculated as follows [275]:

$$y_i'' = \frac{w}{n} \sum_{j=\frac{n}{w}(i-1)+1}^{\frac{n}{w}i} y_j' \tag{9.2}$$

Step 4: Discretize with SAX. Apply Symbolic Aggregate approXimation (SAX) [273] to transform each window of the length w into a "word" of the same length using symbols from an alphabet of size a. SAX determines "breakpoints" that produce a equal-sized areas under the Gaussian curve. By using these breakpoints, we can produce symbols with equiprobability (since the PAA-transformed time series follows the normal distribution).

Breakpoints are a sorted list of numbers $B = \beta_1, \ldots, \beta_{a-1}$ such that the area under the $N(0, 1)$ Gaussian curve from β_i to $\beta_{i+1} = 1/a$ (β_0 and β_a are defined as $-\infty$ and ∞, respectively) [275]. For instance, for the alphabet $a = 4$ used in Fig. 9.3, we would have the breakpoints $\beta_1 = -0.67$, $\beta_2 = 0.00$, and $\beta_3 = 0.67$. As a result, the two windows presented in the figure would be transformed into words *bdab* and *cdba*. It might surprising because the original windows differ only at a single position (week no. 8) but after transforming them to words three out of four symbols would not match. This is the results of mapping between the values and symbols using the probability distributions. The value observed for the last week in the second window could be considered as an outlier in the context of the first window. As a result, the shapes of the probability distributions of both windows differ visibly. However, this phenomenon will be less visible when we increase the window size because we will get more accurate (and stable) approximations of the probability distributions.

Step 5: Calculate SimSAX$_{n,w,a}$(A,B). Having transformed each window into a word, we can assess the similarity between pairs of words. In this paper, we use a simple similarity measure, which is the rate of corresponding symbols being the same in both compared words. We assume that the windows are similar (are motifs) if the similarity between words is equal to 1 (a perfect match of symbols). However, one can use other similarity measures and define own thresholds, e.g., scoring functions and DNA sequence alignment algorithms, e.g., Needleman-Wunsch algorithm [334] or the MINDIST similarity measure proposed by Lin et al. [275] that takes into account differences in levels between the SAX-generated symbols. For instance, the symbol sequence for two windows presented in Fig. 9.3 matches only on a single position, therefore, they are indicated as non-similar.

Finally, we can calculate $SimSAX_{n,w,a}(A,B)$ as the percentage of weeks covered by the windows coming from the time series A that were indicated as similar to at least one window from time series B (being a motif), and do the same for B. Therefore, the result of calculating $SimSAX_{n,w,a}(A,B)$ is a tuple (X, Y), where X and Y are the percentages of weeks covered by at least one motif in A and B, respectively. For instance, having $SimSAX_{n,w,a}(A,B) = (100\%, 20\%)$ would mean that there is not any novelty in defect-inflow profile A with respect to B, while defect-inflow B has 80% of weeks covered by subsequences not observed in A.

We implemented an open-source tool allowing to calculate $SimSAX_{n,w,a}(A,B)$, and made it publicly available on GitHub.[1]

9.5 Research Design

9.5.1 Goal and Research Questions

The goal of this study is to design a measure that would allow measuring the similarity between the ways of working in software projects based on defect inflows. To achieve this goal, we need to answer two research questions:

- RQ1: How to quantify the defect-inflow profiles into a sequence of symbols to calculate the similarity in percentage?
- RQ2: How well does the measure work on software development projects?

In order to address RQ1, we adapted methods used for time series and sequences analysis and defined the $SimSAX_{n,w,a}$ measure presented in Sect. 9.4. Depending on the values of parameters n, w, and a, the measure can be more or less sensitive to local absolute differences between defect inflows while performing similarity evaluation. For instance, by drastically increasing the ratio between n and w or reducing the size of alphabet a, we can indicate nearly any two non-similar time series as similar (the extreme case is to use $SimSAX_{n,1,1}$—transforming each window into one-symbol word over the one-symbol alphabet). Therefore, we need to perform a simulation to understand the impact of the parameters on the selectiveness of the measure. In particular, we want to find the right combinations where we identify the similarities and do not identify any differences when comparing the same project with and without artificially injected anomalies.

Unfortunately, the generated defect inflow containing anomalies is not entirely representative of projects in industry (it is hard to expect that for any two projects similar segments of their defect-inflow profiles are exactly the same while the different segments differs in such a visible way). Therefore, to answer RQ2, we need to

---

[1] SimSAX tool — https://github.com/mochodek/simsax

evaluate $SimSAX_{n,w,a}$ by applying it to industrial projects. By studying two similar, but distinct, industrial projects, we can validate the similarities with the empirical data about the projects obtained through interviews with the projects' team members.

Finally, we apply $SimSAX_{n,w,a}$ to additional five industrial and six large open source projects to validate the measure on a larger sample of projects.

9.5.2 Research Procedure

Our research procedure is presented in Fig. 9.4. It is divided into three main stages: (1) data collection and exploratory interview (a pilot interview) to identify the right projects to study, (2) simulation study to find the most accurate parameters, and (3) series of interviews to evaluate the choice of the parameters on two subsequent projects at the company.

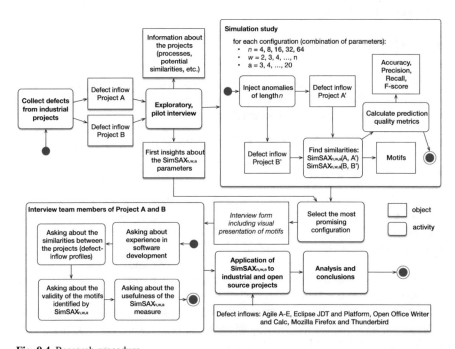

Fig. 9.4 Research procedure

Data Acquisition and Pilot Interview

In the first phase, we collect data about defects from two large projects run by our industrial partner—a large infrastructure provider company. We refer to these projects as Project A and B. Both of them were conducted according to waterfall processes and were aimed at developing two releases of a mature product and its components. The releases were consecutive. The size of the studied embedded software products were several million lines of code, written in C and C++. Since the projects are commercial, the defect databases are professionally structured and managed, thus providing high-quality data for our study. After transforming the collected data into defect inflows, we conduct an exploratory interview with one of the experts in the company, who has more than 15 years of experience and participated in both project A and B. The goal of the interview is to collect information about the projects (their business context, processes, teams, similarities between them, etc.) and collect first insights about the potential for using the $SimSAX_{n,w,a}$ measure and its parameters. During the interview, we present and discuss the similarities found by calculating the measure for a few selected configurations (combinations of parameters).

Simulation Study

In the second phase, we conduct a simulation study. The goal is to find configurations that allow identifying known similarities between the defect-inflow profiles while also correctly ignoring artificially injected anomalies.

We run the simulation procedure for each of the following configurations:

- window length (n) — 4, 8, 16, 32, 64 (consecutive powers of two),
- word length (w) — 2, 3, . . . , n, and
- alphabet size (a) — 3, 4, . . . , 20 (the number of symbols—letters in the Latin alphabet).

In each run, we firstly generate a new defect-inflow profile by injecting anomalies (shapes that do not appear in the original time series) of a given length n so they all cover 64 weeks of the defect inflow (A → A' and B → B'). We preserve a minimum distance of n weeks between each of the injected anomalies so there is enough space to locate at least one motif between them. The examples of the resulting defect inflows with anomalies are presented in Fig. 9.5. Then, we calculate $SimSAX_{n,w,a}$ to find similarities between the original and generated defect-inflow time series, e.g., $SimSAX_{64,8,4}(A, A')$. Since we know which weeks are covered by the similar windows (are motifs), we evaluate the accuracy of the measure in finding these weeks and calculate typically used prediction quality measures, such as Accuracy, Precision, Recall, and F-score. However, we focus entirely on analyzing F-score since it reflects the capability of detecting true similarities (Recall) while minimizing the number of false positives (Precision).

The results of simulation allows us to indicate the most promising configurations, i.e., the parameters for which F-score $\simeq 1.0$, which indicates that all (or nearly all) similar weeks are found (Recall $\simeq 1.0$) with zero (or nearly zero) false positives (Precision $\simeq 1.0$). We then plan to combine information from the exploratory interview and the results of the simulation to select a single configuration to discuss the outcomes of applying the measure procedure with the use of these parameters during the interviews.

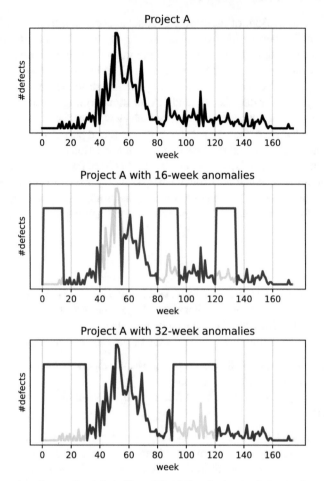

Fig. 9.5 Examples of anomalies injected into defect inflow in the simulation study

Interviews

The next phase of our study is to verify that using selected configuration, indeed, find relevant changes and similarities for industry projects. First, we conduct a pilot interview to validate the interview materials (visualizations and questions) and check whether all parameters are relevant. Based on that we can find whether the prepared materials do not introduce bias and then we interview other experts who participated in Project A and B.

Each interview consists of four stages.[2] Firstly, (1) we ask interviewees about their experience in software development (performed role, number of years in a similar role, number of years with the evaluated products). During the second stage, (2) we

---

[2] The interview materials are available at https://1drv.ms/w/s!Avcq_JfcNezZgqdWmZA1 ysawYmbNJw.

show the interviewees both the defect-inflow time series presented vertically next to each other and ask the following questions regarding the similarity of both projects:

- How similar do you think these two projects are?
- How similar do you think these two projects are in percentage?
- Show areas in the diagram which are similar.
- Can you explain why they are similar (geometrically and empirically)?

After that, (3) the interviewee is presented with a series of motifs (one at the time) found in both defect-inflow time series by using the selected configuration. For each such plot, we ask two questions:

- Are these two highlighted areas similar?
- Where these two periods in the project similar to one another?

During the third stage of an interview, (3) we present a series of plots, each presenting all windows (standardized) indicated as instances of the same motif. The interviewees are asked to point out the plots that present time series similar to each other and to motivate their choices.

Finally, (4) we ask the interviewees if they find this way of measuring and presenting similarity useful to they work, and if so, how.

The selected subjects were managers of the software development projects considered in the study. One person was the program manager who was in charge of the entire software development. One was an integration manager with the responsibility for the process of integrating subsystems to the entire product. The third interviewee was the release manager of the project, responsible for the final stages of testing and preparation of the deployment of the product. These three roles had the best overview of the integrated functionality in the product and could provide us with the information regarding the details of the project, confirming or rejecting the periods identified as similar/different between the project. Although there were over 100 designers in the project, none of the other roles had the required information regarding the projects and the ways of working in the company at the time.

Scaling-up Research

In the final phase of our study, we apply $SimSAX_{n,w,a}$ to additional five industrial projects, owned by the company, and to six large open source projects. We validate the measure on a larger sample of projects. We use the simulation procedure to calibrate $SimSAX_{n,w,a}$ for each of the comparison and discuss the results by referring to facts we have learned about the projects.

The selected industrial projects were conducted at different stages of the waterfall-to-agile transformation that took place in the company:

- Agile A — it is the oldest, and one of the first agile projects executed by the company. Its timeline partially overlaps with the waterfall projects introduced in the simulation study. The overlap is the maintenance phase from the waterfall project overlapping the beginning of the new project.

- Agile B — it is the next agile project. In the project, the ways-of-working have evolved since the first project.
- Agile C — it is one of the longest agile projects in the company. It started two years later than Agile A and one year later than Agile B.
- Agile D and E — these are two more recent agile projects that were concurrently run by the company.

By analyzing these projects, we can observe how the changes in the ways-of-working are reflected in the defect-inflow profiles of these projects.

The selected open source projects are developed by different open-source communities and were chosen because of the following characteristics:

- Eclipse JDT and Platform — these are two core Eclipse plugins that have been developed since the first releases of the programming platform. We limit the analysis to two 3-year periods to reduce the number of potentially-found motifs so we can easier visualize and discuss them. We collected the data on defects for the period between 2001 and 2019 and took the first and last three years.
- Open Office Calc and Writer — these are two flagship products from the Open Office suite. We analyze the defect-inflow profiles for the periods when Open Office was owned by Sun Microsystems / Oracle Corporation and when it was developed only by Apache Software Foundation (after IBM withdrew from the product development).
- Mozilla Firefox and Thunderbird — these are two popular Mozilla products. However, apart from being owned by the same foundation, the products do not have much in common—the former is a web browser and the latter is a mailbox client. Therefore, we could expect a limited set of commonalities.

By analyzing these projects, we can observe whether the measure can be useful in finding similarities between open source projects where defects are reported by community members and users rather than by testers or other team members, as it is in industrial projects.

9.6 Results and Discussions

We present the results in the same order as our research procedure—starting with the pilot interview, through the simulations and ending with the evaluation interviews. Then, we discuss the threats to validity of our study, and finally, we present practical recommendations on using $SimSAX_{n,w,a}$.

9.6.1 Pilot Interview

The goal of the pilot interview was to collect information about the projects and similarities between them from the development process point of view. We were also interested in obtaining first feedback from the practitioner regarding the effectiveness and usefulness of the $SimSAX_{n,w,a}$ measure in finding similarities between the defect inflows depending on the parameters. Finally, we wanted to investigate how to visually present the similarities found by the method (motifs) so it is easy to follow by practitioners we planned to interview in the post-simulation interviews.

We found that the development process was the same for both projects, and the differences in the defect-inflow profiles were caused by the differences in the quality of the product, which in turn was caused by the differences in functionality. Our interviewee has provided us with the information about these processes and about the milestones, such as the end of the development phase and the beginning of the testing phase (and milestones separating different test phases, such as system integration or field testing).

Also, the interviewee shared remarks about the effectiveness and usefulness of the measure depending on the parameters. We used the method to find similarities using a single configuration for each length of window ($n = 4, 8, 16, 32, 64$). We set the remaining parameters (w and a) based on our observations so we have samples approximating the possible space of configurations. After reviewing the plots, the opinion of the interviewee was that using short-length windows ($n = 4$ or 8) was neither effective in finding similarities nor useful from the practical point of view. The number of windows indicated as similar (motifs) was too large and most of the found similarities seemed to be random and could not be explained by any events in the projects. On contrary, according to the interviewee, around 80% of motifs found by the method using longer windows ($n=32$ and 64) reflected true similarities between the ways of working in the projects.

Finally, we have learned that presenting multiple motifs on a single plot (see Fig. 9.6) was distracting and conceptually tiresome. We observed that the interviewee made a comparison between the projects when evaluating the first motifs and used that information when evaluating other motifs—the interviewee knew which parts were similar and then only checked which motifs covered those periods.

9.6.2 Simulation Study

We executed 4,284 simulation runs for all configurations defined in Sect. 9.5.2.

Figure 9.7 presents the relationship between the $SimSAX_{n,w,a}$ parameters and F-score—the subfigure (a) shows the relationship between all the parameters and F-score while the subfigures (b) to (d) use boxplots to present the variability of F-score depending on the values of particular parameters in isolation (n, w, or a). Since the number of weeks covered by anomalies was always the same and equal to 64 weeks (e.g., 16×4-week anomalies, or 2×32-week anomalies) the minimal F-score for both projects was ca. 0.77. It corresponds to the situation when all weeks were recognized as similar (Recall = 1.0 and Precision of $\simeq 0.63$). We can learn from these figures that the selectiveness of $SimSAX_{n,w,a}$ depends on the choice of parameters, and for some configurations, the measure might treat both similar segments and

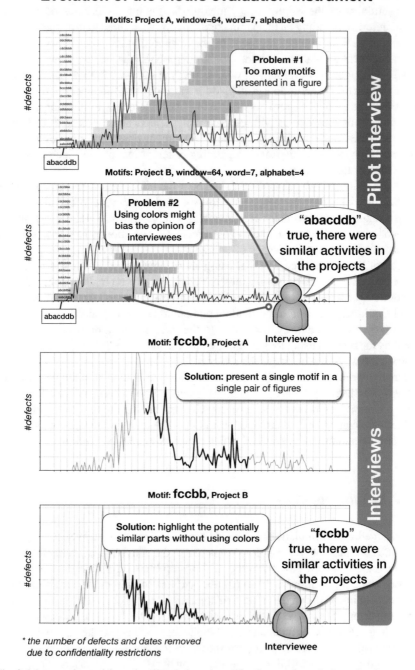

Fig. 9.6 Lessons learned from the pilot study and modifications made to the interview instrument

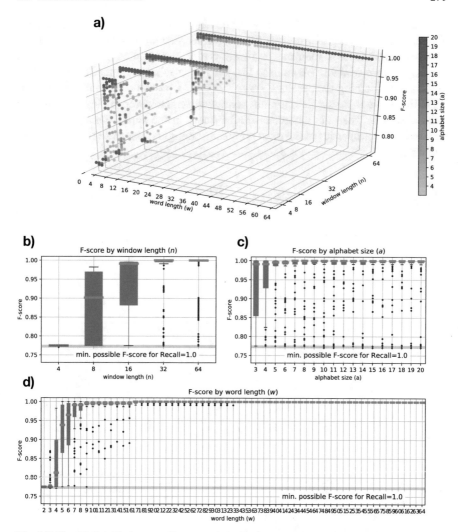

Fig. 9.7 The relationship between F-score and the SimSAX$_{n,w,a}$ parameters

anomalies as similar to each other. For instance, all of the configurations for 4-week windows failed to distinguish between the anomaly and none-anomaly segments of defect inflows. Also, it is visible that the selectiveness of the measure increases when the parameters are set to higher values.

We can see that there is no single, optimal configuration since there are many configurations allowing to achieve obtaining F-score $\simeq$ 1.0. Subfigures (a) to (e) in Fig. 9.8 show all possible combinations of parameters w and a that allow achieving the highest possible selectiveness of the measure for a given window length. Each green circle in the plots ($\bullet$) represents a single configuration. We can see that for 4-week windows, the maximum achieved F-score was nearly the same as the minimal

possible one. Also, none of the configurations for 8-week windows allowed reaching
the maximum F-score of 1.0, however, we can see that increasing the alphabet size
or word length close to their maximum allowed values resulted in achieving nearly
perfect F-score of 0.98. We can see that for longer windows, more configurations
resulted in obtaining the perfect F-score. Therefore, based on these results, we can
state that there is no single optimum configuration. However, by investigating the
relationship between the parameters and F-score in the simulation study, we can
determine the properties of the most promising configurations to be used in real-life
use cases.

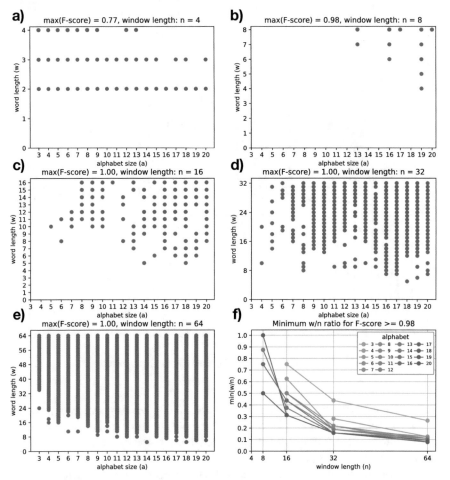

Fig. 9.8 Configuration parameters allowing to achieve a maximum F-score for given window length
n—subfigures a to e; f—minimum w/n ratio for different window lengths n and alphabet sizes a
allowing to achieve the maximum F-score ≥ 0.98

By analyzing the subfigure (f), we can see how the ratio between window length and word length (w/n) affects the selectiveness of the measure. Taking into account that in the simulation study every pair of windows that was supposed to be similar was, in fact, the same, we might want to set the smallest possible values of the parameters to achieve a measure that is selective-enough but still robust to some minor differences in the defect inflows. It means that we are interested in finding the smallest w/n ratio that allows achieving a nearly perfect F-score. As it is shown in subfigure (f), the ratio between w and n decreases asymptotically to zero with the increase of window length. By investigating the plot, it seems that a sensible configuration should have the word/window lengths ratio of ca. 0.18 for $n = 32$ and ca. 0.08 for $n = 64$, while keeping the alphabet size a reasonably small, e.g., between 5 and 8. The alphabet of size 5 is the smallest one allowing to achieve the median F-score close to 1.0 with small variance—see Fig. 9.7(c).

9.6.3 Interviews

The results from the simulation study provided us with a spectrum of the SimSAX$_{n,w,a}$ configurations that cover the similarities and differences between projects in a reasonable way. However, different configurations result in the identification of different similarities. Therefore, we evaluate which of these configurations align best with the practitioners' understanding of the similarities.

Overall Similarity Between the Projects

We interviewed three members of the projects A and B teams (see Sect. 9.5.2). When we asked them about the overall similarity between the projects, they unanimously stated that the projects were "quite similar" and estimated their similarity to 80%, 80%, and 85%. They were convergent in marking the periods when similar activities took place in both projects. According to their opinions, the first halves of both projects were very similar.

Validity of the Motifs and Measurement

The pilot interview indicated that it was difficult to keep track of the similarities when visualizing all similarities in one diagram using the green areas. Therefore, we changed the visualization to one motif per diagram (see Fig. 9.6). A side effect was that it resulted in more diagrams to present. We also noticed that there is no added value in using different configurations because the interviewee analyzed the projects' similarity at the first configuration (diagram) and then used that opinion when checking other configurations (diagrams). Therefore, we decided to use only one configuration SimSAX$_{64,5,6}$ ($n = 64$, $w = 5$, $a = 6$). F-score obtained for this configuration in the simulation study was ca. 0.99 while the w/n ratio was ca. 0.08, which made it one of the reasonable candidates. When applied to compare defect-inflow profiles of projects A and B, it resulted in 17 motifs being found by the method. We also considered 4 more configurations for the same window length $n = 64$ and (w, a) equal to (5,7), (8,6), (8,5), and (5,5) that had similar properties. However, for these configurations, the number of identified motifs was lower (from 3 to 14). We decided to select the configuration that yielded the largest number of motifs since presenting interviewees more (even partially overlapping) motifs could increase the chances of capturing the boundaries of truly similar regions in both defect-inflow profiles.

The details of how the interviewees (I1, I2, and I3) evaluated each of the motifs found by the measurement method are presented in Table 9.2. They were evaluating similarity in terms of shapes of defect-inflow profiles and activities performed in both projects. From the results, we can see that the interviewees were convergent in their opinions, especially for the motifs found in the first halves of the projects' timeliness. This part of the projects corresponded to the phases related to requirements engineering and software implementation. These two phases were similar and the methods and tools used in these two projects were almost identical.

The three motifs located in the middle part of the defect-inflow profiles (fdbbb, fccbb, and fcccb) were also indicated as being true positives. They corresponded to the phases related to unit, component and system testing (and the related defect removal). In particular, the distinct two peaks showed the first testing phase, defect removal and re-testing.

Interestingly, some of the motifs located at the end of the projects' timeliness were also evaluated as correctly describing the reality (eeccb, edccb, and edcbb) by some of the experts, even though when discussing similarities of both projects at the beginning of the interview, the interviewees did not mark these segments of defect inflows as similar. These last phases of the projects corresponded to the functional testing and field testing. As the functionality of the two releases was different, the testing process was partially different and thus the defect inflow was partially different. The experts did not agree on these periods as they focused mostly on describing the different functionality—i.e., they focused on the product and not the process.

The similarity measured as the percentage of weeks covered by the motifs indicated by $SimSAX_{64,5,6}$ was 93% and 100% for projects A and B, respectively. Interestingly, the same measure calculated only for the motifs evaluated by the interviewees were true positives were different than their initial assessment of the projects' similarity (before they were shown the motifs). For the first interviewee, the calculated similarity was slightly lower (A: 68%, B: 72%) but for the remaining *two* experts, it was higher and the same as indicated by $SimSAX_{64,5,6}$ (A: 93%, B: 100%). Therefore, it seems that by showing the motifs to experts they could find projects' similarities that were not obvious to them when they inspected the defect-inflow profiles as a whole.

Table 9.2 Evaluation of the motifs by the interview participants I1, I2, I3 (++ yes, + partially yes, − rather no, − − no)

Motif	Project A/B	Similarity of shapes			Similarity of activities		
		I1	I2	I3	I1	I2	I3
abdfd		++	++	++	++	++	++
abefc		++	+	++	++	++	++
acfeb		++	++	+	++	++	+
befcb		++	+++	+	++	++	+
efcbb		++	++	+	++	+	++
eecbb		− −	− −	− −	− −	− −	− −
fdbbb		− −	++	++	++	++	+
fccbb		− −	++	++	− −	++	++
fcccb		− −	++	++	++	++	++
ecccc		− −	− −	− −	− −	− −	− −
cedcb		− −	− −	− −	− −	− −	− −
ddecb		− −	− −	− −	− −	− −	− −
dddcb		− −	− −	− −	− −	− −	− −
eeccb		− −	++	− −	− −	++	− −
edccb		− −	+	++	− −	+	++
edcbb		− −	− −	++	− −	− −	++
fdccb		− −	− −	− −	− −	− −	−

Usefulness of SimSAX$_{n,w,a}$

The interviewees perceived the way of measuring and presenting similarities as potentially useful in their work. They shared opinion that "*given that the next coming project uses the same ways of working one could use it to estimate defect inflow for the next coming project*" and that it could make it "*easier to perform time/resource estimations, and easier to forecast resource availability for the next-next coming project."*

9.6.4 Scaling-up Research

We applied $SimSAX_{n,w,a}$ to find the similarities between the industrial and open source projects. When calibrating the measure, we performed the simulation and followed the lessons learned from the simulation study. The configuration parameters n, w, a were selected strictly using the following procedure:

1. We run the simulation for $n = 64$ weeks, $w = 2, 3, \ldots, n$, and $a = 3, 4, \ldots, 20$.
2. The results of the simulation were sorted by F-score in the descending order.
3. Following our findings from the simulation study on Project A and B, we always selected the top-ranked configuration for which the ratio between w and n was around 0.08 (this translated to $w \in \{5, 6, 7\}$) and a was between 5 and 8.

The results of selected comparisons between industrial projects are presented in Fig. 9.9. The subfigures (a) to (c) show the similarities between waterfall (Project A) and early agile projects (Agile A, B, and C) identified by $SimSAX_{n,w,a}$. As we can see, the number of motifs found between these projects decreases with time. Agile A was one of the first projects to incorporate agile practices, however, its development process shared many commonalities with the waterfall projects. This was correctly captured by the measure. Agile B was the next agile project and some similarities between this project and the waterfall one were also found. The last project, Agile C, was the youngest one among the three agile projects. For that project, no similarities with the waterfall project were identified. We obtained similar results for the comparison between the agile projects and the second waterfall project (Agile B).

Since projects Agile A, B, and C took place at different stages of the waterfall-to-agile transformation in the company, their development processes differed as a result of continuous improvement. As shown in the subfigures (d) to (f), $SimSAX_{n,w,a}$ did not find similarities between these projects.

However, when the measure was applied to the more recent agile projects (D, E), the measure indicated high similarities between their defect-inflow profiles, as visible in the subfigure (g).

The results of the comparative analysis of the open source projects are presented in Fig. 9.10. The subfigure (a) compares the first three years of Eclipse development reflected in defect-inflows of Eclipse JDT and Platform plugins. The first version of Eclipse (1.0) was released on 2001-11-07 which corresponds to the week number 3 in the figure. The second major version of Eclipse (2.0) was released on 2002-06-27 (week no. 36). From this moment, the development process started to stabilize with one major and two minor versions releases per year. For instance, the version 2.1 was released on 2003-03-27 (week no. 75) and two minor versions 2.01 and 2.02 were released on 2002-08-29 (week no. 45) and 2002-11-07 (week no. 55). In the

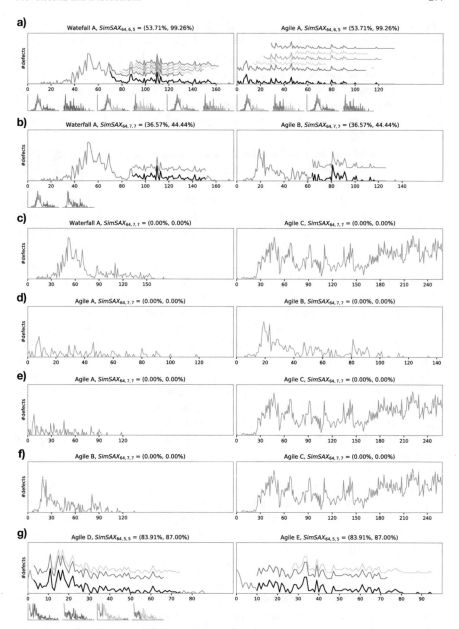

Fig. 9.9 The results of applying SimSAX$_{n,w,a}$ to the selected company's projects using the simulation and recommendations

following year, three minor versions were released 2.1.1, 2.1.2, and 2.1.3 (the last one was released on 2004-03-10; week no. 129). It was an exceptional situation of having three minor releases in that year which proceeded the release of version 3.0 on 2004-06-25 (week no. 140). The whole period between the release of the versions 2.0 and 2.1.3 was indicated as similar by $SimSAX_{n,w,a}$. As it is visible in the subfigure (a), the defect-inflow profiles for the last period before the release of Eclipse 3.0 (between the weeks 129 and 140) differed visibly and was indicated as non-similar by the measure.

We performed a similar analysis for the last three years of Eclipse development (2016-01-04–2018-12-24). It spans through the releases of the versions 4.5.2 to 4.9. As we can see in the subfigure (b), the two defect-inflow profiles share fewer similarities than for the first years, when the development of the plugins was far more active. Also, we can see in the subfigure (c) that the process reflected by the defect-inflow profiles changed visibly between the first and last years of Eclipse development. Therefore, the lack of similarities found by $SimSAX_{n,w,a}$ seems justified.

The second pair of projects analyzed with the use of $SimSAX_{n,w,a}$ were Open Office Writer and Calc. In the subfigure (d), we present the comparison of the defect-inflow profiles for the period when Open Office was owned by Sun Microsystems/Oracle Corporation (2000–2011). As expected, we see many similarities between the defect-inflow profiles which were also indicated by $SimSAX_{n,w,a}$.

The subfigure (e) presents the results of comparing the Writer's defect-inflow profiles for the Sun Microsystems / Oracle Corporation era and after the Open Office trademarks were contributed to the Apache Software Foundation and when IBM finally withdrew from supporting the product development in 2014. The results of applying $SimSAX_{n,w,a}$ suggest that there were no major changes in the ways of working for the latter period of the project since it is nearly fully covered by motifs found in both defect-inflow profiles. Also, we can observe that these motifs appear in the ending part of the Sun/Oracle period what seems rationale because of its close proximity to the Apache period.

The results of comparing the last pair of open source projects being Mozilla Firefox and Thunderbird are presented in the subfigure (f). Although both projects are owned by the Mozilla Foundation, they are very different products what could justify the fact that $SimSAX_{n,w,a}$ did not find any motifs when comparing their defect-inflow profiles.

The results of the conducted analyses show that $SimSAX_{n,w,a}$ could be used to find similarities between ways of working in software projects. Although in the case of open source projects we could not confirm that the similarities found in their defect-inflow profiles reflect the similarities in the ways the development is organized in these projects, their presence could be traced to some facts about these projects and partially explained. In the case of industrial projects, the (dis) similarities found between the projects seem to reflect the reality.

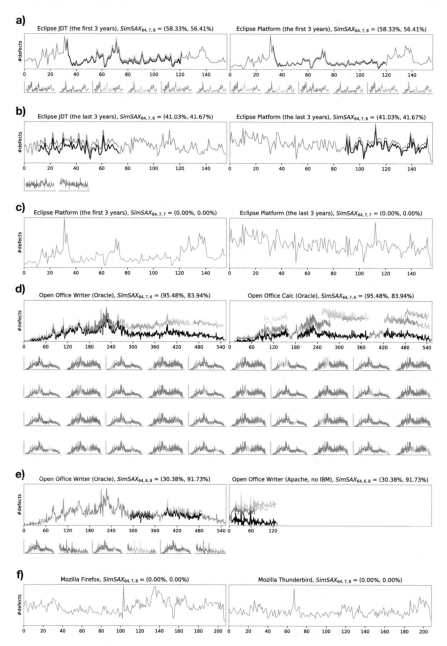

Fig. 9.10 The results of applying $\text{SimSAX}_{n,w,a}$ to selected open source projects using the simulation and recommendations

9.6.5 *Threats to Validity*

Since our study combines empirical and simulation methods, we analyzed the threats to validity of our study using two frameworks, the one proposed by Wohlin et al. [483] and the framework dedicated to simulation studies proposed by de França and Travassos [138].

Construct Validity

These kinds of threats regard misunderstanding or improper use of concepts/terms in the study. For the simulation study, the threats relate to the fact that a defect-inflow profile provides only a reflection of real activities performed in the project. Therefore, finding similar segments in such profiles is insufficient to claim that the method allows identifying similarities in the projects' ways of working. To mitigate this threat, we interviewed projects' team members to create a ground truth of the similarities between both projects in time. However, it triggers another threat to validity related to the knowledge of the practitioners and their perception of the project activities. To minimize this threat, we selected team members that have the necessary knowledge about the projects to answer our questions (i.e., fulfilled management roles) and interviewed three of them to triangulate the observations being made. As it is presented in Table 9.2, the interviewees were convergent in their opinions. Another threat to construct validity regards the procedure of injecting anomalies into defect-inflow profiles during the simulation study. These anomalies were artificially generated to assure that they do not accidentally match with other parts of time series. However, because of that, they may not reflect the kinds of differences normally observed in defect inflows and should be perceived as "extreme" cases. Consequently, the parameters we obtained as optimal should be treated as the upper boundary while configuring the method to be applied in a particular context.

Internal Validity

One of the threats that could affect the outcomes of the study without our awareness is selection bias. We used convenience sampling when selecting both projects and experts. The rationale behind choosing the projects was that both of them were developed using the same waterfall-based process in close time proximity. We assumed that because of the waterfall nature of the projects, the activities performed in the projects would be well-reflected (and separated) in the defect-inflow profiles. Consequently, it would make it easier for practitioners to determine the ground truth. The selection of the experts to be interviewed was partially determined by the projects selection. However, we decided to interview members of the projects' teams that had sufficient knowledge to answer our questions about the activities performed in the projects.

We performed the pilot interview to validate the interview instrument since we expected that the way the defect-inflow profiles and motifs are presented to the interviewees could introduce some bias into their answers. We have learned from the pilot study that we should not overwhelm interviewees with the information and present only one pair of motifs in a single diagram. Also, using colors to highlight motifs occurrences might suggest the interviewees whether they are true or false positives. We incorporated all these observations when preparing the instrument for the main interview study.

Conclusion Validity

The recommendations on choosing the $SimSAX_{n,w,a}$ parameters (e.g., w/n ratio) could be affected by the number of configurations tested in the simulation study. We investigated (in a systematic way) 4284 configurations that allow observing the effect that the w/n ratio and alphabet size (a) has on the selectiveness of the method (see Fig. 9.8).

External Validity

The most important threat to the generalizability of our findings relates to the fact that we performed our study on a limited sample of projects. However, during the simulation and interview studies on two projects, we showed that the measure can be calibrated to detect certain similarities in defect-inflow profiles that reflect the similarities in the activities performed in the projects. By applying the measure to eleven more projects, we showed that it can be calibrated to find similarities between other projects as well. Although the measure parameters determined during the calibration of the measure with the data from the new projects were convergent with the findings from the simulation study, we cannot claim that the parameters obtained during the simulation will be effective for any type of projects (or shapes found in defect-inflow profiles) without the need for re-calibrating the measure.

Reliability

Although $SimSAX_{n,w,a}$ is deterministic, its effectiveness may depend on the quality of input data (e.g., how defects are reported). Both of the studied projects were developed by the same, mature organization, which has a professionally structured defect database. Also, the information about the defects is automatically collected and stored in one of the measurement systems maintained by the company [433].

9.6.6 Recommendations on Applying SimSAX

Based on the results of the simulations and interviews, we provide the following recommendation on applying $SimSAX_{n,w,a}$ to find commonalities between software projects.

When selecting window length (n), we recommend to begin with the length equal to 32 weeks or even more if enough data are available. If there is a fixed and known duration of iterations in the projects, choose n that is at least equal or longer than the duration of a single iteration (if durations are different for each of the compared projects, choose the longer one). The same applies when we search for similarities of a known a priori duration. For instance, we modified the software development process X weeks ago and we want to observe if these changes are reflected in the defect inflows.

When selecting word length (w), the preferable option is to conduct a similar simulation to the one presented in this study. After deciding on the window length, inject n-week anomalies to both compared defect-inflow profiles so they cover approximately half of the profiles. Calculate F-score and determine the minimum w/n ratios allowing to achieve high-selectiveness of the measure (see Fig. 9.8). Alternatively, consult Fig. 9.8 to find a minimum ratio between w and n for the selected window length (n) in our study. Use this ratio to calculate w. When selecting the alphabet size (a), we recommend starting from 5 symbols. To ease the calibration of the measure, we implemented a calibration tool available in the project's GitHub repository.

Calculate $SimSAX_{n,w,a}$ and analyze each of the identified motifs by visualizing them in the original defect-inflow profiles (see Fig. 9.6 and Table 9.2). If there are too many false positives perform either/or of the following actions and re-calculate the measure:

- windows that were falsely identified as motifs differ too much with regard to the number of defects in the corresponding weeks (unacceptable differences in amplitudes) — increase the alphabet size (a),
- windows that were falsely identified as motifs contain different "shapes" — increase the word length (w).

9.7 Conclusions

We proposed a similarity measure called $SimSAX_{n,w,a}$ that allows finding similarities in projects by comparing software defect-inflow profiles (software defects reported per week and collected over time). The measurement procedure converts a defect inflow into a series of overlapping windows of length n and then transforms each of them into a sequence of symbols of length w over an alphabet of size a. $SimSAX_{n,w,a}$ calculated for the defect inflows of two projects A and B indicates the percentage similarity between them (a pair of percentage values, each one giving the percentage of weeks in the project's defect inflow covered by similar sequences occurring in both defect inflows).

We performed a simulation study on two large industrial projects to calibrate the measure and find optimal sets of parameters n, w, and a. After that, we interviewed three members of the projects' teams to validate the measure by investigating whether the similarities found by the measure have practical meaning. Finally, we applied the measure to find similarities in eleven more projects (both industrial and open source).

The results of the study allowed us the formulate the following conclusions regarding the proposed measure:

- $SimSAX_{n,w,a}$ allows finding similarities in software defect inflows that might reflect similarities between the teams' ways of working,
- $SimSAX_{n,w,a}$ provides the best results for longer windows (n), i.e., 32 or more weeks; using shorter windows can result in finding too many false-positive similarities,
- when selecting the word length (w), we recommend keeping $w \ll n$—i.e., keeping the w/n ratio small—e.g., ca. 0.18 for 32-week windows and ca. 0.08 for 64-week windows,
- we recommend choosing alphabet size (a) between 5 and 8.
- the calculation of $SimSAX_{n,w,a}$ should be followed by direct comparison of the identified motifs (similar windows) since we observed that such analysis can reveal not obvious true-positive similarities between projects.

Future Research

As the next step, we would like to use the experience from this study regarding the selection of measure parameters and apply the measure to compare more projects of the company or developed as open source. Also, we would like to define similar measures to $SimSAX_{n,w,a}$ allowing to find similarities between other types of time-series measures in software projects.

Part IV

Customer Data and Ecosystem Driven Development

Introduction to the Customer Data and Ecosystem-Driven Development Theme

Helena Holmström Olsson (Theme Leader 2015–)

1 Introduction

In many ways, digitalization has confirmed that the success of new technologies and innovations is fully realized only when these are effectively adopted and integrated into the daily practices of a company. During the last decade, we have seen how the speed of technology developments only accelerates, and there are numerous examples of innovations that have fundamentally changed businesses as well as everyday life for the customers they serve. In the manufacturing industry, automation is key for improving efficiency as well as for increasing safety. In the automotive domain, electrification of cars and autonomous drive technologies are replacing mechanical power and human intervention. In the telecom domain, seamless connectivity and digital infrastructures allow systems to adapt and respond within the blink of an eye. In the security and surveillance domain, intelligent technologies provide organizations with the ability to detect, respond, and mitigate potential risks and threats with an accuracy and preciseness we could only dream about a few decades ago. While these are only a few examples, they reflect how digital technologies, and the ever-increasing access to data, are transforming businesses to an extent that we have only seen the beginnings of.

Besides the huge potential residing in the technologies themselves, digitalization involves new and endless opportunities related to value creation and value capture. If looking at the Gartner definition of digitalization, it is *". . . the use of digital technologies to change a business model and provide new revenue and value-producing opportunities: it is the process of moving to a digital business"*. With this in mind, technology advancements are critical as the basis for digitalization. However, to utilize and maximize the benefits from these, companies need ways to effectively explore, evolve, and monetize the many opportunities created by new technologies. Therefore, the ability to adjust existing ways-of-working, the ability to adopt novel ways-of-working, and the ability to select the optimal methods, processes, and tools for developing, evolving, and scaling new technologies is key for staying competitive in a digital world. In addition, digitalization brings with it an even stronger need for companies to continuously reinvent and reposition themselves. Each new technology brings new competitors, and to not only survive and avoid disruption but to also increase and strengthen power and position, companies need effective means for how to align with, and maximize the benefits of, the surrounding business ecosystem within which they operate.

During the last 10 years, the "Customer Data and Ecosystem-Driven Development" research theme has had the privilege of conducting research in close collaboration with the Software Center companies with a focus on the engineering practices and processes in these companies. Key to the theme has been to help the Software Center companies accelerate the digital transformation process by improving their existing ways-of-working as well as accelerating the adoption of new practices. Already at the start, and as pictured in the "Stairway to Heaven" model [343], we believed that companies need to evolve from traditional and waterfall development towards what we term R&D as an "experiment system." This means that continuous integration and deployment practices are in place and that companies can act based on instant customer feedback and data collected from products in the field.

To achieve this, and to successfully manage digital transformation of large embedded systems, our research has focused on development methods, process improvement, R&D management, and business strategy. In particular, we have studied topics such as requirements engineering in large-scale agile development, development and deployment of API strategies, adoption of data-driven development practices, and the role and potential of the surrounding business ecosystem. In addition, and due to the increasing need to navigate in a fast-changing business environment, we have studied how to achieve, maintain, and improve business agility. Due to the profound impact of digitalization, and the effects digital technologies have on teams, on companies, and on entire business ecosystems, our research shows how the concept of business agility will increasingly involve continuous alignment between different digital (and nondigital) technologies, mechanisms for continuous value delivery to customers, and finally, the adoption of continuous business models that support continuous value capture from new revenue streams created by software, data, and AI.

2 From Waterfall to Agile Development

If we look back, we started out when most of the Software Center companies were implementing agile development into their organizations and when the concept of cross-functional teams and iterative development of software features was still new. At that time, most companies had only a few agile teams, and the key challenge was how to introduce an agile mindset and culture into a large, and typically hierarchical, organization in which waterfall development had so far been the primary approach to system development. While the introduction of agile methods involved a tremendous change to many of the existing practices, one of the key challenges to solve was how to manage requirements in such a way that these could be continuously introduced and evaluated during agile sprints in which slices of software features were built incrementally. While requirements engineering was already complex, it constituted a key concern to address to successfully transition from a sequential approach to software development with upfront identification and analysis of requirements towards an agile and sprint-based approach in which a large number of development teams need support for continuous identification, analysis, and implementation of requirements. In addition, a large-scale agile setting requires effective ways for teams to communicate requirements as well as maintain traceability of requirements.

With regards to data, all Software Center companies were collecting huge amounts of data already a decade ago when our research started. Typically, this data was product data, and it was collected for quality assurance and diagnostics of systems. As such, it served as the basis for trouble shooting, bug fixing, and feature improvements conducted by R&D teams. At that time, the main concerns were related to collection and analysis practices and how to manage the balance between unstructured data collection, i.e., collecting as much data as possible to allow for as many use cases as possible, and structured data collection, i.e., collecting only the data you know you need for certain types of use cases. While data was effectively exploited as the basis for A/B testing and experimentation in other domains, e.g., in online systems, this was not the case in development of software-intensive and safety-critical embedded systems.

Finally, and with regards to ecosystem management practices, most companies had well-established relationships and large networks of partners already when our research collaborations were initiated. For all of them, the surrounding business ecosystem was, and had always been, critical for success. As a key focus at that time, we explored strategies for how to organize development in the different ecosystems a company operates in, i.e., the innovation ecosystem, the differentiating ecosystem, and the commodity ecosystem. With this research, our intention was to provide companies with comprehensive support for strategy selection as existing practices proved to be more ad hoc rather than strategic in terms of ecosystem partner selection and engagement.

3 From Traditional to Digital Companies

When looking at where the Software Center companies are today and where they are going, the research we now conduct and the challenges we now explore have changed and are continuously evolving to reflect the impressive and on-going transformation the companies have undertaken. Today, large-scale agile practices are adopted across domains, and what used to be a transition toward agile development of software (with practices such as DevOps) is today a transition toward agile and continuous development, deployment, and evolution involving other digital technologies as well (including practices such as DataOps and MLOps).

Besides development practices becoming increasingly continuous in nature, the business models companies use for engaging with customers have also changed. As one of the predominant trends, value is shifting from products to services, with software being the main driver for this. Up until today, the Software Center companies have successfully focused their value creating activities on physical products involving primarily mechanics and electronics components. For decades, product sales have been, and currently are, where the primary revenue is generated. However, with digitalization and with new technologies such as software, data, and artificial intelligence (AI) being introduced, the Software Center companies are in the midst of complementing their physical products with software-driven services and solutions that extend and improve previous products as well as the turnaround time of these. In these new service-oriented offerings, software is the enabler for innovative digital offerings in which data and AI technologies play an increasingly critical role. This involves not only a change of revenue models and value creation opportunities, but also a fundamental shift in the relationship to partners and customers and the ability to quickly respond to market needs. In all Software Center companies, we notice how digitalization is allowing a shift of value delivery from today's transactional business models toward more value-based models with an opportunity to establish a continuous relationship with customers. In such a relationship, the product becomes an enabler for selling complementary services and digital products. As a few examples of the many new ways in which companies monetize their products, we see, e.g., car sharing where customers join a service to get reduced upfront costs but where they pay a regular fee; complementary services that range from offering accessories of the product in a rental model to providing information and advisory services to improve efficiency or quality; customer-oriented business models in which companies monetize based on how well they fulfill customer KPIs, e.g., number of successful deliveries without delays; reduction in customer churn or reaction time gained by earlier detection, etc.; and finally, two-sided market models in which a company develops a second customer base where it can monetize the data generated from its primary customer base.

The advancements described above are all examples of how embedded systems companies are evolving towards digital companies. And although this journey has only started, we already see tremendous progress just by looking at the topics of interest and key challenges the Software Center companies seek to address. Today, these concern, e.g., architectures for new business options; business models for selling services and solutions; monetization of digitalized products; data management practices including, e.g., data access, data utilization, cloud, and data strategies; and finally, effective strategies for development and evolution of autonomous systems that adapt and adjust based on the data it receives.

In the following chapters, we present some of our most influential research within the "Customer Data and Ecosystem Driven Development" research theme. In the first chapter, Kasauli et al. identify challenges and present best practices for requirements engineering in large-scale agile development. In the second chapter, Mattos et al. derive a process for how to deploy and run continuous experiments with customers in the B2B domain and in relation to mission-critical systems. In the third chapter, Fabijan et al. explore the process of moving from ad hoc customer data analysis toward continuous and controlled experimentation at scale. Together, these chapters reflect some of the research we have had the opportunity to conduct together with the Software Center companies and in relation to two areas of key interest, i.e., large-scale agile development and data-driven continuous experimentation.

On behalf of theme 4, a big thank you to all Software Center companies for great collaboration during the last 10 years. And when looking at the results we achieved together, we did not only improve the ways-of-working in the member companies, we also reinvented the ways-of-working in academic research. With 6-month research sprints, continuous collaboration, and frequent delivery of results, and using the Ops terminology denoting continuous practices, we are as close to "ResearchOps" as can ever be. We look forward to future collaborations around the opportunities that new technologies bring and that will keep changing the world.

Chapter 10
Requirements Engineering Challenges and Practices in Large-Scale Agile System Development

Rashidah Kasauli, Eric Knauss, Jennifer Horkoff, Grischa Liebel, and Francisco Gomes de Oliveira Neto

Abstract

Context: Agile methods have become mainstream even in large-scale systems engineering companies that need to accommodate different development cycles of hardware and software. For such companies, requirements engineering is an essential activity that involves upfront and detailed analysis which can be at odds with agile development methods.

Objective: This paper presents a multiple case study with seven large-scale systems companies, reporting their challenges, together with best practices from industry. We also analyse literature about two popular large-scale agile frameworks, SAFe® and LeSS, to derive potential solutions for the challenges.

Method: Our results are based on 20 qualitative interviews, five focus groups, and eight cross-company workshops which we used to both collect and validate our results.

Results: We found 24 challenges which we grouped in six themes, then mapped to solutions from SAFe® , LeSS, and our companies, when available.

Conclusion: In this way, we contribute a comprehensive overview of RE challenges in relation to large-scale agile system development, evaluate the degree to which they have been addressed, and outline research gaps. We expect these results to be useful for practitioners who are responsible for designing processes, methods, or tools for large scale agile development as well as guidance for researchers.

Acknowledgments

We thank all participants in this study for their great support, deep discussions, and clarifications. This work was supported by Software Center Project 27 on RE for Large-Scale Agile System Dev. and the Sida/BRIGHT project 317 under the Makerere-Swedish bilateral research program 2015-2020.

Reprinted with permission from Elsevier. Originally published in Journal of Systems and Software, Volume 172, 2021. DOI: 10.1016/j.jss.2020.110851

J. Bosch et al. (eds.), *Accelerating Digital Transformation*,
https://doi.org/10.1007/978-3-031-10873-0_14

10.1 Introduction

Despite wide criticism, agile approaches have significantly contributed to the way software is developed [321]. While initially focused on small teams [32, 223, 321, 349], success stories have led to their application at large-scale [91, 262, 387] and in system development (i.e., large, complex systems which mix software and hardware) [34, 108, 262], an environment that is characterized by long lead times [34] and stable, sequential engineering practices [355]. These complex, agile environments often involve many challenges which fall under the umbrella of Requirements Engineering (RE), including understanding product value, communicating product purpose, dealing with cross-cutting concerns [231], and managing requirements [389]. Because of these and other challenges, companies struggle to implement efficient RE in a large-scale agile context [69, 260, 479].

Existing work looking at RE-related challenges arising from agile methods, i.e. agile RE (e.g., [40, 176, 368]), mostly focus on proposing new approaches, practices, and artifacts [175]. There is however a lack of empirical studies that investigate the phenomenon of RE in relation to agile methods, particularly in the domain of large-scale system development [175, 176, 203]. This gap is a major obstacle when transitioning to agile system development at scale, considering the extraordinary demands on long-term maintenance, synchronisation of different development cycles (e.g. between hardware, mechanics, and software), and often safety concerns of today's systems. Therefore, in this work we report the RE-related challenges of large-scale agile system development and their solution candidates.

Through a multiple case study of seven large-scale system development cases, based on five focus groups, eight cross-company workshops and 20 semi-structured interviews, as well as a review of state-of-the-art large-scale agile frameworks, this paper makes three contributions from an RE perspective. First, we present a report of industrial RE challenges related to applying agile development in large-scale systems. The identified challenges fall roughly into the areas of building and maintaining shared knowledge, representing that knowledge, as well as integrating it into the process and organization.

Second, the paper provides candidate solutions to the challenges identified under each of the challenge areas. The solutions are obtained from the use of established large-scale agile frameworks and additional solutions from best practices in industry provided by our industry partners.

Finally, we are also highlighting the need for systematic approaches to engineering requirements, even in an agile context. Thus, we hope that our work helps to establish RE practices that better support agility within large-scale system development.

This paper revises and extends our previous work [231] by two more six-month iterations with three additional companies.

This paper is organized as follows. In Sect. 10.2, we discuss the background of large-scale agile development and the related works to our study. Section 10.3 presents the research questions as well as the methodology we used including data collection, analysis and validity threats. We provide study context and case company agile pervasiveness in Sect. 10.4. In Sect. 10.5, we report the results to our research questions. We discuss our results in Sect. 10.6, before concluding our article in Sect. 10.7.

10.2 Related Work

We refer to large-scale agile system development as the development of a product consisting of software, hardware and potentially mechatronic components that includes more than six development teams [91] and is aligned with agile principles [321]. To that effect, this section discusses the background of RE and agile development in large-scale systems engineering companies. We start by giving the background of agile development in large-scale systems engineering. We then discuss the background of RE and agile development while also identifying related works in that context. A summary of the related work with respect to our research then concludes the section.

10.2.1 Large-Scale Agile

Agile methods like Scrum and XP are being adopted in large-scale system development companies [387], even though they were originally intended for use on a small scale [32, 223, 349]. Existing work on this topic shows that companies successfully adopt agile methods, but that several challenges remain. In a survey with 13 organizations in 8 European countries and 35 individual projects on the adoption of XP and Scrum, Salo and Abrahamsson [387] report successful adoption of these methods and appreciation among practitioners. Lindvall et al. [279] study the potential of adopting agile methods with ABB, DaimlerChrysler, Motorola, and Nokia. The authors' conclusion is that, overall, agile methods could suit the needs of large organizations, in particular for small and collocated teams. However, integrating agile into the company environment could be challenging. Lagerberg et al. [262] report based on a survey at Ericsson that applying agile on a large scale facilitated knowledge sharing and effective coordination. Additionally, through a questionnaire based survey of 101 Norwegian projects, Jørgensen [221] analyse agile methods' use for large software projects and conclude that increased use of agile methods in large-scale projects reduces failure risk.

In a systematic literature review on the adoption of agile methods at scale, Dikert et al. [91] identify 35 challenges, e.g., coordination in a multi-team environment with hierarchical management and organizational boundaries. In a structured literature review on challenges of large-scale agile, Uludag et al. [461] identify 79 stakeholder specific challenges e.g., coordinating multiple agile teams that work on the same product, which was deemed specific to program managers. In a position paper by Eklund et al. [108], research challenges of scaling agile in embedded organizations are presented. These challenges include, e.g., coordination of work between agile teams or taking into account existing ways of working for systems engineering. Similarly, Berger and Eklund [34] present, based on a survey with 46 participants, expected benefits and challenges of scaling agile in mechatronic organizations, including efficiently structuring the organization, understanding of agile along the value chain, and adaptation to frequent releases.

In an attempt to address these challenges, several companies are adopting large-scale agile frameworks [103] such as Scaled Agile Framework (SAFe®)[248, 269] and Large-Scale Scrum (LeSS) [264]. These frameworks offer a series of practices, principles, and methods for large-scale agility, e.g., sprint-review bazaars, enabler user stories, guilds and chapters. Given the attention that these large-scale agile frameworks currently receive, we aim in this paper to discuss RE-related challenges with the principles and practices suggested by SAFe® and LeSS. We avoid giving a full summary of these complex frameworks here, but refer to and briefly describe various specific practices and principles which address our identified challenges.

10.2.2 RE and Agile

In the past, agile methods and requirements were often perceived as conflicting, particularly if RE is seen narrowly as a set of "the system shall. . . " statements, which agile's de-emphasis on documentation recommends to avoid. However, RE is a wide field covering requirements of all formats, implicit or explicit, including sharing and coordination of functionality, quality, or value-related knowledge. Although there is less work on the relationship between agile and RE, compared to work focusing solely on agile, existing work has commented on synergies and conflicts of traditional RE thinking with agile methods.

Based on a mapping study with 28 analyzed articles, Heikkilä et al. [175] find that there is no universal definition of agile RE. Furthermore, they report several problematic areas in agile RE such as the use of customer representatives, prioritization of requirements or growing technical debt. In a case study by the same authors at Ericsson, the flow of requirements in large-scale agile is studied [176]. Perceived benefits include increased flexibility, increased planning efficiency, and improved communication effectiveness. However, the authors also report problems such as overcommitment, organizing system-level work, and growing technical debt. Similarly, Bjarnason et al. [40] investigate the use of agile RE in a case study with nine practitioners at one large-scale company transitioning to agile. The authors report that agile methods can address some classical RE challenges, such as communication gaps, but cause new challenges, such as ensuring sufficient competence in cross-functional teams. In a case study with 16 US-based companies, Ramesh et al. [368] identify risks with the use of agile RE. These are, e.g., the neglection of non-functional requirements or customer inability. A systematic literature review on agile RE practices and challenges reports eight challenges posed by the use of agile RE [203], such as customer availability or minimal documentation. However, the authors also report 17 challenges from traditional RE that are overcome by the use of agile RE. The authors conclude that there is more empirical research needed on the topic of agile RE.

Other studies have addressed the use of traditional RE practices and agile RE. Paetsch [350] provide a comparison between traditional RE approaches and agile software development while identifying possible ways in which agile software development can benefit from RE methods. The authors conclude that agile methods and RE are pursuing similar goals in key areas like stakeholder involvement. The major difference is the emphasis on the amount of documentation needed in an effective project. Meyer, in contrast, regards the relationship between RE and agile more critical, describing the discouragement of upfront analysis and the focus on scenario based artifacts (i.e. user stories) as harmful [321], however not based on empirical data.

10.2.3 Summary of Related Work

In summary, there is substantial existing work on the adoption of large-scale agile in system development, including empirical studies. However, existing work either focuses on identifying and evaluating agile RE practices [175, 203], or at presenting the current state of practice at single companies [176] and without explicitly targeting system development [40]. Hence, additional empirical work is needed to understand the complex phenomenon of agile methods and RE in the domain of large-scale system development. Our study contributes with a cross-case analysis of large-scale agile development. The study extends our preliminary work presented in [231] as follows:

- We refined and expanded the catalogue of challenges by talking to the initial four companies plus additional three companies with comparable context.
- We used the expanded catalogue to run a workshop on RE practices in large-scale agile system development where companies described their ways of working, relating to the challenges. This activity contributed new potential best practices.
- We analysed documentation of SAFe® and LeSS to understand to what extent we can rely on these scaled frameworks for addressing our challenges. The analysis together with feedback from the workshop provided potential solutions to our identified challenges.

10.3 Research Methodology

We have conducted our multiple-case study [386] in two rounds with several points of elicitation and validation in each round. Overall, the elicitation took place over a period of two years, with data analysis and writing continuing for another year. In Round 1, we investigated four companies with a series of focus groups and interviews, the results of which have been summarized in [231]. In Round 2, new to this paper, we continue to investigate the four original companies, and a further three companies, running a series of cross-company and individual company workshops - gathering challenges and solutions and presenting and validating our findings with the case companies. The final results provide insights regarding our two research questions:

RQ1: *Which requirements-related challenges exist in large-scale agile system development?* Given the scope of agile development at the different case companies, we categorize and describe the challenges provided by our case companies.

RQ2: *Which approaches have been proposed in popular literature and which approaches are used by practitioners to address the challenges identified in RQ1?* Using the results from RQ1 as a benchmark, we aim to provide a set of solutions from proposals presented by practitioners as well as those offered by well-known large-scale agile frameworks, particularly LeSS [264] and SAFe® [248].

10.3.1 Case Companies

Our study includes one telecommunications company (referred to as Telecom in this paper), two automotive companies (Automotive1 and 2), one company developing software-intensive embedded systems (Technology1), another technology and engineering company (Technology2), one manufacturing company (Manufacturing) and one processing company (Processing). Both Manufacturing and Processing have significant software components. All seven cases represent large, international companies developing products and systems that include a significant amount of software, hardware, and typically mechanical components. All case companies have experience with agile software teams and have the goal to further speed up the development of their software-intense systems. We elaborate on the specific cases in Sect. 10.4.

10.3.2 Sampling and Data Collection

In order to answer our research questions, we collected data both from our company cases and from the literature concerning scaled agile frameworks. Generally, we relied on semi-structured interviews (one or more interviewers interact with one or more interviewees based on an interview guide), workshops (a group meets to jointly work on creating a defined result), and focus groups (for a given scope, representative stakeholders are invited to discuss current challenges and future opportunities). In order to coordinate the multiple-case study, we relied on special cross-company workshops (XComp WS) for scoping of work, validation of results, and planning of next steps across participating companies. The elicitation and validation for this study was conducted in two rounds as elaborated in Sects. 10.3.2.1 and 10.3.2.2.

Table 10.1 Data Sources First Round (Reported in [231])

Type	Company	Role(s)	Label
Focus Group	Telecom	2xTest Architect, System Manager	FG-1
Focus Group	Automotive 1	Process Manager, Specialist Platform Software	FG-2
Focus Group	Telecom	2xTest Architect, System Manager	FG-3
Focus Group	Automotive 2	System Responsible, 2x Function Owner, System Quality Engineer	FG-4
Focus Group	Technology 1	RE Change Agent, Chief Engineer	FG-5
WS	Automotive 1 Telecom	Verification Manager, Specialist Platform Software Test Architect, System Manager	XComp 1
WS	Automotive 1 Telecom Automotive 2 Technology 1	Verification Manager, Specialist Platform Software Test Architect, System Manager Test Architect, System Manager Chief Engineer Software	XComp 2
Int	Telecom	Test Architect (TA), System Manager (SysM) x2, Developer (T-Dev), Scrum Master (ScrM), Area Product Owner (APO), Operational Product Owner (OPO),	T-*
Int	Automotive 1	Safety Technology Specialist (TS),	A1-TS
Int	Automotive 2	Component Design Engineer (CDE),System Design Engineer (SDE), Function Owner x2 (FO), Software Developer x2 (SD), Product Owner (PO), Scrum Master (SM), System Tester (ST), Functional Tester (FT), Software Quality Expert (SQE)	A2-*
Int	Technology 1	Requirements responsible	Tec-SRR

10.3.2.1 Round One Elicitation and Validation

Figure 10.1 gives an overview of our research design for the first round of elicitation and validation, as presented in [231], and Table 10.1 presents a summary of the individual elicitation events.

Starting from a common case study design and common research questions, we conducted a cross-company scoping workshop (XComp 1 Scoping WS) to secure commitment from participating companies, align the goals of the study and finalize the research design. We then scheduled individual scoping workshops (Scoping WS) with each company, except for Technology1 which, despite genuine interest in the study, could not free up resources for this study at that time. During these scoping workshops, we selected with the help of our company contacts the most appropriate case in terms of availability and available experience on the topic, e.g., a specific product or component (partially) developed with the use of agile methods. These cases were selected to accommodate two aspects: *variation* to allow better

Table 10.2 Data Sources Second Round

Type	Company	Role(s)	Label
WS	All companies invited	Many roles, see below	XComp PV
WS	Telecom	Verification Manager, System Architect	TelWS
WS	Technology 1	Project Manager, Chief Engineer, Requirements Manager, Technical Integrator (2x), Product Manager	TechWS
WS	Automotive 2	Project Manager (Process/Methods/Tools) 3x (OD, SW-Dev, Sys-Dev), Technical Expert	Auto1WS
WS	Manufacturing	Project Manager x2, Chief Engineer, Electronic Developer, Technical Integrator x2	ManWS
WS	Processing	System Engineer x3, Technology Specialist x2, Project Manager, Requirement Manager	ProcWS
WS	Telecom, Technology 1, Technology 2, Automotive 1, Automotive 2, Processing	Toolchain and Processes, Requirements Expert, Process/Method/Tools(SysEng) x4, Process/Methods/Tools (SW) SW Reqt Eng. x3, Architect x2, System Manager	XComp 3
WS	Telecom, Technology 1, Technology 2, Automotive 2	System Engineer x2, Agile Team Lead, Product Owner x2, Agile Expert x2, Requirements Engineer x3	XComp 4

generalization of results and *convenience*, since there was an interest to investigate the research questions in each particular case. This allowed us to cover a variety of perspectives during data collection, i.e., system overview, customer experience, development, integration, and testing.

Upon selecting the appropriate case, we started data collection through the use of interviews and focus groups. Our generic data collection instrument for Round 1 of our study can be found online.[1] Data collection was adjusted according to each individual case based on resource availability and commitment. For instance, the Telecomcase relates to a large product development by many Scrum teams and we relied on a focus group followed by interviews (denoted *Int* in the figure) with a variety of roles (see Table 10.1). In contrast, the Automotive1 case relates to one Scrum team and we chose a focus group with the entire team, complemented with an interview of a safety expert. Interviews lasted approximately one hour and followed a similar interview instrument for all companies with domain specific adjustments for each company. For focus groups and cross-company workshops we scheduled three hours.

---

[1] http://www.cse.chalmers.se/~knauss/2020-AgileREChallenges/KGLKK_re_agile.pdf

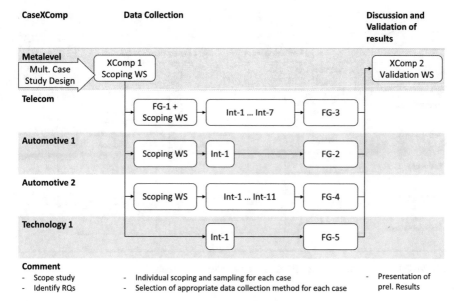

Fig. 10.1 Overview of multiple case study research design - Round 1

10.3.2.2 Round Two Elicitation and Validation

In the second round of data collection, summarized in Fig. 10.2, with elicitation events listed in Table 10.2, we relied mainly on workshops to expand and validate our data. We did Round 2 over a period of one and a half years divided into three six-month cycles (each column in Fig. 10.2). This round includes regular cross-company workshops, labelled XComp PV (Planning and Validation), that served as checkpoints to validate our findings with our industry partners and plan together the upcoming cycles. These XComp PV workshops gave us an opportunity to continually present our findings, receiving feedback. Round 1 (Fig. 10.1) covers six months and Round 2 (Fig. 10.2) covers one and a half years, making a total of two years composed of four 6-month cycles for the entire investigation.

We started Round 2 with a cross-company workshop (XComp PV) at which we presented and received feedback on our previous findings, making plans for further investigation with each company. We then conducted a number of individual workshops with each company, following a standard workshop instrument.[2] The general purpose of the instrument was to both orient the new companies to the project and to go through the RE-related challenges found in the previous round of the study. In order to make the workshops more concrete, we elicited RE-related artifacts (e.g., product backlogs, feature descriptions), and understood how each artifact would relate to the challenges we had discovered. Using this instrument

---

[2] http://www.cse.chalmers.se/ knauss/2020-AgileREChallenges/SWC27-Sprint12-Interview- Instrument.pdf

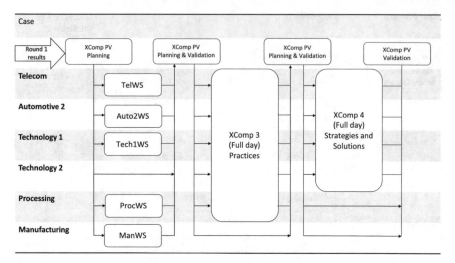

Fig. 10.2 Overview of multiple case study research design - Round 2

as a guide, we conducted five company workshops (TelWS, TechWS, Auto1WS, ManWS, ProcWS) confirming, expanding and collecting challenges and solutions. Each workshop lasted three hours and was hosted by the case company.

At this stage, with a tentative list of challenges and potential solutions from industry, we sought for solutions from available literature. In order to extract potential solutions provided in literature for large-scale agile development, we selected two popular large-scale agile frameworks to include in our analysis: LeSS [264] and SAFe® [248]. Two authors read both sources and independently created a matrix relating challenges found with our companies to potential solutions suggested by either source. Our matrices were discussed and merged, and the results are presented as part of our findings, addressing RQ2.

We then conducted two, full day cross-company workshops, XComp 3 and XComp 4, with a focus on finding and developing solutions and strategies to our discovered challenges. At these workshops, we presented an overview of current findings, including updated challenges, collected solutions from the companies, and the challenge-solution matrix obtained from the analysis of scaled agile frameworks, then discussed companies' RE practices via individual presentations and a world cafe[3] focusing on selected issues. Depending on availability, not all case companies could send representatives to each workshop, but each workshop had at least four companies represented (see Fig. 10.2).

---

[3] The world cafe method allows to effectively host large group discussions http://www.theworldcafe.com/key-concepts-resources/world-cafe-method/

10.3.3 Data Verification

Not all researchers participated in all interviews, workshops and focus groups. In Round 1 we had one dedicated researcher present in all data collection events. In Round 2, we had at least two out of three principle investigators present in all workshops, after calibrating our efforts via our research instrument. We recorded interviews and focus groups where possible and had at least two researchers take notes otherwise. Collected data was verified at multiple points with case company representatives through follow-up workshops.

10.3.4 Data Analysis

For data analysis, we relied on a thematic coding approach [151]. For each case in Round 1, at least two researchers familiarized themselves with the data and highlighted noteworthy statements and assigned a label or code to each. Based on a card sorting approach, the authors of [231] discussed and iteratively combined codes into 30 candidate themes, from which we derived four high-level clusters containing 3–5 themes each. In our expanded data collection, we processed the material collected from company workshops in the same manner, i.e., with two researchers sorting and updating findings to create the updated list of issues and solutions presented in Sect. 10.5. In order to validate the clusters in each round, we discussed the outcome of our analysis in a reporting workshop (XComp 2 Validation WS for Round 1 and XComp PV for Round 2) with all participating companies.

As an example of our coding process, in Round 1, interview A2-PO said the following, "I don't think traceability is not required or something like that. It's just that my focus hasn't been on documenting the function." These and other quotes led to the creation of code (challenge) 'C3.c Creating and Maintaining Traces'. In Round 2, as part of our discussions with Manufacturing, we made the note "Reusable modules = requirements and solutions", providing a potential solution for our earlier C3.c challenge. These and other items are described in Sect. 10.5.3.3. As a third example, our notes from the ProcWS included the following statement: "Product focus means little reuse of requirements. How to reuse existing requirements in a new product? Beyond copy and paste. . . ". This and other supporting quotes and notes caused us to create a new code (challenge), compared to the Round 1 results in [231], 'C2.c Avoid Re-specifying, Encourage Re-use', and is integrated with the other explanatory text in Sect. 10.5.2.3.

Overall, comparing Round 1 to Round 2, we re-worded and re-organised several challenges, as well as adding many new categories and sub-categories. Of the six challenge categories with 24 sub-challenges presented in this work, two of the challenges categories and roughly 11 of the sub-categories appeared already in the Round 1 results (details can be found in [231]). As such, roughly half of the challenges arose in Round 2, and are new to this work. Overall, due to the extensive changes, categories and challenges from Round 1 appear in a more elaborate context and are adjusted accordingly, which makes a clear mapping between Round 1 and Round 2 results difficult.

Once the challenges were established, we repeated the analysis process going through material collected from company workshops and the LeSS [264] and SAFe® [248] sources, looking for potential solutions which mapped to our identified challenges. Two researchers did this mapping individually. The results were merged and differences discussed. Section 10.5 presents both the challenges, updated from [231], along with potential mapped solutions, extracted from the company interactions and SAFe® and LeSS materials. This list of potential solutions, mapped to challenges, was also presented back to company participants in a cross-company workshop, collecting feedback and making updates to the findings.

10.3.5 Threats to Validity

By design, the external validity of case studies is low. Hence, generalization of our findings might not be possible to different companies or domains. In particular, we cannot reason about challenges for small-scale or pure software development. We believe that while some challenges might be visible there as well, they can likely be managed ad hoc or within the scope of agile practices. We designed our study to identify common challenges across participating companies. Thus, our research method does not support any deep argument about differences between companies, domains, and market positions. However, given that we found similar themes in all cases, we expect that these apply similarly to other companies or projects in large-scale systems engineering.

To increase internal validity, we regularly discussed the results of our analysis in multiple cross-company workshops (XComp 2 Validation WS, XComp PV). The workshops included key roles from each company that were already involved in the study. We also used the workshops to discuss underlying root causes and challenges that are shared by all companies.

To avoid a too restricted view on smaller parts of a project or a product, we selected interviewees from different parts of the development, including at least one team and several system level roles in each case. Workshops often involved a variety of roles from a variety of divisions/areas within the companies. We relied on a convenience sample and companies provided us with access to dedicated company experts in the areas of agile transformation and RE, with a genuine but diverse interest in the field. While we hope that this improved internal validity, it might have introduced a selection bias, which we tried to mitigate by encouraging participation of both proponents and opponents of agile/RE. Our contact persons at the case companies all have substantial knowledge in the area of agile transformation. Therefore, we expect that they were able to select suitable participants.

To mitigate threats to construct validity, we designed and improved the interview guides in multiple iterations and with correspondence from the company contacts that, as mentioned, are knowledgeable with agile transformation. During the interviews, workshops and focus groups, we gave explanations where concepts were not clear and asked participants or interviewees for elaborations in case of an ambiguous answer. Data was collected from multiple sources including different companies and existing literature (SAFe® and LeSS) which helped us ensure we identified the challenges correctly. During data analysis, we used data triangulation between interviews, company workshops, and the literature. Further, in case of ambiguous statements, we would contact the interviewee or include a discussion of these statements in the next XComp workshop. While it is important to maintain a chain of evidence from the data to findings, we did not attempt to connect all found challenges to specific cases. Since many data points came from cross-company workshops or focus groups with many participating companies, it was not always possible to clearly decide which company had this challenge. We could have tried to establish these connections, e.g., by following up with a survey. However, we refrained from doing so to avoid confirmation bias or bandwagon effect, i.e., that company representatives would agree to challenges simply because they sound likely and because others experience them as well.

Reliability is hard to achieve in qualitative studies. However, we tried to describe our study design, in particular the data collection and analysis procedures, in a detailed fashion and shared the various instruments used for data collection. At least two researchers were involved in all interviews, focus groups, and workshops, to reduce the impact of subjectivity. Similarly, we analysed all data involving at least two researchers at a time. With all case companies, we have a prolonged involvement leading to mutual trust among the parties.

The potential solutions proposed in Sect. 10.5 are based on our own reasoning, claims in related work (that these solutions help with a certain challenge), and on discussions with the case companies. Thus far, we have not applied the solutions from the literature in the case companies, or solutions suggested by one company in further companies. Further validation of the collected solutions is needed.

10.4 Study Context: Pervasiveness of Agile Development

Before answering the RQs as outlined in Sect. 10.3, we need to get an overview of how the case companies work with agile in a large-scale, setting the context of the study. For this, we analyzed our collected data and confirmed our summaries with the company representatives. We found it challenging to characterize the state of agility in potential case companies. Especially at scale, it becomes very hard to give an overview of concrete practices being applied within a development organization. As one of our company contacts stated:

> I suspect that our organization is very agile when judged on what is found on powerpoint level, but hardly agile at all when judged on how agile practices are implemented. — Anonymous interviewee

The challenges we discuss in this paper may offer potential explanations for why adopting satisfactory agile practices is so hard. They should not be seen as

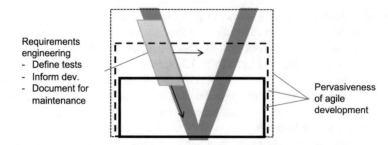

Fig. 10.3 Different scopes of agile development within system development and a typical V model. (Light grey box denotes RE, arrows indicate how requirements are used for informing developers about what to implement, testers about what to test, and for documenting the system for maintenance. Three black boxes show the different agile scopes discussed in this case study)

challenges that only occur once a company has completely transitioned to agile, but more generally as challenges that companies need to consider when they aim to be agile.

In addition to the practices being followed, we found it important to distinguish how widespread agile approaches are in the company. Figure 10.3 is a simplified visualization of the different states we found within the case companies. For some, agile practices are only applied by software teams, for others, they span the development of complete functions (incl. hardware and potentially mechanics), and for some, the full development organization aims for continuous and agile development. Note that not only do the companies differ in the way they (aim to) implement agile practices, but that there is also a huge variation within the individual companies' products, services and structures. This section provides an overview of the contexts of our case companies.

Telecom Company

The Telecomcase relates to the development of one major product. More than 30 Scrum teams develop in parallel based on a scaled agile approach (adapted from SAFe® [270]). Scrum sprints are based on a backlog and a hierarchy of product owners breaks down product requirements and customer visible features to backlog items. While these product owners represent the customer requirements towards the product development, system managers represent a system requirements perspective. The overall effect is a continuous development stream and feature flow, which is supported by a powerful infrastructure that enables continuous integration and testing. Pre-development generates knowledge about new features, which enables effective planning for continuous delivery.

Particular to the Telecomcase, hardware development is largely decoupled from the software development. New hardware becomes available with a regular, but low frequency. Thus, the software development sets the pace of system development, which can be seen as continuous and agile, in that it embraces agile values as much as possible. In Fig. 10.3 this is shown by the largest outer box encompassing the entire V model, which implies that the whole scope of a traditional V model is covered.

Automotive Company 1

In Automotive1, agile methods have been successfully applied to in-house development of software components. In the light of growing competition from software-centric companies, e.g., on autonomous driving, there is a desire to scale up these fast-paced approaches from developing software components to developing complete functions, thus including agile development of hardware and mechatronic. The selected case is a pilot project that re-implements a whole customer function in an agile way. Integration of this function into a real vehicle requires additional verification with respect to safety and overall system behavior. Thus, we would characterize this situation with the second largest box in Fig. 10.3, where a function owner takes responsibility for one particular function and implements it with an agile team.

Automotive Company 2

With Automotive2, we selected a case responsible for safety critical functionality developed in house. As with Automotive1, agile teams develop software within a development process that still corresponds to the V model. Within the agile software teams, software requirements are transformed into backlog items. In order to speed up development of this differentiating functionality, different measures have been taken to speed up the overall system development, such as introducing a shared information model that supports storing requirements, design elements, tests, and implementation models throughout the system development. Since this helps shortening development time significantly, participants referred to this approach as *narrow V model* (comparable to *agile loop* in [108]) in FG-4. In Fig. 10.3, we describe this as the smallest box, not to refer to overall development speed, but to the fact that hand-over between plan-driven and agile development happens on a low level of abstraction.

Technology Company 1

Technology1 develops mechatronic products, both for consumer markets and for industrial development and manufacturing, as well as for OEM system integrators. Their system development is decomposed into several system elements. Software development is mostly confined to two of these elements, both of which are characterized by agile methods and practices such as Scrum and Continuous Integration. As with Automotive2, we refer to this situation with the smallest box in Fig. 10.3, as

Technology1 enables agile work of more than 20 Scrum teams within a plan-driven system development organization.

Technology Company 2

Technology2 develops advanced systems both for consumer markets and for OEMs, including systems that are safety critical. In order to better serve their customers, TechnologyCompany 2 is increasing their agile development competency. Especially for interacting with OEMs, this entails challenging established ways of working throughout the company, and at the time of this investigation, we discussed agility on the scale of a full customer project.

Manufacturing Company

The Manufacturing company, develops high-tech products of supreme complexity and very large software parts for the medical domain. In order to decrease lead-time for delivering new features and to increase throughput, continuous development paradigms have been embraced throughout the R&D department. Agile principles and practices are considered on all levels, yet must be carefully considered due to regulatory requirements and the very large scale of the development effort. The software development is to a good extent independent from hardware development cycles and can be considered very large scale. It is increasingly organized according to large-scale agile development frameworks and continuous software development paradigms and at this scale, we would characterize its level of agility to correspond with the second largest box in Fig. 10.3.

Processing Company

The processing company, Processing, offers components, services, and management for production and factories. Services provide detailed intelligence about physical processes within a factory or plant. The company has adopted agile ways of implementing software based services, which however rely on capabilities of physical components within a factory or plant. Thus, the scope of agility roughly relates to the smaller box of Fig. 10.3, when considering a complete facility as the system.

Summarizing the seven cases, we recognize that some case companies have come a long way towards continuous software engineering and enterprise-wide adoption of agile [420]. Others are currently moving in that direction. Our research aims for common themes, regardless of the pervasiveness of agile adoption or agile maturity (which we did not explicitly investigate in this study). In the analysis of interview and workshop data, we uncovered challenges and practices that relate to the application of agile methods in these contexts, described in the next section.

10.5 Challenges and Potential Solutions (RQ1 and RQ2)

With respect to RQ1, we see 24 challenges that we group into six areas of challenges: *Build and Maintain Shared Understanding of Customer Value, Support Change and Evolution, Build and Maintain Shared Understanding about System, Representation for Requirements Knowledge, Process Aspects* and *Organizational Aspects*. For each challenge, we also discuss potential solutions from literature and practice to answer RQ2.

In this section, we present the challenges along with solutions candidates from SAFe® and LESS, and, when available, solutions suggested by our participating companies. It is our goal to provide a comprehensive overview. Although we have tried to organize the challenges in similar areas to facilitate understanding, the areas are not independent, and often there is overlap between areas and challenges. Fig. 10.4 provides an overview of the categories and challenges, and, in addition, we summarize challenges, potential solutions, and research gaps for each category in six summary tables, Table 10.3 to 10.8. Readers can either follow our report sequentially, or use the figure and the tables as a starting point to directly jump to a challenge of interest.

(C1) Build and maintain shared understanding of customer value
a) Bridge gap to customer
   i. Make team understand customer value
   ii. Unable to express value in user stories
   iii. Feedback and clarification
b) Building long-lasting customer knowledge

(C2) Support Change and Evolution
a) Managing experimental requirements
b) Synchronization of development
c) Avoid re-specifying, encourage re-use
d) Updating requirements

(C3) Build and maintain shared understanding about system
a) Documentation to complement tests and stories
b) System vs. component thinking
c) Creating and maintaining traces
d) Learning and long-term knowledge
e) Backward compatibility

(C4) Representation of reqts knowledge
a) Manage levels vs. decomposition
b) Quality reqts as thresholds
c) Tooling not fit for purpose
d) Accommodate different representations
e) Consistent reqts quality

(C5) Process aspects
a) Prioritization of distributed functionality
b) Manage completeness
c) Consistent requirements processes
d) Quality vs. time-to-market

(C6) Organizational aspects
a) Bridge plan-driven and agile
b) Plan V&V based on reqts
c) Time for invention and planning
d) Impact on infrastructure

Fig. 10.4 Challenging Areas of RE for Large-Scale Agile System Development. Updated from [231]

10.5.1 Build and Maintain Shared Understanding of Customer Value

10.5.1.1 C1.a: Bridge Gap to Customer

> C1.a: In large organizations, it is challenging to achieve sufficient customer collaboration. It is hard to make teams understand customer value, express actual customer value in terms of user stories that can be implemented in a single sprint, as well as to provide feedback to and obtain clarifications from the customer.

Despite the close customer relations advocated by agile, study participants indicate a large distance between customers and developers. In all our cases we found dedicated roles that channel information from multiple stakeholders down to the teams. It is not trivial to bridge that gap, direct interaction of teams and stakeholders can lead to chaos when established plans are circumvented or on-site customers are not an option. Teams want to be agile, but do not focus on customer value.

i. Make Team Understand Customer Value

Independent of distance/gap, the teams struggle to understand their customers' view and cannot describe how their work provides customer value. Teams work with sub-features and tasks that can be finished during a typical sprint as opposed to the bigger features in order to ensure frequent delivery, a practice noted from all our case companies, although the methods used differ. However, one interviewee (T-ScrM) pointed out that *a feature is what is sold to the customer*. It thus becomes hard to gauge what the value of a sub-feature is. One participant (XComp 1) claimed that the focus on agile practices occupied the teams so much that this caused a neglect of product value. *Teams just want to be agile.* However, value creation is not solely the teams' responsibility as the requirements breakdown starts from the customer units, as in the Telecomcase, or from the function management units, in the Automotivecases. One interviewee (T-APO-1) pointed out that it is hard to break down the requirements such that they carry user value, a challenge also recognized in other cases (Automotive1 and Technology1).

ii. Unable to Express Value in User Stories

Due to complexity of systems it is hard to write user stories that can be addressed by one team in one sprint and at the same time relate to value that could be recognized by a user/customer. User stories provide a fast means to share knowledge both on a high and a low level in an agile system development. In the Telecomas well as in the two Automotivecases, user stories are used for two purposes:

... so there are user stories that of course take the view from the end customer and describe what the end customer wants from our system and why. But then there are other user stories that are more like work descriptions of what the team should achieve and those could be like internal things that need to be developed in order to keep the architecture constrained. — T-SysM

A Function Owner in Automotive2 specifically expressed that high-level user stories could help to communicate value early. However, it is particularly difficult to write user stories that have direct value for the user. Such user stories would typically be too large to be completed and demonstrated in one sprint. Yet, breaking it into more user stories or more detailed requirements could deteriorate requirements quality since not enough effort goes into maintaining the requirements. This also creates traceability challenges, as it is hard to understand which high-level user story can be traced to detailed requirements. We discuss traceability further in challenge *C3.c Creating and maintaining traces*. In summary, user stories are hard to write at the scale and complexity of the cases in our study, yet they offer a unique opportunity to bridge distances between customer and developer.

iii. Feedback and Clarification

Our teams suffer from long feedback cycles, which are a consequence of (a) dependence on slow hardware development/deployment, (b) customers not being agile, (c) large numbers of stakeholders. In several companies, study participants raised the issue of long or complicated feedback cycles. At Automotive1, one study participant named *slow mechanical or hardware development* as one of the main reasons for long feedback cycles. If software has to be tested together with actual hardware, feedback on software functionality is postponed until the hardware is ready. One study participant stated a second reason — often *customers are not agile* and take a long time to try out and approve new features. By the time feedback then reaches the agile teams, they are already working on another part of the product and do not remember exactly what the feedback is about. That is, for the teams the feedback comes too late, while customers do not see value in giving quick and frequent feedback, even on smaller increments. This challenge is especially encountered if the system under development is supposed to be integrated into a larger system at the customer site, as for example in the Telecomand Technologycases. A third reason for complicated feedback cycles is that there is a *large number of stakeholders*, both external and internal. Due to the complex nature and the scale of the products developed by our case companies, there is rarely a single customer. Instead, requirements inflow occurs from many different sources, e.g., customers, authorities, managing subcontractors and sourcing, or standardization organizations. In many cases, requirements need to be discussed with and communicated to other stakeholders within or outside the organization, delaying feedback.

Potential Solution

In our view, the root cause of these challenges relates to size and complexity of the systems we investigated. In such large-scale systems, customers and end-users cannot easily relate or give feedback on things developers work on.

In our workshops and focus groups, participating companies brought up potential solutions. Many of these relate to facilitating discussion and communication, which could for example be supported through better visualization of requirements (Technology1) or by investing into teams to focus on customer value every sprint (Telecom). Further, the companies suggested that handovers should be reduced, e.g., by introducing cross-functional teams that span traditional levels of abstraction (FG-1 and FG-5) or by keeping the product management close to development teams (ProcWS).

Common frameworks for large-scale agile, such as SAFe® [248] and LeSS [264], focus on customer-value and offer advice that relates to our challenges. SAFe® generally suggests frequent (train) demos as well as to involve customers on every level [248]. Similarly, LeSS recommends organizations to be customer-centric [264]. While we agree with this advice, we suggest that more concrete support must be provided in the light of our challenges. If work provided by an individual team does not clearly relate to a feature for which a customer could care, it will be hard to demo or to involve customers in decisions.

In line with Lean Software Development, SAFe® also suggests that teams take an economic view, which, if sufficiently supported within an organization can help [248, 264]. In addition, SAFe® suggests that teams should cover all necessary roles [248], which might help, but could also be problematic, since the inter-disciplinary nature of large-scale system development may lead to a large number of necessary roles. LeSS offers Sprint-review bazars [264], which might offer teams an opportunity to practice relating their work to customer-value. Other than that, LeSS suggests to rely on product owners to connect teams and customers [264], but does not share concrete advice or tools for product owners to navigate the challenges we bring up.

10.5.1.2 C1.b: Building Long-Lasting Customer Knowledge

C1.b: In complex product families and large stakeholder landscapes, it is hard to maintain reusable knowledge about customers. Thus, each change could result in repeated efforts to acquire similar information from customers.

Even if the challenges related to feedback and clarification can be addressed, gained knowledge must be effectively managed, as pointed out by participants in FG-5 and FG-3.

> The teams have a lot of tacit knowledge, which is not available beyond their scope. But how much ceremony should we force on teams? — FG 3

Even beyond designing a single system, knowledge about customers and their needs should be maintained for future projects. Without a good knowledge management approach, this can collide with the desire to allow empowered component teams to make fast, local decisions. Two aspects of this knowledge management challenge were raised: First, it is unclear where knowledge about a specific customer can be managed beyond the team and current project. Second, in continuous product development, teams might not realize that they have valuable knowledge for other parts of the system development, while those other parts do not know that valuable knowledge is available.

Potential Solution

Both, SAFe® and LeSS focus on short lead-times. It appears that long-term knowledge is mainly captured as (automated) tests and in the product itself, but also maintained within the agile organization. To this end, we find discussions about component and feature teams within the SAFe® community insightful. In particular, the community indicates a slight preference towards feature teams [269].

In contrast, component teams can maintain long-term knowledge about which features their component supports and how this is providing customer value. However, problem-based customer or end-user requirements must be translated into requirements that a particular component should fulfill. This additional indirection is likely to increase the team-customer gap.

We did not find relevant practices specifically for building long-lasting customer knowledge in LeSS. Our participating companies could not provide further potential solutions beyond the use of feature or component teams.

10.5.2 Support Change and Evolution

10.5.2.1 C2.a: Managing Experimental Requirements

> C2.a: When exploring new functionality or product ideas, experimental requirements need to be treated differently from stable requirements. Still, they need to be captured and potentially integrated in the system view at a later time.

Organizations that develop large, complex products have often established significant research and pre-development operations as part of traditional systems engineering. When changing to an agile organization of system development, it is not clear where such activities (which can easily span a year) fit in. Should a particular cross-functional team research, create a prototype, and then develop a specific system function? This does not likely fit well into an agile iteration and release rhythm. Should a specialized market/research department do such activities? This would introduce hand-overs, often including comprehensive documentation, which would appear un-agile.

On the scale of typical system functions or user-visible features, research and pre-development also asks for explicit support for managing experimental requirements. That is, given a current state of the system requirements, it should be able to create a variant, exploring what-if scenarios and identifying potential changes to the overall requirements model that a specific new function or feature might entail. Given the scale of products and their features, it is clear that the current state of the system requirements will evolve during such research and pre-development activities. Thus, our case companies were raising the need to create, synchronize and merge variants of the system requirements.

Potential Solution

In our workshops, participants were considering to introduce specific sprints for learning and increment planning. It seems generally more promising to broaden the views of team-members and allow them to participate in such activities, and by this to reduce hand-overs. With respect to the actual managing of variants, there was a suggestion to manage requirements as part of the product. T-Reqs, a specific solution that we explored, considers to maintain (textual) system requirement in the same repository as tests and source code [249]. This allows to rely on powerful support for branching and merging that modern source control systems such as git provide.

SAFe® proposes some mechanisms that can support the management of experimental requirements, e.g. by relying on enabler stories, architecture, and exploration [248, p. 108]. Further, set-based design allows to some extent to reason about different alternatives during the development flow [248, p. 178]. Input from exploration, research, and pre-development can also be managed as *(variable) solution intents* [248, p. 186ff].

LeSS, in contrast, appears to suggest that this complex topic can be handled using a backlog [264].

In summary, we identify encouraging building blocks for solving the challenge of managing experimental requirements, but have to note that combining them into a convincing strategy remains non-trivial.

10.5.2.2 C2.b: Synchronization of Development

> C2.b: In large organizations, there exists a large variety of stakeholders, teams, projects and features. This variety makes it challenging to synchronize development between teams. A trade-off arises between documenting extensively and specializing teams to take ownership of a single feature or system aspect.

In many of our case companies, teams receive requirements from the product managers through several organizational levels. Furthermore, they often need to exchange information with other teams to synchronize the development. This process of channeling the 'right' information towards and between teams is difficult and time-consuming. Hence, it limits agility and speed of teams.

FG-2 participants wondered whether agile should be limited to the development only, or should start from a feature request. In the former case, developers would receive feature requests in the form of already broken down requirements for implementation. In the latter case, developers would have to do the breakdown of a feature request into smaller units themselves. While both cases seem to be feasible, the question is how teams can be synchronized in any of these cases, especially at scale, where some form of decomposition is required. If requirements are broken down by an external role or team, possibly in a plan-driven way, they can be handed to different agile teams and their work needs to be synchronized. If they are broken down and implemented within one team, multiple agile teams only need to synchronize when there is interaction with or dependencies to features developed by other teams. However, analysis of a user-visible feature with respect to its implications and suitable decomposition takes time and it is not clear how this work can be fit into the tight sprint schedule of agile teams. Awareness about such dependencies is a pre-requisite.

Potential Solution

As described above, our company partners suggest different levels of agile pervasiveness as a way to address this issue, although different choices have different tradeoffs. SAFe® suggests to provide such synchronisation through bi-weekly synchronisation of agile release trains (ART, a set of agile teams that work together towards a shared release schedule) [248]. This is further supported through enabler stories for exploration [248, p.108].

With respect to organizing such synchronisation, SAFe® also suggests tribes (i.e. organizational units of around 100 members in a common scope, such as an ART), chapters (i.e. communities of practices, that can discuss cross-cutting concerns within a tribe), and guilds (allowing to discuss cross-cutting concerns beyond the scope of a single ART or tribe) [64, p.46]. We believe that such structures provide good support for synchronisation of development, mainly however for discussing methods and processes. It remains an open question whether for example a safety or performance guild could also provide value to discuss cross-cutting requirements. Further, the unity hour, a regular meeting meant to bring together a tribe [64, p.33], can be used to make announcements that can foster synchronisation between teams.

LeSS is comparably brief on the synchronisation of development, but suggests aiming for continuous improvement based on reflection, both on team level and overall [264, p.69].

10.5.2.3 C2.c: Avoid Re-specifying, Encourage Re-use

C2.c: Focusing on projects discourages re-use between projects. Defining a strategy to manage existing requirements and encourage their re-use across projects is challenging.

Our company partners have indicated that dealing effectively with legacy systems is becoming more important. Previous approaches which focused on projects instead of products or components lead to re-inventing common requirements. Several of our companies are searching for ways to reuse existing requirements, e.g., beyond copy and paste (Processing). One participant company with a shared requirements database indicated that reusing requirements was still a challenge, as reusing requires a general knowledge of existing features – in order to reuse, one needs to know what is there. Currently, requirements reuse only happens on the lowest levels.

Requirements reuse also potentially involves some level of governance. On one hand, it may be desirable to avoid duplicate or very similar requirements in the repository (e.g., for different projects or products), but on the other hand agile teams want freedom and autonomy in their practices.

Potential Solution

In our workshops, we explored two different approaches to facilitate re-use of requirements: product line engineering and shifting from a project focus to a product focus. While the former approach would aim to group requirements into customer-visible and reuse-oriented features directly linked to existing solutions and components, the latter would bundle key requirements into a core product that can be maintained over longer time.

It appears that both SAFe® and LeSS are assuming a product-focused organization. In such a context, set-based design could facilitate reuse [248, p.75,190]. LeSS suggests to avoid duplicate product functionality as well as a narrow product definition, which could to some extent remove the need to reuse requirements [264, p.159].

Despite these recommendations, SAFe® and LeSS do not go into detail or emphasize systematic reuse in large-scale agile projects.

10.5.2.4 C2.d: Updating Requirements

C2.d: Requirements can be defined at the beginning of the sprint, but often these requirements become out of date, and no longer reflect the solution. This causes issues in organizational memory. It is challenging to understand when and who should update requirements.

In TechWS, the company explained that their requirements and feature models are often old and not up to date. Requirements are not being updated, in part due to the nature of agile work, which does not explicitly factor in activities for keeping requirements up-to-date. This issue was echoed by Telecomand Manufacturing, in the latter case requirements are defined at the beginning of the sprint, but then kept the same; however, the company would like to enable more flexible requirements updates. In the Telecomcase, non-functional requirements are kept in a document originating from before the agile transformation took place and for which there is no obvious way of providing regular updates. In the short term, this works, as these requirements are relatively stable; however, it is not clear within their current processes how to deal with this document becoming slowly out of date. From an agile perspective, perhaps the requirements only serve to get the development started, and it is therefore not important to keep them up to date with the eventual product. However, the overall problem is that having out-of-date requirements can cause confusion, discourage requirements reuse, and prevents companies from using requirements as a form organizational memory, a practice which we found desirable in our subject companies.

Potential Solution

LeSS acknowledges that requirements areas have a lifecycle in which they will change, get less important, or are retired [264, p.105]. This clearly shows that the problem is known, yet there is a lack of concrete guidance on how to do this. We believe that guilds and chapters in SAFe® could be useful for bringing together interested parties in a platform that could make decisions about updates of cross-cutting requirements [64, p.46].

Still, we are surprised about the lack of explicit mechanisms for updating or changing requirements in large-scale agile frameworks. It suggests that epics and user stories do not provide value beyond planning the next releases and that updates from the agile teams (such as hidden dependencies or costs) are irrelevant for updating such planning as well as that no other requirements-related information (beyond for example tests) should be shared between teams. Neither of these suggestions match our data.

One suggestion from our focus groups is again based on T-Reqs, a system that allows cross-functional teams to manage system requirements together with source code and tests in a version control system [249]. T-Reqs allows all teams to update requirements via git and relies on gerrit for peer-reviews, which not only allows to check a team's suggestion for updating or deprecating requirements, but also to share information about such updates with peers. Thus, requirements could be updated or deprecated based on knowledge generated during agile sprints. Note the strong relationship to C4.c *Tooling not fit for purpose*

10.5.3 Build and Maintain Shared Understanding About System

While the C1 challenges focus on building and maintaining shared knowledge of the customer value, these challenges focus on building and maintaining knowledge about the system, a more internal view.

10.5.3.1 C3.a: Documentation to Complement Tests and Stories

> C3.a: For complex systems, user stories and test cases are often insufficient to understand the overall functionality. It is challenging to complement these artifacts with appropriate but yet agile documentation of requirements that provides this understanding.

The idea of using test cases both as actual test artifacts and as requirements documentation is wide-spread in the agile community [321] and was also discussed by several participants. While this was seen as a potential way to reduce documentation effort, several issues with this approach were brought up. According to several study participants, test cases do not carry enough information to serve as a means of documentation:

Tests are written in a pragmatic way. They do not capture the 'why'. — Tec-SRR

Other interviewees throughout the companies added that one would need a number of tests to document any significant requirement, which will then be hard to reconstruct from just reading the tests during maintenance.

Several participants saw similar problems with user stories, as they would only reflect single scenarios. The overall system behavior would then emerge from the synthesis of all these single scenarios. To derive this full picture from tests or user stories only would, however, be too difficult:

If we don't specify this kind of complete [requirements] specification, we could try to use all [..] user stories [..]. But then we must base the understanding on [..] lets say [..] 2000 user stories [..] and try to find a good way of describing the complete system. — T-SysM

It is interesting to note that this challenge surfaces early on, i.e., when an incoming customer request is analyzed. Therefore, if agile teams only develop backlog items based on finished requirements that they receive from other parts of the organization, they might not be aware of this challenge and therefore wrongly consider user stories complemented by test cases to be sufficient.

While in the Telecomcase the issue of understanding system behavior from user stories or tests was mainly discussed with respect to new features, participants in Automotive1 raised this issue especially for system maintenance. FG-2 participants agreed that user stories or test cases would not be appropriate to understand the behavior. They were unsure what form of documentation should be used instead, which level of detail the requirements should be on, and how they could be different from 'traditional' requirements.

Potential Solution

With respect to complementing user stories and tests, the focus groups yielded suggestions relating to two areas: modeling customer-value (see C1.a *Bridge gap to customer* and C1.b *Building lasting customer knowledge*) and modeling (distributed) system behaviour. With respect to the latter, the reasoning is that teams could use models to explicitly describe the intended behaviour of their solutions. However, some of the same challenges with traditional large-scale requirements documents could arise with models, e.g., scalability, and modifiability.

Furthermore, we note that several companies create additional custom requirements documentation to supplement tests and stories. For example, Telecomcreates a one-slide description of a feature, giving a high-level view, and then traces this description down to requirements.

SAFe® provides suggestions to model both interfaces and behaviours to account for their importance. There have also been further suggestions in the large-scale agile literature to use models to analyze requirements [269, pg. 356], however, it is not exactly clear how these models will relate to the requirements information model suggested in SAFe® .

We did not identify artifacts to potentially complement tests and user stories in LeSS. In contrast, the focus on specification by example and acceptance test driven development seems to suggest that such a complement is not anticipated in LeSS.

To summarize, modeling in an agile manner is one possibility to supplement the description of overall system functionality provided by user stories and test cases. Other forms of lightweight textual summaries can also be possible.

10.5.3.2 C3.b: System vs Component Thinking

> C3.b: It is hard to balance system versus component versus feature thinking in complex system development with multiple teams.

Teams typically have specialized knowledge for their scope. However, they may lack the overall system knowledge. This can be problematic when developing a feature in a complex product, as several components might be affected. Our companies had different types of agile software development teams. Some companies relied mainly on component teams, who become experts for their component, but do not necessarily understand all features that are supported by their component or the implications of their design decisions on the overall system. Thus, when reasoning about the quality of a component, teams might sub-optimize with regard to the overall system. Other companies relied mainly on feature teams, which might find an elegant way of implementing a new feature. Such feature teams struggle however to monitor the evolution of all affected components as well as their quality. Often, we even find a mixture of feature and component teams in complex systems, where some of the more sophisticated components are maintained and developed by dedicated teams.

Overall, we find it is challenging to provide teams with system-level knowledge while at the same time maintaining specialized knowledge about features or components in the teams.

Potential Solution

In our focus groups, Automotive2 sees a clear need for a global baseline that allows to reason about the full system. In large system development, requirements can be seen as a way to put tasks on specific sub-organizations. Automotive2 reported that this is not beneficial. Instead, requirements should be split with respect to the product while all parts of the organization should be encouraged to also monitor requirements for the full system, not only for their component. Processingfurther suggested that these ideas should be complemented by a clear model of ownership of requirements on all levels.

System thinking on all levels could, according to our focus groups, be facilitated by placing architects in teams and to take special care with respect to the architectural runway, when planning architectural enablers. Our companies saw the need for active governance of APIs, dependencies, and interfaces between teams, and to manage volatile architectural concepts differently from those that are stable.

It is one strength of SAFe® to provide a clear breakdown hierarchy from enterprise level to teams [248], which, when combined with awareness on how each part fits in the complete picture, could discourage localized thinking. SAFe® does promote system thinking [248, pg. 70f], [264, pg. 12], yet it is hard to deduct from the textbooks on how such thinking will emerge.

It is interesting to look at the discussion of feature or component teams [269], particularly from the perspective of this challenge (systems vs. component-thinking). Clearly, a feature team will find it easier to think about the system and how it relates to a particular feature. Yet, their goal will be primarily to implement the feature. The long-term quality of the different components as well as their role for the overall system is not their main concern. One of the more concrete suggestions with respect to SAFe® is to strive for tribal unity and use regular release train level meetings for communicating the vision [64, pg. 78,83].

Similarly, also LeSS emphasizes the importance of whole product focus [264, pg. 11,78], which is partially provided by multi-team product backlog refinement and the engagement of the product owner with the team to facilitate ownership of the product.

10.5.3.3 C3.c: Creating and Maintaining Traces

> C3.c: Traces are valuable and often required, but rarely provide a direct value to their creators. Thus, they are typically produced inefficiently post-development and not maintained. It is challenging to incentivize the creation and maintenance of trace links.

In several of our companies, we see the existence of both textual requirements and user stories, where requirements are produced in a plan-driven way and provided to teams or organizations, who then create user stories to work locally in an agile way. However, since user stories relate directly to feature implementation they are not always systematically derived from existing requirements. Thus, direct tracing is not always possible.

A similar situation occurs in Automotive2, where product owners write user stories based on plan-driven requirements they receive as an input. These user stories can in fact be rather local development tasks and backlog items that do not require tracing to system requirements. Thus, traces are not systematically managed, which can lead to additional work in cases where such backlog items become relevant for tracing to system requirements. The fact that often only the product owner is aware of which user stories originate from which requirements can slow down collaboration between agile teams and plan-driven RE teams. Interviewees in the agile teams considered tracing user stories to requirements to be documentation, which should not be part of the agile process. Instead they preferred to spend their time on implementation:

> I don't think traceability is not required or something like that. It's just that my focus hasn't been on documenting the function. I just focus on doing implementation and developing the function. — A2-PO

This view was also shared in Automotive1: while participants stated that tracing is valuable, or even required by standards, they felt that right now there is not enough incentive for agile developers to create traces. They wished for an incentive or directly visible benefit for the developers as well as for simplifying trace creation.

Potential Solution

In our focus groups, most focus was on how to reduce the workload related to tracing. One way of doing this could be through a better approach to reuse, where complete features (equal to a group of requirements) are seen as reusable modules, consisting both of reusable requirements (with adequate tracing) and reusable solutions. By moving from project to (long-term) product focus, such reuse could further be facilitated, and agile teams would find themselves integrating existing requirements with strong traceability.

For system engineering companies, it is slightly concerning how little scaled agile frameworks discuss tracing. SAFe® suggests to describe the solution, which will likely result in technical documentation with rich trace links [248, pg. 184ff]. LeSS suggests to link to wiki pages for additional information [264, pg. 33], as well as to suggest to link backlog items to ancestors for maximum three levels [264, pg. 204,222], but does not offer rich details on how and by whom such links are maintained.

10.5.3.4 C3.d: Learning and Long-Term Knowledge

> C3.d: Due to their long lifetime, product families require knowledge to be built up and maintained over longer periods of time and across products. It is challenging to optimize an organization towards generating and maintaining this knowledge, both on system level and on team level.

In the Tech1WS, the company expressed that agile is needed at the beginning of development, but later the need shifts to knowledge management, in part to support the learning of future personnel and other teams. Often requirements management is an activity that is performed at the end of the sprint. Technology1, Manufacturing, and Processingexpressed that spreading knowledge and networking knowledge was a challenge, it is not clear for them how to synchronize knowledge across different teams working in different cycles or on different projects. In the ManWS, the participants discussed the use of specialists to share knowledge (e.g., a specialist in security), but decided that this was not the most effective solution in practice, as often the specialists ended up being rare, and working in too many different contexts.

TelWS brought up the challenging trade-off between feature ownership and documentation. If a feature is strongly owned by an individual or team, it does not need extensive documentation; however, others are then dependent on the team or product owner for anything to do with that feature, and this places the company in a dangerous position in the case of personnel turnover, where important, non-documented knowledge is lost.

Potential Solution

Although turnover is a problem, one solution offered by Telecomis to exploit ownership of features and tools to document less. One way to mitigate personnel loss would be to support ownership by teams rather than individuals.

According to SAFe® , agile release trains should focus on value, not on projects [248]. Thus, knowledge about value for customers can be maintained in such release trains without additional documentation, even with normal amounts of staff turnover. SAFe® also proposes the use of feature or component teams [269]. SAFe® recommends supporting communities of practice, helping to share information in particular areas [248]. The creation of chapters or guilds has also been proposed [64] as a way to support and share specific topical knowledge. LeSS proposes something similar, encouraging experts to teach each other, and to create informal networks.

In addition, SAFe® introduces the idea of enabler stories, user stories that are explicitly aimed for exploration. This allows teams to learn about a particular topic and explore feasibility [248, pg. 108]. LeSS promotes a similar practice by discussing reflection and encouraging improvement experiments [264, p. 7,20]. As a form of learning, LeSS also recommends specification by example, using concrete examples instead of more abstract user stories [264, p.3,254].

10.5.3.5 C3.e: Backward Compatibility

> C3.e: As a part of the maintained product knowledge, teams need to be aware of compatibility issues. In particular, as part of an agile way of working, it is challenging to maintain the knowledge of backwards compatibility as part of the requirements across different products and product versions of a product family.

Several of our companies have indicated the importance of backwards compatibility, particularly for customers.

> But also we use them (detailed requirements) for regression result, to make sure have we . . . its very important for our customers that we don't change backward compatibility, we don't change the behaviour without notifying our customers. — T-APO

In some ways, using an agile way of working makes the preservation of backwards compatibility easier, as developers are given the freedom to handle changes in a way in which compatibility is not broken. However, in cases where the developer does not have this knowledge, if it is not somehow also captured via the requirements, compatibility may be broken

> For me the part of being agile here is that we don't define it (compatibility) on the highest level and just say you never break backward stability but you handle the changes. And of course you can only tolerate (this) to a certain degree. At some point it breaks legacy and then it goes to a level (where) we cannot release software anymore. You need to make sure that doesn't happen. — T-OPO

Potential Solution

We have not found suggestions from the companies for this challenge as part of our interviews or focus groups. Although agility in general can help, the companies are lacking methods to capture backwards compatibility at a higher-level of abstraction, as captured by requirements. Furthermore, we find no potential solutions in SAFe® /LeSS to address backward compatibility issues.

10.5.4 Representation of Requirements Knowledge

While the C3 challenges focus on internal understanding, the C4 challenges focus on how this knowledge can be effectively captured, managed and accessed.

10.5.4.1 C4.a: Manage Levels vs. Decomposition

> In an agile environment, it is hard to map requirements to levels of decomposition. Classic levels (stakeholder, system, system element) do not fit with an agile way of working, since stakeholders can define low-level requirements. Yet the complexity of the software calls for some form of decomposition.

In Tech1WS, the participants explained that requirements from the customer express needs, and are very different from system requirements, which express elements of a solution. This company very much wants stakeholder requirements, they want to always define the problem before the solution, but customers sometimes provide them with detailed solutions instead of describing their problem. Although one can consider this a rather classical requirements problem, it is exacerbated by agility, which discourages many levels of requirements, and does not distinguish between different types of requirements.

In the ProcWS, we covered challenges in consistently breaking down requirements, particularly non-functional requirements, and expressed the need for more levels of classification. They made the point that breaking down requirements is very much experience-based, and is part of the process of building knowledge. Along the same lines, Manufacturingexpressed the problem that requirements are often in the form of system requirements, focusing on a technical thing, and the real customer problem behind this requirement may be lost. They also echoed the challenge that those who describe problems (sales, customers) often have solutions in mind, meaning that the problem may not be captured. Telecomreported something similar, that although they have a means to capture the motivation behind requirements via a one-page slide, sometimes this step is skipped. Often their user stories (despite the name) tend to be more technically focused, and the user value is only implicit.

Potential Solution

One potential solution offered by Technology1 is to allow stakeholders to specify requirements on any level of abstraction, but then use matching between levels to match details to motivations, or point out missing requirements at one level. They also suggest to support distributed requirements analysis, so that stakeholder with different expertise (e.g., problem, solution) can contribute. Traceability was offered as a solution by both Processingand Technology2, allowing for a requirements structure linked via traceability, bearing similarity to the suggestion above.

Automotive2 emphasized the importance of the interplay between requirements and architecture. They suggested to distinguish dimensioning functional requirements (e.g. in form of use cases) and quality attributes and to use both separately as input for a suitable architectural decomposition. As is common practice with quality attributes and quality scenarios, such dimensioning functional requirements would be carefully chosen early on as typical representatives and could be used to reason whether a given architecture is suitable to support such functionality, thus functioning as a blue print for architectural decomposition.

SAFe® suggests having a clear hierarchy of people and roles, from enterprise level to team [248, p.70], complemented by a hierarchical view of requirements in four levels, from epics to capabilities to features to user stories that corresponds to this clear hierarchy [248, p.177-6,104-109]. Based on this hierarchy and requirements information model, SAFe® advises to transport the stakeholder view to components across potential hierarchies [269]. LeSS also provides various splitting and refinement guides using requirement areas, major areas of customer concern, where each area has its own backlog and feature teams [264, p.30]. LeSS advises for traceability of certain items (e.g., product backlog items have requirement area attributes which trace to their associated area) [264, p.216]. However, they advise splitting requirements only to three levels [264, p.222].

Overall, we see potential solutions from both industry and the literature; however, although recommendations are given for limited refinement and traceability, this issue of customer vs. system requirements is not deeply addressed. It seems SAFe® and LeSS may advise to avoid purely system requirements with no links to customer rationale, which does not appear to be good advice for our case companies.

10.5.4.2 C4.b: Quality Requirements as Thresholds

> Often quality targets are within a range. Negotiation of cost-value trade-off is difficult to capture and manage with current representations.

As agile methods recommend various levels of user stories, Tech1WS reported issues with using such presentations for quantitative quality requirements trade-offs. For them, quality requirements are thresholds, and it often takes a lot of time to quantify thresholds for requirements, leaving 'TBD' in the meantime. The systems and representations the company has now are not capable of dealing with these type of thresholds, and they default to a single hard target for requirements. There is also a need for guidance in how to find these boundaries, a process as part of requirements specification. Other companies confirm this challenge.

Potential Solution

The companies offered a few solutions to this challenge. For example, Tele-comdiscusses trade-offs when they are brought up by a team, and these trade-offs are peer-reviewed among teams and system managers in gerrit (a code collaboration tool). Technology1 emphasised that thresholds for quality requirements can be a good way to indicate and moderate price negotiations between different development partners.

In SAFe® , non-functional requirements[4] are constraints on a program level, constraining the backlogs at every level (system, feature, team) [269, p.77,79]. We find no potential solution in LeSS to help with quality requirements.

Overall, one can argue that this issue may occur also in a non-agile context, but use of user stories makes solving this issue more challenging, and current scaled agile frameworks do not offer any specific solutions for it.

10.5.4.3 C4.c: Tooling not Fit for Purpose

Tooling plays a significant role in agile processes, but available tools are often not designed to support large-scale agile practices. Part of the problem is access to requirements, as traditionally tools do not allow access to all requirements, but some form of managed access is often needed.

Agile endeavours to empower teams, but it is challenging to determine the scope of this power. Technology1 has expressed a requirements/tooling access challenge where teams rely on requirements they do not have view or edit access to. These requirements are exported outside of the tool to other formats for them to use as inputs to their process. This requires extra effort and results in inconsistent requirements, but the alternative, to let every team access and edit/refine all requirements, would need to be carefully managed both in terms of processes and tools. Often, teams lack expertise and knowledge to modify requirements that they have not worked closely with, even if they are dependent on those requirements, and would like changes.

This brings up a broader challenge related to the need for specialized tools. Automotive1 have described their used of tooling, at the moment they use traditional tools for requirements management (e.g., Doors), and tools that are aimed for agile

---

[4] For our purposes we treat NFRs and quality requirements as the same, a more detailed debate on this is out of our scope.

(e.g., JIRA). However, these tools are largely separated and not designed to fit a large-scale agile process.

Similarly, in Telecom, current tooling was brought up as a hindrance for speed and agility. Interviewees described the current process of updating system requirements as too slow and cumbersome. They stated that by introducing a more efficient tool solution, engineers could potentially be more motivated to make changes to requirements and by this narrow the gap between agile user stories and requirements.

The need of a tool-chain that better supports agile information flows was further confirmed by other companies.

Potential Solution

There are a few solutions to this challenge suggested by industry: Technology2 suggests that only the product owner updates requirements, and all requests must go through them. Tooling should be updated to support this model. This imposes governance, but may create bottlenecks if change requests are frequent. In Automotive1, 2, and Telecom, it is suggested that the team itself takes the main responsibility to update the requirements. This approach removes bottlenecks, but makes governance more difficult and requires strong support from tooling, especially when knowledge of updates needs to be shared across teams and abstraction levels.

SAFe® offers no solutions to this issue. LeSS advices against using software tools for sprint backlogs [264, p. 18, 281], but discusses tooling for large product backlogs such as boards, wikis, pictures and spreadsheets [264, p. 23, 210]. However, the source does not discuss the issue of tool or requirements access.

To summarize, our companies of study are looking for better tooling and more effective requirements access solutions, and while some custom tools show promise, SAFe® and LeSS do not emphasize tooling or discuss access control.

10.5.4.4 C4.d: Accommodate Different Representations

> Individual teams strive to tailor requirements related artifacts to what works best in their context. This however is seemingly in conflict with the system level goal of keeping artifacts consistent and manageable. Companies experience a lack of support for navigating this conflict.

In Tech1WS, the participants expressed frustration with this challenge. On the one hand, specific teams use a variety of different representations for requirements depending on purpose. Word documents are used for quick exchange with external stakeholders, figures, graphs, and models are used to discuss, and teams use them in the way most promising to get the job done. On the other hand, a consistent view on system level needs to be arranged and there are reasons to limit the flexibility in representations. This is partly due to technical reasons (it is easier to store text requirements in a requirements database, see also Challenge 4.c *tooling not fit for purpose* in Sect. 10.5.4.3) and partly due to organizational reasons (system-level planning demands that certain information is easily accessible, it is easier to share a small number of simple formats across a large organization).

This trade-off demands for an approach that allows starting from a consistent requirements model of the full system, quickly draft sketches in arbitrary representations and coordinate between teams and external stakeholders, and then re-integrate any knowledge gained in the consistent requirements model to evaluate it in the context of system or platform variability constraints.

Potential Solution

We did not find potential solutions to this issue from our participating companies as part of current workshops or interviews. SAFe® advocates for teams to have their own individual user story flavor [248], which to some degree supports freedom in using a format that best fits local work. This goes along with SAFe® 's tendency to emphasize team independence, where teams are responsible for their own way of working. However, SAFe® does recommend some sharing of knowledge and practices using book clubs and guilds [64]. We find no potential solutions for different representations of requirements in LeSS.

10.5.4.5 C4.e: Consistent Requirements Quality

> The quality of requirements artifacts (i.e. user stories, backlogs) differs (e.g. level of detail). This makes working with requirements at higher levels, across teams or boundaries, difficult.

Telecomreports that the quality of requirements differs from system to system, or between roles and sites. They find that the quality of user stories also varies, sometimes they are from the perspective of the user, while often they are phrased like a technical task. Technology1 reports similar findings, with backlogs from different teams relating to the same product or platform having very different styles. Processingsimilarly reports that they lack a common way of working with requirements, which means that some teams try to minimize the requirements they write, while other teams try to specify everything, defining similar requirements over and over across projects or backlogs.

Potential Solution

Manufacturingexpresses the importance of experience in operationalizing requirements in an effective way. As such, either skilled personnel or training may be required. Currently, Telecomare exploring supporting requirements reviews using T-Reqs and gerrit.

SAFe® advocates responsibility for Ways of Working, and other practices such as book clubs and guilds [64], potentially sharing knowledge on ways of working with requirements or ideas on requirements quality. Similarly, SAFe® supports the formation of community of practices to align on needs [248, p.25,43,290]. Less offers no potential solution to help with requirements quality. Overall, some practices are suggested by our industry sources and the large-scale agile literature, but the challenge is not yet sufficiently addressed.

10.5.5 Process Aspects

10.5.5.1 C5.a: Prioritization of Distributed Functionality

> The frequency of dependencies in large-scale agile makes prioritization of products or requirements between teams difficult. Bottom-up prioritization is not working well, since teams tend to start with simpler tasks.

In TelWS, participants reported that, before their agile transition, they had spent a lot of time analyzing features that did not end up in the product. They see an improvement on this using a more agile approach. However, a potential drawback brought up at our case companies relates to features that have a scale at which many teams or even several release trains need to be included. Each of these teams or release trains usually has a full backlog and when coordinating functionality, each involved party has their own critical parts to consider.

In ManWS, participants complained that developers often do not take on the highest priority task first, often because they are lacking expertise. When prioritizing their backlog, teams consider which of the tasks they can do in the time available provides most value. A particular complex task may therefore not be touched, since the team considers the time to implement it to be in no good relation to the value they could provide with other tasks. This can be a problem when considering highly complex products. A complex feature then might take a very long time to be deployed, since teams go for "lower hanging fruits" and are unable to consider the cost this delay creates. This becomes a problem, especially if other teams or release trains have already committed to develop their part of the complex feature, as their effort then does not generate business value (since the overall feature is still incomplete).

Simplifying, one could summarize this as: Letting individual teams prioritize (bottom-up prioritization) is not working well, as teams tend to favor simple tasks.

Potential Solution

Although our participating companies have prioritization with coordination as a challenge, they also offer several potential solutions. Manufacturingprioritizes their release backlog based on a business dashboard, including items such as commitments to customer. Automotive2 aims to address this challenge by introducing a clear product owner hierarchy and puts the focus on interfaces instead of requirements. This helps address prioritization as teams can articulate their needs towards other teams and interface issues can be addressed with high priority. Through appropriate architectural decomposition, complex requirements will inform changes on interface definitions and concrete requirements on team level. Processinghas developed a system with some success, prioritizing by risk, and working on the next part with the highest technical risk. They calculate risk via a system design meeting focusing on technical needs. They also have forums with both business and technical experts, focusing on a bidirectional flow between both roles. Technical risks are transferred in technical review meetings, helping awareness.

The large-scale agile frameworks also offer some solutions. SAFe® describes techniques such as combining "weighted shortest job first", "portfolio backlog", and "program kanban" to support cross-cutting initiatives towards prioritization [248, p.65,104,212]. It also advocates the combination of team backlog, business values and an "interaction backlog" [248, p.109,127,137] and sequencing tasks based on the cost of delay [248, p.175]. However, it's not clear how to combine all these suggestions together into one coordinated process. LeSS recommends that one product owner acts as a single source of prioritization, and that a multi-site product backlog review is used to help prioritization across products [264].

Overall, this is a challenge that comes with a lot of potential solutions; however, there is a lack of empirical evidence or proven strategies to inform companies on which approach may work best in a particular context.

10.5.5.2 C5.b: Manage Completeness

> In a large-scale agile context, it is not clear when requirements are complete enough. It is also not clear on what level to judge completeness: per sprint? per product? per system? Which view is the most important for completeness?

The ProcWS participants described their agile transition in relation to requirements completeness goals. Initially, they wanted to have complete requirements, but it was difficult to have an overview. They questioned how many requirements they could manage in a sprint. The ManWS participants expressed similar difficulties with their specification of system control, the requirements could not cover everything, but instead focused on the algorithm and control.

Potential Solution

Generally, for our companies that mentioned this as an issue, the goal of complete requirements was relaxed for something more manageable. SAFe® offers no potential solution, in fact, by advocating building incrementally and producing minimal viable products (MVPs) as principles, SAFe® actually recommends against requirements completeness [248, p.77]. Similarly, LeSS recommends to "take a bite", analyzing and implementing small parts of the problem, forgoing completeness in requirements [264, p.3,202].

Taking an agile mindset, one can argue that requirements completeness should not be a goal; however, at least two of our companies have struggled with this even in an agile context. Even working incrementally, it's not clear how complete or detailed requirements for an increment should be.

10.5.5.3 C5.c: Consistent Requirements Processes

> Different teams create and manage their requirements using different processes, tools and level of detail. Coordination and sharing is difficult.

The TelWS participants indicated that distributed development in different countries with different cultures has made consistency in requirements processes difficult. Some locations are embracing agile, with others still want a more procedural approach with document approval. Processinghas addressed similar frustrations, but with tooling. People are reluctant to stop using common tools like Excel and migrate to modern requirements management tools. The result ranges from full to partial migration, sometimes moving between the tool and Excel, with the Excel version updated more frequently. The problem persists due to usability complaints about the new tool as well as management not enforcing its use. If some migrate and some do not, inconsistency is the result, hampering coordination. Technology1 sees similar tool-related migration and consistency problems. This challenge relates strongly to both Challenge 4.c (requirements quality) and 4.e (tooling).

Potential Solution

Telecomsuggested that requirements consistency could be managed similarly to code and test consistency. Therefore, they aimed for a system were requirements are stored in the same repository as code and test, be consistently updated during sprints, and peer-reviewed to ensure comparability. This would then lead to a more consistent requirements process.

With respect to SAFe® , the recommendation for a clear hierarchy, from the enterprise level to team, may help to promote consistent processes [248, 269]. However, SAFe® also advocates for team independence, with responsibility for their own way of working. Coordination mechanisms like book clubs and guilds can help to share best practices, even given independence between teams [64]. LeSS does not appear to directly address this issue.

Overall, the level of consistency needed between teams is an open question, likely depending on context.

10.5.5.4 C5.d: Quality vs Time-to-Market:

> It is often not clear what quality level (of requirements, products, deliverables) is good enough. It is not clear when to continue improving or when to release, particularly on a large-scale.

Given the aim to shorten time-to-market, answering the question of what is good-enough quality is becoming a challenge for our case companies. This challenge holds for the releases of the actual product, but also for intermediate deliverables, such as requirements. It is one of the agile dogmas that one should not invest time into high-quality specifications of requirements that then might never be implemented. The same holds for products: there is a widely spread idea that it is better to have a first version of the product in the market and then iteratively improve it to achieve good fitness for purpose without overshooting the required quality.

This view however raises practical concerns, especially when embracing agility at scale. Telecomand Automotive2 did indicate that sometimes requirements were not of sufficient quality to allow testing. While in small-scale agile, this could be mitigated through intra-team communication, at large-scale there must be a form of moderation to ensure that lack of information can be articulated and fixed between teams and release trains.

Technology1 indicated a related challenge with respect to releases of products. Obviously, quality comes at a price which could manifest in product cost, time-to-delivery, or a combination of both. However, it is very hard to discuss this with customers, since for large-scale products it is difficult to make customers aware of the price. Thus, when discussing with customers about quantitative quality requirements on systems that include hardware or software components, customers usually strongly demand very high quality, even beyond what they actually need or can afford for a concrete business case.

Often, there is also a reluctance to record a number on quality requirements, as then there is a level of commitment for this number, when agility demands flexibility. Yet, for many qualities, it will be difficult to address them late in the development without careful planning. While for example functionality can be added later, fixing major performance or usability problems late can entail major refactoring and rework. In addition, customer expectations about quality remain rather constant.

Potential Solution

Relying on frequent reviews of requirements as part of sprint deliverables can be a good way to establish a feedback channel about requirements quality and lack of information, as brought up by Telecom. This could help teams to find over time a good balance on providing just enough requirement quality: missing information might delay development, while to elaborate requirements will unnecessarily lengthen time-to-market.

SAFe® advocates for built-in-quality as part of the agile process [248, p.23, 140], and provides guidance for reducing time-to-market through value stream mapping [248, p.298], but does not explicitly address the trade offs between time and quality. We did not identify concrete guidance for this challenge within LeSS.

Generally, there is a trade-off between product quality and time-to-market, for products and releases as well as for deliverables and artifacts needed during development. There is a lack of guidance to balance this trade-off.

10.5.6 Organizational Aspects

10.5.6.1 C6.a: Bridge Plan-Driven and Agile

> It is hard to bridge the gap between plan-driven, document-centric approaches on system level and value-driven, agile approaches on team level. Companies struggle to stay pro-active on system level as well as to leverage knowledge about requirements that is generated on team level.

From a product perspective, a plan-driven or stage-gate approach is important. Release of a new product needs to be planned and longer development cycles for hardware and mechanical components need to be scheduled. All of our case companies have agile software development teams that operate within the context of a larger system engineering process, which one interviewee described as agile islands:

It feels like agile islands in a waterfall. — FG 2

The challenge we found here regardless of agile scope in the specific case is continuous information exchange between plan-driven and agile parts of an organization. Incubation of new innovative ideas, facilitating quick feedback loops, and quick learning on potential business value are important assets to remain competitive, yet they are hard to integrate into the overall system development approach in all our cases.

In the Telecomcase, we found that system managers feel disconnected from the agile teams. Their role is to be experts on a certain part of the system and support teams with their knowledge of the system requirements. However, as one interviewee stated they currently cannot be in contact with all teams and might therefore not get a notification if something has been changed with respect to existing requirements.

> If [..] a team updates a past requirement, perhaps I should get like a notification on that so I can ask them 'Have you forgotten X?'. — T-SysM

Similar challenges exist with the other companies, e.g. in the Automotive2 case where agile teams can add new backlog items or change existing ones in collaboration with the product owner. However, since agile teams do not interact directly with system requirements (see *C3.c creating and maintaining traces*), they do not consider knowledge about them to be of importance. Further, backlog items are easy to understand, even for stakeholders not directly involved, and allow them to share their opinion. While this is generally perceived positively by the interviewees, it was also brought up that this can cause the function owner to be overexposed to change requests. One function owner expressed this as follows.

> The more people look into requirements, the more they read them, the more iterations it will become. [..] there is going to be more opinions, comments and also more work. — A2-FO

As this can lead to inconsistencies between changed and new backlog items and the system requirements, e.g., in the case where a system requirement related to a new user story already existed, increased gate-keeping becomes necessary. This generates effort for backlog grooming by the (agile) product owner, and managing of system requirements by the (plan-driven) function owner. The current separation between both worlds does not seem to be ideal, since product and function owner can easily become bottlenecks, and late resolution of inconsistencies can create additional effort. If the actual implementation deviates from the original requirement or when some requirements are not implemented, this will surface as problems during system integration and testing. Tests are developed against the plan-driven requirements and are therefore in need of an up-to-date version.

> If I have a requirement saying this thing should happen, when I test it, I find out that what is supposed to happen doesn't happen. [..] And then I find out the requirement wasn't updated. So actually the implementation was correct but the requirement isn't matching the implementation. — A2-ST

Further, if the system has to be evolved or maintained in the future, outdated requirements can cause misunderstandings.

Potential Solution

In our focus groups, the governance of requirements between system level planning and agile teams was raised as a key issue. Telecomemphasized that the team should be enabled to update the requirements during sprints, similarly to source code, tests, and documentation. TReqs as a tool solution was again mentioned as potential enabler [249]. In contrast, Technology2 placed the responsibility of updating requirements with the product owner.

While we did not identify related practices in LeSS, we believe that SAFe® offers good advice on governance of requirements and related knowledge across levels in that it provides a clear hierarchy from enterprise level to individual teams [248, 269]. Yet, mastering this part will require significant effort by any company transitioning into agile development, as we found few concrete practices and guidelines in the agile frameworks.

While transitioning from plan-driven to large-scale agile, companies start to rethink the role of systems engineering artifacts. While many of these artifacts (including requirements specifications on various levels) have been static documents, agile development now demands for actively managed artifacts that help with the coordination of agile teams within a plan-driven system engineering organization. We believe that this will be a challenge even for fully agile system development.

10.5.6.2 C6.b: Plan V & V Based on Requirements

In the past, verification and validation (V & V) was planned based on requirements. Now that requirements are inherently incomplete and incremental throughout development, how does one plan for testing? Particularly, it is hard to provide guidelines and traceability, to allocate resources, manage test artifact information for decision making, and align requirements with system tests.

Using the V model, our case companies were used to a tight link between requirements and tests. As the nature of requirements changes, these links must be rethought. However, planning of test activities is still critical, particularly in order to allocate resources (time, hardware, people, etc.), and can be costly. Manufacturinghas indicated that following new agile practices means there is only partial traceability between tests and requirements. High-level artifacts are used to define test guidelines (boundaries on tests); however, these are hard to follow, as for example, a wide range of test oracles needs to be taken into account, which vary from numbers (dimensions or signals) to user action responses. More guidelines are needed in testing. In this company, system engineers are responsible for the V & V strategy, while the project managers, who are more in line with the agile processes, do not do such planning. This gap between agility and the testing team causes challenges.

More generally, this requires to rethink traceability and one has to discuss the different information items in relation to the roles that use them. In our large-scale agile system development cases, we find a very complex picture and it is partially unclear how information items relate and which stakeholder needs could be satisfied through traceability. Several interviewees in the Telecomcase stated that their system requirements work as a documentation of what the system is doing, rather than a plan of what shall be implemented.

> You can't really afford to have this kind of static requirements work upfront which will be a waste anyway when you implement stuff. The way we handle requirements now is more like a system description. — T-TA

Yet, as mentioned before, user stories and tests are not enough (C3.a), thus there is a need to document any assumptions or decisions taken during testing, which can be interpreted as requirements that the system should fulfil from now on.

Potential Solution

Manufacturinghas partially addressed this challenge by establishing virtual test rigs and simulation models, reducing the cost of testing and at the same time making testing infrastructure more directly available to development teams. Telecomsuggested to include system requirements in the same repository as code and tests and to make sure that the same quality assurance mechanisms are applied. Ideally, this ensures that tests and requirements are consistent, as they are modified at the same time, and traced, as they share the same commit as well as explicit trace links.

SAFe® recommends duality in backlog items and tests, and describes solution intents as linking specifications to tests [248, p.187]. Adopting a more cross-functional organization, including testers or system engineers in the agile teams, would also help to alleviate these issues [248, p.97]. LeSS does not offer any specific solution here.

Despite these promising suggestions, the planning of validation and verification remains a huge challenge especially in system engineering and its various disciplines. Empirical evidence about the proposed practices and proven approaches are currently lacking.

10.5.6.3 C6.c: Time for Invention and Planning

> Research activities and exploration are hard to fit into development sprints but offer fundamental information towards requirements.

Study participants in Automotive1 reported that an exploration of solution space is difficult within agile sprints, as it would be impossible to commit to a fixed schedule without deep knowledge about new features. Pre-development is required to better understand the impact of new features. If this is done by a dedicated group, this would imply documentation and hand-over of results and slow down the process. If it were done by the developers the development process would be slowed.

Potential Solution

As a remedy, specific exploration sprints were brought up. Another solution could be to transfer engineers between pre-development and agile system development, so that they can also share their knowledge with team members.

SAFe® again recommends capturing the solution intent, including a repository of current and future solution behaviours [248, p.20]. SAFe® also describes both enabler stories, stories that explicitly support exploration [248, p.108] and iterations dedicated to innovation and planning [248, p.96,154]. LeSS offers no potential solution.

In summary, there is a lack of experience or evidence with respect to the proposed practices. For a company transitioning towards large-scale agile, this challenge requires careful scoping of agility within system development.

10.5.6.4 C6.d: Impact on Infrastructure

> When neglecting upfront analysis, the impact on infrastructure might become obvious too late. Then, updating infrastructure (e.g., improving labs for testing) increases cycle time and time-to-market.

In system development, integration testing often depends on a strong laboratory setup that allows testing hardware, software, and potentially mechanics together. Although this relates to challenge C6.b, required infrastructure changes may go beyond testing infrastructure. While a new feature might mainly depend on changes of software and can be provided in an incremental, fast-paced way, it could require an update of the test environment, which may include sophisticated hardware and environment models. However, changing the test environment might take as long as finishing the software components, thus introducing delays, if not started in due time. Similar concerns relate to other infrastructure for continuous integration, delivery, and deployment.

Potential Solution

From a testing prospective, as mentioned in C6.b, companies can make use of virtual test rigs and simulation models to avoid physical infrastructure changes. Peer-reviewing of requirements can raise awareness about potential impact on infrastructure early on.

SAFe® recommends having a cross-functional organization, which can help teams to understand the wider impact of their features and changes, including impact on infrastructure [248, p.97]. We do not find a potential solution in LeSS.

This challenge shows that independent of the pervasiveness in Fig. 10.3, there is a need to maintain a system-level perspective beyond self-organized teams and to allow requirements related information to escalate to this level as early as possible.

10.6 Discussion and Implications

Table 10.3 Summary of results for Challenge Area 1: Build and maintain shared understanding of customer value

ID Challenge	Proposed practices from case companies	Proposed practices from SAFe	Proposed practices from LeSS	Research gap in large-scale agile
1.a Bridge gap to customer	→Visualization of requirements to facilitate discussion; →Reduce handovers, XFTs across levels; →Keep product management close; →Focus on value every sprint.	→Frequent (train) demos; →Customer involved at every level; →Teams take economic view; →Team covers all necessary roles.	→Customer-centric; →Sprint-Review bazaar; →PO connects teams / customer	→Provide concrete advice and tools for establishing, managing, and validating shared understanding of customer value.
1.b Building long-lasting customer knowledge	-	→Feature teams; →Component teams.	-	→Research gap similar to 1.a, but with long-term memory in mind.

Even though the seven cases differ in their context, i.e., domain and pervasiveness of agile methods within system development, we found common concerns and challenges with respect to RE. As our investigation reveals, systems companies face severe challenges that are not sufficiently covered by common large-scale agile frameworks. Generally this suggests that in order to yield their full benefits, agile practices must be combined with a sufficiently strong mechanism to manage requirements and related knowledge. We found challenges in six different areas and while we could derive potential solutions from data collected with our case companies as well as from our analysis of agile frameworks, we see a significant need for future research. We will discuss each of the challenge areas and their implications for future research in the following.

10.6.1 Build and Maintain Shared Understanding of Customer Value

Managing customer value is usually assumed to be the core strengths of agile approaches and we identified potential solutions both in LeSS and SAFe® . Yet, we found in all our case companies that the distance between the customers and the development is perceived to be too large (summarized in Table 10.3). In particular, it was described as difficult to break down a feature request into small packages that both have customer value and can be delivered in small iterations. However, agile values such as individuals and interactions [113] as well as agile practices such as continuous delivery [231] depend on a good notion of value. Yet, we found this particularly hard to establish in large-scale system development, because of unclear customer role and scale. The customer role is often unclear, since development teams do not only need to produce value to external customers, but also to other roles within the company, e.g., in order to prepare for maintenance.

In case of an external customer, any customer-visible feature will imply more work than can be done within one sprint or by one team, at the scale of our case companies. This makes feature decomposition necessary and it is impossible for a single team to demonstrate customer value at the end of a typical sprint. Related work in this direction has, in particular, pointed out challenges with the practice of customer representatives [175, 203, 368], but it seems that the notion of value itself is problematic and a shared language for discussing value is needed [192, 231, 238] as well as approaches to systematically enable, build, and assess shared understanding [28]. Without those concepts, our case companies struggle to establish, manage, and validate a shared understanding of customer value throughout the development organization and we see the need for future research to address these challenges.

10.6.2 Support Change and Evolution

As summarized in Table 10.4, our results indicate that sufficient facilities for updating system requirements based on agile learning are currently missing affecting managing experimental requirements, synchronizing development, re-using requirements, and managing the lifecycle of requirements. Thus, such updates are a result of manual work, leading to inconsistencies, which are expensive to remove and can be considered waste in the overall development process. In addition, developers have little intrinsic motivation to update requirements models based on updates to user stories, as they are not part of their delivery (usually code and tests). If, however, requirements updates were not propagated, the system requirements view

Table 10.4 Summary of results for Challenge Area 2: Support change and evolution

ID Challenge	Proposed practices from case companies	Proposed practices from SAFe	Proposed practices from LeSS	Research gap in large-scale agile
2.a Managing experimental requirements	→Introduce Learning and increment planning Sprints; →T-Reqs: Use git branching and merging.	→Combine enabler stories, architecture, and exploration; →Set-based design; →(Variable) solution intent.	→Use backlog	→Design and evaluate an approach to manage experimental requirements.
2.b Synchronization of development	→Differing levels of agile pervasiveness	→Biweekly ART sync; →F2f PI planning; →Enabler stories (Exploration); →Tribes, chapters, guilds; →Unity hour	→Continuous improvement; →Retrospectives (Team+overall).	→Design and evaluate an approach to synchronize development based on promising ideas in literature.
2.c Avoid re-specifying encourage re-use	→Product-line engineering; →Move from project to product focus.	→Product-focused; →Set based design.	→Product-focused; →Avoid duplicate product functionality; →Avoid narrow product definition.	→Strategies and guidance for systematic reuse and agile product-line engineering at scale.
2.d Updating requirements	→T-Reqs: Reviews supported by git and gerrit.	→Guilds and chapters.	→Requirement areas will change, will get less important, have a lifecycle, be retired.	→Provide concrete advice and tools for updating requirements and to establish awareness of the current state.

would become quickly obsolete and detached from the real system. Consequently, roles responsible for customer and high-level system requirements (product owners, function owners, system managers) fear a loss of important knowledge for later maintenance of the systems. A more systematic approach to manage requirements updates received from agile teams would make their jobs much easier.

We believe that more research on these aspects is urgently needed to provide better guidance, approaches and tools to manage evolving requirements. In line with

Cockburn, we believe that agility is a game on two levels: not only should one aim to deploy features to the market quickly, but one should also increase the organizations ability to provide value to customers in the future [72].

10.6.3 Build and Maintain Shared Understanding About System

Our third challenge area relates to building and maintaining a shared understanding about the system and is summarized in Table 10.5. Historically, plan-driven approaches suggest to distinguish between requirements specified from a user perspective (user or customer requirements specification) and those specified from a system perspective (system or supplier requirements specification) [416]. Agile methods mainly concern themselves with customer or user value, thus covering the content of a user requirements specification and even going beyond by focusing on the value that is generated for users and customers. There is virtue in such value- or problem-based specifications [265, 266], and we agree that user or customer value is an important knowledge area with respect to requirements. We found, however, that system requirements knowledge is crucial for large-scale system development as well, especially considering the very long maintenance cycles.

We generally find this perspective of requirements with a particular system or solution in mind to be underrepresented in scaled agile frameworks. User stories have been found insufficient to cover such knowledge [175] and (automated) test cases are often named as an alternative [39, 175], especially for small-scale projects. Our findings suggest that using test cases, even in combination with user stories, is not sufficient, in particular with respect to supporting the understanding of a system's current functionality. Specifically, we identify a lack of guidance in agile frameworks with respect to capturing a comprehensive big picture of requirements and their rationale, a finding in agreement with Heikkila et al. [176]. Because of this lack it is challenging to support systems thinking and requirements governance, to provide (often required) traceability, and to manage long-term knowledge as well as backwards compatibility. Therefore, we see the need for more work investigating the use of different notations, techniques or methods to inform early analysis of incoming requirements.

Even though such documentation and management of system requirement may feel non-agile by nature, it becomes crucial to support agile systems development. While significant work exists in the area of agile modeling [13, 383], our focus companies do not report experiences with these solutions. We distinguish therefore between *agile requirements engineering* as covered in most of the related work [203] and *requirements engineering for agile system-development (RE4agile)*, where we do not require an agile approach to engineering requirements. We see RE4agile as a fundamental service to provide crucial requirements knowledge so that agile teams can perform. Our findings suggest that such support cannot be offered sufficiently by traditional, upfront RE, as indicated [176, 321]. Similarly, we did not find any specific roles that emerge in the large-scale agile environment comparable to the roles presented in [184].

Our results suggest that continuous and agile development methods on a large scale require new concepts. Hybrid approaches [257] that aim to combine strengths of both plan-driven (waterfall) and value-driven (agile) paradigms may offer inspiration, but are at this point not sufficiently documented through empirical studies to relate them to our findings. In more recent parallel work with the same companies [278, 485], we have been exploring theories and methods to manage and govern shared objects such as requirements, architecture descriptions, APIs, and user documentation. Interpreting such items as *boundary objects* can help link individual teams to shared views of vision of the whole system and ultimately lead to effective agile approaches to manage such knowledge at scale [485]. We have explored this approach with respect to strategic API management and governance [278] and we are confident that this research direction will yield useful concepts and theories to tackle this challenge area.

10.6.4 Representation of Requirements Knowledge

The fourth challenge area includes challenges that relate to the representation of requirements knowledge (see Table 10.6). One underlying observation of the challenges in this area relates to the shared responsibility for requirements knowledge. In particular, scaled agile appears to imply that teams take more responsibility for both customer and system requirements. This in turn implies a bi-directional flow of requirements knowledge. On the one hand, it must both be relayed top-down, from system level planning to teams. On the other hand, it must flow bottom-up, from teams that explore the best way of satisfying a customer need through incremental and iterative work. We discovered challenges with both directions.

Bottom-up, the current tooling is not fit for purpose, since it does not allow teams to create and share knowledge efficiently. In addition, teams are expected to take responsibility for their own ways of working and to establish suitable flavours of requirements artifacts. How can individual teams have their own specialized requirements representations and still relate to the overall system-level requirements model? Top-down, a suitable decomposition of requirements is hard to achieve, especially since agile frameworks do not cover the duality of customer and system requirements. It is also difficult to establish a consistent requirement quality. Related work by Wohlrab et al. suggests that diversity and alignment of representations can be balanced, especially when taking into account information and consistency needs on different levels of abstractions and at different times during the development cycle [484].

Challenges with this shared responsibility for generating and managing requirements-related knowledge surfaces in difficulties to establish thresholds for quality requirements. How does a large-scale organization align on such threshold and manage their evolution when new knowledge becomes available?

We have been evaluating the use of T-Reqs, an approach to manage textual requirements in git version control together with tests and source code [249]. Custom tools such as T-Reqs can be accessible across an organization, and allow for customized access to requirements and peer-reviews of requirements changes by other teams and system managers. Existing work in the requirements literature has recognized that user story quality in practice can be problematic and has introduced various quality frameworks and tools to manually and automatically detect quality issues, e.g., [286], which in our view would integrate well with such peer-reviews. Such an approach promises to help with giving teams access to requirements tooling, supporting quality assurance, and even with re-negotiating quality thresholds and we encourage further research in this area.

As our results suggest, it is crucial to establish suitable exchange and management of knowledge throughout large-scale agile system development. Agile development works best with a continuous inflow of new requirements and can in turn help to resolve ambiguities and refine requirements just in time, as new knowledge becomes available. However, it is important to support updating system requirements models and to coordinate the information flow between parallel teams.

This finding suggests that communication issues continue to be relevant in large-scale agile RE, in contrast to what is suggested by related studies, e.g., [40, 203].

10.6.5 Process Aspects

Our fifth challenge area relates to the process of working with requirements. As the previous challenge areas indicate that requirements knowledge is not only continuously evolving, but also spread between customer value and system requirements as well as between a consistent requirements model of the complete system and specialized views of individual teams, it becomes clear that strong, continuous, and distributed processes must be established. Within this problem-space, the well-known challenge of *just enough requirements engineering* [85] reappears with force: how can a developing organization with dozens of agile teams find this fine balance where time-to-market is neither impacted by too much missing information nor excessive requirements work?

A concrete challenge relates to distributed prioritization [40, 175, 203]. While this is certainly challenging, it appears that prioritization by risk rather than value can be a good practice in many cases. This suggestion is in line with recent research by Hadar et al. [167], suggesting to use risk for prioritization. They suggest that risk is in many cases easier to quantify than value, thus providing a strong prioritization criteria, if applicable.

Further, requirements processes are expected to help establishing a meaningful concept of completeness as well as consistency. Yet, they must enable agile teams to take responsibility for their own ways of working. Recent works on boundary objects [396, 485] and bridging methodological gaps between different scopes in large-scale agile [232] may offer useful guidelines.

10.6.6 Organization Aspects

Related to the process aspects, our final challenge area includes challenges that relate to the overall organization in which requirements engineering is practiced. It is inherent to systems engineering that some long-term planning is needed, especially to plan for facilities to manufacture and test hardware and mechanics, but also to coordinate the integration of components across disciplines. Our challenges here relate to bridging between such system-level planning and agile work in software teams, to the planning of integrated system testing, to manage the research and pre-development, and to identify impacts on critical infrastructure in good time.

At the moment, we are not aware of proven approaches, neither through empirical evidence nor within agile frameworks, that can address these challenges. As with our challenges related to process aspects, we believe that recent research around boundary objects could offer a framework to encourage self-organization in system development [396, 485]. If constructively used to establish boundary objects as means of coordination between plan-driven and agile areas of an organization, we expect a positive impact on organizational aspects with engineering requirements in scaled-agile system development [232]. Our works on T-Reqs can be seen as a special boundary objects, where teams can communicate critical requirements changes early on and spread awareness through peer reviews [249].

10.6.7 Challenges Beyond the Scope of This Study

Through the transition to large-scale agile, many aspects of the overall processes, organization and ways of working of our case companies were under consideration at the time of our investigation. Requirements are of critical importance to all of our case companies and they traditionally relate directly or indirectly to all aspects of system development. Thus, we found at several times during this investigation that we needed to sharpen the scope. We wanted to create a catalogue of general requirements-related challenges that are relevant to system development of organizations that have transitioned or desire to transition to large-scale agile.

One big challenge that we ultimately excluded from the scope relates to the development of safety-critical or regulated systems. It is an exciting research field, but deserves a dedicated space. Our challenges of large-scale agile system development also apply if safety-critical systems are developed, yet, safety and regulation bring in an additional level of complexity to an already complex topic. We will instead spend a few lines here to relate our findings to safety-critical systems.

Traditionally, long upfront analysis and planning aimed to address these needs [321]. However, as companies try to speed up their development, research needs to investigate new ways of dealing with documentation of such cross-cutting issues. Ensuring qualities and addressing non-functional requirements has been brought forward as a challenge in agile RE [175, 203], and first works exist to address regulations in agile [128, 169]. This is an interesting area, since it allows to look at requirements practice in large-scale agile as a spectrum, where regulation or safety demand for a more formal approach. Several of our case companies develop such systems and participants repeatedly expressed concerns that the development of safety critical software together with corresponding standards could impede agile development.

As examples, the participants expressed the need for documentation and tracing that is required by several standards, such as ISO26262 [206]. However, an expert for functional safety in Automotive 1 stated that the need for documentation and tracing is related more to the size of the company and the system rather than regulations.

> Many see that as a problem. Many say that it's safety problem, it is a 26262 problem. But we say [..] we need to document anyway since then half a year later it is a different team [working on the same software] — A1-TS

According to our interviewees, standard conformance could be combined with agile development if only this was planned in a systematic fashion, e.g., by sandboxing safety critical parts. Further, our case companies discussed a spectrum of requirements method ranging from full-scale for regulated and safety-critical systems to lightweight for unregulated and non-critical systems. Yet, it is unclear which concrete practices and approaches are distributed over this spectrum in large-scale agile, which is confirmed by our parallel work on safety in agile system development [230, 441].

10.7 Conclusion and Outlook

We presented our results from a multiple-case study with seven systems engineering companies on the interaction of RE and agile methods in large-scale development. We studied the pervasiveness of agile methods adoption, requirements-related challenges of large-scale agile systems development and solutions from best practices in industry as well as those provided by SAFe® and LeSS. In all case companies, the way plan-driven and agile development currently co-exist within the systems engineering environment limits the potential development speed. We found that in all companies, there is a need for strong requirements engineering approaches, especially with respect to documenting a system's behavior for future feature requests or maintenance. The pervasiveness of agile implementation in the case companies differs, ranging from agile development on team-level embedded in an overall plan-driven process up to agile development for the entire product development. Despite the difference in pervasiveness, we observed similar challenges in all companies. These relate to establishing a shared view of value from the customer and other stakeholders down to development, supporting change and evolution, building up and maintaining a shared understanding about the system, representation of requirements knowledge, as well as dealing with process and organizational aspects. Proposals to mitigate these challenges have been extracted from SAFe® and LeSS, and we have collected further practices from the companies. Despite these proposals and practices, we note that many challenges remain open or have solutions without realistic evaluation.

At the time of this investigation, we conclude that neither traditional requirements engineering nor scaled-agile frameworks provide satisfying concepts to manage requirements knowledge effectively, when developing at the scale and speed that our case companies desire. Thus, each organization must find workarounds for their particular context. Our results facilitate the search for such individual solution strategies by providing a comprehensive overview of challenges. In particular, it helps to design solutions that do not over-optimize solving one challenge at the expense of a different challenge. Further inspiration is provided by listing relevant solution candidates. Yet, more general and reusable approaches are desperately needed. Therefore, we encourage future work to not only produce further practices to solve open challenges, but also focus on evaluation of existing large-scale agile proposals from a requirements perspective. Ideally, this will allow large-scale system development efforts to fully benefit from agile methods, while still systematically managing knowledge about customer value and the system under construction.

Table 10.5 Summary of results for Challenge Area 3: Build and maintain shared understanding about system

ID Challenge	Proposed practices from case companies	Proposed practices from SAFe	Proposed practices from LeSS	Research gap in large-scale agile
3.a Documentation to complement tests and stories	→Use models for interfaces and behaviors, additional text summaries.	→Use models to analyse requirements.	-	→Methods to capture comprehensible big picture of agile requirements and motivations.
3.b System vs. component thinking	→Need (global) baseline; →Requirements for product, not organization; →Establish ownership on all levels; →Architects on each team.	→Clear breakdown from enterprise level to team; →Feature and component teams; →Systems thinking; →Tribal unity; →Communicating the vision.	→Principle: Whole product focus; →Multi-team product backlog refinement; →PO engages team to own product.	→Provide and evaluate concrete advice and tools to support systems thinking on all levels as well as governance of requirements.
3.c Creating and maintaining traces	→Reuse features(= groups of reqs); →Reusable modules (= requirements and solutions); →Move from project to product focus.	→Describe the solution (Documentation).	→Link to wiki pages; →Backlog items to ancestors, max. 3 levels.	→Provide guidance and tools for large-scale agile traceability.
3.d Learning and long-term knowledge	→Exploit ownership of feature and tools to document less.	→ART focus on value, not project; →Enabler stories (Exploration); →Feature and Component teams; →Community of practice, chapters, guilds.	→Reflection + improvement experiments; →Experts teach each other, informal networks; →Specification by example.	→New approaches towards requirements as a knowledge management problem.
3.e Backward compatibility	→Push responsibility (and freedom) to developer.	-	-	→Strategies and guidance for systematic management of backwards compatibility.

Table 10.6 Summary of results for Challenge Area 4: Representation of requirements knowledge

ID Challenge	Proposed practices from case companies	Proposed practices from SAFe	Proposed practices from LeSS	Research gap in large-scale agile
4.a Manage levels vs. decomposition	→ Allow stakeholders to specify on any level of abstraction, e.g. through traceability and reqts structure; →Support distributed reqts analysis; →Distinguish dimensioning FR and NFR.	→Clear hierarchy, from enterprise level to team; →Requirements information model (epic-capability-feature-story): transport stakeholder view to components.	→Various splitting and refinement guides with depth 3 limit.	→Strategies and guidance for requirements decomposition, including how to manage customer and system requirements as well as on how to inter-relate them.
4.b Quality requirements as thresholds	→Thresholds to negotiate prizes; →Trade-offs brought up by team and peer-reviewed by teams and system managers.	→NFR are constraints on program level, constraining (a) the system and the product backlog or (b) a feature and the team backlog.	-	→Strategies and guidance on managing and evolving quality requirements.
4.c Tooling not fit for purpose	→PO updates requirements; →Team updates requirements.	-	→No software tools for sprint backlog; →Tools for large product backlogs (boards, pictures, wikis, spreadsheets).	→Tools specifically designed for large-scale scale agile practices, including reqts access control.
4.d Accommodate different representations	-	→Teams can have individual user stories flavour; →Emphasize team independence; →Responsibility for Ways of Working, book clubs, guilds.	-	→Strategies and guidance to balance independence of teams and system level consistency.
4.e Consistent requirements quality	→Operationalizatic from experience; →Peer-reviews by teams and system manager.	→Responsibility for Ways of Working, book clubs, guilds; →Community of practice to align on what is needed.	-	→Ways to share experiences on quality; →Empirical evaluation of suggested methods in practice.

Table 10.7 Summary of results for Challenge Area 5: Process aspects

ID Challenge	Proposed practices from case companies	Proposed practices from SAFe	Proposed practices from LeSS	Research gap in large-scale agile
5.a Prioritization of distributed functionality	→Business dashboard to help rank reqts; →Clear product owner (hierarchy); →More focus on interfaces, less on reqts; →Estimation by risk.	→Combining "weighted shortest job first", 'Portfolio backlog", and "Program Kanban" to support cross-cutting initiatives; →Combine team backlog, business value, and interaction backlog; →Sequencing based on cost of delay.	→One PO single source of prio.; →Multi-site product backlog review; →Challenge: Join the split-to-see problems.	→Empirical evidence and proven strategies on what works in specific context.
5.b Manage completeness	-	→No potential solution found in SAFe. Instead, build incrementally (Principle) and MVP suggest the opposite.	→LeSS-Guideline "take a bite".	→Provide a clear taxonomy or language to reason about requirements completeness in incremental work at scale.
5.c Consistent requirements processes	→Delivery = code, test, and reqt (update).	→Clear hierarchy, from enterprise level to team; →Emphasis on team independence; →Responsibility for WoW, book clubs, guilds.	-	→Strategies and guidelines to balance alignment and diversity of reqts practices.
5.d Quality vs time-to-market	→Frequent reviews of reqts in relation to Sprint deliverables.	→Clear hierarchy, from enterprise level to team; →Built-in-quality; →Reduce time-to- market: Value stream mapping.	-	→Guidelines to achieve just-enough quality of requirements, products, deliverables in order to reduce time-to-market.

Table 10.8 Summary of results for Challenge Area 6: Organisational aspects

ID Challenge	Proposed practices from case companies	Proposed practices from SAFe	Proposed practices from LeSS	Research gap in large-scale agile
6.a Bridge plan-driven and agile	→Dedicated governance of reqts across levels; →Team updates requirements; →PO updates requirements.	→Clear hierarchy, from enterprise level to team.	-	→Strategies and guidelines to replace static documents with actively managed boundary objects to allow coordination across levels.
6.b Plan V&V based on reqts	→Establish virtual test rigs and simulation models; →Manage reqts and tests together.	→Solution intent links specifications to tests; →Duality of backlog items and tests; →Cross-functional org.	-	→Empirical evidence and proven approaches.
6.c Time for invention and planning		→Solution intent, a repository of current and future solution behaviors; →Innovation and planning iterations; →Enabler stories.	-	→Empirical evidence and proven approaches.
6.d Impact on infrastructure	→Establish virtual test rigs and simulation models.	→Feature teams; →Component teams; →Cross-functional org.	-	→Proven strategies for achieving system- level awareness about critical reqt changes.

Chapter 11
Experimentation for Business-to-Business Mission-Critical Systems: A Case Study

David Issa Mattos, Anas Dakkak, Jan Bosch, and Helena Holmström Olsson

Abstract Continuous experimentation (CE) refers to a group of practices used by software companies to rapidly assess the usage, value and performance of deployed software using data collected from customers and the deployed system. Despite its increasing popularity in the development of web-facing applications, CE has not been discussed in the development process of business-to-business (B2B) mission-critical systems. We investigated in a case study the use of CE practices within several products, teams and areas inside Ericsson. By observing the CE practices of different teams, we were able to identify the key activities in four main areas and inductively derive an experimentation process, the HURRIER process, that addresses the deployment of experiments with customers in the B2B and with mission-critical systems. We illustrate this process with a case study in the development of a large mission-critical functionality in the Long Term Evolution (4G) product. In this case study, the HURRIER process is not only used to validate the value delivered by the solution but to increase the quality and the confidence from both the customers and the R&D organization in the deployed solution. Additionally, we discuss the challenges, opportunities and lessons learned from applying CE and the HURRIER process in B2B mission-critical systems.

11.1 Introduction

In the current competitive software market, companies are expected to continuously evolve and deliver fast, high-quality software that provides value to customers in an ever-changing operational environment. For example, in the telecommunication domain, mobile networks are continuously evolving to support new user equipment

Reprinted with permission from ACM. Originally published in Proceedings of the International Conference on Software and System Processes, pp. 95–104, June 2020. DOI: 10.1145/3379177.3388902

(such as consumer electronics, medical equipment, payment and navigation systems) and to improve the quality of the delivered service to their customer and final users. The deployed software is becoming increasingly complex and has a high degree of interdependence with the operating environment in which they operate. These aspects make it hard for the development organization to evaluate in the pre-deployment stage both the delivered value and the quality aspects that depend on the interaction with the operating environment.

Large-scale web-facing companies (such as Google, Amazon, Microsoft, Netflix among others) continuously reporting success stories and the competitive advantage that continuous experimentation (CE) gives them [78, 115, 252], development organizations have been moving towards continuous experimentation practices [19, 127, 277] to rapidly validate the value delivered to customers by software and to assess quality aspects that cannot be verified during internal development and pre-deployment quality assurance activities [391]. CE has been primarily focused on Software-as-a-Service and web-facing systems, in both research and industry [19]. Despite a few papers that discuss the introduction of CE in a business-to-business (B2B) context [374, 489, 490], no publications explore or discuss the industrial usage of a CE experimentation process in a B2B mission-critical systems.

This work refers to mission-critical systems as: in the presence of failures or degradation in the system can lead to property damage, reputation damage as well as preventing the main task to be successfully completed [134]. Fowler also points that such systems are often subject to regulations and standards (e.g. the 3GPP specification [112]). Mobile communication is an integral part of payment and banking systems, medical and transportation devices and others which if disrupted can lead to severe-major failures for different business and society [134]. Experimentation in the B2B and mission-critical systems domain have different characteristics compared to most web-facing applications such as the difference between customer and users, ownership of the product and the data, who has control over new deployments, service level agreements, presence of risk analysis and the impact of failure as well as strategies to overcome them among others. In the mobile communication domain, even if the mobile operator receives software updates frequently they are in control and which version of the software will be deployed, how and when the deployment will take place, which systems will be updated based on risk and how the software will be verified before full deployment to a whole network. Therefore any experimentation activity requires in-depth collaboration between the development organization and the customers.

To investigate the use of CE in B2B and mission critical-systems we conducted a case study in collaboration with Ericsson. Ericsson is a multinational networking and telecommunications company, with a R&D organization of over 24000 people.[1] Ericsson is arguably one of the largest software development company operating in the B2B domain. By observing the CE practices of different teams, we were able to identify the key activities and inductively derive an experimentation process that addresses the deployment of experiments with customers in the B2B and with

---

[1] https://www.ericsson.com/en/about-us/company-facts

mission-critical systems. In this paper, we present the HURRIER process (**H**igh valUed softwa**R**e th**R**ough cont**I**nuous Expe**R**imentation). We describe the process as a set of generic activities organized in four main areas, implemented by both the R&D organization as well as the customers. We illustrate this process with a case study in the development of a large mission-critical functionality in the Long Term Evolution (4G) product. This case study shows how the HURRIER process is implemented and how it is used to increase quality and confidence in the deployed solution, by validating it in terms of value delivered and functionality coverage.

The contribution of this paper is three-fold. First, we present the HURRIER process, a process that combines different experimentation techniques to deliver high-quality solutions that are valued by the customers. Second, we demonstrate the usage of HURRIER in the context of a B2B mission-critical functionality deployed in a complex environment. Thus, making this research, to the best of our knowledge, the first to discuss CE in B2B mission-critical systems. Third, we discuss challenges, opportunities and lessons learned of applying CE and the HURRIER process in B2B mission-critical system.

The rest of this paper is organized as follows. Section 11.2 presents background information in CE and related work in CE in the B2B domain. Section 11.3 describes the research method and validity considerations. Section 11.4 presents the HURRIER process and its activities. Section 11.5 illustrates the HURRIER framework in the development of a large mission-critical functionality in the Long Term Evolution (4G) product. Section 11.6 presents a discussion on the results, as well as lessons learned and opportunities of CE in the B2B and mission-critical systems. Finally, Sect. 11.7 concludes the paper and discusses future work.

11.2 Background

Fitzgerald and Stol [127] provide a review on a number of different initiatives around the term continuous. They present a holistic view of the different software development activities throughout the entire software life cycle. These activities are divided into three phases: business strategy and planning, development and operations. Continuous experimentation acts as a link between the strategy and operations and the development, where repeated cycles of build, measure and learn [14] guide the product improvement, evolution and innovation inside the company.

CE aims at minimizing the risk of developing software that does not deliver value to the customer, through continuously identifying, prioritizing and validating critical product assumptions during all development phases [277]. A significant amount of research has been conducted in the context of continuous experimentation. Auer and Felderer [19] performed a systematic mapping study in CE from 2007 to 2017 and identified a total of 82 publications. They identified that most of the research with industry participation is in the context of web-facing companies such as Microsoft, Yandex, Facebook, Google and LinkedIn. Additionally, CE is discussed mainly through randomized controlled experiments (A/B testing). However, CE constitutes a group of techniques that goes beyond randomized controlled experiments [114, 391], and that can encompass many other activities and techniques.

Schermann et al. [391] identify two groups of goals when conducting CE activities. The first group, business-driven experiment, is aimed at evaluating, in terms of the delivered value, the development ideas, business changes and design decisions. The second, regression-driven experiment, is aimed at identifying and mitigating the impact of software changes in existing behavior, functional and non-functional bugs that evaded or can not be detected in the pre-deployment quality assurance activities, and scalability issues.

One important aspect of CE in the business-to-business domain is the difference between customers and users. Customers acquire or subscribe to a product or service for the users [277, 374]. On the other hand, in the business-to-customer domain, the customers are also the users, and generally acquires or subscribe to the product for themselves. Therefore, in the B2B domain, vendors usually sell products and services to other companies that sell products or services to users. A distinctive factor is that user data, product usage, and user feedback are not readily or easily available for the vendors without prior agreements. This can restrict the data collection, user feedback and even new deployments aimed at product improvement.

Yaman et al. [490] describe the process of introducing continuous experimentation in companies with an established development process using two company cases with pure software products, Ericsson and a digital business consulting company. The study investigates the introduction of experimentation in a cloud service platform, describing relevant decision points taken (such as the target of the experiment, how to update the experiment design, etc), benefits from the experiment (new insights, reduced development effort etc) and challenges (access to end-users, inexperience with experimentation, length of the process, etc). Rissanen and Münch [374] investigate challenges, benefits and organizational aspects when introducing CE in the B2B domain. They identified that customers play a major role when designing and deploying an experiment.

A comparison of the HURRIER framework with related frameworks from the literature is provided in Sect. 11.6.

11.3 Research Method

The purpose of this research is to gain an in-depth understanding of the continuous experimentation process, its challenges, advantages when it is applied in mission-critical functionalities in the B2B domain. Based on the study goals, we formulated the following research questions:

- **RQ1**: How can CE be used in mission-critical features in the B2B domain?
- **RQ2**: What are the challenges and opportunities for CE for mission-critical features in B2B contexts?

11.3.1 The Case Study

This study was founded on a qualitative case study design for two main reasons. First, it allows the researchers to study and understand the phenomenon in its context in more depth [492]. Second, since CE in mission-critical and B2B systems, to the best of our knowledge, has not been discussed and investigated in research, a case study is an appropriate method for understanding a particular phenomenon in an industrial context [384].

We followed the five steps for a case study using the guidelines proposed by Runeson and Höst [384]: (1) case study design: the objectives are defined and the study is planned, (2) preparation for data collection: procedures and protocols for data collection are defined, (3) collecting evidence: execution with data collection on the study case, (4) analysis of the collected data and (5) reporting of the results.

11.3.1.1 Case Company

This research was conducted at Ericsson AB, which is a multinational networking and telecommunications company that develops, produces and sells telecommunication equipment, services, software and infrastructure to telecommunication operators in both mobile and fixed broadband. Ericsson employs over 95,000 people in around 180 countries. Over the last 10 years, Ericsson started the transition from traditional development to agile and towards DevOps. In the last 3 years, CE started to get attention and promotion inside Ericsson, and although continuous experimentation is not a well-defined process throughout the company, several teams independently conduct over a thousand field experiments a year, in different products and parts of the system. Experiments in Ericsson are used in a large number of use cases ranging from innovation and new feature development to legacy assurance and performance optimization. Although this case study was conducted with a single company, we investigated CE practices in multiple teams, areas and products.

11.3.1.2 Data Collection

The data collected in this case study consists of a mix of different data sources, including transcripts of semi-structured interviews, notes from meetings, emails, documentation and presentations. The first author is conducting research embedded in Ericsson and he has access to an Ericsson facility and internal documents. The second author is employed by Ericsson. He was involved in several of the project meetings and was also responsible for the selection of the interviews for this study.

We utilized a combination of criterion sampling with convenience sampling, where we interviewed the practitioners who were knowledgeable and accepted to participate in this study. We interviewed both participants that were part of the development and design of the case study feature as well as participants that were not involved but had extensive experimentation experience inside Ericsson.

Table 11.1 Overview of the interviews

Interview	N. Interviewees	Role	Location site	Years of exp.
A1	1	Operational prd. owner	L1	3
B	1	Test manager	L2	28
C	1	Program manager	L2	23
D	1	Technical specialist	L2	15
E1	6	Developers and testers	L1	3–5
F1	1	Prd. guardian	L1	6
G	1	Prd. introduction manager	L2	20
H	1	Prd. introduction manager	L2	19
I	1	Prd. manager	L6	12
J	1	Prin. project manager	L2	23
K	1	Program manager for field analysis	L2	22
L	1	Customer solutions manager	L3	7
M	2	Operational Prd. Owner, Developer	L4	8, 12
N	1	Customer support manager	L2	22
O	1	Release manager	L2	24
P1	4	Technical coord., Field feature tester, CD for customer support, Project manager support	L5	3–15
A2	1	Operational prd. owner	L1	3
E2	6	Developers and testers	L2	3–5
F2	1	Product guardian	L2	6
P2	2	Technical coord., Field feature tester	L5	3–15

We conducted semi-structured individual and group interviews, both in site and phone-conference with 25 practitioners, distributed in six locations in four countries, with experience ranging from 3 to 25 years working in a range of different roles, as shown in Table 11.1. The interviews were conducted in English, were designed to last approximately one hour and had an average duration of 55 min with a minimum duration of 41 min and a maximum duration of 1 hour and 8 min. The interviews were conducted between December 2018 and May 2019.

Since, at the time of the interviews, part of the interviewees were actively engaged in the deployment of a mission-critical feature that was being deployed and validated with the aid of field experiments, we conducted additional four follow-up interviews with 10 members after the project was concluded, as discussed in Sect. 11.5. These interviews were used to evaluate the experience with the experimentation processes in this mission-critical feature. In Table 11.1, the follow-up interviews are identified in the second part of the table.

At least two authors were present in all interviews. Interview guides were created depending on the role of the interviewee, to focus on their expertise and knowledge in the particular part of the experimentation process.

All interviewees were asked about their background and experience with customer experiments, live trials, data collection and feedback from both customers and users. Relevant concepts to continuous experimentation already identified in literature such as gradual releases, dark deployments were also asked whether the subjects had previous experience with these concepts or related ones. For all participants that have conducted entirely or partially projects with an experimentation component, we asked more in-depth questions about the process used, project timeline, impediments, lessons learned, perception of the benefits and the disadvantages. For the interviews with the subjects that were involved in the case study development, additional questions regarding the feature, the impact of the feature in the 4G product, the specific experimentation process used, results, lessons learned among others. For interviewees in managing positions, we also asked their reflections on experimentation projects they supervised or followed and how the development organization was moving towards experimentation. For participants in customer units, we asked questions regarding customer feedback and perception in experimentation projects, data collection and their current and future interest in collaborating in experimentation activities. The additional 10 interviews of the case study were intended to evaluate the use of experimentation in a mission-critical feature. Therefore for them, we asked specific questions about the project, the results, customer perception and feedback, lessons learned and impediments created by the use of a CE process and its application in a mission-critical feature.

For all interviews, the academic purpose of the study and a statement about participants' anonymity in the analysis and results were explicitly shared before the start of the interview and agreed by the participants. For the qualitative analysis, all interviews were recorded and transcribed, both the questions and participants' answers. Since all authors have non-disclosure agreements with Ericsson, the interviewees could utilize internal examples and freely discuss their experiences and practices.

Additionally, we collected data from over 30 documents including project documentation, feature development plans, solutions and product presentations for both internal employees and external customers. These additional documents were shared, mentioned or discussed during the interviews, meetings or emails and were available to the authors through the internal network. These documents contained detailed information about the development and release process of different features and products, the sequence of steps taken, customer feedback on both the continuous experimentation process and specific feedback used by the development team (e.g. feedback given in the customer feedback channel of the HURRIER process). We utilized these documents as a triangulation source to support the data collected from the interviews, in particular, to help the ordering and timeline of activities to induct the HURRIER process. The described collected data was the main source of information to answer both research questions, as discussed in Sect. 11.6.

11.3.1.3 Data Analysis

All data collected described previously were added to the qualitative analysis software NVivo, where a thematic coding analysis was utilized, according to the six-phase process by Braun and Clark [52]. We utilized inductive thematic coding, as the themes were first identified and linked to the data, rather than being based on previous subject coding frames.

The first phase consists of familiarizing with the data. This was done by the authors in several ways, such as participating in the interview process, the transcription process, reading the transcriptions and interview notes. In the second phase, we generated the first set of codes, representing interesting concepts and ideas captured in the interviews or discussed in the additional documents. These codes identified in the interviews the goal of the experiment, perceived advantages and disadvantages, technical limitations, organizational limitations, deployment and experimentation techniques, customer perception, steps taken, deployment prerequisites, showstoppers etc. In the third phase, we discussed potential themes for the identified codes. In the fourth phase, we reviewed the potential themes and merged similar codes when possible and classified them as part of the theme-groups: experimentation activities, B2B challenges, mission-critical challenges, perceived advantages, customer involvement, etc. In the fifth phase, we analyzed each theme individually, generating the main results and discussion points to answer each research question. The last phase consists of this publication, where the results are presented and the research questions explicitly answered in the discussion. At the webpage: https://github.com/davidissamattos/public_documents/blob/master/coding.pdf we show an example of how the empirical data was coded and then grouped into themes.

11.3.2 Identification of the HURRIER Process

The HURRIER process was identified by observing the CE practices of different projects, teams and products. Utilizing the thematic coding approach describe earlier, we were able to identify the key activities performed by each team, the order of these activities, techniques used, pre-conditions, challenges and impediments, results and lessons learned. We ordered all these activities in time and in terms of importance. From these, we inductively derive an experimentation process that addresses the deployment of experiments for all of the analyzed teams and features involved in this research. All were developed in the context of B2B while some of them are not mission critical, over half are considered mission-critical. In Sect. 11.5, we illustrate the HURRIER process in one mission-critical project. The HURRIER process itself did not trigger the CE process used in this example but rather conceptualizes the CE process used in this and other projects and features.

11.3.3 Validity Considerations

External validity: This case study was conducted within multiple teams, areas and products in a single software company. To minimize the bias of working with a single team inside the company, the HURRIER process was based on the experimentation practices of several teams located in four countries. The presented process is used in its entirety or a subset of it by the different teams and parts of the organization. We abstracted the activities of the HURRIER process performed by Ericsson in terms of common development activities that are used in different industries and in research, such as continuous integration, passive launch, simulations laboratory evaluations, gradual rollouts etc. Although identified in Ericsson, the HURRIER process does not restrict specifically to Ericsson or to the telecommunication industry, and therefore can be instantiated, used or adapted by other software companies striving to introduce CE in mission-critical in the B2B domain. However, we do not claim generalization of the process to the entire software industry. *Construct validity:* The authors of this paper are well familiar with continuous experimentation practices and related research. However, the participants not always utilized the same nomenclature as research in continuous experimentation. To mitigate the threat to construct validity, the second author who works as full-time employee at Ericsson, was present in all interviews. When the practitioners asked for clarification or misunderstood a question, the second author explained or rephrase questions and concepts in the technical vocabulary used internally and given examples of well-known internal practices at Ericsson that exemplified the concept or question.

11.4 The HURRIER Process

The deployment of new software in B2B and mission-critical systems, unlike many web-facing applications, requires extensive verification, risk analysis and customer approvals. The R&D organization must comply with specifications, pre-established testing procedures and service level agreements. In these situations, field experiments must be planned and agreed in collaboration with the customers to ensure that the R&D organization receives adequate field feedback and to minimize the risk imposed on the service provided by the customer. In this section, and based on the empirical data, we present the HURRIER process for conducting experimentation in mission-critical features in the B2B domain. The HURRIER process was identified and formulated based on the current experimentation practices of different teams inside Ericsson. The process is used in its entirety or just a subset of its activities depending on the scope and area of the development project.

The process is composed of a set of generic activities that can be organized in four main areas around two feedback channels. The areas are: (1) the R&D organization, (2) the internal validation, (3) single customer validation and (4) multiple customer validation. Next, we discuss each of these groups in detail together with the set of activities commonly found in these groups and the feedback channel. Figure 11.1 shows an overview of the HURRIER process. In this process, the square boxes represent activities, thin arrows indicate the sequence of the activities inside an area. The thick arrows represent feedback data. At any point in this process and based on the feedback data, an activity can be interrupted and returned to the R&D organization, either in the form of new requests and ideas, by adding new use-cases and providing additional data for the pre-study activity, or providing continuous feedback for the incremental development activity.

11.4.1 The R&D Organization

The R&D organization is responsible for the development of the feature or change that is going to be deployed. The R&D starts after a development idea is generated. These development ideas can come from different sources such as direct customer request, market needs, competition, innovation or to meet the internal goals of the R&D organization.

11.4.1.1 Pre-study

The pre-study activity consists of scoping the project and planning its development. Metrics and success criteria are determined, as well as the expected improvement in both system internal metrics and customer level metrics. The feature is divided into incremental steps that can be rapidly evaluated in the field in collaboration with the customer. In this activity, potential customers are selected to evaluate the

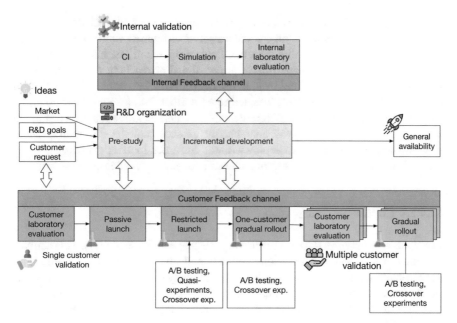

Fig. 11.1 The HURRIER Process. The different activities in the process can be organized in four main areas: (1) the R&D organization (in gray), (2) internal validation (in orange), (3) single customer validation (in green) and (4) multiple customer validation (in blue). The internal feedback channel provides continuous feedback from the quality assurance activities while the customer feedback channel provides feedback from field experiments back to the R&D organization

first experiments. These customers usually have a significant interest in the specific feature, either because it was their request or because of potential benefits. Customers in this step can have different degrees of interaction, from an observer role to a more active role in the design of field experiments.

11.4.1.2 Incremental Development

After the initial planning and the selection of a customer to run the field experiments, the development activities start. The feature is divided to be implemented incrementally and with constant feedback validation from both the internal procedures as well as from feedback from the field in close collaboration with the customer.

11.4.2 The Internal Validation

The internal validation consists of quality assurance activities. These activities are performed both before and in parallel with the customer validation and the field experiments. Before the internal development reaches the customer for a field experiment, the R&D organization conducts a series of internal validation procedures to guarantee a minimum quality for a first field deployment. The internal validation before the customer field experiments is not aimed at reaching a high degree of coverage as provided by a field evaluation. Instead, this internal validation aims at capturing integration problems, interaction with other features and other common implementation errors. The first iterations of the internal validation are considered a fast procedure, as it is target at guaranteeing an acceptable level of quality while minimizing the leading time to deploy with the customer. In parallel to the customer validation activities, quality assurance teams incrementally validate the development.

11.4.2.1 Continuous Integration

Continuous integration (CI) is a mandatory internal validation activity. This activity is aimed at identifying integration problems and interaction of the feature under development with a range of other features and many different hardware configurations. This activity is part of all deployment processes at Ericsson, regardless of the presence of field experiments or not. Continuous integration at Ericsson, has been discussed extensively in [422].

11.4.2.2 Simulation

The development of some features can be verified using simulators. Ericsson has modeled several characteristics of its products and of the different environments that the products can be deployed. The development of a simulator is an intensive activity that requires extensive validation. Additionally, not all conditions can be easily simulated or have a simulator available, and for those conditions, an internal validation with simulation is not used.

11.4.2.3 Internal Laboratory Evaluation

Similar to the simulation activity, Ericsson has several laboratory testing environments. The laboratory environments are designed to capture and verify a large number of use cases including software and hardware integration. These cases give a good indication of how the deployed system will perform under controlled circumstances. However, sometimes the feature under development addresses corner cases or requires the complex interaction of live network traffic. Those cases are often hard and expensive to recreate in a environment laboratory, and in those cases, the feature requires field experiments for validation.

11.4.3 Single Customer Validation

The internal validation provides software with enough quality and verification to be deployed in the field. However, as discussed previously, internal validation activities cannot cover all the quality aspects of the system. Time and costs constraints impose a limited number of scenarios that can be run in simulation and laboratory evaluation. Additionally, controlled environments lack the high complexity and variability seen in a field deployment, such as in traffic patterns, in types and number of user equipment among others and cannot assess customer-specific KPIs (key performance indicators). The first field validation is done in collaboration with a single customer and it is usually the same one that has been involved since the beginning in the pre-study phase. This customer has a high interest in the development and the success of the field experiment and therefore collaborates in sharing field data both in terms of qualitative and quantitative feedback.

11.4.3.1 Customer Laboratory Evaluation

The first activity after the internal verification is the deployment of the software for evaluation in the customer laboratory. The customer laboratory is run by the customer and contains specific configurations to replicate its own network. In the laboratory, the customer can verify the software with its internal test procedures and Key Performance Indicators (KPIs). This step gives confidence for the customer to deploy the software in its own network. This evaluation is also considered a fast procedure since it does not cover all cases.

11.4.3.2 Passive Launch

Passive launch, also known as a dark launch or a dark deployment [378, 391], is a CE technique that consists of deploying the new feature or change in parallel with the existing system. The new feature performs its task in the background and it is executed by the same traffic profile and inputs of the system. However, its output and its main functionality is not exposed to the users. It is used to provide an open loop verification of how the feature would behave in production in systems where response parity is necessary and correctness of the response can be evaluated. This activity is not mandatory, and it is often seen as a time-consuming activity for smaller features and changes. However, in mission-critical development, a passive launch can increase the confidence level in the deployment, verify the system response, memory and CPU usage, and the quality of the response with minimal to no risks for the end-users.

11.4.3.3 Restricted Launch

Restricted launch corresponds to the deployment of the system in a low-risk scenario that can help validate the development. The restricted scenario can be the selection of systems in a way that if they fail, then the impact is small on the final users (such as systems with high redundancy and safe fails). Additionally, the restricted scenario can be a restriction in time so that the new feature is deployed only in periods of low-risk, such as maintenance hours or low traffic hours. If the deployed systems in the restricted launch are compared to other equivalent systems, the customers and the R&D organization usually follow a quasi-experimental design [399]. If the system metrics are compared with the historical metrics or metrics after the restricted launch, the R&D organization and customers plan for a cross-over experimental design [216]. If KPIs that are being tracked are end-user dependent, the R&D organization and the customers can utilize A/B testing or another randomized factorial design to evaluate the impact of the feature. In this last case, negative movements are further investigated, while statistically non-significant and positive significant movements give confidence for proceeding towards a larger experiment.

11.4.3.4 One Customer Gradual Rollout

After a successful restricted launch, the customer has enough confidence to make the gradual rollout of the feature to the whole network. This rollout can be randomized, from lower to higher risk systems, or use another pre-established procedure. The mobile operator together with the manufacturer can decide to run cross-over experiments or A/B experiments between each ramp-up, or select two previously known regions with high correlation to evaluate the deployment. At the last stage of the gradual rollout, a full experiment is conducted to evaluate the deployment. This evaluation can be used to verify the value of the deployment and the quality aspects of the deployment. At this stage, the R&D organization can decide to continually develop the feature towards its full scope running additional single and multiple customer experiments or abandon the idea and development, and move to the next feature.

11.4.4 Multiple Customer Validation

If the field experiments with the first customer already provide enough coverage and confidence in the solution, in terms of quality or value, the R&D organization can decide to mark the feature for general availability (GA) which means that the feature has the adequate quality and therefore ready to be deployed by any customer. However, often a single customer cannot cover all the necessary validation aspects of the feature and the R&D organization may select a number of additional customers that can increase this coverage for more field experiments. Since the feature has already gone through field validation and has higher confidence some steps such as the passive and restricted launch are usually not covered. The customer laboratory and the gradual rollout are similar to the single customer validation. However, the R&D organization may focus in identifying the corner cases to increase the feature coverage and the delivered value by choosing different experimental designs. Additionally, due to the significant differences between each customer network, the result of these experiments are analyzed individually and not combined.

After the multiple customer validation, the feature is fully documented and marked for GA. At this stage, other customers can acquire or deploy the feature in their own networks fully or partially, gradually or at once. However, the feedback to the R&D organization takes longer, as the development has moved towards a new idea and other experiments.

11.4.5 The Internal and the Customer Feedback Channels

In the B2B context, the software manufacturer is not always allowed to have direct access to field data or user data. To make sure the development team has access to all necessary field data to drive the product and feature development in a fast way, the HURRIER process center all activities around two main feedback channels.

The internal feedback channel consists of reports and communication between the development teams and the operation teams. This feedback channel provides quantitative data from the quality assurance teams, such as continuous integration status, simulation reports and laboratory test reports.

The customer feedback channel is an agreed communication channel between customers and the R&D organization. It serves as a central source of feedback information that developers can get from the field validations activities with customers. The provided feedback can be both quantitative and qualitative data. The customers can control directly what information they provide, facilitating compliance with specific regions' regulations, such as GDPR, guaranteeing the anonymity and privacy of their users and controlling business-sensitive information. In case a particular development activity requires sensitive data from users, the customers can agree to run analyses scripts on the data and only provide the results as feedback. The customer feedback channel can be implemented in several ways, from both automated data collection of instrumented software, direct contact between developers and customers, or through specialize customer units.

11.5 Illustrating HURRIER

This case study investigates the adopted experimentation practices in the context of the Long Term Evolution (4G) system. In particular, we investigate the usage of CE in a project that consists of the refactoring of a framework that implements several functionalities of the 3GPP specification [112]. This framework is used to increase speed, coverage and capacity of mobile communication systems and is considered a mission-critical system in the LTE context, i.e. without proper function of this framework, key functionalities of the 4G are compromised with possible mobile traffic disruptions for the affected region. The refactoring procedure aims at increasing performance, scalability of the system for new solutions and specification modifications, support for number of new future user equipment, and to open the space for new machine-learning and artificial intelligence solutions. The importance and critical aspect of the framework are captured in the quote:

> This is one of the most important features that we have in LTE . . . as it has a great impact for the end-user — Interview F

The framework is highly complex as it interacts with over 20 different functionalities in the LTE system and it needs to interact and perform well with over the 5000 different configurations of user equipment available in the 3GPP specification and with the additional new 5G systems. Combined with the different traffic profiles and optimizations that mobile operators can have, verification and validation of this system in all different conditions in-house is unfeasible, in terms of cost to create such testing facility, the evolution of the testing facility to include the continuously increasing number of user equipment and the time to validate the solution. Internal testing of the framework can verify functionality interaction of the framework with new features and how new features can impact the framework. However, it is not possible to achieve high coverage and quantify the improvement of the solution without running field experiments in a customer network. This project involved design teams, development units and customer units in 4 different countries.

> We want to test it in the field with the customers. . . the main reason is that the feature that we are working on is highly dependable on the configuration that is used in the field, and the configuration is different in different countries, it is different between operators in the same country, it is different between different types of user equipment that we have on the market. And due to that, it is very hard and probably impossible to verify all the functionality with internal testing, or in our lab. In our lab, we only have a limited set of user equipment, a limited set of configurations. So to secure the quality of the product that we are delivering, we want to have the ability to deploy that in some of the customers' networks, before we go full scale. — Interview F

During the pre-study phase, it was identified one mobile operator that had a network profile that could be used to validate a large part of the refactored framework and that had a high interest in the evolution of the system after the framework has been deployed. The operator provided initial field data to aid the initial stages of the development. Following an incremental approach, the first version of the new framework was developed. In parallel, the R&D organization worked on securing that internal verification is set up to cover major use cases and obvious configurations. The internal feedback channel was implemented with the existing Ericsson procedures for quality assurance, including CI reports, simulation status and laboratory validation tests.

We tested (the feature) in our internal tests and run regression tests in the virtual environment. The field is a second step for validating. The customers want to be safe, to be sure that everything is fine (before the field experiments). — Interview E

The customer feedback was implemented together with the local customer unit. It contains both automated data collection of the instrumented software in addition to an ad-hoc manual collection of further performance and diagnostic data, if necessary. Because of the critical aspects of the framework, the single customer validation followed all activities. After passing the customer laboratory evaluation, the passive launch activity allowed benchmarking the responses from the new framework with the existing one. This activity allowed the R&D organization to identify corner cases from the live network traffic, that were not covered during the internal validation and customer laboratory. The frequent feedback and iterations allowed the software to have enough confidence for a restricted launch in the live network.

The passive deployment was a very valuable activity. Besides the validation, we could also collect a lot of data to support other development activities in future iterations of this project. — Interview F2

The restricted launch enabled the framework only during maintenance hours for a week. Maintenance hours, correspond to lower traffic and requirements on the network, making it a lower risk scenario in cases of faults. The analysis of the restricted launch was made by comparing key metrics and time series of the maintenance hours of the experiment week against a control week with the old framework. When the new framework reached enough quality level in terms of key metrics it proceeded to the gradual rollout.

The field deployment (in maintenance hours) allowed us to identify a problem that none of our existing internal testing could identify — Interview F2

The gradual rollout followed the existing customer deployment plans for new software, where the software is deployed in groups and the performance of each group regarding KPIs is measured before the deployment of the next group occurs. In this stage, quantitative feedback regarding the KPIs ensured that the new framework behaved as designed.

Later on we are going to run experiments with other customers and in other countries. The reason for that is that the framework has a huge number of interactions with other functionalities that we have in our software. So that means that the one customer that we are going to start with does not have all the configurations that we would like to test. ... If we get positive results from this first customer we want to expand that to the other customers — Interview A

In parallel with the first (single) customer validation, the R&D organization contacted other customers for further field experiments. The contacted customers, that also showed great interest in the framework, had different network profiles to increase the coverage of the solution. Since the first customer validation already validated the most critical aspects of the framework, the R&D organization performed the gradual rollout (after the customer verify the software in their own laboratories). Therefore, these new field experiments with multiple customers were aimed at increasing the coverage and confidence in the framework in special and corner cases.

The field experiments with multiple customers generated enough data and evidence for the R&D organization to proceed towards final documentation and release of the framework in GA for other customers.

11.6 Discussion

In this section, we discuss the research questions and also on the challenges and lessons learned from the use of the HURRIER process in the refactoring project discussed in Sect. 11.5, as well as the usage of CE in the other development projects.

RQ1: How can CE be used in mission-critical features in the B2B domain?

By observing the CE practices of different teams, we were able to observe the key activities that compose an experimentation process in the B2B domain. This set of activities including how experimentation is used in mission-critical features led to the development of the HURRIER process model. The HURRIER process represents a superset of the activities that are performed by these different teams. The requirements and the available tools (such as simulators and test rigs) in both the R&D organization and in the customers determine which set of activities are instantiated.

The key aspects when deciding upon the activities and instantiating the process are the time-length of the activity, the value it delivers when verifying the system. Deployment activities, such as network optimization, depend heavily upon the existing conditions of the operator's network. In those cases, extensive laboratory testing and simulation activities deliver little value compared to field experiments. The internal validation is kept to a minimum, the software is validated only in terms of quality, guaranteeing that it does not influence or deteriorate other features.

On the other hand, the development of mission or even safety-critical features requires more extensive and lengthy internal validation, including following specifications and legislation. In this case, simulations and laboratory evaluations play a major role in increasing confidence before the field deployment. However, simulations and laboratory evaluations should be kept to the minimum necessary to guarantee the safety and basic functionality of the feature. Field experiments present a fast way to evaluate the feature and increase coverage in the operating conditions, which is often not feasible, costly and time consuming to implement in laboratory conditions. Deploying the mission-critical feature in the field within maintenance hours where traffic is minimal, is another way used to minimize the risk when the implementation to be deployed in the field for the first time. Therefore, it is not only that the feature is deployed to a small subset of the network, but also done at different times to reduce the risk further.

The feature should be implemented incrementally, so its value can be faster evaluated. Any evaluation of the delivered value should be left for the field experiments. In case the minimum functionality of the feature does not deliver the expected value, the feature can be abandoned without the need to go through all the extensive work of developing, verifying and even certifying the full feature.

> we always start with understanding the problem and trying to solve it in the simplest possible way, and then before we start an expensive simulation or a study how this interact with everything else to fully understand it, we try to build a prototype and test it (in the field), the minimum scope, with tremendous amount of limitations. Possibly, the prototype does not work with this or that feature, but at least we can test if there is a gain or not... We are not more efficient when it comes to building time, but we know in advance that it works (in the real-world). That is the benefit of prototyping and experimenting. — Interview I

RQ2: What are the challenges and opportunities for CE for mission-critical features in B2B contexts? Running CE in the B2B domain and in mission-critical features presents many opportunities and challenges for both the company and the customers.

A challenge in CE in the B2B domain is that any new deployment requires explicit approval and consent of the customers. For that, the customer needs to understand the need for the deployment, have a clear vision of how it can impact the system and what are the potential benefits. However, successful experiments and transparency between the R&D company and the customer can help to build a trust relationship. A high trust relationship can facilitate running field experiments and evaluating new ideas for which the direct benefit is not yet clear for the customer. CE in the B2B domain also requires close collaboration between companies and customers, since the field experiments are run in the customer premises. The collaboration happens from the pre-study to gradual the rollout phase.

Depending on the level of interaction, trust between the R&D team and the customer and the level of interest in the feature, customers can help to shape the development activities and even to steer the development of the feature.

> Now, we have some experiments with teams and customers where they have the customer involvement all the way. The problem with that is that we develop features that are supposed to be globally and possible to use for all our customers. — Interview B

In mission-critical features, CE practices allow higher coverage and confidence in the development solution, reducing the number of problem reports after general availability, and minimizing the costs of developing and maintaining an extensive simulation and laboratory solution. However, the responsibility for managing the risks of a field experiment in the B2B context relies on the customers, which requires the company to have a close collaboration and build a high-trust relationship.

CE is not seen only as positive for the company but also the customers. For the company, CE helps to reduce the time-to-market as features are continuously validated with field data in terms of value and functionality. Other perceived advantages are the reduced time for a problem report to be addressed by the development team; an increased sense of accomplishment, as the functionality is seen in the field in a shorter period; and the higher sense of autonomy that comes with a higher trust from the customers, as the development teams can propose and test new ideas in the field faster. For the customer, CE has allowed them to test new functionalities, evaluate ideas and understand the impact of those ahead of the release, give them a competitive advantage on their corresponding markets.

Some customers understand the need for field experiments in their network. Because with experiments they can access earlier the latest functionalities and improvements of our software.
— Interview C

Several academic publications discuss the process used in introducing and deploying experiments in online systems [120, 308, 345]. The processes follow a generic iterative three-step structure of build-measure-learn, where experiments are associate in measuring and learning. The proposed HURRIER process does not contradict existing experimentation processes such as the HYPEX [345] the RIGHT model [120] since it is built on top of those models. The HURRIER adds and reinforces specific activities for the deployment of software that needs to have high-quality assurance and in the B2B context. For example, the execution step of an experiment iteration in the RIGHT model is broken down into several activities such as customer laboratory evaluation, passive launch, restricted launch and one-customer gradual rollout. These activities although necessary for the context of mission-critical systems and B2B context, might not be relevant for startup experiments or web-facing companies that usually have lower risks involved in the deployment and are more in control of the data collection and deployment strategy than the customers. The HURRIER process emphasizes that to continuously deliver high quality and validated solutions, not only continuous integration and delivery process should be integrated, but also that customer feedback and exposure of the system to live contexts in collaboration with customers give much faster and valuable feedback than focusing only in in-house validation and predefined testing scenarios.

11.7 Conclusion

In collaboration with Ericsson, we conducted a case study to understand how to CE can be used in the B2B domain, and investigate how this process can be used with mission-critical features. The contributions of this paper is three-fold. First and based on the existing CE practices and their usage at Ericsson, we inductively derived the HURRIER process. This process describes the deployment of experiments within the B2B domain and also takes into account considerations for running experiments with mission-critical features. Second, we illustrate the HURRIER process with the development of a large mission-critical functionality in the Long Term Evolution (4G) product. The HURRIER process helped the R&D organization to validate feature functionality and increase coverage and confidence in solutions much faster than without the field experiments. Finally, we discuss lessons learned, challenges and opportunities within CE in B2B and mission-critical features. CE has the potential to deliver valuable and higher quality solutions. However, in the B2B domain, this can only be achieved with a high trust and close collaboration with the customers. Although, the HURRIER process was identified in the context of Ericsson and in the telecommunication domain, we believe that a similar process could benefit other companies in other domains. As future work, we plan to introduce and evaluate this process in other industries.

Acknowledgements

This work was partially supported by the Wallenberg Artificial Intelligence, Autonomous Systems and Software Program (WASP) funded by the Knut and Alice Wallenberg Foundation and by the Software Center. The authors would also like to express their gratitude for all the support provided by Ericsson.

Chapter 12
The Evolution of Continuous Experimentation in Software Product Development: From Data to a Data-Driven Organization at Scale

Aleksander Fabijan, Pavel Dmitriev, Jan Bosch, and Helena Holmström Olsson

Abstract Software development companies are increasingly aiming to become data-driven by trying to continuously experiment with the products used by their customers. Although familiar with the competitive edge that the A/B testing technology delivers, they seldom succeed in evolving and adopting the methodology. In this paper, and based on an exhaustive and collaborative case study research in a large software-intense company with highly developed experimentation culture, we present the evolution process of moving from ad-hoc customer data analysis towards continuous controlled experimentation at scale. Our main contribution is the "Experimentation Evolution Model" in which we detail three phases of evolution: technical, organizational and business evolution. With our contribution, we aim to provide guidance to practitioners on how to develop and scale continuous experimentation in software organizations with the purpose of becoming data-driven at scale.

12.1 Introduction

Software development organizations and their product development teams are increasingly using customer and product data to support decisions throughout the product lifecycle [116, 353]. Data-driven companies acquire, process, and leverage data in order to create efficiencies, iterate on and develop new products, and navigate the competitive landscape [353]. Digitally adept and technology driven companies are as much as 26 percent more profitable than their competitors [475]. Recent software engineering research reflects this situation with a number of publications on how to change and efficiently conduct controlled experiments to become data-driven

Reprinted with permission from IEEE. Originally published in Proceedings of the 39th International Conference on Software Engineering, 2017, pp. 770–780. DOI: 10.1109/ICSE.2017.76

J. Bosch et al. (eds.), *Accelerating Digital Transformation*,
https://doi.org/10.1007/978-3-031-10873-0_16

[119, 120, 252, 345, 346]. The role of data scientists is increasingly gaining momentum in large software companies [243]. However, despite having data, the number of companies that efficiently use it and that successfully transform into data-driven organizations stays low and how this transformation is done in practice is little studied [117, 378].

In this paper, we present the phases that teams at Microsoft evolved through in order to become data-driven at scale by establishing a controlled experimentation platform and a data-driven mindset. The impact of scaling out the experimentation platform across Microsoft is in hundreds of millions of dollars of additional revenue annually. The journey from a company with data to a data-driven company, however, was not a jump but rather an evolution over a period of years. This development occurs through phases and we illustrate this process by creating the "Experimentation Evolution Model". With this model, we describe the steps to take while evolving data-driven development practices towards continuous experimentation at scale. With our contribution, we aim to provide guidance to practitioners on how to develop and scale continuous experimentation in software organizations and thus become truly data-driven.

The paper is organized as follows. In Sect. 12.2 we present the background and the motivation for this study. In Sect. 12.3, we describe our research method, the data collection and analysis practices and our case company. Our empirical findings are in Sect. 12.4. In Sect. 12.5, we present our main contribution – the "Experimentation Evolution Model". Finally, we conclude the paper in Sect. 12.6.

12.2 Background

Rapid delivery of value to customers is one of the core priorities of software companies [120]. With this goal in mind, companies typically evolve their development practices. At first, they inherit the Agile principles within the development part of the organization [297] and expand them to other departments [343]. Next, companies focus on various lean concepts such as eliminating waste [330], removing constraints in the development pipeline [153] and advancing towards continuous integration [419] and continuous deployment of software functionality [378]. Continuous deployment, however, is characterized by a bidirectional channel that enables companies not only to send data to their customers to rapidly prototype with them [373], but also to receive feedback data from products in the field. The intuition of software development companies on customer preferences can be wrong as much as 90% of the time [66, 71, 292]. The actual product usage data has the potential to make the prioritization process in product development more accurate as it focuses on what customers do rather than what they say [49, 344]. Controlled experimentation is becoming the norm in advanced software companies for reliably evaluating ideas with customers in order to correctly prioritize product development activities [119, 120, 252, 345, 346].

12.2.1 Controlled Experiments

In a controlled experiment, users are randomly divided between the variants (e.g., the two different designs of a product interface) in a persistent manner (a user receives the same experience multiple times). Users' interactions with the product are instrumented and key metrics are computed [76, 252]. One of the key challenges with metrics is to decide on which to include in an Overall Evaluation Criteria (OEC). An OEC is a quantitative measure of a controlled experiment's objective [469] and steers the direction of the business development. In controlled experimentation, it is intuitive to measure the short-term effect, i.e., the impact observed during the experiment [186]. Providing more weight to advertisement metrics, for example, makes businesses more profitable in the short-term. However, the short-term effect is not always predictive of the long-term effect and consequently should not be the sole component of an OEC [251]. Defining an OEC is not trivial and should be conducted with great care. Kohavi et al. [251, 252] in their papers present common pitfalls in the process of establishing a controlled experimentation system and guidance on how to reliably define an OEC.

Research contributions with practical guides on how to develop an experimentation system have previously been published both by Microsoft [250, 252] and Google [453]. The Return on Investment (ROI) of controlled experimentation has been discussed a number of times in the literature [76, 252]. However, the count of companies that successfully developed an experimentation culture and became data-driven remains low and limited to other web service companies such as Facebook, Google, Booking, Amazon, LinkedIn, Etsy, Skyscanner [250, 378]. We believe that the reason for this unsuccessful adoption of continuous experimentation resides in the lack of knowledge on how the transition can be done in practice. Companies have the necessary instrumentation in place [25], are able to gather and analyze product data, but they fail to efficiently utilize it and learn from it [343].

The research contributions from Google and Microsoft provide guidance on how to start developing the experimentation platform. However, they do not provide guidance on which R&D activities to prioritize in order to incrementally scale the experimentation across the organization. This technical research contribution is aiming to address this gap and provide guidance on how to evolve from a company with data to a data-driven company. We focus on technical challenges (e.g. the necessary platform features that are required for successful scaling) as well as the organizational aspects (e.g. how to integrate data scientists in product teams) and business aspects (e.g. how to develop an Overall Evaluation Criteria). This leads to the following research question:

RQ: "How to evolve controlled experimentation in software-intensive companies in order to become data-driven at scale?"

To address this research question, we conducted a mixed methods study of how continuous experimentation scaled at Microsoft. We describe the research method in detail next.

12.3 Method

This research work is an inductive case study and was conducted in collaboration with the Analysis and Experimentation (A&E) team at Microsoft. The inspiration for the study originates from an internal model used at A&E, which is used to illustrate and compare progress of different product teams on their path towards data-driven development at scale. The study is based on historical data points that were collected over a period of two years and complemented with a series of semi-structured interviews, observations, and meeting participations. In principle, it is an in-depth and single case study [384], however, our participants are from different organizational units and product teams with fundamentally different product and service offerings. Several of the participants worked in other data-driven organizations before joining the Microsoft A&E team. The A&E team provides a platform and service for running controlled experiments for customers. Its data scientists, engineers and program managers are involved with partner teams and departments across Microsoft on a daily basis. The participants involved in this research work are primarily collaborating with the following Microsoft product and services teams: Bing, Cortana, Office, MSN.com, Skype and Xbox.

12.3.1 Data Collection

The data collection for this research was conducted in two streams. The first stream consisted of collection of archival data on past controlled experiments conducted at Microsoft. The first author of this paper worked with the Microsoft Analysis & Experimentation team for a period of 10 weeks. During this time, he collected documents, presentations, meeting minutes and other notes available to Microsoft employees about the past controlled experiments, the development of the experimentation platform and organizational developments conducted at Microsoft A&E over the last 5 years. In cumulative, we collected approximately 130 pages of qualitative data (including a number of figures and illustrations).

The second stream consisted of three parts. The first author (1) participated in weekly experimentation meetings, (2) attended internal training on controlled experimentation and other related topics, and (3) conducted a number of semi-structured interviews with Microsoft employees. In all three data collection activities, the first author was accompanied by one of the other three authors (as schedules permitted). At all meetings and training, we took notes that were shared between us at the end of each activity. The individual interviews were recorded and transcribed by the first researcher.

The second author of this paper has been working with the Analysis & Experimentation team at Microsoft for a period of six years. He was the main contact person for the other three researchers throughout the data collection and analysis period and advised the diverse selection of data scientist, managers and software engineers that we interviewed. In total, we conducted 14 semi-structured interviews (1 woman, 13 men) using a questionnaire guide with 11 open-ended questions. The participants that work with different product teams were invited for a half an hour interview by the first two authors. The interview format started with an introduction and a short explanation of the research being conducted. Participants were then asked on their experience with conducting controlled experiments, how they document learnings from those experiments, and how their practices changed over time. We also asked for examples of successes, pitfalls, and pain points that they experience while conducting controlled experiments. We provide a detailed list of our interviewees, their roles and their primary product teams in Table 12.1 below. The ones with n/a do not collaborate with product teams directly, but are rather focusing on platform development and other activities within the A&E team.

Table 12.1 Interview participants

Interview	Role	Length (min)	Product
1	Senior Data Scientist	45	Skype
2	Data Scientist	45	Skype
3	Principal Group Engineering Mgr.	30	n/a
4	Principal Data Scientist	30	Bing
5	Senior Software Engineer	30	n/a
6	Senior Data Scientist	45	MSN
7	Principal Data Scientist Mgr.	30	Office
8	Principal Data Scientist Mgr.	30	Office
9	Principal Data Scientist & Architect	30	Bing
10	GPM Program Manager	30	n/a
11	Principal Software Engineer	30	Bing
12	Senior Applied Researcher	30	Ads
13	Senior Program Manager	30	Bing
14	Senior Program Manager	30	Cortana

12.3.2 Data Analysis

We analyzed the collected data in two steps. First, we grouped the data that belonged to a certain product. Next, we grouped products in 4 buckets based on the number of experiments that their product teams are capable of executing per annum (i.e. 1–9, 10–99, 100–999, and 1000+). Second, and with the goal to model the evolution of continuous experimentation, we performed inductive category development [312]. In the first step, we emerged with three high level definitions of categories that represent our research interest (namely technical evolution, organizational evolution and business evolution). Next, we formulated the categories under each of the three categories by reading through the collected data and assigning codes to concepts that appeared in it. This approach is similar to the Grounded Theory approach as we didn't have preconceptions on which categories to form beforehand [107]. The final categories are visible in our model in Fig. 12.5. To develop the content of the table, we backtracked the codes within the buckets. Using a 'venting' method, i.e. a process whereby interpretations are continuously discussed with professional colleagues, we iteratively verified and updated our theory on the content for each of the four phases of our models in Fig. 12.5. The A&E team provided continuous feedback on the developing theory and helped to clear any discrepancies in the raw data.

12.3.3 Validity Considerations

12.3.3.1 Construct Validity

To improve the study's construct validity, we complemented the archival data collection activities with individual semi-structured interviews, meetings and trainings. This enabled us to ask clarifying questions, prevent misinterpretations, and study the phenomena from different angles. Meeting minutes and interview transcriptions were independently assessed by three researchers to guarantee inter-rater reliability. Since this study has been conducted in a highly data-driven company, all the participants were familiar with the research topic and expectations between the researchers and participants were well aligned. The constructed artifact was continuously validated with the A&E team members during the study.

12.3.3.2 External Validity

The main result of this paper details an evolution towards becoming a data-driven company as experienced at Microsoft. The first author conducted this research while collaborating with the second author who is permanently employed at the case company. This set-up enabled continuous access and insight. However, and since this approach differs from a traditional case study [384], the contributions of this paper risk being biased from this extensive inside view. The main contribution can thus not directly translate to other companies. However, we believe that the phases of our model, especially the dimension concerning the technical evolution, are similar to the ones that other software companies traverse on their path towards becoming data-driven. The 'Experimentation Evolution Model' can be used to compare other companies and advise them on what to focus on next in order to efficiently scale their data-driven practices. The embedded systems domain is one example area where companies are aiming to become data-driven and that we previously studied [46, 117, 118]. The phases of our model can be applied to this domain.

In the next section, we show the empirical data by describing four controlled experiments from different product teams.

12.4 Empirical Foundation

In this section, we briefly present examples of controlled experiments conducted at Microsoft. The space limitations make it difficult to show all the depth and breadth of our empirical data. Due to this limitation, we select four example experiments. With each of them, we aim to illustrate the capabilities and limitations that product teams at Microsoft experience as they evolve their data-driven practices. We start with Office, where data-driven development is beginning to gain momentum and where the first controlled experiments were recently conducted. Next, we present an example from Xbox and an example from MSN where the experimentation is well established. Finally, we conclude the section by providing an illustrative experiment from Bing where experimentation is indispensable and deeply embedded in the teams' development process.

12.4.1 Office Contextual Bar Experiment

Microsoft Office is a well-known suite of products designed for increasing work productivity. Data-driven practices in Office product teams are in the early stages. The product team responsible for the edit interface in Office mobile apps recently conducted a design experiment on their Word, Excel, and PowerPoint apps. They believed that introducing a Contextual Command Bar (see Fig. 12.1 below) would increase the engagement compared to a version of the product without the contextual bar. Their hypothesis was that mobile phone users will do more editing on the phone because the contextual command bar will improve editing efficiency and will result in increased commonality and frequency of edits and 2-week retention.

During the set-up of the experiment, the team ran into issues with measuring the number of edits. The instrumentation was still in the early stages, and the telemetry teams did not accurately log the edit events. These issues had to be fixed prior to the start of the experiment. The results of a two-week experiment indicated a substantial increase in engagement (counts of edits), but no statistically significant change in 2-week retention. The experiment provided the team with two key learnings: (1) Proper instrumentation of existing features and the new feature is essential for computing experiment metrics, (2) It is important to define global metrics that are good leading indicators and that can change in a reasonable timeframe.

12.4.2 Xbox Deals for Gold Members

Xbox is a well-known platform for video gaming. Experimentation is becoming well established with this product and their teams have been conducting experiments on several different features.

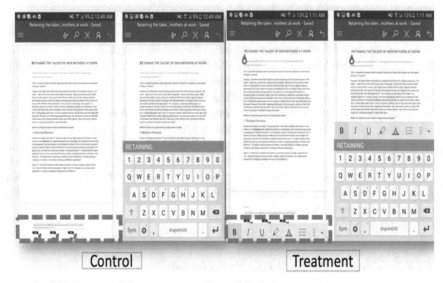

Fig. 12.1 The "Contextual Bar" experiment on Word mobile app

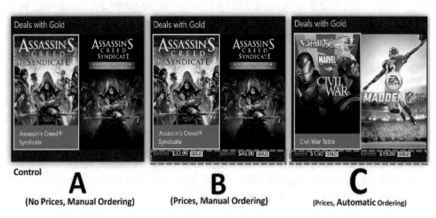

Fig. 12.2 The "Xbox deals" experiment

In one of the experiments, a product team at Xbox aimed to identify whether showing prices (original price and the discount) in the weekly deals stripe, and using algorithmic as opposed to editorial ordering of the items in the stripe impacts engagement and purchases. They experimented with two different variants. On Fig. 12.2, we illustrate the experiment control (A) and both of the treatments (B, C).

At Xbox, instrumentation is well established and a reliable pipeline for data collection exists. Metrics that measure user engagement and purchases are established and consist of a combination of different signals from the logs aggregated per user, session and other analysis units. In contrast to the Office Word experiment above, the Xbox team autonomously set-up their experiments, however, they still require assistance on the execution and monitoring of the experiment and at the analysis stage to interpret results. The two-week experiment showed that, compared to control, treatment B decreased engagement with the stripe. The purchases, however, did not decrease. By showing prices upfront treatment B provided better user experience by engaging the users who are interested in a purchase and sparing a click for those not interested. Treatment C provided even greater benefit, increasing both engagement with the stripe and purchases made. In this experiment the team learned that (1) Showing prices upfront results in better user experience, and (2) Algorithmic ordering of deals beats manual editorial ordering.

12.4.3 MSN.com News Personalization

In contrast to Office Word and Xbox where experimentation is primarily conducted with features focusing on design changes, teams at MSN.com experiment with most feature changes. In one of the recent experiments, they aimed to test a personalization algorithm developed within Microsoft Research for their news page. The hypothesis was that user engagement with the version that uses the machine learning personalization algorithm would increase in comparison to the manually curated articles. In contrast to Word and Xbox teams, the MSN product team autonomously set-up and execute experiments. A number of Data Scientists were hired in their product team and they partner with the central Analysis and Experimentation team to interpret and analyze complex experiments. Contrary to the expectations, in the initial iteration of the experiment machine learning algorithm performed worse than the manual ordering. After some investigation, a bug was found in the algorithm. The bug was fixed and several subsequent iterations of the experiment were run to tune the algorithm. At the end, the algorithmic ordering resulted in a substantial lift in engagement. In Fig. 12.3 below we show an example screenshot from one of the iterations.

12.4.4 Bing Bot Detection Experiment

Bing is a search engine developed by Microsoft. On this product, several teams at Microsoft conduct over 10.000 experiments per year ranging from large design modifications to every bug fix or minor improvement. In contrast to the previous examples, teams at Bing set-up, execute and analyze experiments autonomously and without the help of the Analysis & Experimentation data scientists. At any given point in time, almost every user of the product is in at least a few of the experiments simultaneously. As users are put into more and more concurrent experiments, the chance of unexpected interactions between those experiments increases, which can lead to bad user experience and inaccurate results. Preventing interactions where possible, and detecting where not (alerts fire automatically when experiments hurt

Fig. 12.3 The "MSN.com personalization" experiment

the user experience, or interact with other experiments) has been a critical element for delivering trustworthy, large-scale experimentation.

The core purpose of Bing is to provide search results to its users. Finding relevant results, however, is a computational operation that extensively consumes infrastructure capacity. One way to save on resources is to prevent computer bots from performing the actual search by e.g. returning results from a smaller in-memory index that is orders of magnitude cheaper to serve. The experiment that we briefly present in this section targeted exactly this scenario. The hypothesis was that with an improved and more pervasive bot-detection algorithm, human users will not be harmed and fewer resources will be used for the computation of search results. Conducting such experiments, however, involves the use of advanced features that prevent potentially harmful variants (see e.g. Fig. 12.4 below) from affecting a large population by automatically checking alerts and incrementally ramping the number of users assigned to the treatment.

The results of the particular experiment indicated a 10% saving on infrastructure resources without introducing user harm. Screenshot on Fig. 12.4 is, however, a part of another experiment with a slightly different outcome.

Fig. 12.4 An archival experiment with Bing that introduced user harm

12.5 The Experimentation Evolution Model

In this section, and based on the empirical presentation of products and related experiments in Sect. 12.4, we present the transition process model of moving from a situation with ad-hoc data analysis towards continuous controlled experimentation at scale. We name this process the "Experimentation Evolution Model" and use this term to describe the phases that companies and their product teams follow while evolving their data-driven development practices towards continuous experimentation at scale. It is based on the empirical data collected at Microsoft and inspired by a model developed internally at A&E.

In our model, and after listing a number of prerequisites for experimentation, we present three dimensions of evolution: technical, organizational and business evolution. In the technical evolution part, we focus on the technical aspects such as the complexity of the experimentation platform, the pervasiveness of experimentation in product teams, and the overall focus of the development activities. The organizational evolution focuses on the organization of the data science teams and their self-sufficiency for experimentation. Finally, in the business evolution part, we discuss the focus of the Overall Evaluation Criteria.

The four phases of the "Experimentation Evolution Model", namely "crawl", "walk", "run" and "fly", are summarized on Fig. 12.5 below and described in detail in the remainder of this section.

	Category/Phase	Crawl	Walk	Run	Fly
Technical Evolution	Technical focus of product dev. Activities	(1) Logging of signals (2) Work on data quality issues (3) Manual analysis of experiments. Transitioning from the debugging logs to a format that can be used for data-driven development.	(1) Setting-up a reliable pipeline (2) Creation of simple metrics. Combining signals with analysis units. Four types of metrics are created: debug metrics (largest group), success metrics, guardrail metrics and data quality metrics.	(1) Learning experiments (2) Comprehensive metrics. Creation of comprehensive set of metrics using the knowledge from the learning experiments.	(1) Standardized process for metric design and evaluation, and OEC improvement
	Experimentation platform complexity	No experimentation platform. An initial experiment can be coded manually (ad-hoc).	Platform is required. 3rd party platform can be used or internally developed. The following two features are required: • Power Analysis • Pre-Experiment A/A testing	New platform features. The experimentation platform should be extended with the following features: • Alerting • Control of carry-over effect • Experiment iteration support	Advanced platform features. The following features are needed: • Interaction control and detection • Near real-time detection and automatic shutdown of harmful experiments • Institutional memory
	Experimentation pervasiveness	Generating management support. Experimenting with e.g. design options for which it's not a priori clear which one is better. To generate management support to move to the next stage.	Experiment on individual feature level. Broadening the types of experiments run on a limited set of features (design to performance, from performance to infrastructure experiments)	Expanding to (1) more features and (2) other products. Experiment on most new features and most products.	Experiment with every minor change to portfolio. Experiment with any change on all products in the portfolio. Even to e.g. small bug fixes on feature level.
Organizational Evolution	Engineering team self-sufficiency	Limited understanding. External Data Scientist knowledge is needed in order to set-up, execute and analyse a controlled experiment.	Creation and set-up of experiments. Creating the experiment (instrumentation, A/A testing, assigning traffic) is managed by the local Experiment Owners. Data scientists responsible for the platform supervise Experiment Owners and correct errors.	Creation and execution of experiments. Includes monitoring for bad experiments, making ramp-up and shut-down decisions, designing and deploying experiment-specific metrics.	Creation, execution and analyses of experiments. Scorecards showing the experiment results are intuitive for interpretation and conclusion making.
	Experimentation team organization	Standalone. Fully centralized data science team. In product teams, however, no or very little data science skills. The standalone team needs to train the local product teams on experimentation. We introduce the role of Experiment Owner (EO).	Embedded. Data science team that implemented the platform supports different product teams and their Experiment Owners. Product teams do not have their own data scientists that would analyse experiments independently.	Partnership. Product teams hire their own data scientists that create a strong unity with business. Learning between the teams is limited to their communication.	Partnership. Small data science teams in each of the product teams. Learnings from experiments are shared automatically across organization via the institutional memory features.
Business Evolution	Overall Evaluation Criteria (OEC)	OEC is defined for the first set of experiments with a few key signals that will help ground expectations and evaluation of the experiment results.	OEC evolves from a few key signals to a structured set of metrics consisting of Success, Guardrail and Data Quality metrics. Debug metrics are not a part of OEC.	OEC is tailored with the findings from the learning experiments. Single metric as a weighted combination of others is desired.	OEC is stable, only periodic changes allowed (e.g. 1 per year). It is also used for setting the performance goals for teams within the organization.

Fig. 12.5 The "Experimentation Evolution Model"

12.5.1 Prerequisites

Although most of the requirements for successful experimentation arise while we scale the number of experiments and teams, a few need to be fulfilled beforehand. To evaluate the product statistics, skills that are typically possessed by data scientists [243] are required within the company. Here, we specifically emphasize the understanding of hypothesis testing, randomization, sample size determination, and confidence interval calculation with multiple testing. For companies that lack these skills and wish to train their engineers on these topics, online resources and kits are available.[1] Combining these skills with domain knowledge about the product will enable companies to generate the first set of hypotheses for evaluation. The second major prerequisite is the availability of accessing the product instrumentation data. We discuss how to implement the instrumentation in the following sections, however, companies first need to have policies in place that allow them to provide experimenters access to the data. In some domains, this is a serious concern and needs to be addressed both on legal and technical levels.

12.5.2 Crawl Phase

As the starting point on the path towards continuous experimentation at scale, product teams start by configuring the first experiment.

12.5.2.1 Technical Aspect

Focus:

The technical focus of this phase is twofold. First, and the main focus of this phase is the implementation of the logging system. In non-data driven companies, logging exists for the purpose of debugging product features [25, 140, 494]. This is usually very limited and not useful for analyzing how users interact with the products. Logging procedures in the organization need to be updated by creating a centralized catalog of events in the form of class and enumeration, and implemented in the product telemetry. The goal of such systematic logging is that a data scientist, analyst, or anyone else in the organization who is not familiar with the feature or the product itself, can understand what action or event was triggered and logged by simply looking at the name of the event. Names for events should be consistent across products and platforms so that it is easy to search for them and link them with tangible actions in the product. We name the data collected or sent from a product or feature for the purpose of data-driven development signals. Examples of signals are clicks, swipes over an image, interactions with a product, time spent loading a

---

[1] http://www.experimentationhub.com/hypothesis-kit.html

feature, files touched, etc. Based on the complete set of signals, an analyst should be able to reconstruct the interactions that a user had with the product.

Second, any quality issues with writing and collecting signals need to be solved. The goal is to have a reliable system where events are consistently logged and repetitive actions result in identical results.

Experimentation Platform Complexity:

In this initial phase, an experimentation platform is not required. With signals systematically collected, a product team can perform the first controlled experiment manually. They can do this by splitting the users between two versions of the same product and measuring how the distribution of signals differs between the versions, for example. Practitioners can use the guidance on how to calculate the statistics behind a controlled experiment in [252]. In summary, if the difference between the values for the Treatment group and the Control group is statistically significant, we conclude with high probability that the change introduced in the treatment group caused the observed effect. Conventionally, a 95% confidence interval is used.

Experimentation Pervasiveness:

Experiments in this phase are for targeted components of a product and are not pervasive. Typically, product teams should start to experiment with a feature where multiple versions are available. The main purpose of the first experiments is to gain traction and evangelize the results to obtain the necessary funding needed to develop an experimentation platform and culture within the company. As an example, product teams can start with a design experiment for which it is not a priori clear which of the variants is better. The results of the first experiment should not be trusted without assuring that the data quality issues have been addressed.

Engineering Team Self-Sufficiency

In this initial phase, experiment set-up, execution and analysis is conducted by a data scientist team. Product teams typically do not possess the necessary skills to conduct trustworthy controlled experiments and correctly analyze the results on their own. We use the term Experiment Owner (EO) to refer to one or more individuals from the product team involved with the experiment. Experiment Owners are the individuals that understand both the product and the experiment, and are used as the main contact between the data science team and the product teams for set up and interpretation of the experiments and their results. (e) Experimentation team organization: In this phase, product teams require training and help from a standalone data scientist team. This organization of data scientists allows freedom for generating ideas and long-term thinking that are needed for development of the experimentation platform.

12.5.2.2 Business Aspect

Overall Evaluation Criteria:

The aim of the "Crawl" phase is to define an OEC for the first set of experiments that will help ground expectations and evaluation of the experiment results. In concept, an OEC stands for Overall (in view of all circumstances or conditions), Evaluation (the process determining the significance, worth, or condition of something by careful appraisal and study) and Criteria (a standard on which a judgment or decision may be based). In practice, and for the first experiments, data scientists and Experiment Owners should collaborate on defining the OEC from a few key signals. An OEC should typically be closely related to long-term business goals and teams should be informed upfront that it will develop over time.

12.5.3 Walk Phase

After the initial logging and instrumentation have been configured, the focus of the R&D activities transitions towards defining metrics and an experimentation platform.

12.5.3.1 Technical Aspect

Focus:

In contrast to the "crawl" phase where experiments were evaluated by comparing the volume and distribution of signals such as clicks and page views, the focus in this phase is on defining a set of metrics combined from those signals. Metrics are functions that take signals as an input and output a number per unit. Signals should first be categorized into classes and combined into metrics by being aggregated over analysis units. Microsoft recognizes three classes of signals for their products: action signals (e.g. clicks, page views, visits, etc.), time signals (minutes per session, total time on site, page load time, etc.), and value signals (revenue, units purchased, ads clicked, etc.). The units of analysis vary depending on the context and product. The following apply at Microsoft for web products: per user (e.g. clicks per user), per session (e.g. minutes per session), per user-day (e.g. page views per day), and per experiment (e.g. clicks per page view).

For other types of products, units of analysis might be different. For a well-known video-conferencing Microsoft product, "per call" is a useful unit of analysis. And by combining signals with units of analysis, simple metrics are created. Microsoft typically aims to construct four types of metrics: success metrics (the ones that we will intend to improve), guardrail metrics (constraints that are not allowed to be changed), data quality metrics (the metrics that ensure that the experiments will be set-up correctly), and debug metrics (the ones that help deeper understanding and drill down into success and guardrail metrics). A popular research contribution from Google provides practical guidance on the creation of these metrics for measuring user experience on a large scale [377].

Experimentation Platform Complexity:

With more experiments being run, a need for an experimentation platform arises. Software development organizations can decide to either start developing their own experimentation platform or utilize one of the commercial products designed for this purpose. Several third party experimentation platforms are available to software companies out of the box.[2, 3, 4] Regardless of the decision, the experimentation platform should have two essential features integrated in this phase. (1) Power Analysis and (2) pre-experiment A/A testing.

- Power analysis. This is a feature that is used to determine the minimal sample size for detecting the change in an experiment and it should be implemented early in order to automate decisions on the duration of the experiments. This will prevent some of the common pitfalls (e.g. running experiments longer than required in order to find the change or having an under-powered experiment) [5].
- Pre-experiment A/A testing. An A/A feature assigns to the treatment group the same experience as the control group is being exposed to. Data is collected and its variability is assed for power calculations and to test the experimentation system (the null hypothesis should be rejected about 5% of the time when a 95% confidence level is used). After ensuring that there is no imbalance on key OEC metrics, one of the A's is reconfigured into B – the A/B test is started on the same population. The number of experiments in this phase is relatively low. This allows for central planning and scheduling of experiments to avoid interactions. Each experiment is still closely monitored to detect user harm or data quality issues.

Experimentation Pervasiveness:

In contrast to the "crawl" phase where experiments were mostly with design variants or features with alternative implementations, product teams in this phase move on to different types of experiments with the same product. From design focused experiments (testing a set of design alternatives) the teams advance to performance experiments (testing performance between different variants of the same feature). Infrastructure experiments (testing resource alternatives) are another example of advancing the experimentation within the product domain.

12.5.3.2 Organizational Aspect

Engineering Team Self-Sufficiency:

In this phase, EO's responsibility for creating the experiments (scheduling the experiment, performing the power analysis etc.) is transitioning from a data science expert to a product/program manager employed in the product team. However, the execution, monitoring, and analysis of the experiments is still the responsibility of the data scientists.

Experimentation Team Organization:

The results should be evangelized across the team and bad practices should be disputed (e.g. experimenting only on preview audience). We recommend embedded organization of data scientists that support product teams with increasing data quality, metrics creation and developing an Overall Evaluation Criteria. Embedded data scientists in the product teams can hold the role of Experiment Owners or work closely with other product team members that have this role. They communicate and work with the central platform team. The products within organizations will typically share certain characteristics. With this organization, a bridge in transferring learnings from one embedded data science product team to another is established.

12.5.3.3 Business Aspect

Overall Evaluation Criteria:

Most investments by feature and product teams in this phase are to address data quality issues and instrumentation to build an initial set of metrics. It is important to understand and document metric movements, validate findings, and build experimentation muscle within the product and feature team. The initial Overall Evaluation Criteria should be improved with the findings from multiple experiments and supported by multiple metrics. In contrast to the "crawl" phase, the OEC will evolve from a few key signals to a structured set of metrics consisting of success metrics (the ones we intend to improve), guardrail metrics (constraints that are not allowed to be changed) and data quality metrics (the metrics that ensure that the experiments were set-up correctly and results can be trusted). It is very important to work close with many product team members and reach agreement on the OEC. When disagreements occur, the OEC should be backtracked and concerns addressed.

12.5.4 Run Phase

In the Run Phase, product teams ramp up the number of experiments and iterate quickly with the purpose of identifying the effect of the experiments on the business.

12.5.4.1 Technical Aspect

Focus:

In the "walk" phase, product teams started to merge signals into metrics. In the "Run" phase, however, these metrics should evolve and become comprehensive. Metrics should evolve from counting signals to capturing more abstract concepts such as "loyalty" and "success", closely related to long-term company goals [486]. To evaluate the metrics product teams should start running learning experiments where a small degradation in user experience is intentionally introduced for learning purposes (e.g. degradation of results, slow down of a feature). With such learning experiments, teams will have a better understanding of the importance of certain features and the effect that changes have on the metrics. Knowingly hurting users slightly in the short-term (e.g., in a 2-week experiment) enables teams at Microsoft to understand fundamental issues and thereby improve the experience in the long-term [250].

Experimentation Platform Complexity:

To scale above 100 data-driven experiments per year, the power analysis and pre-experiment A/A features that were implemented in the "Walk" phase will not be sufficient. The experimentation platform needs to be extended with additional features that will both (1) prevent incidents and (2) increase the efficiency of product teams by automating certain aspects of the workflow. We describe the new features next:

- Alerting. With an increasing number of experiments, having a manual overview review of metric movements will become a resource-demanding task for Experiment Owners. Automated alerting should be introduced together with the ability to divert traffic to control if an emergency situation occurs (e.g. a decrease of an important metric). The naïve approach to alerting on any statistically significant negative metric changes will lead to an unacceptable number of false alerts and make the entire alerting system overloaded and hard to interpret. Detailed guidance on how to avoid this situation and develop alerting that works is available in [250].
- Control of carry-over effects. Harmful experiments have an effect on the population that may carry over into the follow-up experiments and cause biased results. A feature that re-randomizes the population between experiments should

be implemented in order to prevent a high concentration of biased users in either treatment or control.

- Experiment iteration support. This is a feature that enables re-iteration of an experiment. Initially, experiments in this phase should start on a small percentage of traffic (e.g. 0.5% of users assigned to treatment). The reason is that, as it gets easier to configure and start an experiment, the risk of user harm also increases (changes to production software risk the introduction of degradations). Over time, the percentage should automatically increase (by e.g. running a new iteration of the experiment with a higher setting) if no alerts on guardrail metrics were triggered beforehand. The benefit of this feature is twofold. First, it offers assurance that the impact of a harmful experience will be limited to a low number of users. Second, it optimizes the time to ramp to full power, which minimizes the time to analysis of experimentation results.

Experimentation Pervasiveness:

In contrast to the "Walk" phase where experiments were conducted on a single product, in the "Run" phase companies aim to expand the scope of controlled experimentation. They can achieve this by expanding (1) to more features within the products and more importantly, (2) to other product teams. Product teams should be experimenting with every increment to their products (e.g. introductions of new features, algorithm changes, etc.). Experimenting should be the norm for identifying the value of new features as well as for identifying the impact of smaller changes to existing features. Past experiment data can be used to understand the correlation and relationship between movements in different business goals.

12.5.4.2 Organizational Aspect

Engineering Team Self-Sufficiency:

Experiment Owners that were introduced in the "Crawl" phase and the ones that were responsible for the creation of experiments in the "Walk" phase now receive the complete responsibility to execute their experiments. The execution of experiments includes running power analysis to determine treatment allocation, monitoring for bad experiments (e.g. the ones with triggered alerts), making shut-down and ramp-up decisions, and resolution of errors. However, the analysis of results should still be supervised by the data scientists.

Experimentation Team Organization:

We recommend to keep a partnership approach to the arrangement of data scientist teams by assigning a fixed number of data scientists to work with product teams (they are employed in the product teams directly). They review experiments, decide on the evaluation criteria, and are trained by the central platform data science team to become local operational data scientists capable of setting-up the experiments, executing them, and resolving basic alerts.

12.5.4.3 Business Aspect

Overall Evaluation Criteria:

The purpose of this phase is to tailor OEC using the knowledge obtained from the learning experiments. Typically, and as presented in the "Walk" phase, OEC will be a combination of success, guardrail and data quality metrics. In the "Run" phase, however, it will be evolved to capture concepts such as "loyalty" and "success", and corrected with the findings from learning experiments. Selecting a single metric, possibly as a weighted combination of objectives is highly desired. The reason for that is that (1) single metric forces inherent tradeoffs to be made once for multiple experiments and (2) it aligns the organization behind a clear objective. A good practice in this phase is to also start accumulating a corpus of experiments with known outcomes and re-run the evaluation every time changes are introduced to an OEC. A good OEC will correctly determine the outcome.

12.5.5 Fly Phase

In the "Fly" phase, controlled experiments are the norm for every change to any product in the company's portfolio. Such changes include not only obvious and visual changes such as improvements of a user interface, but also subtler changes such as different machine learning and prediction algorithms that might affect ranking or content selection. However, with such pervasiveness, a number of new features are needed in the experimentation platform and new responsibilities are assigned to experiment owners.

12.5.5.1 Technical Aspect

Focus:

In the previous phases, technical activities focused on implementing reliable instrumentation, creating comprehensive metrics and conducting learning experiments. In the "Fly" phase, however, we recommend to focus on standardizing the process for the evaluation and improvement of the Overall Evaluation Criteria. An OEC should be used as a foundation to define the direction for teams developing the product. At the same time, and since customers' preferences change over time [486], a product team should invest in standardizing metric design and evaluation practices and scheduling the activities for updating the existing OEC. See [486] for details.

Experimentation Platform Complexity:

In addition to the features introduced in the previous phases, advanced features such as interaction control and detection, auto-detection and shut-down of harmful experiments, and institutional memory collection are needed. These features will enable experiment owners to conduct a larger number of experiments and protect users from harm. We describe them briefly below:

- Interaction control and detection. A statistical interaction between two treatments A and B exists if their combined effect is not the same as the sum of two individual treatment effects [252]. This is a feature that prevents such experiments with conflicting outcomes to run on the same sets of users (e.g. one experiment is changing the background color to black, another the text to gray). Control for such interactions should be established and handled automatically. After detecting an interaction, the platform should send an alert to the experiment owners. Detailed guidance on how to implement this feature is available in [252].
- Near real-time detection and automatic shutdown of harmful experiments. In the "Run" phase alerting was configured by periodically (e.g. bi-hourly) calculating scorecards on critical guardrail metrics. In the "Fly" phase, and with thousands of experiments simultaneously active, the detection of harmful experiments should be near real-time and automatic emergency shutdown functionality should be implemented (the time to exclude users minimized).
- Institutional Memory. To prevent an experiment owner from repeating an experiment that someone else previously conducted, an institutional memory of experimentation should be kept. It should be searchable and include all the essential metadata of the experiment (e.g. hypothesis, experiment outcome, selected markets and execution date).

Experimentation Pervasiveness:

In contrast to the previous phases where controlled experiments were primarily used to support decisions on new feature introductions and deletions, in the "Fly" phase every small change to any product in the portfolio (e.g. a minor bug fix) should be supported by data from a controlled experiment. Advanced features described above enable product teams to experiment at this scale and expand their experimentation capabilities to cover the complete portfolio.

12.5.5.2 Organizational Aspect

Engineering Team

self-sufficiency: In contrast to the previous phase where the analysis of experiment results was supported by a data science team, Experiment Owners in this phase work autonomously. They create, execute and analyze the results of the experiments. The central data science team reviews experiments only on demand.

Experimentation Team Organization:

The partnership approach to the arrangement of data scientist teams will be efficient at this scale. Local product teams with their operational data science teams are empowered to run experiments on their own. A central data science team should be in charge of the experimentation platform and leasing its individual data scientists to cooperate with product teams to resolve issues and share experience.

12.5.5.3 Business Aspect

Overall Evaluation Criteria:

The OEC at this phase should be rather stable and well defined. The OEC is used for setting the performance goals for teams within the organization. In contrast to the previous phases where the OEC was evolving, changes to the overall evaluation criteria in the "Fly" phase should occur only periodically (e.g. once per year) and follow and standardized process. This gives independent teams across the product portfolio a chance to focus their work on understanding how the features they own affect the key metrics, prioritizing their work to improve the OEC.

12.6 Conclusions

Controlled Experimentation is becoming the norm in the software industry for reliably evaluating ideas with customers and correctly prioritizing product development activities [49, 119, 120, 252, 345, 346]. Previous research publications by Microsoft [250, 252], Google [453] and academia [119, 120, 345, 346] reveal the essential building blocks for an experimentation platform; however, they leave out the details on how to incrementally scale (e.g. which technical and organizational activities to focus on at what phase). With our research contribution, which is based on an extensive case study at Microsoft, we aim to provide guidance on this topic and enable other companies to establish or scale their experimentation practices. Our main contribution is the "Experimentation Evolution Model". In the model, we summarize the four phases of evolution and describe the focus of technical, organizational and business activities for each of them. Researchers and practitioners can use this model to position other case companies and guide them to the next phase by suggesting the necessary features.

In future research, we plan to (1) research the impact of controlled experimentation with respect to the four phases from the "Experimentation Evolution Model" and (2), validate our model in other companies.

Acknowledgements

We wish to thank Brian Frasca, Ronny Kohavi and others at Microsoft that provided the input for and feedback on this research. Ronny Kohavi was the creator of a similar model used internally in A&E that was used as inspiration for this work. The first author of this paper would also like to thank the A&E team for the invaluable opportunity to work with them during his research internship at Microsoft.

Part V
AI Engineering

Introduction to the AI Engineering Theme

Jan Bosch (Theme Leader 2019–)

1 Introduction

The term artificial intelligence (AI) triggers many things in terms of its inherent meaning and potential. The notion of a machine with the same level of intellect as a human or even far exceeding it is enthralling and scary at the same time. Several science fiction movies build on the HAL 9000 or Terminator theme of artificial intelligence bent on controlling or even exterminating humankind.

The reality of contemporary AI is of course that general AI is still far off, if we ever reach that point, but narrow AI has proven to have great potential in a variety of domains. Narrow AI builds on techniques that have been developed for decades or, in some cases, even centuries but are now coming to fruition because of two main developments. First, the Big Data era has increased the availability of large data sets with orders of magnitude compared to earlier. As machine learning (ML) algorithms and especially deep learning (DL) perform better as the amount of training data increases, the availability of data has been a major driver in the success of ML/DL. Second, Moore's law and especially massively parallel computing architectures such as those found in graphical processing units (GPUs) provide a compute infrastructure that allows us to conduct the computations required to enable ML/DL algorithms at scales that were unfathomable in earlier decades.

Although the likelihood of Skynet taking over the world remains as close to zero as one can hope, narrow AI and specifically ML/DL have established themselves as wonderful technologies complementary to traditional software technologies. Ranging from recommendation engines to house price prediction and from automatic fault detection in production lines to autonomous robotaxis, we can see ML/DL emerging in a variety of use cases across all industries.

The success of ML/DL has caused an enormous upswing in the interest and investment in AI, but one can see that the majority is focused on ML/DL algorithms and achieving optimal outcomes in terms of accuracy, recall, and F1 scores. Although this is important, it is easy to forget that ML/DL models operate in a context that is critical to get in place if one hopes to have a production deployment of these models. This includes data pipelines for feeding the models, monitoring and logging, automatic retraining solutions, etc.

In our research with the Software Center companies as well as others, we found that the development of ML/DL models was only a small part of the overall development and evolution process. In fact, most effort was spent, e.g., on collecting and labeling suitable training data, setting up data pipelines, creating infrastructure for storing data sets, and interfacing the ML/DL model with the rest of the system. To provide a perspective and a focus for all the work outside of model development, we defined the term "AI engineering" to indicate all the engineering work that has to take place to create production deployments of ML/DL models in software-intensive systems.

The fifth theme of Software Center is concerned with this challenge of AI engineering and the chapter in this part provide a research agenda as well as cases of research where we have addressed some of the AI engineering challenges. The remainder of this chapter is organized as follows. In the next section, we introduce the HoliDev model that provides a structure to place AI into, next to other types of development. The section after that raises some of the AI engineering challenges that we have identified in our research with the Software Center companies. Subsequently, we provide an overview of the chapters in this part. Before concluding, however, we look into the future and discuss some of the ongoing developments that will cause significant transitions in the way companies work with AI, specifically around the shift from offline to online training.

2 HoliDev Model

The first challenge that many struggle with when working with artificial intelligence is that the resulting ML/DL models need to operate in a software-intensive system that contains components that were developed in different ways. The system as a whole is likely to contain mechanical and electronics components and subsystems that are subject to very different constraints and development processes. However, software can also be developed in very different ways and it is important to recognize this.

In Fig. 1, three types of development are explicitly considered and each of these have their own unique characteristics. These types include:

- **Requirements**: Development driven by requirements simply follows the specifications as provided by customers or product management. Building to requirements is the oldest way of building software as it does not require anything beyond a customer signing off on the result of a development effort. Requirements have ample challenges, including the difficulty of writing clear and unambiguous specifications, the challenges of misinterpreting requirements by developers as well as customers realizing after the fact that the specification did in fact not address their needs.

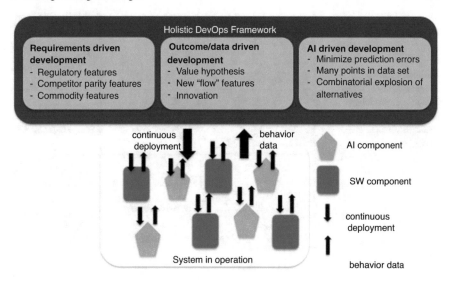

Fig. 1 The HoliDev Model

- **Outcome**: The outcome- or data-driven development model is where the team is asked to optimize some value hypothesis. Typically, this type of development is used for new functionality where the team is not clear on the best way to realize the functionality, even if they are able to clearly define what they are optimizing for. Typical techniques in this context include A/B testing. Here, teams develop hypotheses on improving one or more KPIs and use the A/B test to quantitatively establish which alternative is superior.

- **AI**: Finally, AI-driven development is concerned with building, training, evaluating, and evolving ML/DL models that match large data sets from a prediction, classification, or regression perspective. Several metrics can be used to determine the suitability of a model, including accuracy, recall, and F1 scores, but the basic principle is that the model is trained by the data rather than by human effort.

The figure indicates not only that the three types of development result in components that end up in the same system and consequently need to integrate so that each can contribute optimally to the successful operation of the system. It also shows that each of the components is subject to continuous deployment and constant monitoring and logging in order to collect behavioral data from the system.

3 AI Engineering Challenges

Over the last several years, we have worked with most of the companies in Software Center as well as other companies on challenges related to industrial deployment of ML/DL models. As shown in Fig. 2, we worked with several cases in these companies

cases	identified problems		strategic focus
Real Estate Valuation	Lack of labelled data	Data drift	
Predicting Oil and Gas Recovery	Lack of metadata	Data dependencies	
Predicting User Retention	Shortage of diverse samples	Managing categorical data	data quality
Weather Forecasting	Heterogeneity in data	Managing sequences in data	management
Credit Card Fraud Detection	Data granularity	Deduplication complexity	
	Imbalanced data sets	Data streams for training	
Poker Bot Identification	Experiment management	Lack of modularity	
Media Recommendations	Dependency management	Sharing and tracking techn.	
Sensor data (automotive)	Unintended feedback loops	Reproducibility of results	design methods
Sentiment analysis	Effort estimation	Data extraction methods	and processes
	Cultural differences	Tooling	
Manufacturing optimization	Specifying desired outcome		
Training data annotation	Overfitting	Limited transparency	
Failure prediction (telecom)	Scalable ML pipeline	Training/serving skew	model performance
OoO reply analysis	Quality attributes	Sliced analysis of final model	
	Statistical Understanding		
Search engine optimization	Monitoring and Logging	Privacy and data safety	
Wind power prediction	Testing	Data silos	deployment &
Skin lesion classification	Troubleshooting	Data storage	compliance
	Data sources and distribution	Resource limitations	
	Glue code and support		

Fig. 2 Overview of AI Engineering Challenges

and identified a variety of different challenges that companies are struggling to address.

We have structured these challenges around the key phases of a ML/DL project, i.e., data management, model design and evolution, training and evaluating, and, finally, deploying. As the figure shows, there are several challenges that companies struggle with. In one of the chapters in this part, we discuss these challenges in more detail, but here we discuss some of the more prominent ones.

One of the hardest challenges for our industrial partners is the management of data, including its collection, labelling in order to be able to use the data for training, implicit dependencies on data that messes up training, dealing with time series, and managing windows of data in data streams. As ML and even more so DL deeply depends on the quality of the data it is served for training, validation, and operations, it is critical to get this right. Companies have of course gone through the Big Data era and have worked with data for analysis by data analysts for years, but still maintaining high data quality levels remains a complex challenge for most companies.

When it comes to designing and evolving models, the interesting learning that we got is that the development of the model itself is actually a quite well understood activity. The main challenges companies face have to do with the infrastructure around the modeling, such as experiment management, unintended feedback loops, and sharing and tracking models in teams. In addition, topics such as effort estimation, lack of modularity, complicating the scaling of work among multiple individuals, and tooling are raised as concerns.

Training models is largely an automated activity and at the heart of machine learning. The key challenges of our industrial partners were concerned with scaling the ML pipeline, dealing with quality attributes such as performance and robustness, difficulties due to training/serving skew, causing a model to do well in training but poorly in production, and overfitting due to limited data sets. Overall, due to the limited access to trained data scientists, incorrect interpretation of training results due to a lack of statistical understanding was quite common, leading to suboptimal outcomes.

Finally, deployment of ML/DL models in production is fraught with challenges and is, together with data management, the hardest challenge faced by the collaborating companies. Developing reliable solutions to test and monitor deployments, to log results, and to troubleshoot whenever there are issues during operations proves to be difficult. This is complicated as these systems often contain significant amounts of glue code and are subject to strict data privacy and security constraints.

Concluding, for all the benefits that machine learning and deep learning provide, it proves to be challenging to reap the benefits. The development and training of models on a standard data set is trivial, but scaling this to production-quality, industry strength deployment and supporting continuous evolution in the context of MLOps is a whole different ball game.

4 The Chapter in This Part

Despite the AI Engineering theme being the newest theme in Software Center, we have accumulated quite a number of publications already in the last years. This is among others due to the fact that several PhD students have been working with us on a variety of topics in the theme. Consequently, it is hard to make a selection, and we prioritized only a single chapter that captures a spectrum of research results from the theme.

The selected chapter [48] presents a research agenda for engineering AI systems. It structures the agenda around the aforementioned phases of a ML/DL project, i.e., data management, model design and evolution, training and evaluation, and deployment. Orthogonal to that, it presents challenges around architecture, development, and process. In each of the cross sections of these two dimensions, the research agenda presents the most important challenge to be addressed by research. It also captures key challenges for some specific domains, including cyber-physical and safety-critical systems. The research agenda is based on dozens of case studies and even more identified challenges in industrial practices, and the empirical basis makes it a well-founded agenda.

5 Future of AI

Claiming to know the future of artificial intelligence is of course a very dangerous proposition, and I will refrain from even claiming such clairvoyance. Having said that, there are two main trends in the Software Center companies that will likely influence the future of AI for these companies. The first trend is the increasing concern and frustration with the unwieldiness and cost associated with centralized, offline training of ML/DL models. Especially for very complex problems, such as autonomous driving, the size of the data, the infrastructure for training models, and challenge of working with all that data is so hard and expensive that companies will increasingly look for alternative approaches. As embedded systems obviously have computation resources in each device, it is an obvious avenue for companies to explore ways to move towards "in situ' rather and "in vitro" training.

One obvious example to shift training to the edge and to the devices themselves is to make use of federated learning. Here we can use part or all of the population of devices to use their local data to train the ML/DL model and to exchange model parameters with the other devices to learn and become better. Federated learning has many advantages, including the significantly reduced bandwidth use and privacy preservation as no data leaves the device living on the edge. Not all use cases fit this model, if only because each device needs to be able to determine the label for the data it is training, but it addresses many of the concerns associated with offline, centralized training.

The second approach is reinforcement learning. Here each device operates in a context and learns from its actions by observing the effect of each action, resulting in a reward. Over time, each action becomes associated with an expected reward. The reinforcement learning algorithm initially balances exploration, i.e., learning the effect of randomly selected actions, and exploitation, i.e., optimizing the reward from actions that it already knows the reward for. Once the exploration results in less learning, the algorithm increasingly seeks to optimize its total reward.

Especially in contexts where suboptimal actions may result in significant consequences for the system or users around the system, we need techniques to ensure that the worst-case outcome of an exploratory action is bounded, which requires forms of prediction. One effective technique is to first train the model to a sufficient level of proficiency offline and then to use online training to improve.

Of course, reinforcement learning and federated learning can be combined, and one can view the holy grail of AI for several of the Software Center companies to be a situation where their entire population of devices deployed in the field is continuously getting better through experimentation through reinforcement learning and the sharing of these learnings using federation.

The second trend is that the Software Center companies are in the process of adopting DevOps or have already done so. As ML/DL models also are software, we see that these are basically dragged along by the DevOps ways of working. This translates itself into the introduction of DataOps and MLOps as more formalized frameworks to work with data and ML/DL models in the same iterative, continuous ways of working as what we have for traditional software. So, we will increasingly also see the ML/DL models being subject to continuous evolution, requiring techniques such as A/B testing and multi-armed bandits to gradually introduce new versions of ML/DL models, parallel to the older version, with the intent of determining that the new model not only performs better in training but also in production.

6 Conclusion

Although the likelihood of Skynet taking over the world remains as close to zero as one can hope, narrow AI and specifically ML/DL have established themselves as powerful technologies providing many benefits. The success of ML/DL has resulted in significant interest and investment in AI. Currently, however, the main focus is on ML/DL algorithms and achieving optimal outcomes in terms of accuracy, recall, and F1 scores. Although this is important, it is easy to forget that ML/DL models operate in a context that is critical to get in place if one hopes to have a production deployment of these models. This includes data pipelines for feeding the models, monitoring and logging, automatic retraining solutions, etc.

In our research with the Software Center companies as well as others, we found that the development of ML/DL models was only a small part of the overall development and evolution process. In fact, most effort was spent on collecting and labeling suitable training data, setting up data pipelines, creating infrastructure for storing data sets, interfacing the ML/DL model with the rest of the system, etc. To provide a perspective and a focus for all the work outside of model development, we defined the term "AI engineering" to indicate all the engineering work that has to take place to create production deployments of ML/DL models in software-intensive systems.

The AI Engineering theme in Software Center studies the challenges associated with developing, deploying, and evolving ML/DL models in production. In this part, we provide a research agenda, an overview of challenges and available solutions, and a first exploration in one of the approaches that we consider to be highly relevant for the Software Center companies, i.e., federated learning.

Chapter 13
Engineering AI Systems
A Research Agenda

Jan Bosch, Helena Holmström Olsson, and Ivica Crnkovic

Abstract Artificial intelligence (AI) and machine learning (ML) are increasingly broadly adopted in industry, However, based on well over a dozen case studies, we have learned that deploying industry-strength, production quality ML models in systems proves to be challenging. Companies experience challenges related to data quality, design methods and processes, performance of models as well as deployment and compliance. We learned that a new, structured engineering approach is required to construct and evolve systems that contain ML/DL components. In this chapter, we provide a conceptualization of the typical evolution patterns that companies experience when employing ML as well as an overview of the key problems experienced by the companies that we have studied. The main contribution of the chapter is a research agenda for AI engineering that provides an overview of the key engineering challenges surrounding ML solutions and an overview of open items that need to be addressed by the research community at large.

13.1 Introduction

The prominence of artificial intelligence (AI) and specifically machine- and deep-learning (ML/DL) solutions has grown exponentially [15], [35]. Because of the Big Data era, more data is available than ever before, and this data can be used for training ML/DL solutions. In parallel, progress in high-performance parallel hardware such as GPUs and FPGAs allows for training solutions of scales unfathomable even a decade ago. These two concurrent technology developments are at the heart of the rapid adoption of ML/DL solutions.

Reprinted with permission from IGI Global. Originally published in Artificial Intelligence Paradigms for Smart Cyber-Physical Systems, Ashish Kumar Luhach and Atilla Elçi IGI Global, 2021. DOI: 10.4018/978-1-7998-5101-1.ch001

Virtually every company has an AI initiative ongoing and the number of experiments and prototypes in industry is phenomenal. Although earlier the province of large Software-as-a-Service (SaaS) companies, our research shows a democratization of AI and broad adoption across the entire industry, ranging from startups to large cyber-physical systems companies. ML solutions are deployed in telecommunications, healthcare, automotive, internet-of-things (IoT) as well as numerous other industries and we expect an exponential growth in the number of deployments across society. As examples, ML solutions are used in the automotive industry to explore autonomous driving and as a means to increase efficiency and productivity. In domains such as e.g. mining, autonomous vehicles are currently being used in under-ground operations where human safety is a concern and in situations where there is a risk of accidents. Similarly, self-driving trucks can operate largely automatically within e.g. harbor or airport areas which helps to increase both productivity and safety. In the defense domain, AI segmentation is used to identify buildings, roads or any type of land at pixel level from a great height. In addition, AI technologies provide a range of opportunities in a fast-moving emergency where there is conflicting information and where there is a need to rapidly establish an understanding of the current situation, as well as for prediction of future events.

Across industries, image recognition capabilities are key and as an example from the packaging domain, ML is used for checking the inner sides of packages to detect any flaws or deviations in sealings and for analyzing temperature, anomalies and edges to ensure quality. Unfortunately, our research [18, 288, 332] shows that the transition from prototype to production-quality deployment of ML models proves to be challenging for many companies. Though not recognized by many, the engineering challenges surrounding ML prove to be significant. In our research, we have studied well over a dozen cases and identified the problems that these companies experience as they adopt ML. These problems are concerned with a range of topics including data quality, design methods and processes, performance of models as well as deployment and compliance.

To the best of our knowledge, no research exists that provide a systematic overview of the research challenges associated with the emerging field of AI engineering, which we define as follows: *AI Engineering is an engineering discipline that is concerned of all aspects of development and evolution of AI systems, i.e. systems that include AI components. AI engineering is primary an extension of Software Engineering, but it also includes methods and technologies from data science and AI in general.*

In this chapter, we provide a research agenda that has been derived from the research that we have conducted to date. The goal of this research agenda is to provide inspiration for the software engineering research community to start addressing the AI engineering challenges.

The purpose and contribution of this chapter is threefold. First, we provide a conceptualization of the typical evolution patterns concerned with adoption of AI that companies experience. Second, we provide an overview of the engineering challenges surrounding ML solutions. Third, we provide a research agenda and overview of open items that need to be addressed by the research community at large.

The remainder of this chapter is organized as follows. In the next section, we present the background, followed by a section presenting the research method underlying the research in this chapter. In Sect. 13.4, we present on overview of the problems that we identified in our earlier research as well as a model capturing the evolution pattern of companies adopting AI solutions. Subsequently, we present our research agenda in Sect. 13.5. Finally, we discuss future research directions in Sect. 13.6 and conclude the chapter in Sect. 13.7.

13.2 Background

For decades, software engineering (SE) research has been concerned with processes and methods that are used in designing, developing and maintaining software. Typically, SE research seeks to create tool-supported methods and techniques to ensure robust and reliable design of software and with major efforts spent on supporting and advancing requirements-driven development approaches in which specification, testing and traceability of requirements is key [288]. For companies in the software-intensive industry, the applicability and adoption of novel software engineering practices is critical as a means to stay competitive and to continuously improve product performance.

However, today's software-intensive business is in the midst of profound changes in relation to development of software systems. With rapid pace, and across industry domains, sophisticated technologies for data collection and analysis are implemented to provide developers with real-time input on how the systems they develop perform in the field. Fueled by the increasing availability and access to data, artificial intelligence (AI) and technologies such as machine learning (ML) and deep learning (DL) are rapidly adopted in a variety of domains. Recent years show an increasing use of these technologies in industry with companies such as e.g. Google, Apple and Facebook leading the way but with software-intensive companies in the embedded systems domain as fast adopters. For these companies, ML/DL components are rapidly complementing the traditional software components in the systems they develop, and we can already see how companies across domains have started complementing their requirements-driven development approaches with novel approaches such as outcome driven and AI driven development approaches [47]. Machine learning (ML) and Deep Learning, as a rapidly developing branch of AI, provides the companies with key capabilities for improving and accelerating innovation in their offerings based on operational system data. The application areas of ML/DL to real-world problems are vast and range from large use in recommendation systems of social media [276] and e- commerce [281] services, to highly regulated products, such as autonomous vehicle prototypes.

For a number of years, the field of SE has benefited from ML research by having various ML techniques applied to the activities of SE [459]] such as defect prediction, test-case generation and refinement in software testing [54], [97]. A number of studies report on improved software quality and decreased development efforts as the primary benefits of applying ML techniques to solve problems in existing software development processes [457]. In our research, and in contrast to research that focuses on how AI technologies help SE, we focus on how the traditional approach to SE is changing as new components, such as AI components, are introduced into software-intensive systems. Practice has shown that building ML/DL-based systems involves challenges that go beyond ML techniques and algorithms [394], [82] and that include the integration and evolution of these models as part of larger software-intensive systems. As a consequence, and due to the specific characteristics and complexities involved in the development of ML/DL components, the entire software development process requires new methods and new ways-of-working [306], [15]. Going forward, competitive advantage will involve more than mastering the requirements-driven approach to software engineering. As argued in this paper, it will involve the engineering of systems that include software as well as ML/DL components and that requires novel engineering approaches.

Although there are state-of-the-art surveys in the area of ML covering the general use of ML techniques [171] and its application in domains such as e.g. automotive [287]] and telecommunication [247], these studies tend to focus on the technical aspects of ML rather than the role these play in software-intensive embedded systems and how to effectively engineer systems consisting of technologies with very different characteristics. Up to date, there are a few studies that report on the end-to-end development process of ML-based systems in embedded systems industrial contexts, e.g. [214, 215, 333, 366]. However, to the best of our knowledge, there is no study that provides a systematic overview of the research challenges associated with the emerging field of AI engineering (which we define as an extension of Software Engineering with new processes and technologies needed for development and evolution of AI systems). In what follows, and in order to address this shortcoming, we report on the challenges we identified in relation to the transition from prototype to production-quality deployment of ML models in large-scale software engineering and we provide a research agenda for how to address what we define as AI engineering challenges.

13.3 Research Method

In the context of Software Center1, we work with more than a dozen large international Cyber-physical systems (CPS) and embedded systems (ES) companies, including Ericsson, Tetra Pak, Siemens, Bosch, Volvo Cars, Boeing and several others around, among other topics, the adoption of ML/DL technologies. In addition, we frequently have the opportunity to study and collaborate with companies also outside of Software Center that operate as SaaS companies in a variety of business domains.

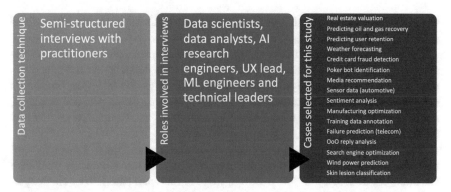

Fig. 13.1 Roles and cases that were selected as the empirical basis for this study

For the purpose of this chapter, we have selected a set of 16 primary cases as the foundation for the challenges we identify and the research agenda we outline. However, it should be noted that the work reported on in this chapter is based also on learning from more than 20 companies from around the world, though with a focus on the software-intensive embedded systems industry in Europe, mostly Nordic countries. With this as our empirical basis, we believe that the challenges we identify, and the research agenda we outline, reflect the key engineering challenges that companies in a variety of domains experience when employing and integrating ML/DL components in their systems. Below, we present the research approach adopted in this work and the cases we selected as the basis for this chapter.

13.3.1 Research Approach and Selected Cases

The goal of this research is to provide an understanding of the typical evolution patterns that companies experience, and the challenges they face, when adopting and integrating ML/DL components in their systems. Based on this understanding, we develop a research agenda in which we identify the open research questions that need to be addressed by the research community.

In alignment with this research goal, our research builds on multiple-case study research [130, 310] with semi-structured interviews and observations as the primary techniques for data collection. The findings we present build on a total number of 16 cases representing startups as well as large multinational companies in domains such as e.g. real estate, weather forecasting, fraud detection, sentiment analysis and failure prediction. Each case represents a software-intensive system that incorporates ML and DL components and involves challenges ranging from data management and data quality to creation, training and deployment of ML/DL models. For data collection, we used semi-structured interviews with data scientists, data analysts, AI research engineers, UX lead, ML engineers and technical leaders. The research approach as well as the roles and cases that were selected as the basis for this study are outlined in Fig. 13.1.

For analysis and coding of the empirical data, we adopted a thematic data analysis approach [289]. Following this approach, all cases were documented and interviews were recorded. During analysis of our empirical findings, the interview transcripts were read carefully by the researchers to identify recurring elements and concepts, i.e. challenges experienced by the practitioners in the case companies we selected for this study [107, 310].

The details of the case studies, as well as a number of additional cases that were not selected for this particular chapter, can be found in our previously published research [18, 288, 332]. In this research, we identified and categorized challenges, and in particular data management challenges, that practitioners experience when building ML/DL systems and we concluded that there is a significant need for future research on this topic. In this chapter, and to build on and advance our previous research, we map the challenges we identified to a set of strategic focus areas that we recognize in industry. Furthermore, and based on this mapping, we outline a research agenda for AI engineering research to help the research community structure and conceptualize the problem space. As recommended by [472], the generalizations made based on case study research should be viewed as insights valuable for contexts with similar characteristics. With the opportunity to work closely with more than a dozen large CPS and SaaS companies, we believe that the insights we provide on the challenges these companies experience when building ML/DL systems will be valuable also outside the specific context of these companies. In addition, and as the main contribution of this chapter, we believe that the research agenda we present will provide support and structure, as well as inspiration, for the research community at large.

13.4 The Challenge of AI Engineering

Engineering AI systems is often portrayed as the creation of a ML/DL model and deploying it. In practice, however, the ML/DL model is only a small part of the overall system and significant additional functionality is required to ensure that the ML/DL model can operate in a reliable and predictable fashion with proper engineering of data pipelines, monitoring and logging, etc. [35, 394]. To capture these aspects of AI engineering we defined the Holistic DevOps (HoliDev) model [47], where we distinguish between requirements-driven development, outcome-driven development (e.g. A/B testing) and AI-driven development. In the model, we outline requirements-driven development as an approach in which software is built to specification and an approach predominantly used when new features or functionality are well understood. Outcome-driven development refers to an approach where development teams receive a quantitative target to realize and are asked to experiment with different solutions to improve the metric. Typically, this development approach is used for new and for innovation efforts. The third approach is AI-driven development

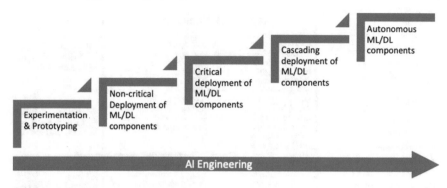

Fig. 13.2 The AI adoption evolution model

where a company has a large data set available and use ML/DL solutions to create components that act based on input data and that learn from previous actions. We conclude that the selection and combination of development approaches will be key for competitive advantage.

13.4.1 AI Adoption in Practice

The challenge of AI engineering is that the results of each of the aforementioned type of development end up in the same system and are subject to data collection, monitoring of behavior as well as continuous deployment of new functionality. In industrial deployments that we have studied, also AI models are constantly improved, retrained and redeployed and consequently follow the same DevOps process as the other software components.

In a transformation to AI-driven development, companies, over time, tend to develop more skills, capabilities and needs in the ML/DL space and consequently they evolve through several stages. In the AI Evolution model in Fig. 13.2, we illustrate how companies, based on our previous research [288, 332], evolve over time. The maturity of companies concerning AI evolves through five stages:

- **Experimentation and prototyping**: This stage is purely exploratory and the results are not deployed in a production environment. Consequently, AI engineering challenges are not present in this stage.
- **Non-critical deployment**: In this stage, a ML/DL model is deployed as part of a product or system in a non-critical capacity, meaning that if the model fails to perform, the overall product or system is still functional and delivers value to customers.
- **Critical deployment**: Once the confidence in the ML/DL models increases, key decision makers become sufficiently comfortable with deploying these models in a critical context, meaning that the product or system fails if the ML/DL model does not perform correctly.

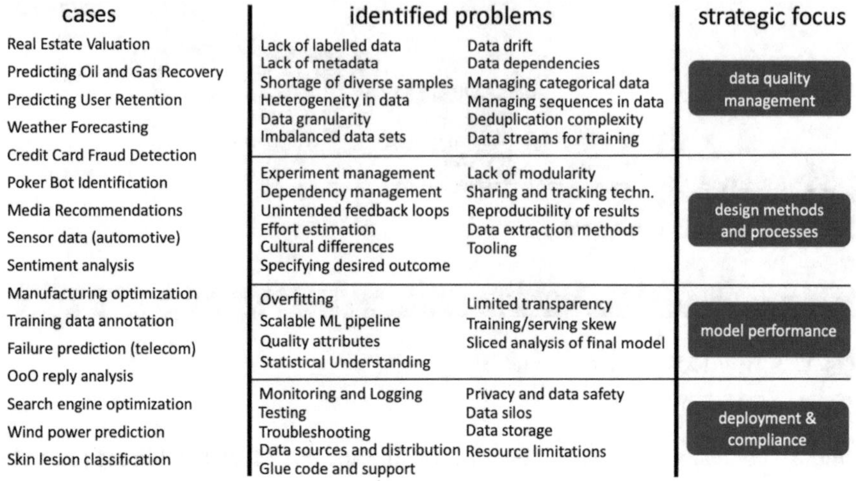

cases	identified problems		strategic focus
Real Estate Valuation Predicting Oil and Gas Recovery Predicting User Retention Weather Forecasting Credit Card Fraud Detection	Lack of labelled data Lack of metadata Shortage of diverse samples Heterogeneity in data Data granularity Imbalanced data sets	Data drift Data dependencies Managing categorical data Managing sequences in data Deduplication complexity Data streams for training	data quality management
Poker Bot Identification Media Recommendations Sensor data (automotive) Sentiment analysis	Experiment management Dependency management Unintended feedback loops Effort estimation Cultural differences Specifying desired outcome	Lack of modularity Sharing and tracking techn. Reproducibility of results Data extraction methods Tooling	design methods and processes
Manufacturing optimization Training data annotation Failure prediction (telecom) OoO reply analysis	Overfitting Scalable ML pipeline Quality attributes Statistical Understanding	Limited transparency Training/serving skew Sliced analysis of final model	model performance
Search engine optimization Wind power prediction Skin lesion classification	Monitoring and Logging Testing Troubleshooting Data sources and distribution Glue code and support	Privacy and data safety Data silos Data storage Resource limitations	deployment & compliance

Fig. 13.3 Overview of cases and identified problems

- **Cascading deployment**: With the increasing use of ML/DL models, the next step is to start to use the output of one model as the input for the next model in the chain. In this case, monitoring and ensuring correct functioning of the system becomes more difficult as the issues may be emergent, rather than directly associated with a specific ML/DL model.
- **Autonomous ML/DL components**: In the final stage, ML/DL models monitor their own behavior, automatically initiate retraining and are able to flag when the model observes that, despite retraining using the latest data, it does not provide acceptable accuracy.

Each of the steps above requires increased activities of "AI engineering", i.e. a set of methods and tools that originated from software engineering in a system life cycle, and procedures, technologies and tools from data science and AI. While the first step, which is today state of the practice, typically covers the end-to-end ML development cycle (data acquisition, feature engineering, training and evaluation, and deployment), the next steps require the existing approaches from software engineering (e.g. system testing) as well as completely new methods that will need to become an integrated part of software and AI engineering (e.g. continuous training, or version management of code and data).

13.4.2 AI Engineering Strategic Focus

During our research, we worked with a variety of companies and identified over 30 problems that are a concern in multiple cases that we studied. We have presented some of these in detail in earlier publications, specifically [18, 288, 332], so we will not discuss each identified problem in this chapter. Instead, we provide an overview in Fig. 13.3 and we present a categorization of the identified problems. The categories represent four strategic focus areas that relate to the typical phases of a ML project. These four areas are the following:

- **Data quality management**: One of the key challenges in successful AI projects is to establish data sets and streams that are of sufficient quality for training and inference. Specifically, data sets tend to be unbalanced, have a high degree of heterogeneity, lack labels, tend to drift over time, contain implicit dependencies and generally require vast amounts of pre-processing effort before they are usable.
- **Design methods and processes**: Although creating an ML model is relatively easy, doing so at scale and in a repeatable fashion proves to be challenging. Specifically, managing a multitude of experiments, detecting and resolving implicit dependencies and feedback loops, inability of tracing data dependency, estimating effort, cultural differences between developer roles, specifying desired outcome and tooling prove to be difficult to accomplish efficiently and effectively.
- **Model performance**: The performance of ML/DL models depends on various factors, both for accuracy and for general quality attributes. Some of the specific problems that we have identified include a skew between training data and the data served during operation, lack of support for quality attributes, over-fitting of models and scalable data pipelines for training and serving.
- **Deployment & compliance**: Finally, one area that is highly underestimated is the deployment of models. Here, companies struggle with a multitude of problems, including monitoring and logging of models, testing of models, troubleshooting, resource limitations and significant amounts of glue code to get the system up and running.

13.5 AI Engineering: A Research Agenda

The subject of AI and the notion of engineering practices for building AI systems is a multi-faceted and complex problem. Consequently, few, if any, models exist that seek to create a structure and conceptualization of the problem space. In this section, we provide a structured view on the challenge of AI engineering and we provide a research agenda (Fig. 13.4). In the research agenda, we organize the challenges into two main categories, i.e. generic AI engineering and domain specific AI engineering. Within generic AI Engineering (AI Eng.), we categorize the challenges into to three main areas, i.e. architecture, development and process. For domain specific AI Engineering (D AI Eng.), we have identified one set of challenges for each domain that we have studied in the case study companies.

As a second dimension, we follow the strategic focus areas that are related directly to the four main phases of a typical ML/DL project, i.e. data quality management (related to assembling data sets), design methods and processes (related to creating and evolving ML/DL models), model performance (related to training and evaluating) and finally deployment and conformance, related to the deploy phase. In Fig. 13.4, the model is presented graphically. In the remainder of the section, we discuss the key research challenges in more detail.

As the data science activities shown in Fig. 13.4 are the regular AI/data science activities, we will discuss these only briefly:

- **Assemble data sets**: The first activity in virtually any ML/DL project is to assemble the data sets that can be used for training and evaluation and to evaluate these in order to understand the relevant features in the data.
- **Create & evolve ML/DL model**: After analyzing the data sets, the next step is to experiment with different ML algorithms or DL models and to select the most promising one for further development.
- **Train & evaluate**: Once the model has been developed, the next step is to train and validate the model using the data.
- **Deploy**: Once the model has been trained and is shown to have sufficient accuracy, recall and/or other relevant metrics, the model is deployed in a system where it typically is connected to one or more data streams for the purpose of inference.

The data science process above has many additional aspects and is typically conducted in an iterative manner. In Fig. 13.4, we show two of these iterations, i.e. between training and modeling and between deployment and the assembling of new data sets. However, as this paper is concerned with AI engineering and not with the specific data science aspects, we do not discuss these aspects in more detail.

13.5.1 AI Engineering: Architecture

In the context of AI engineering, architecture is concerned with structuring the overall system and decomposing it into its main components. Constructing systems including ML/DL components require components and solutions not found in traditional systems and that need to address novel concerns. Below we describe the primary research challenges that we have identified in our research.

- **Data versioning & dependency management**: The quality of the data used for training is absolutely central for achieving high performance of models. Especially in a DevOps environment, data generated by one version of the software is not necessarily compatible with the software generated by the subsequent version. Consequently, versioning of data needs to be carefully managed. In addition, systems typically generate multiple streams of data that have dependencies on each other. As data pipelines tend to be less robust than software pipelines [332], it is important to provide solutions for the management of data quality. This can be concerned with simple checks for data being in range or even being present or more advanced checks to ensure that the average for a window of data stays constant over time or that the statistical distribution of the data remains similar. As ML/DL models are heavily data dependent, the data pipelines needed for feeding the models as well as the data generated by the models need to be set up. This can be particularly challenging when different types of data and different sources of data are used; in addition to questions of availability, accuracy, synchronization and normalization, significant problems related to security and privacy appear.

- **Federated learning infrastructure**: Most of the cases that we studied concern systems where ML models are deployed in each instance of the system. Several approaches exist for managing training, evaluation and deployment in such contexts, but one central infrastructure component is the support for federated learning. As it often is infeasible to move all data to a central location for training a global model, solutions are needed for federated learning and the sharing of model parameters such as neural network weights as well as selected data sets that, for instance, represent cases not well handled by the central model. Federated learning requires an infrastructure to achieve the required quality attributes and to efficiently and securely share models and data.

- **Storage and computing infrastructure**: Although many assume that all ML/DL deployments operate in the cloud, our interaction with industry shows that many companies build up internal storage and computing infrastructure because of legal constraints, cost or quality attributes. Developing these infrastructures, for example for the development of autonomous driving solutions, is a major engineering and research challenge. Typically, collection and storing of data is organized centrally on the enterprise level, while development of AI solutions is distributed over several development teams.

- **Deployment infrastructure**: Independent of the use of centralized or federated learning approaches, models still need to be deployed in systems in the field. As most case study companies have adopted or plan to soon adopt DevOps, it is important for a deployment infrastructure to reliably deploy subsequent versions of models, measure their performance, raise warnings and initiate rollbacks in the case of anomalous behavior. This infrastructure is by necessity of a distributed nature as it requires functionality both centrally as well as in each system that is part of the DevOps approach. Deployment of MD/DL models may require substantial change in the overall architecture of the system.

13.5.2 AI Engineering: Development

Building and deploying successful ML/DL components and systems requires more than data science alone. In this section we focus on the development of systems including ML/DL components. This is important because also ML/DL models, in most cases that we have studied, are subject to the same DevOps activities as the other software in systems, meaning that models evolve, are retrained and deployed on continuous basis. Based on our case study research, we present the four primary research challenges concerning development in AI engineering below.

- **DataOps**: Although considered a buzzword by some, DataOps raises the concern of managing everything data with the same structured and systematic approach as that we manage software within a traditional DevOps context. As typical companies ask their data scientists to spend north of 95% of their time on cleaning, pre-processing and managing data, there is a significant opportunity to reduce this overhead by generating, distributing and storing data smarter in the development process. DataOps requires high levels of automation, which requires alignment and standardization in order to achieve continuous value delivery.

- **Reuse of pre-developed models**: Most companies prefer to employ models developed by others or that have been developed earlier inside the company. However, reuse of existing ML/DL models is not trivial as the separation between the generic and specific parts of the model are not always easy to separate, in particular when the run-time context is different from that used in training phase.

- **Quality attributes**: In data science, the key challenge is to achieve high accuracy, recall or other metrics directly related to the ML performance of the machine learning model. In an AI engineering context, however, several other quality attributes become relevant including the computation performance, in terms of the number of inferences per time unit the system can manage, the real-time properties, robustness of the system in case of data outside the scope of training set, etc. Ensuring satisfactory adherence to the quality requirements on the ML components in the system is a research challenge that is far from resolved.

- **Integration of models & components**: As we discussed earlier in the paper, ML/DL models need to be integrated with the remainder of the system containing regular software components. However, it is not always trivial to connect the data-driven ML/DL models with the computation-driven software components. Also, traditional testing and evaluation of the models must be integrated in such a way that software methods and data-science evaluation methods are combined seamlessly. Depending on the criticality of the ML/DL model for the overall performance of the system, the validation activities need to be more elaborate.

13.5.3 AI Engineering: Process

Although the notion of process has gone out of vogue with the emergence of agile, it is hard to argue that no process is required to align the efforts of large groups of people without prohibitively high coordination cost. The context of AI engineering is no different, but there are surprisingly few design methods, processes and approaches available for the development and evolution of ML/DL models. Experienced data scientists do not need these, but with the rapidly growing need for AI engineers, many less experienced data scientists and software engineers are asked to build these models. These professionals would very much benefit from more methodological and process support. We have identified four main process related challenges that require significant research efforts to resolve in a constructive and efficient way. Below we describe each of these in more detail.

- **Automated labelling**: As the data sets that a company starts with are limited sources for training and validation, ideally, we want to collect the data sets for

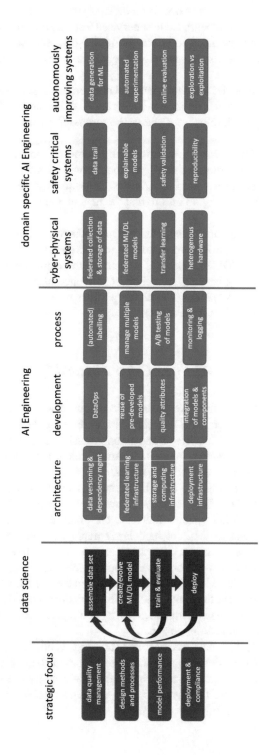

Fig. 13.4 Research agenda for AI engineering

training evolving models during operation in deployment. Although it is easy to collect the input data, the labels used in supervised learning are often much harder to add. Consequently, we need solutions for, preferably, automated labelling of data so that we have a constant stream of recent data for training and validation purposes during evolution.

- **Manage multiple models**: The first concern that often surfaces in teams working on ML/DL models is that it is difficult to keep track of all the models that are being considered during the development phase. We discussed parts of this challenge in [35].
- **A/B testing of models**: During evolution, the improved model is deployed for operation. However, experience shows that models that perform better in training do not necessarily perform better in operations. Consequently, we need solutions, often variants of A/B testing, to ensure that the new model also performs better in deployment.
- **Monitoring & logging**: Once the model is deployed and used in operation, it is important to monitor its performance and to log events specific to the performance of the model. As ML/DL models tend to lack on the explainability front, the monitoring and logging is required to build confidence in the accuracy of the models and to detect situations where the performance of a model starts to deteriorate or is insufficient from the start.

13.5.4 Domain-Specific AI Eng.: Cyber Physical Systems

In the remainder of this section, we present the unique research topics for three application domains in which ML/DL technologies are being deployed, i.e. cyber physical systems, safety critical systems and autonomously improving systems. Our research shows that each domain brings with it a set of unique activities and research challenges associated with AI engineering topics.

Although the recent emergence of ML/DL models in industry started in the online SaaS world, this has been rapidly followed by increasing interest in the software-intensive embedded systems industry. The main difference with cloud-based deployments is that the ML/DL models are deployed in embedded systems out in the field such as base stations, cars, radars, sensors and the like.

Cyber physical systems are often organized around three computing platforms, i.e. the edge device where the data for ML/DL is collected, an on-premise server of some kind and the infrastructure in the cloud. Each of these platforms has its own characteristics in terms of real-time performance, security and privacy, computational and storage resources, communications cost, etc.

The consequence is that data management, training, validation and inference associated with ML/DL models has a tendency to become federated as it requires these three computing platforms as most capabilities that customers care about will cross-cut all three platforms. This leads to a set of unique research challenges for this domain that we discuss below.

- **Federated/distributed storage of data**: Parallel to the model, the data used for training and inference needs to be managed in a distributed and federated fashion. Local storage on device instances minimizes communication cost but tends to increase the bill-of-materials for each device and these architectural drivers need to be managed.
- **Federated/distributed model creation**: Due to the presence of multiple computing platforms, the architect or data scientist needs to distribute the ML/DL model over these computing platforms, resulting in a federated model. This is an open research area related to the system and data lifecycles, performance, availability, security, computation, etc.
- **Transfer learning**: Especially for companies that have thousands or millions of devices deployed in the field, the challenge is the balancing between centralized and decentralized learning. The most promising approach is to distribute centrally trained models and to allow each individual device to apply its local learnings to the centrally trained model using transfer learning approaches. However, more research is needed.
- **Deploy on heterogeneous hardware**: Finally, because of both cost and computational efficiency, embedded systems often use dedicated hardware solutions such as ASICs and FPGAs. Additionally, MD/DL models require huge amounts of parallel computation, both during training and implementation, realized in e.g. GPUs. These execution platforms use different development environments, programming languages, and execution paradigms. Embedded systems tend to have constraints on computational and storage resources as well as power consumption. Deploying ML/DL models on these types of hardware frequently requires engineering effort from the team as there are no generic solutions available.

One challenge that is not yet one of the primary ones but that has appeared on the horizon is mass-customization of ML/DL models. As some CPS companies have many instances of their products in the field, the ML/DL models deployed in these instances should, ideally, adjust their behavior to the specifics of the users using the instance, i.e. mass-customization. However, there are few solutions available for combining both continuous deployment of centrally trained models with the customization of each product instance.

13.5.5 Domain-Specific AI Eng.: Safety-Critical Systems

A special class of cyber physical systems are safety-critical systems, i.e. those systems whose failure or malfunction may result in significant bodily, environmental or financial harm. The community struggles with balancing two forces. On the one hand, we seek to avoid harm by taking conservative approaches and introducing new technologies only after careful evaluation. On the other hand, the slow introduction of new technologies may easily cause harm in that the new technologies can help avoid safety issues that were not possible to avoid with conventional technologies only.

One of these new technologies is, of course, ML/DL. In the automotive industry, among others, the use of ML/DL allows for advanced driver support functions as well as fully autonomous driving. The open challenge is establishing the safety of these systems. In our research, we have defined the four primary research challenges specific for safety-critical AI-based systems.

- **Data trail**: One of the key challenges in safety critical systems is that the collection of safety-related evidence before the deployment of systems and the creation of a data trail during operations in order to ensure safe operation of the system. In the context of ML/DL models, this requires maintaining a clear trail of the data that was used for training as well as the inferences that the model provided during operation. Little research exists that addresses this challenge for AI components and consequently this is a significant research challenge.
- **Explainable models**: As it is virtually impossible to test a system to safety, the community often uses various approaches to certify systems. This is performed by assessors who need to understand the functionality of the system. This requires that ML/DL models are explainable, which today is unsolvable or at least a non-trivial problem for most models.
- **Validation of safety-critical systems**: The basic enabler for deployment of ML/DL models in safety critical systems is the validation of these systems. Validation concerns both the correct behavior in situations where application should act, but we also need to show that the system will not engage in situations where it is not necessary or even dangerous to do so. Validation of safety-critical systems starts from requirements of justifiable prediction and of deterministic system behavior, while ML/DL solutions are based on statistical models, so in principle non-deterministic behavior. In practice, the ML/DL models can be more accurate and reliable, but justification of these models requires new approaches, methods, and standards in the validation process.
- **Reproducibility**: For a variety of factors, a ML/DL model may end up looking different when it is given a different seed, order of training data, infrastructure it is deployed on, etc. Especially for safety critical systems, it is critical that we can reproduce the model in a predictable manner, independent of the aforementioned factors.

13.5.6 Domain-Specific AI Eng.: Autonomously Improving Systems

There is an emerging category of systems that uses ML/DL models with the intent of continuously improving the performance of the system autonomously. In practice, there are humans involved in the improvement of the system, but the system employs mechanisms for experimentation and improvement that do not require human involvement.

The primary way for systems to achieve this is through the use of ML/DL models that analyze the data, train using it and then provide interference. This requires forms of automated experimentation where the system itself generates alternatives and, for example, deploys these alternatives in A/B testing or similar contexts and measures the impact of these changes. There are four research challenges that need to be addressed for autonomously improving systems:

- **Data generation for machine learning**: Traditional ML/DL model development requires data scientists to spend significant amounts of time to convert available data sets that often are intended for human consumption into data sets that are usable for machine learning. In autonomously improving systems, the data that is generated by the system needs to be machine interpretable without any human help. How to accomplish this, though, is an open research question.
- **Automated experimentation**: Although the notion of automated experimentation is conceptually easy to understand, actually realizing systems that can operate in this fashion is largely an open research challenge where little work is available.
- **Online evaluation**: As autonomously improving systems generate alternatives for evaluation at run-time, these alternatives need to be deployed and evaluated during the regular operation of the system. This requires solutions for dynamically adjusting the behavior of the system to select, for a small percentage of the cases, the new alternative for evaluation as well as to keep track of statistical validity of the test results associated with each alternative.
- **Exploration vs exploitation**: In autonomously improving systems, the system autonomously experiments with different responses to the environment in which it operates with the intent of improving its performance. The challenge is that some or even many of these experiments will result in worse performance than the current default response. This is referred to as regret in optimization theory. The challenge is that it is impossible to find better ways of doing things without trying out these new ways, but especially in embedded systems there is a limit to how poor the alternative can be. This means that we need research to help assess the worst-case outcomes for each experiment with the intent of balancing the cost of exploration with the cost too much exploitation.

13.5.7 Other Domain Specific Systems

We described the domain specific research challenges for building ML/DL systems for specific types of systems. There of course are other domains that likely have specific research challenges as well. These challenges might be the same as for non AI-based systems, but new methods must be developed to meet these challenges (for example develop new methods to ensure system reliability, availability, security, reusability, or other non-functional properties). However, in many cases introducing ML/DL solutions cause new challenges such as quality of data, real-time data access, increase in efforts in the development life cycle as well as challenges in combination of security, functionality and privacy, etc.

13.6 Future Research Directions in AI Engineering

In the previous section we have provided a research agenda with an exhaustive list of topics relevant for research in AI Engineering. The identified problems (Fig. 13.3) indicate the currently important research directions. The topics related to a) data quality management, b) design methods and processing, c) model performance and d) deployment & compliance are recognized by industry as big challenges and even possible showstoppers of AI-based development in large. AI Engineering, forming as a new discipline, includes a number of research challenges related to system and software architecture, development methods and theologies, and processes, as shown on Fig. 13.4. Many of these challenges are new, not previously present in software engineering (for example, data versioning and dependencies, managing multiple models, A/B testing of AI-based components), while others are related to known challenges (for example safety, reliability, real-time requirements) that require new methods and processes to obtain the solutions.

In addition to these research directions that originate from the concrete problems the industry faces today, there are a number of meta-level challenges that originate from the AI/ML nature – dependence of data and algorithm and generality. While the domain-specific problems related to the algorithms and procedures can be generalised, it is significantly more difficult with data-related problems, as it is more difficult to generalise and abstract data on which the ML models depend. Examples of these challenges are related to following questions: a) How to manage data and algorithms versions? b) How to relate changes in data to changes in ML models? c) How to measure when changes of data require new ML-models? How to synchronize run-time context changes with re-training frequency?

While AI is not a new research discipline, its application in different domains and the operational aspects are new, which leads to many unpredictable results. A typical example is that a ML model works perfectly in a training/evaluation environment, while in operation the system become unreliable, and its development unpredictable. One of the sources of this challenge is inability of data science to manage the problem. In the development process, a domain knowledge is inevitable for providing the proper semantics of the results provided by data-related and statistical methods. The other challenge is related to the complexity and ineffectiveness of software that is used as a glue code and additional logic required to connect results from ML-based models. That requires interdisciplinary research, and by that research about roles and impact on different stakeholders in the development and operational process.

During at least a decade the topics from the present research agenda will be highly prioritised in the research community and in the industry.

13.7 Conclusion

Artificial intelligence, and specifically machine- and deep-learning, has, over the last decade, proven to have the potential to deliver enormous value to industry and society. This has resulted in most companies experimenting and prototyping with a host of AI initiatives. Unfortunately, our research [18, 288, 332] shows that the transition from prototype to industry-strength, production-quality deployment of ML models proves to be very challenging for many companies. The engineering challenges surrounding this prove to be significant [54], even if many researchers and companies fail to recognize this.

To the best of our knowledge, no papers exist that provide a systematic overview of the research challenges associated with the emerging field of AI engineering. In this chapter we provide a conceptualization of the typical evolution patterns that companies experience when adopting ML, we present an overview of the problems that companies experience based on well over a dozen cases that we studied and we provide a research agenda that was derived from the research that we conducted to date and that needs to be addressed by the research community at large. The goal of this research agenda is to provide inspiration for the software engineering research community to start addressing the AI engineering challenges.

AI and ML have the potential to greatly benefit industry and society at large. For us to capture the value, however, we need to be able to engineer solutions that deliver production-quality deployments. This requires research to address the AI engineering challenges that we present in this paper. In future work, we aim to address several of these research challenges in our research and our collaboration with industry. In particular collaboration with industry in real industrial settings is crucial since ML methods build upon empirical methods and directly depend on the amount and types of data. For this reason, we frequently organize events in the Nordics and at international conferences to create awareness for the identified challenges and to encourage other researchers to join us in addressing these.

Acknowledgement

The research in this paper has been supported by Software Center, the Chalmers Artificial Intelligence Research Center (CHAIR) and Vinnova.

References

1. Ablett, R., Sharlin, E., Maurer, F., Denzinger, J., Schock, C.: Buildbot: Robotic monitoring of agile software development teams. In: RO-MAN 2007-The 16th IEEE International Symposium on Robot and Human Interactive Communication, pp. 931–936. IEEE (2007)
2. Abrahamsson, P.: Is management commitment a necessity after all in software process improvement? In: Proceedings of the 26th Euromicro Conference. EUROMICRO 2000. Informatics: Inventing the Future, vol. 2, pp. 246–253. IEEE (2000)
3. Abrahamsson, P.: Measuring the success of software process improvement: the dimensions. arXiv preprint arXiv:1309.4645 (2013)
4. Abrahamsson, P., Warsta, J., Siponen, M., Ronkainen, J.: New directions on agile methods: a comparative analysis. In: Proceedings of the International Conference on Software Engineering, pp. 244–254 (2003). DOI 10.1109/ICSE.2003.1201204
5. Abran, A.: Software metrics and software metrology. John Wiley & Sons (2010)
6. Agarwal, A., Shankar, R., Tiwari, M.: Modeling the metrics of lean, agile and leagile supply chain: An anp-based approach. European Journal of Operational Research **173**(1), 211–225 (2006)
7. Agarwal, P.: Continuous scrum: agile management of saas products. In: Proceedings of the 4th India Software Engineering Conference, pp. 51–60 (2011)
8. Aghabozorgi, S., Shirkhorshidi, A.S., Wah, T.Y.: Time-series clustering–a decade review. Information Systems **53**, 16–38 (2015)
9. Albuquerque, C., Antonino, P., Nakagawa, E.: An investigation into agile methods in embedded systems development. In: Computational Science and Its Applications, *Lecture Notes in Computer Science*, vol. 7335, pp. 576–591. Springer (2012). URL http://www.springerlink.com/content/38uk703767811277/abstract/
10. Allamanis, M., Barr, E.T., Bird, C., Sutton, C.: Learning natural coding conventions. In: Proceedings of the 22nd ACM SIGSOFT International Symposium on Foundations of Software Engineering, pp. 281–293. ACM (2014)
11. Alshayeb, M., Li, W.: An empirical study of system design instability metric and design evolution in an agile software process. Journal of Systems and Software **74**(3), 269–274 (2005)
12. Alyahya, S., Ivins, W.K., Gray, W.: A holistic approach to developing a progress tracking system for distributed agile teams. In: 2012 IEEE/ACIS 11th International Conference on Computer and Information Science, pp. 503–512. IEEE (2012)
13. Ambler, S.: Agile modeling: effective practices for extreme programming and the unified process. John Wiley & Sons (2002)
14. Ambler, S.W., Lines, M.: Disciplined Agile Delivery, 1 edn. IBM Press (2012). URL http://disciplinedagiledelivery.wordpress.com/

© The Author(s), under exclusive license to Springer Nature Switzerland AG 2022
J. Bosch et al. (eds.), *Accelerating Digital Transformation*,
https://doi.org/10.1007/978-3-031-10873-0

15. Amershi, S., Begel, A., Bird, C., DeLine, R., Gall, H., Kamar, E., Nagappan, N., Nushi, B., Zimmermann, T.: Software engineering for machine learning: A case study. In: 2019 IEEE/ACM 41st International Conference on Software Engineering: Software Engineering in Practice (ICSE-SEIP), pp. 291–300. IEEE (2019)
16. Antinyan, V., Staron, M.: Rendex: A method for automated reviews of textual requirements. Journal of Systems and Software **131**, 63–77 (2017)
17. Arazy, O., Kopak, R.: On the measurability of information quality. Journal of the American Society for Information Science and Technology **62**(1), 89–99 (2011)
18. Arpteg, A., Brinne, B., Crnkovic-Friis, L., Bosch, J.: Software engineering challenges of deep learning. In: 2018 44th Euromicro Conference on Software Engineering and Advanced Applications (SEAA), pp. 50–59. IEEE (2018)
19. Auer, F., Felderer, M.: Current state of research on continuous experimentation: a systematic mapping study. In: 2018 44th Euromicro Conference on Software Engineering and Advanced Applications (SEAA), pp. 335–344. IEEE (2018)
20. Avgeriou, P., Kruchten, P., Ozkaya, I., Seaman, C.: Managing technical debt in software engineering (dagstuhl seminar 16162). In: Dagstuhl Reports, vol. 6. Schloss Dagstuhl-Leibniz-Zentrum fuer Informatik (2016)
21. Axelsson, S., Baca, D., Feldt, R., Sidlauskas, D., Kacan, D.: Detecting defects with an interactive code review tool based on visualisation and machine learning. In: the 21st International Conference on Software Engineering and Knowledge Engineering (SEKE 2009) (2009)
22. Bach, J.: Exploratory Testing. https://www.satisfice.com/exploratory-testing (2020). [Online; accessed July 18, 2020]
23. Baldassarre, M.T., Caivano, D., Visaggio, G.: Comprehensibility and efficiency of multiview framework for measurement plan design. In: Empirical Software Engineering, 2003. ISESE 2003. Proceedings. 2003 International Symposium on, pp. 89–98. IEEE (2003)
24. Bardsiri, V.K., Jawawi, D.N.A., Hashim, S.Z.M., Khatibi, E.: Increasing the accuracy of software development effort estimation using projects clustering. IET Software **6**(6), 461–473 (2012)
25. Barik, T., DeLine, R., Drucker, S., Fisher, D.: The bones of the system: A case study of logging and telemetry at microsoft. In: 2016 IEEE/ACM 38th International Conference on Software Engineering Companion (ICSE-C), pp. 92–101. IEEE (2016)
26. Baskerville, R., Wood-Harper, A.T.: A Critical Perspective on Action Research as a Method for Information Systems Research. Journal of Information Technology **11**(2), 235–246 (1996)
27. Basri, S., Dominic, D.D., Murugan, T., Almomani, M.A.: A proposed framework using exploratory testing to improve software quality in sme's. In: International Conference of Reliable Information and Communication Technology, pp. 1113–1122. Springer (2018)
28. Batsaikhan, O., Lin, Y.: Building a shared understanding of customer value in a large-scale agile organization: A case study. Master's thesis, Chalmers—University of Gothenburg, Dept. of Computer Science and Engineering (2018)
29. Baumeister, J., Reutelshoefer, J.: Developing knowledge systems with continuous integration. In: Proceedings of the 11th International Conference on Knowledge Management and Knowledge Technologies, pp. 1–4 (2011)
30. Beaumont, O., Bonichon, N., Courtès, L., Dolstra, E., Hanin, X.: Mixed data-parallel scheduling for distributed continuous integration. In: 2012 IEEE 26th International Parallel and Distributed Processing Symposium Workshops & PhD Forum, pp. 91–98. IEEE (2012)
31. Beck, K.: Embracing change with extreme programming. Computer **32**(10), 70–77 (1999)
32. Beck, K.: Extreme programming explained: embrace change. addison-wesley professional (2000)
33. Beck, K., Beedle, M., van Bennekum, A., Cockburn, A., Cunningham, W., Fowler, M., Grenning, J., Highsmith, J., Hunt, A., Jeffries, R., Kern, J., Marick, B., Martin, R.C., Mellor, S., Schwaber, K., Sutherland, J., Thomas, D.: Manifesto for the Agile Software Development (2001)
34. Berger, C., Eklund, U.: Expectations and challenges from scaling agile in mechatronics-driven companies–a comparative case study. In: International Conference on Agile Software Development, pp. 15–26. Springer (2015)

35. Bernardi, L., Mavridis, T., Estevez, P.: 150 successful machine learning models: 6 lessons learned at booking. com. In: Proceedings of the 25th ACM SIGKDD International Conference on Knowledge Discovery & Data Mining, pp. 1743–1751 (2019)
36. Besker, T., Martini, A., Bosch, J.: A systematic literature review and a unified model of atd. In: 2016 42th Euromicro Conference on Software Engineering and Advanced Applications (SEAA), pp. 189–197. IEEE (2016)
37. Besker, T., Martini, A., Bosch, J.: The pricey bill of technical debt: When and by whom will it be paid? In: 2017 IEEE International Conference on Software Maintenance and Evolution (ICSME), pp. 13–23. IEEE (2017)
38. Bisio, R., Malabocchia, F.: Cost estimation of software projects through case base reasoning. In: International Conference on Case-Based Reasoning, pp. 11–22. Springer (1995)
39. Bjarnason, E., Unterkalmsteiner, M., Borg, M., Engström, E.: A multi-case study of agile requirements engineering and the use of test cases as requirements. Information and Software Technology **77**, 61–79 (2016)
40. Bjarnason, E., Wnuk, K., Regnell, B.: A case study on benefits and side-effects of agile practices in large-scale requirements engineering. In: proceedings of the 1st workshop on agile requirements engineering, pp. 1–5 (2011)
41. Boehm, B.: Get ready for agile methods, with care. Computer **35**(1), 64–69 (2002)
42. Boehm, B.W., et al.: Software engineering economics, vol. 197. Prentice-hall Englewood Cliffs (NJ) (1981)
43. Boetticher, G., Menzies, T., Ostrand, T.: Promise repository of empirical software engineering data. West Virginia University, Department of Computer Science (2007)
44. Booch, G.: Object oriented design with applications. Benjamin-Cummings Publishing Co., Inc. (1990)
45. Bosch, J.: Building products as innovation experiment systems. In: International Conference of Software Business, pp. 27–39. Springer (2012)
46. Bosch, J., Eklund, U.: Eternal embedded software: Towards innovation experiment systems. In: International Symposium On Leveraging Applications of Formal Methods, Verification and Validation, pp. 19–31. Springer (2012)
47. Bosch, J., Olsson, H.H., Crnkovic, I.: It takes three to tango: Requirement, outcome/data, and ai driven development. In: SiBW, pp. 177–192 (2018)
48. Bosch, J., Olsson, H.H., Crnkovic, I.: Engineering ai systems: A research agenda. In: Artificial Intelligence Paradigms for Smart Cyber-Physical Systems, pp. 1–19. IGI Global (2021)
49. Bosch-Sijtsema, P., Bosch, J.: User involvement throughout the innovation process in high-tech industries. Journal of Product Innovation Management **32**(5), 793–807 (2015)
50. Bowyer, J., Hughes, J.: Assessing undergraduate experience of continuous integration and test-driven development. In: Proceedings of the 28th international conference on Software engineering, pp. 691–694 (2006)
51. Brar, H.K., Kaur, P.J.: Static analysis tools for security: A comparative evaluation. International Journal **5**(7) (2015)
52. Braun, V., Clarke, V.: Using thematic analysis in psychology. Qualitative research in psychology **3**(2), 77–101 (2006)
53. Briand, L., El Emam, K., Morasca, S.: Theoretical and empirical validation of software product measures. International Software Engineering Research Network, Technical Report ISERN-95-03 (1995)
54. Briand, L.C.: Novel applications of machine learning in software testing. In: 2008 The Eighth International Conference on Quality Software, pp. 3–10. IEEE (2008)
55. Briand, L.C., Morasca, S., Basili, V.R.: Property-based software engineering measurement. Software Engineering, IEEE Transactions on **22**(1), 68–86 (1996)
56. Briand, L.C., Wüst, J., Daly, J.W., Victor Porter, D.: Exploring the relationships between design measures and software quality in object-oriented systems. Journal of systems and software **51**(3), 245–273 (2000)
57. Brooks, G.: Team pace keeping build times down. In: Agile 2008 Conference, pp. 294–297. IEEE (2008)

58. Brown, N., Cai, Y., Guo, Y., Kazman, R., Kim, M., Kruchten, P., Lim, E., MacCormack, A., Nord, R., Ozkaya, I., et al.: Managing technical debt in software-reliant systems. In: Proceedings of the FSE/SDP workshop on Future of software engineering research, pp. 47–52 (2010)
59. Brun, Y., Ernst, M.D.: Finding latent code errors via machine learning over program executions. In: Proceedings of the 26th International Conference on Software Engineering, ICSE '04, pp. 480–490. IEEE Computer Society, Washington, DC, USA (2004). URL http://dl.acm.org/citation.cfm?id=998675.999452
60. Bruneliere, H., Burger, E., Cabot, J., Wimmer, M.: A feature-based survey of model view approaches. Software & Systems Modeling (2017). DOI 10.1007/s10270-017-0622-9
61. Buglione, L., Abran, A.: Introducing root-cause analysis and orthogonal defect classification at lower cmmi maturity levels. Proc. MENSURA p. 29 (2006)
62. Bures, M., Frajtak, K., Ahmed, B.S.: Tapir: Automation support of exploratory testing using model reconstruction of the system under test. IEEE Transactions on Reliability **67**(2), 557–580 (2018)
63. Calpur, M.C., Arca, S., Calpur, T.C., Yilmaz, C.: Model dressing for automated exploratory testing. In: 2017 IEEE International Conference on Software Quality, Reliability and Security Companion (QRS-C), pp. 577–578. IEEE (2017)
64. Campbell-Pretty, E.: Tribal unity: Getting from teams to tribes by creating a one team culture (2016)
65. Cannizzo, F., Clutton, R., Ramesh, R.: Pushing the boundaries of testing and continuous integration. In: Agile 2008 Conference, pp. 501–505. IEEE (2008)
66. Castellion, G.: Do it wrong quickly: how the web changes the old marketing rules by mike moran (2008)
67. Catal, C., Diri, B.: A systematic review of software fault prediction studies. Expert systems with applications **36**(4), 7346–7354 (2009)
68. Chappelly, T., Cifuentes, C., Krishnan, P., Gevay, S.: Machine learning for finding bugs: An initial report. In: Machine Learning Techniques for Software Quality Evaluation (MaL-TeSQuE), IEEE Workshop on, pp. 21–26. IEEE (2017)
69. Chow, T., Cao, D.B.: A survey study of critical success factors in agile software projects. Journal of systems and software **81**(6), 961–971 (2008)
70. Cicchetti, A., Ciccozzi, F., Pierantonio, A.: Multi-view approaches for software and system modelling: a systematic literature review. Software & Systems Modeling pp. 1–27 (2019). DOI 10.1007/s10270-018-00713-w
71. Clancy, T.: The standish group report. Chaos report (1995)
72. Cockburn, A.: Agile software development: the cooperative game. Pearson Education (2006)
73. Codabux, Z., Williams, B.: Managing technical debt: An industrial case study. In: 2013 4th International Workshop on Managing Technical Debt (MTD), pp. 8–15. IEEE (2013)
74. Cohan, S.: Successful customer collaboration resulting in the right product for the end user. In: Agile 2008 Conference, pp. 284–288. IEEE (2008)
75. Cook, T.D., Campbell, D.T., Day, A.: Quasi-experimentation: Design & analysis issues for field settings, vol. 351. Houghton Mifflin Boston (1979)
76. Cossio, M., et al.: A/b testing-the most powerful way to turn clicks into customers, vol (2012)
77. Mascarenhas Hornos da Costa, J., Oehmen, J., Rebentisch, E., Nightingale, D.: Toward a better comprehension of lean metrics for research and product development management. R&D Management (2014)
78. Crook, T., Frasca, B., Kohavi, R., Longbotham, R.: Seven pitfalls to avoid when running controlled experiments on the web. In: Proceedings of the 15th ACM SIGKDD international conference on Knowledge discovery and data mining, pp. 1105–1114. ACM (2009)
79. Cunningham, W.: The wycash portfolio management system. ACM SIGPLAN OOPS Messenger **4**(2), 29–30 (1992)
80. Cusomano, M., Selby, R.: Microsoft secrets—how the world's most powerful software company creates technology, shapes markets, and manages people (1995)
81. Dagan, I., Engelson, S.P.: Committee-based sampling for training probabilistic classifiers. In: Machine Learning Proceedings 1995, pp. 150–157. Elsevier (1995)

82. Dahlmeier, D.: On the challenges of translating nlp research into commercial products. In: Proceedings of the 55th Annual Meeting of the Association for Computational Linguistics (Volume 2: Short Papers), pp. 92–96 (2017)

83. Dajsuren, Y., Gerpheide, C., Serebrenik, A., Wijs, A., Vasilescu, B., van den Brand, M.: Formalizing Correspondence Rules for Automotive Architecture Views. In: Proceedings of the 10th international ACM Sigsoft conference on Quality of software architectures, pp. 129–138. ACM (2014). DOI 10.1145/2602576.2602588

84. Daskalantonakis, M.K., Yacobellis, R.H., Basili, V.R.: A method for assessing software measurement technology. Quality Engineering 3(1), 27–40 (1990)

85. Davis, A.M.: Just Enough Requirements Management: Where Software Development Meets Marketing. Dorset House Publishing (2005)

86. Desharnais, J.M., Abran, A.: How to succesfully implement a measurement program: From theory to practice. In: Metrics in Software Evolution, pp. 11–38. Oldenbourg Verlag, Oldenburg (1995)

87. Dess, G.G., Shaw, J.D.: Voluntary turnover, social capital, and organizational performance. Academy of Management Review 26(3), 446–456 (2001)

88. D'haeseleer, P.: What are dna sequence motifs? Nature biotechnology 24(4), 423 (2006)

89. Di Nucci, D., Palomba, F., Tamburri, D.A., Serebrenik, A., De Lucia, A.: Detecting code smells using machine learning techniques: are we there yet? In: 2018 IEEE 25th International Conference on Software Analysis, Evolution and Reengineering (SANER), pp. 612–621. IEEE (2018)

90. Diaz-Ley, M., Garcia, F., Piattini, M.: Implementing a software measurement program in small and medium enterprises: a suitable framework. IET Software 2(5), 417–436 (2008)

91. Dikert, K., Paasivaara, M., Lassenius, C.: Challenges and success factors for large-scale agile transformations: A systematic literature review. Journal of Systems and Software 119, 87–108 (2016)

92. DingsÃ¿yr, T., Nerur, S., Balijepally, V., Moe, N.B.: A decade of agile methodologies: Towards explaining agile software development. Journal of Systems and Software 85(6), 1213–1221 (2012). DOI 10.1016/j.jss.2012.02.033. URL http://www.sciencedirect.com/science/article/pii/S0164121212000532

93. Dösinger, S., Mordinyi, R., Biffl, S.: Communicating continuous integration servers for increasing effectiveness of automated testing. In: 2012 Proceedings of the 27th IEEE/ACM International Conference on Automated Software Engineering, pp. 374–377. IEEE (2012)

94. Downs, J., Hosking, J., Plimmer, B.: Status communication in agile software teams: A case study. In: 2010 Fifth International Conference on Software Engineering Advances, pp. 82–87. IEEE (2010)

95. Downs, J., Plimmer, B., Hosking, J.G.: Ambient awareness of build status in collocated software teams. In: 2012 34th International Conference on Software Engineering (ICSE), pp. 507–517. IEEE (2012)

96. Dubinsky, Y., Talby, D., Hazzan, O., Keren, A.: Agile metrics at the israeli air force. In: Agile Conference, 2005. Proceedings, pp. 12–19. IEEE (2005)

97. Durelli, V.H., Durelli, R.S., Borges, S.S., Endo, A.T., Eler, M.M., Dias, D.R., Guimarães, M.P.: Machine learning applied to software testing: A systematic mapping study. IEEE Transactions on Reliability 68(3), 1189–1212 (2019)

98. Durisic, D., Staron, M., Tichy, M., Hansson, J.: Assessing the impact of meta-model evolution: a measure and its automotive application. Software & Systems Modeling 18(2), 1419–1445 (2019)

99. Duvall, P.M., Matyas, S., Glover, A.: Continuous integration: improving software quality and reducing risk. Pearson Education (2007)

100. Dybå, T., Dingsøyr, T.: Empirical studies of agile software development: A systematic review. Information and Software Technology 50(9-10), 833–859 (2008). DOI 10.1016/j.infsof.2008.01.006. URL http://www.sciencedirect.com/science/article/pii/S0950584908000256

101. Dyer, R., Nguyen, H.A., Rajan, H., Nguyen, T.N.: Boa: A language and infrastructure for analyzing ultra-large-scale software repositories. In: Proceedings of the 2013 International Conference on Software Engineering, pp. 422–431. IEEE Press (2013)

102. Dzamashvili Fogelström, N., Gorschek, T., Svahnberg, M., Olsson, P.: The impact of agile principles on market-driven software product development. Journal of software maintenance and evolution: Research and practice 22(1), 53–80 (2010)

103. Ebert, C., Paasivaara, M.: Scaling agile. Ieee Software 34(6), 98–103 (2017)

104. Egyed, A.: Automatically Detecting and Tracking Inconsistencies in Software Design Models. IEEE Transactions on Software Engineering 37(2), 188–204 (2010). DOI 10.1109/tse.2010.38

105. Ehrig, H., Ehrig, K., Hermann, F.: From Model Transformation to Model Integration based on the Algebraic Approach to Triple Graph Grammars. Electronic Communications of the EASST 10 (2008)

106. Eiffel protocol. https://github.com/eiffel-community/eiffel

107. Eisenhardt, K.M.: Building theories from case study research. Academy of management review 14(4), 532–550 (1989)

108. Eklund, U., Olsson, H.H., Strøm, N.J.: Industrial challenges of scaling agile in mass-produced embedded systems. In: International Conference on Agile Software Development, pp. 30–42. Springer (2014)

109. Emanuelsson, P., Nilsson, U.: A comparative study of industrial static analysis tools. Electronic notes in theoretical computer science 217, 5–21 (2008)

110. Ernst, N.A., Bellomo, S., Ozkaya, I., Nord, R.L., Gorton, I.: Measure it? manage it? ignore it? software practitioners and technical debt. In: Proceedings of the 2015 10th Joint Meeting on Foundations of Software Engineering, pp. 50–60 (2015)

111. Esling, P., Agon, C.: Time-series data mining. ACM Computing Surveys (CSUR) 45(1), 12 (2012)

112. ETSI: 3GPP Technical Specification Release 14 - ETSI TS 136 300. Tech. Rep. Release 14, ETSI, Valbonne, France (2017)

113. Evbota, F., Knauss, E., Sandberg, A.: Scaling up the planning game: Collaboration challenges in large-scale agile product development. In: International Conference on Agile Software Development, pp. 28–38. Springer, Cham (2016)

114. Fabijan, A., Dmitriev, P., McFarland, C., Vermeer, L., Holmström Olsson, H., Bosch, J.: Experimentation growth: Evolving trustworthy a/b testing capabilities in online software companies. Journal of Software: Evolution and Process 30(12), e2113 (2018)

115. Fabijan, A., Dmitriev, P., Olsson, H.H., Bosch, J.: The evolution of continuous experimentation in software product development: from data to a data-driven organization at scale. In: 2017 IEEE/ACM 39th International Conference on Software Engineering (ICSE), pp. 770–780. IEEE (2017)

116. Fabijan, A., Olsson, H.H., Bosch, J.: Customer feedback and data collection techniques in software r&d: a literature review. In: International Conference of Software Business, pp. 139–153. Springer (2015)

117. Fabijan, A., Olsson, H.H., Bosch, J.: The lack of sharing of customer data in large software organizations: challenges and implications. In: International Conference on Agile Software Development, pp. 39–52. Springer (2016)

118. Fabijan, A., Olsson, H.H., Bosch, J.: Time to say'good bye': Feature lifecycle. In: 2016 42th Euromicro Conference on Software Engineering and Advanced Applications (SEAA), pp. 9–16. IEEE (2016)

119. Fagerholm, F., Guinea, A.S., Mäenpää, H., Münch, J.: Building blocks for continuous experimentation. In: Proceedings of the 1st international workshop on rapid continuous software engineering, pp. 26–35 (2014)

120. Fagerholm, F., Guinea, A.S., Mäenpää, H., Münch, J.: The right model for continuous experimentation. Journal of Systems and Software 123, 292–305 (2017)

121. Fatima, A., Bibi, S., Hanif, R.: Comparative study on static code analysis tools for c/c++. In: Applied Sciences and Technology (IBCAST), 2018 15th International Bhurban Conference on, pp. 465–469. IEEE (2018)

122. Feldmann, S., Herzig, S., Kernschmidt, K., Wolfenstetter, T., Kammerl, D., Qamar, A., Lindemann, U., Krcmar, H., Paredis, C., Vogel-Heuser, B.: A Comparison of Inconsistency Management Approaches Using a Mechatronic Manufacturing System Design Case Study. In: 2015 IEEE International Conference on Automation Science and Engineering (CASE), pp. 158–165. IEEE (2015). DOI 10.1109/coase.2015.7294055

123. Feldmann, S., Wimmer, M., Kernschmidt, K., Vogel-Heuser, B.: A Comprehensive Approach for Managing Inter-Model Inconsistencies in Automated Production Systems Engineering. In: 2016 IEEE International Conference on Automation Science and Engineering (CASE), pp. 1120–1127. IEEE (2016). DOI 10.1109/coase.2016.7743530

124. Fenton, N., Bieman, J.: Software metrics: a rigorous and practical approach. CRC Press (2014)

125. Feyh, M., Petersen, K.: Lean software development measures and indicators-a systematic mapping study. In: Lean Enterprise Software and Systems, pp. 32–47. Springer (2013)

126. Fisher, R.A.: On the Interpretation of χ^2 from Contingency Tables, and the Calculation of P. Journal of the Royal Statistical Society **85**(1), 87 (1922). DOI 10.2307/2340521. URL http://www.jstor.org/stable/2340521?origin=crossref

127. Fitzgerald, B., Stol, K.J.: Continuous software engineering: A roadmap and agenda. Journal of Systems and Software **123**, 176–189 (2017)

128. Fitzgerald, B., Stol, K.J., O'Sullivan, R., O'Brien, D.: Scaling agile methods to regulated environments: An industry case study. In: 2013 35th International Conference on Software Engineering (ICSE), pp. 863–872. IEEE (2013)

129. Flick, U.: An introduction to qualitative research. Sage Publications Ltd (2009)

130. Flick, U.: Designing qualitative research. Sage (2018)

131. Fontana, F.A., Mäntylä, M.V., Zanoni, M., Marino, A.: Comparing and experimenting machine learning techniques for code smell detection. Empirical Software Engineering **21**(3), 1143–1191 (2016)

132. Fontana, F.A., Roveda, R., Zanoni, M.: Tool support for evaluating architectural debt of an existing system: An experience report. In: Proceedings of the 31st Annual ACM Symposium on Applied Computing, pp. 1347–1349 (2016)

133. Fontana, F.A., Zanoni, M., Marino, A., Mantyla, M.V.: Code smell detection: Towards a machine learning-based approach. In: Software Maintenance (ICSM), 2013 29th IEEE International Conference on, pp. 396–399. IEEE (2013)

134. Fowler, K.: Mission-critical and safety-critical development. IEEE Instrumentation & Measurement Magazine **7**(4), 52–59 (2004)

135. Fowler, M.: Continuous Integration. https://martinfowler.com/articles/continuousIntegration.html (2006). [Online; accessed 30-January-2013]

136. Frajtak, K., Bures, M., Jelinek, I.: Model-based testing and exploratory testing: Is synergy possible? In: 2016 6th International Conference on IT Convergence and Security (ICITCS), pp. 1–6. IEEE (2016)

137. Frajtak, K., Bures, M., Jelinek, I.: Exploratory testing supported by automated reengineering of model of the system under test. Cluster Computing **20**(1), 855–865 (2017)

138. Bernard Nicolau de França, B., Horta Travassos, G.: Simulation based studies in software engineering: A matter of validity. CLEI electronic journal **18**(1), 5–5 (2015)

139. Freitas, A.A.: Comprehensible classification models: a position paper. ACM SIGKDD explorations newsletter **15**(1), 1–10 (2014)

140. Fu, Q., Zhu, J., Hu, W., Lou, J.G., Ding, R., Lin, Q., Zhang, D., Xie, T.: Where do developers log? an empirical study on logging practices in industry. In: Companion Proceedings of the 36th International Conference on Software Engineering, pp. 24–33 (2014)

141. Fu, T.c.: A review on time series data mining. Engineering Applications of Artificial Intelligence **24**(1), 164–181 (2011)

142. Fu, Y., Zhu, X., Li, B.: A survey on instance selection for active learning. Knowledge and information systems **35**(2), 249–283 (2013)

143. Gatrell, M., Counsell, S., Hall, T.: Empirical support for two refactoring studies using commercial c# software. In: 13th International Conference on Evaluation and Assessment in Software Engineering (EASE), pp. 1–10 (2009)

144. Gebizli, C.S., Sözer, H.: Improving models for model-based testing based on exploratory testing. In: 2014 IEEE 38th International Computer Software and Applications Conference Workshops, pp. 656–661. IEEE (2014)

145. Gebizli, C.Ş., Sözer, H.: Automated refinement of models for model-based testing using exploratory testing. Software Quality Journal **25**(3), 979–1005 (2017)

146. Gebizli, C.Ş., Sözer, H.: Impact of education and experience level on the effectiveness of exploratory testing: An industrial case study. In: 2017 IEEE International Conference on Software Testing, Verification and Validation Workshops (ICSTW), pp. 23–28. IEEE (2017)

147. Geels, F.W., Kemp, R.: Dynamics in socio-technical systems: Typology of change processes and contrasting case studies. Technology in Society **29**(4), 441 – 455 (2007). DOI http://dx.doi.org/10.1016/j.techsoc.2007.08.009

148. Gestwicki, P.: The entity system architecture and its application in an undergraduate game development studio. In: Proceedings of the International Conference on the Foundations of Digital Games, pp. 73–80 (2012)

149. Ghazi, A.N., Garigapati, R.P., Petersen, K.: Checklists to support test charter design in exploratory testing. In: International Conference on Agile Software Development, pp. 251–258. Springer (2017)

150. Ghazi, A.N., Petersen, K., Bjarnason, E., Runeson, P.: Levels of exploration in exploratory testing: From freestyle to fully scripted. IEEE Access **6**, 26416–26423 (2018)

151. Gibbs, G.R.: Analyzing qualitative data, vol. 6. Sage (2018)

152. Gilb, T.: Software metrics. Winthrop Publishers (1977)

153. Goldratt, E.M., Cox, J.: The goal: a process of ongoing improvement. Routledge (2016)

154. Goodman, D., Elbaz, M.: "it's not the pants, it's the people in the pants" learnings from the gap agile transformation what worked, how we did it, and what still puzzles us. In: Agile 2008 Conference, pp. 112–115. IEEE (2008)

155. Goodman, L.A.: Snowball Sampling. The Annals of Mathematical Statistics **32**(1), 148–170 (1961)

156. Goodman, P.: Practical implementation of software metrics. International software quality assurance series. McGraw-Hill, London (1993). Lc92042989 Paul Goodman

157. Goodman, P.S., Bazerman, M., Conlon, E.: Institutionalization of planned organizational change. In: Research in Organizational Behavior, pp. 215–246. JAI Press,Greenwich (1980)

158. Goodman, P.S., Dean Jr, J.W.: Creating long-term organizational change. In: Change In Organizations. Carnegie-Mellon Univ Pittsburgh, PA, Graduate School of Industiral Administration (1982)

159. Goodman, R.M., Steckler, A.: A framework for assessing program institutionalization. Knowledge in Society **2**(1), 57–71 (1989)

160. Gould, E., Marcus, A.: Company culture audit to improve development team's collaboration, communication, and cooperation. In: Design, user experience, and usability. Theory, methods, tools and practice, pp. 415–424. Springer (2011)

161. Gregory, J., Crispin, L.: More agile testing: learning journeys for the whole team. Addison-Wesley Professional (2014)

162. Gryce, C., Finkelstein, A., Nentwich, C.: Lightweight Checking for UML Based Software Development. In: Workshop on Consistency Problems in UML-based Software Development., Dresden, Germany (2002)

163. Guinan, P.J., Cooprider, J.G., Faraj, S.: Enabling software development team performance during requirements definition: A behavioral versus technical approach. Information Systems Research **9**(2), 101–125 (1998)

164. Guo, Y., Seaman, C., Gomes, R., Cavalcanti, A., Tonin, G., Da Silva, F.Q., Santos, A.L., Siebra, C.: Tracking technical debt—an exploratory case study. In: 2011 27th IEEE international conference on software maintenance (ICSM), pp. 528–531. IEEE (2011)

165. Guo, Y., Spínola, R.O., Seaman, C.: Exploring the costs of technical debt management–a case study. Empirical Software Engineering **21**(1), 159–182 (2016)

166. Gyimothy, T., Ferenc, R., Siket, I.: Empirical validation of object-oriented metrics on open source software for fault prediction. Software Engineering, IEEE Transactions on **31**(10), 897–910 (2005)

167. Hadar, E., Hassanzadeh, A.: Big data analytics on cyber attack graphs for prioritizing agile security requirements. In: 2019 IEEE 27th International Requirements Engineering Conference (RE), pp. 330–339 (2019). DOI 10.1109/RE.2019.00042

168. Hall, T., Beecham, S., Bowes, D., Gray, D., Counsell, S.: A systematic literature review on fault prediction performance in software engineering. Software Engineering, IEEE Transactions on **38**(6), 1276–1304 (2012)

169. Hanssen, G.K., Haugset, B., Stålhane, T., Myklebust, T., Kulbrandstad, I.: Quality assurance in scrum applied to safety critical software. In: International Conference on Agile Software Development, pp. 92–103. Springer, Cham (2016)

170. Hartmann, D., Dymond, R.: Appropriate agile measurement: using metrics and diagnostics to deliver business value. In: Agile Conference, 2006, pp. 6–pp. IEEE (2006)

171. Hatcher, W.G., Yu, W.: A survey of deep learning: Platforms, applications and emerging research trends. IEEE Access **6**, 24411–24432 (2018)

172. Hause, M.: The SysML Modelling Language. In: Fifteenth European Systems Engineering Conference, vol. 9, pp. 1–12. Citeseer (2006)

173. Heidenberg, J., Porres, I.: Metrics functions for kanban guards. In: Engineering of Computer Based Systems (ECBS), 2010 17th IEEE International Conference and Workshops on, pp. 306–310. IEEE (2010)

174. Heidenberg, J., Weijola, M., Mikkonen, K., Porres, I.: A metrics model to measure the impact of an agile transformation in large software development organizations. In: International Conference on Agile Software Development, pp. 165–179. Springer (2013)

175. Heikkilä, V.T., Damian, D., Lassenius, C., Paasivaara, M.: A mapping study on requirements engineering in agile software development. In: 2015 41st Euromicro conference on software engineering and advanced applications, pp. 199–207. IEEE (2015)

176. Heikkilä, V.T., Paasivaara, M., Lasssenius, C., Damian, D., Engblom, C.: Managing the requirements flow from strategy to release in large-scale agile development: a case study at ericsson. Empirical Software Engineering **22**(6), 2892–2936 (2017)

177. Hellmann, T.D., Maurer, F.: Rule-based exploratory testing of graphical user interfaces. In: 2011 Agile Conference, pp. 107–116. IEEE (2011)

178. Hendrickson, E.: Explore it!: reduce risk and increase confidence with exploratory testing. Pragmatic Bookshelf (2013)

179. Herzig, S., Qamar, A., Paredis, C.: An approach to Identifying Inconsistencies in Model-Based Systems Engineering. Procedia Computer Science **28**, 354–362 (2014). DOI 10.1016/j.procs.2014.03.044

180. Hetzel, B.: Making software measurement work: Building an effective measurement program. John Wiley & Sons, Inc. (1993)

181. Highsmith, J., Cockburn, A.: Agile software development: The business of innovation. Computer **34**(9), 120–127 (2001)

182. Hill, J.H., Schmidt, D.C., Porter, A.A., Slaby, J.M.: Cicuts: combining system execution modeling tools with continuous integration environments. In: 15th Annual IEEE International Conference and Workshop on the Engineering of Computer Based Systems (ecbs 2008), pp. 66–75. IEEE (2008)

183. Hochstein, L., Basili, V.R., Zelkowitz, M.V., Hollingsworth, J.K., Carver, J.: Combining self-reported and automatic data to improve programming effort measurement. In: ACM SIGSOFT Software Engineering Notes, vol. 30, pp. 356–365. ACM (2005)

184. Hoda, R., Noble, J., Marshall, S.: Self-organizing roles on agile software development teams. IEEE Transactions on Software Engineering **39**(3), 422–444 (2013). DOI 10.1109/TSE.2012.30

185. Hoffman, B., Cole, D., Vines, J.: Software process for rapid development of hpc software using cmake. In: 2009 DoD high performance computing modernization program users group conference, pp. 378–382. IEEE (2009)

186. Hohnhold, H., O'Brien, D., Tang, D.: Focusing on the long-term: It's good for users and business. In: Proceedings of the 21th ACM SIGKDD International Conference on Knowledge Discovery and Data Mining, pp. 1849–1858 (2015)

187. Holck, J., Jørgensen, N., et al.: Continuous integration and quality assurance: A case study of two open source projects. Australasian Journal of Information Systems **11**(1) (2003)
188. Holmes, A., Kellogg, M.: Automating functional tests using selenium. In: AGILE 2006 (AGILE'06), pp. 6–pp. IEEE (2006)
189. Holmström Olsson, H., Alahyari, H., Bosch, J.: Climbing the "stairway to heaven". In: Proceeding of the Euromicro Conference on Software Engineering and Advanced Applications. Cesme, Izmir, Turkey (2012)
190. Holvitie, J., Leppänen, V.: Debtflag: Technical debt management with a development environment integrated tool. In: 2013 4th International Workshop on Managing Technical Debt (MTD), pp. 20–27. IEEE (2013)
191. Holvitie, J., Leppänen, V., Hyrynsalmi, S.: Technical debt and the effect of agile software development practices on it-an industry practitioner survey. In: 2014 Sixth International Workshop on Managing Technical Debt, pp. 35–42. IEEE (2014)
192. Horkoff, J., Lindman, J., Hammouda, I., Knauss, E.: Experiences applying e^3 value modeling in a cross-company study. In: International conference on conceptual modeling, pp. 610–625. Springer (2018)
193. Huang, H.Y., Liu, H.H., Li, Z.J., Zhu, J.: Surrogate: A simulation apparatus for continuous integration testing in service oriented architecture. In: 2008 IEEE International Conference on Services Computing, vol. 2, pp. 223–230. IEEE (2008)
194. Huang, Q., Shihab, E., Xia, X., Lo, D., Li, S.: Identifying self-admitted technical debt in open source projects using text mining. Empirical Software Engineering **23**(1), 418–451 (2018)
195. Hudson, J., Denzinger, J.: Risk management for self-adapting self-organizing emergent multi-agent systems performing dynamic task fulfillment. Autonomous Agents and Multi-Agent Systems **29**(5), 973–1022 (2015)
196. Humble, J., Farley, D.: Continuous delivery: reliable software releases through build, test, and deployment automation. Pearson Education (2010)
197. Humphrey, W.S., Chick, T.A., Nichols, W.R., Pomeroy-Huff, M.: Team software processâĎă(tspâĎă) body of knowledge (bok). Tech. rep., Carnegie Mellon University (2010)
198. Huzar, Z., Kuzniarz, L., Reggio, G., Sourrouille, J.L.: Consistency Problems in UML-Based Software Development. In: UML Modeling Languages and Applications, pp. 1–12. Springer (2005). DOI 10.1007/978-3-540-31797-5_1
199. Idri, A., Abran, A.: Evaluating software project similarity by using linguistic quantifier guided aggregations. In: IFSA World Congress and 20th NAFIPS International Conference, 2001. Joint 9th, vol. 1, pp. 470–475. IEEE (2001)
200. Idri, A., azzahra Amazal, F., Abran, A.: Analogy-based software development effort estimation: A systematic mapping and review. Information and Software Technology **58**, 206–230 (2015)
201. Idri, A., Zahi, A., Abran, A.: Software cost estimation by fuzzy analogy for web hypermedia applications. In: Proceedings of the International Conference on Software Process and Product Measurement, Cadiz, Spain, pp. 53–62 (2006)
202. IEEE Standard Glossary of Software Engineering Terminology (1990). IEEE Standards Board/American National Standards Institute, Std. 610.12-1990
203. Inayat, I., Salim, S.S., Marczak, S., Daneva, M., Shamshirband, S.: A systematic literature review on agile requirements engineering practices and challenges. Computers in human behavior **51**, 915–929 (2015)
204. International vocabulary of basic and general terms in metrology (1993). International Organization for Standardization
205. Irwin, W., Churcher, N.: A generated parser of c++. NZ Journal of Computing **8**(3), 26–37 (2001)
206. ISO: Iso 26262: 2018:"road vehicles—functional safety" (2018)
207. ISO/IEC/IEEE Systems and software engineering – Architecture description (2011). DOI 10.1109/IEEESTD.2011.6129467
208. ISO/IEC 15939: Systems and Software Engineering - Measurement Process (2007)

209. Itkonen, J., Mantyla, M.V., Lassenius, C.: How do testers do it? an exploratory study on manual testing practices. In: 2009 3rd International Symposium on Empirical Software Engineering and Measurement, pp. 494–497. IEEE (2009)
210. Itkonen, J., Mäntylä, M.V., Lassenius, C.: The role of the tester's knowledge in exploratory software testing. IEEE Transactions on Software Engineering **39**(5), 707–724 (2012)
211. Jacquet, J.P., Abran, A.: From software metrics to software measurement methods: a process model. In: Third IEEE International Software Engineering Standards Symposium and Forum – Emerging International Standards, ISESS, pp. 128–135. IEEE (1997)
212. Janus, A., Dumke, R., Schmietendorf, A., Jäger, J.: The 3c approach for agile quality assurance. In: 2012 3rd International Workshop on Emerging Trends in Software Metrics (WETSoM), pp. 9–13. IEEE (2012)
213. Jenkins. http://jenkins-ci.org. [Online; accessed 30-January-2013]
214. John, M.M., Olsson, H.H., Bosch, J.: Ai on the edge: Architectural alternatives. In: 2020 46th Euromicro Conference on Software Engineering and Advanced Applications (SEAA), pp. 21–28. IEEE (2020)
215. John, M.M., Olsson, H.H., Bosch, J.: Developing ml/dl models: A design framework. In: Proceedings of the International Conference on Software and System Processes, pp. 1–10 (2020)
216. Johnson, D.E.: Crossover experiments. Wiley Interdisciplinary Reviews: Computational Statistics **2**(5), 620–625 (2010)
217. Johnson, P.M.: Project hackystat: Accelerating adoption of empirically guided software development through non-disruptive, developer-centric, in-process data collection and analysis. Department of Information and Computer Sciences, University of Hawaii **22** (2001)
218. Johnson, P.M., Kou, H., Agustin, J., Chan, C., Moore, C., Miglani, J., Zhen, S., Doane, W.E.: Beyond the personal software process: Metrics collection and analysis for the differently disciplined. In: Proceedings of the 25th international Conference on Software Engineering, pp. 641–646. IEEE Computer Society (2003)
219. Johnson, T., Kerzhner, A., Paredis, C., Burkhart, R.: Integrating Models and Simulations of Continuous Dynamics into SysML. Journal of Computing and Information Science in Engineering **12** (2012). DOI 10.1115/1.4005452
220. Jorgensen, M.: Software quality measurement. Advances in Engineering Software **30**(12), 907–912 (1999)
221. Jørgensen, M.: Do agile methods work for large software projects? In: International Conference on Agile Software Development, pp. 179–190. Springer (2018)
222. Jung, H.W., Kim, S.G., Chung, C.S.: Measuring software product quality: A survey of iso/iec 9126. IEEE software **21**(5), 88–92 (2004)
223. Kahkonen, T.: Agile methods for large organizations-building communities of practice. In: Agile development conference, pp. 2–10. IEEE (2004)
224. Kai, G.: Virtual measurement system for muzzle velocity and firing frequency. In: 8th International Conference on Electronic Measurement and Instruments, pp. 176–179 (2001)
225. Kaisti, M., Mujunen, T., Mäkilä, T., Rantala, V., Lehtonen, T.: Agile principles in the embedded system development. In: Agile Processes in Software Engineering and Extreme Programming, *Lecture Notes in Business Information Processing*, vol. 179, pp. 16–31. Springer, Rome, Italy (2014). DOI 10.1007/978-3-319-06862-6_2
226. Kaner, C.: Testing computer software. TAB Books (1988)
227. Kaner, C., Bach, J., Pettichord, B.: Lessons learned in software testing. John Wiley & Sons (2001)
228. Kaplan, B., Maxwell, J.A.: Qualitative research methods for evaluating computer information systems. In: Evaluating the organizational impact of healthcare information systems, pp. 30–55. Springer (2005)
229. Kaplan, R.S., Norton, D.P.: Putting the balanced scorecard to work. Performance measurement, management, and appraisal sourcebook **66** (1995)
230. Kasauli, R., Knauss, E., Kanagwa, B., Nilsson, A., Calikli, G.: Safety-critical systems and agile development: A mapping study. In: 2018 44th Euromicro Conference on Software Engineering and Advanced Applications (SEAA), pp. 470–477 (2018). DOI 10.1109/SEAA.2018.00082

231. Kasauli, R., Knauss, E., Nilsson, A., Klug, S.: Adding value every sprint: A case study on large-scale continuous requirements engineering. In: REFSQ Workshops (2017)

232. Kasauli, R., Wohlrab, R., Knauss, E., Steghöfer, J.P., Horkoff, J., Maro, S.: Charting coordination needs in large-scale agile organisations with boundary objects and methodological islands. In: Proceedings of the International Conference on Software and System Processes, ICSSP '20, p. 51–60. Association for Computing Machinery, New York, NY, USA (2020). DOI 10.1145/3379177.3388897. URL https://doi.org/10.1145/3379177.3388897

233. Kazman, R., Cai, Y., Mo, R., Feng, Q., Xiao, L., Haziyev, S., Fedak, V., Shapochka, A.: A case study in locating the architectural roots of technical debt. In: 2015 IEEE/ACM 37th IEEE International Conference on Software Engineering, vol. 2, pp. 179–188. IEEE (2015)

234. Keogh, E., Lin, J.: Clustering of time-series subsequences is meaningless: implications for previous and future research. Knowledge and information systems 8(2), 154–177 (2005)

235. Kerievsky, J.: Industrial XP: Making XP work in large organizations. Executive Report Vol. 6, No. 2, Cutter Consortium (2005). URL http://www.cutter.com/content-and-analysis/resource-centers/agile-project-management/sample-our-research/apmr0502.html

236. Kettunen, P.: Adopting key lessons from agile manufacturing to agile software product development—a comparative study. Technovation 29(6), 408–422 (2009)

237. Kettunen, P., Laanti, M.: Combining agile software projects and large-scale organizational agility. Software Process: Improvement and Practice 13(2), 183–193 (2008). DOI 10.1002/spip.354. URL http://onlinelibrary.wiley.com/doi/10.1002/spip.354/abstract

238. Khurum, M., Gorschek, T., Wilson, M.: The software value map—an exhaustive collection of value aspects for the development of software intensive products. Journal of software: Evolution and Process 25(7), 711–741 (2013)

239. Kilpi, T.: Implementing a software metrics program at nokia. IEEE Software 18(6), 72–77 (2001)

240. Kim, D.K., Lee, L.S.: Reverse engineering from exploratory testing to specification-based testing. International Journal of Software Engineering and Its Applications 8(11), 197–208 (2014)

241. Kim, E.H., Na, J.C., Ryoo, S.M.: Implementing an effective test automation framework. In: 2009 33rd Annual IEEE International Computer Software and Applications Conference, vol. 2, pp. 534–538. IEEE (2009)

242. Kim, E.H., Na, J.C., Ryoo, S.M.: Test automation framework for implementing continuous integration. In: 2009 Sixth International Conference on Information Technology: New Generations, pp. 784–789. IEEE (2009)

243. Kim, M., Zimmermann, T., DeLine, R., Begel, A.: The emerging role of data scientists on software development teams. In: 2016 IEEE/ACM 38th International Conference on Software Engineering (ICSE), pp. 96–107. IEEE (2016)

244. Kim, S., Park, S., Yun, J., Lee, Y.: Automated continuous integration of component-based software: An industrial experience. In: 2008 23rd IEEE/ACM International Conference on Automated Software Engineering, pp. 423–426. IEEE (2008)

245. Kitchenham, B.: Procedures for performing systematic reviews. Keele, UK, Keele University 33(2004), 1–26 (2004)

246. Kitchenham, B.: What's up with software metrics?–a preliminary mapping study. Journal of systems and software 83(1), 37–51 (2010)

247. Klaine, P.V., Imran, M.A., Onireti, O., Souza, R.D.: A survey of machine learning techniques applied to self-organizing cellular networks. IEEE Communications Surveys & Tutorials 19(4), 2392–2431 (2017)

248. Knaster, R., Leffingwell, D.: SAFe 4.0 distilled: applying the Scaled Agile Framework for lean software and systems engineering. Addison-Wesley Professional (2017)

249. Knauss, E., Liebel, G., Horkoff, J., Wohlrab, R., Kasauli, R., Lange, F., Gildert, P.: T-reqs: Tool support for managing requirements in large-scale agile system development. In: 2018 IEEE 26th International Requirements Engineering Conference (RE), pp. 502–503. IEEE (2018)

250. Kohavi, R., Deng, A., Frasca, B., Walker, T., Xu, Y., Pohlmann, N.: Online controlled experiments at large scale. In: Proceedings of the 19th ACM SIGKDD international conference on Knowledge discovery and data mining, pp. 1168–1176 (2013)

251. Kohavi, R., Deng, A., Longbotham, R., Xu, Y.: Seven rules of thumb for web site experimenters. In: Proceedings of the 20th ACM SIGKDD international conference on Knowledge discovery and data mining, pp. 1857–1866 (2014)

252. Kohavi, R., Longbotham, R., Sommerfield, D., Henne, R.M.: Controlled experiments on the web: survey and practical guide. Data mining and knowledge discovery **18**(1), 140–181 (2009)

253. Kolovos, D., Paige, R., Polack, F.: The Epsilon Object Language (EOL). In: European Conference on Model Driven Architecture-Foundations and Applications, pp. 128–142. Springer (2006). DOI 10.1007/11787044_11

254. Kolovos, D., Paige, R., Polack, F.: Detecting and Repairing Inconsistencies Across Heterogeneous Models. In: 2008 1st International Conference on Software Testing, Verification, and Validation, pp. 356–364. IEEE (2008). DOI 10.1109/icst.2008.23

255. Kruchten, P., Nord, R.L., Ozkaya, I.: Technical debt: From metaphor to theory and practice. Ieee software **29**(6), 18–21 (2012)

256. Kuhn, A.: On extracting unit tests from interactive live programming sessions. In: 2013 35th International Conference on Software Engineering (ICSE), pp. 1241–1244. IEEE (2013)

257. Kuhrmann, M., Diebold, P., Münch, J., Tell, P., Garousi, V., Felderer, M., Trektere, K., McCaffery, F., Linssen, O., Hanser, E., Prause, C.R.: Hybrid software and system development in practice: Waterfall, scrum, and beyond. In: Proceedings of the 2017 International Conference on Software and System Process, ICSSP 2017, p. 30–39. Association for Computing Machinery, New York, NY, USA (2017). DOI 10.1145/3084100.3084104. URL https://doi.org/10.1145/3084100.3084104

258. Kumar, S., Wallace, C.: Guidance for exploratory testing through problem frames. In: 2013 26th International Conference on Software Engineering Education and Training (CSEE&T), pp. 284–288. IEEE (2013)

259. Kunz, R.F., Kasmala, G.F., Mahaffy, J.H., Murray, C.J.: On the automated assessment of nuclear reactor systems code accuracy. Nuclear Engineering and Design **211**(2-3), 245–272 (2002). TY - JOUR

260. Laanti, M., Salo, O., Abrahamsson, P.: Agile methods rapidly replacing traditional methods at nokia: A survey of opinions on agile transformation. Information and Software Technology **53**(3), 276–290 (2011)

261. Lacoste, F.J.: Killing the gatekeeper: Introducing a continuous integration system. In: 2009 agile conference, pp. 387–392. IEEE (2009)

262. Lagerberg, L., Skude, T., Emanuelsson, P., Sandahl, K., Ståhl, D.: The impact of agile principles and practices on large-scale software development projects: A multiple-case study of two projects at ericsson. In: 2013 ACM/IEEE International Symposium on Empirical Software Engineering and Measurement, pp. 348–356. IEEE (2013)

263. Larman, C.: Scaling lean & agile development: thinking and organizational tools for large-scale Scrum. Pearson Education India (2008)

264. Larman, C., Vodde, B.: Large-scale scrum: More with LeSS. Addison-Wesley Professional (2016)

265. Lauesen, S.: Software requirements: styles and techniques. Pearson Education (2002)

266. Lauesen, S.: Guide to requirements SL-07. Lauesen Publishing (2017)

267. Layman, L., Williams, L., Cunningham, L.: Motivations and measurements in an agile case study. Journal of Systems Architecture **52**(11), 654–667 (2006)

268. Lee, C.L., Yang, H.J.: Organization structure, competition and performance measurement systems and their joint effects on performance. Management Accounting Research **22**(2), 84–104 (2011)

269. Leffingwell, D.: Agile software requirements: lean requirements practices for teams, programs, and the enterprise. Addison-Wesley Professional (2010)

270. Leffingwell, D., et al.: Scaled agile framework 3.0 (2014)

271. Li, Z., Avgeriou, P., Liang, P.: A systematic mapping study on technical debt and its management. Journal of Systems and Software **101**, 193–220 (2015)
272. Lier, F., Wrede, S., Siepmann, F., Lütkebohle, I., Paul-Stueve, T., Wachsmuth, S.: Facilitating research cooperation through linking and sharing of heterogenous research artefacts: cross platform linking of semantically enriched research artefacts. In: Proceedings of the 8th International Conference on Semantic Systems, pp. 157–164 (2012)
273. Lin, J., Keogh, E., Lonardi, S., Chiu, B.: A symbolic representation of time series, with implications for streaming algorithms. In: Proceedings of the 8th ACM SIGMOD workshop on Research issues in data mining and knowledge discovery, pp. 2–11. ACM (2003)
274. Lin, J., Keogh, E., Lonardi, S., Patel, P.: Finding motifs in time series. In: In the 2nd Workshop on Temporal Data Mining, at the 8th ACM SIGKDD International Conference on Knowledge Discovery and Data Mining, pp. 53–68 (2002)
275. Lin, J., Keogh, E., Wei, L., Lonardi, S.: Experiencing sax: a novel symbolic representation of time series. Data Mining and knowledge discovery **15**(2), 107–144 (2007)
276. Lin, J., Kolcz, A.: Large-scale machine learning at twitter. In: Proceedings of the 2012 ACM SIGMOD International Conference on Management of Data, pp. 793–804 (2012)
277. Lindgren, E., Münch, J.: Raising the odds of success: the current state of experimentation in product development. Information and Software Technology **77**, 80–91 (2016)
278. Lindman, J., Horkoff, J., Hammouda, I., Knauss, E.: Emerging perspectives of application programming interface strategy: A framework to respond to business concerns. IEEE Software **37**(2), 52–59 (2020). DOI 10.1109/MS.2018.2875964
279. Lindvall, M., Muthig, D., Dagnino, A., Wallin, C., Stupperich, M., Kiefer, D., May, J., Kahkonen, T.: Agile software development in large organizations. Computer **37**(12), 26–34 (2004)
280. Liu, H., Li, Z., Zhu, J., Tan, H., Huang, H.: A unified test framework for continuous integration testing of soa solutions. In: 2009 IEEE International Conference on Web Services, pp. 880–887. IEEE (2009)
281. Liu, S., Xiao, F., Ou, W., Si, L.: Cascade ranking for operational e-commerce search. In: Proceedings of the 23rd ACM SIGKDD International Conference on Knowledge Discovery and Data Mining, pp. 1557–1565 (2017)
282. Lokan, C., Mendes, E.: Cross-company and single-company effort models using the isbsg database: A further replicated study. In: Proceedings of the 2006 ACM/IEEE International Symposium on Empirical Software Engineering, ISESE '06, pp. 75–84. ACM, New York, NY, USA (2006). DOI 10.1145/1159733.1159747. URL http://doi.acm.org/10.1145/1159733.1159747
283. Lokan, C., Wright, T., Hill, P.R., Stringer, M.: Organizational benchmarking using the isbsg data repository. IEEE Software **18**(5), 26–32 (2001)
284. Long, B.: Managing module dependencies to facilitate continuous testing. Information processing letters **108**(3), 127–131 (2008)
285. Lucas, F., Molina, F., Toval, A.: A systematic review of UML model consistency management. Information and Software Technology **51**(12), 1631–1645 (2009). DOI 10.1016/j.infsof.2009.04.009
286. Lucassen, G., Dalpiaz, F., van der Werf, J.M.E., Brinkkemper, S.: Forging high-quality user stories: Towards a discipline for agile requirements. In: 2015 IEEE 23rd International Requirements Engineering Conference (RE), pp. 126–135 (2015). DOI 10.1109/RE.2015.7320415
287. Luckow, A., Cook, M., Ashcraft, N., Weill, E., Djerekarov, E., Vorster, B.: Deep learning in the automotive industry: Applications and tools. In: 2016 IEEE International Conference on Big Data (Big Data), pp. 3759–3768. IEEE (2016)
288. Lwakatare, L.E., Raj, A., Bosch, J., Olsson, H.H., Crnkovic, I.: A taxonomy of software engineering challenges for machine learning systems: An empirical investigation. In: International Conference on Agile Software Development, pp. 227–243. Springer, Cham (2019)
289. Maguire, M., Delahunt, B.: Doing a thematic analysis: A practical, step-by-step guide for learning and teaching scholars. All Ireland Journal of Higher Education **9**(3) (2017)

290. van Manen, H., van Vliet, H.: Organization-wide agile expansion requires an organization-wide agile mindset. In: Product-Focused Software Process Improvement, Lecture Notes in Computer Science, pp. 48–62. Springer, Helsinki, Finland (2014). URL http://link.springer.com/chapter/10.1007/978-3-319-13835-0_4

291. Mantere, M., Uusitalo, I., Roning, J.: Comparison of static code analysis tools. In: Emerging Security Information, Systems and Technologies, 2009. SECURWARE'09. Third International Conference on, pp. 15–22. IEEE (2009)

292. Manzi, J.: Uncontrolled: The surprising payoff of trial-and-error for business, politics, and society. Basic Books (AZ) (2012)

293. Mårtensson, T., Martini, A., Ståhl, D., Bosch, J.: Excellence in exploratory testing: Success factors in large-scale industry projects. In: International Conference on Product-Focused Software Process Improvement, pp. 299–314. Springer (2019)

294. Mårtensson, T., Ståhl, D., Bosch, J.: Exploratory testing of large-scale systems–testing in the continuous integration and delivery pipeline. In: International Conference on Product-Focused Software Process Improvement, pp. 368–384. Springer (2017)

295. Mårtensson, T., Ståhl, D., Bosch, J.: Enable more frequent integration of software in industry projects. Journal of Systems and Software **142**, 223–236 (2018)

296. Mårtensson, T., Ståhl, D., Bosch, J.: Test activities in the continuous integration and delivery pipeline. Journal of Software: Evolution and Process **31**(4), e2153 (2019)

297. Martin, R.C.: Agile software development: principles, patterns, and practices. Prentice Hall (2002)

298. Martini, A., Besker, T., Bosch, J.: The introduction of technical debt tracking in large companies. In: 2016 23rd Asia-Pacific Software Engineering Conference (APSEC), pp. 161–168. IEEE (2016)

299. Martini, A., Bosch, J.: The danger of architectural technical debt: Contagious debt and vicious circles. In: 2015 12th Working IEEE/IFIP Conference on Software Architecture, pp. 1–10. IEEE (2015)

300. Martini, A., Bosch, J.: An empirically developed method to aid decisions on architectural technical debt refactoring: Anacondebt. In: 2016 IEEE/ACM 38th International Conference on Software Engineering Companion (ICSE-C), pp. 31–40. IEEE (2016)

301. Martini, A., Bosch, J.: A multiple case study of continuous architecting in large agile companies: current gaps and the caffea framework. In: 2016 13th Working IEEE/IFIP Conference on Software Architecture (WICSA), pp. 1–10. IEEE (2016)

302. Martini, A., Bosch, J.: The magnificent seven: towards a systematic estimation of technical debt interest. In: Proceedings of the XP2017 Scientific Workshops, pp. 1–5 (2017)

303. Martini, A., Bosch, J., Chaudron, M.: Investigating architectural technical debt accumulation and refactoring over time: A multiple-case study. Information and Software Technology **67**, 237–253 (2015)

304. Maruping, L.M., Zhang, X., Venkatesh, V.: Role of collective ownership and coding standards in coordinating expertise in software project teams. European Journal of Information Systems **18**(4), 355–371 (2009)

305. Masters, J.: The history of action research. Action research electronic reader **22**, 2005 (1995)

306. Masuda, S., Ono, K., Yasue, T., Hosokawa, N.: A survey of software quality for machine learning applications. In: 2018 IEEE International conference on software testing, verification and validation workshops (ICSTW), pp. 279–284. IEEE (2018)

307. Matsumoto, K., Kibe, S., Uehara, M., Mori, H.: Design of development as a service in the cloud. In: 2012 15th International Conference on Network-Based Information Systems, pp. 815–819. IEEE (2012)

308. Mattos, D.I., Bosch, J., Olsson, H.H.: Challenges and strategies for undertaking continuous experimentation to embedded systems: Industry and research perspectives. In: 19th International Conference on Agile Software Development (2018)

309. Maximilien, E.M., Williams, L.: Assessing test-driven development at ibm. In: Software Engineering, 2003. Proceedings. 25th International Conference on, pp. 564–569. IEEE (2003)

310. Maxwell, J.A.: Qualitative research design: An interactive approach, vol. 41. Sage publications (2012)

311. Maxwell, K.D., Forselius, P.: Benchmarking software development productivity. IEEE Software **17**(1), 80–88 (2000). DOI 10.1109/52.820015

312. Mayring, P.: Qualitative content analysis–research instrument or mode of interpretation. The role of the researcher in qualitative psychology **2**(139-148) (2002)

313. McConnell, S.: Managing technical debt presentation at icse 2013 (2013)

314. McGarry, J.: Practical software measurement: objective information for decision makers. Addison-Wesley Professional (2002)

315. McIntosh, S., Kamei, Y., Adams, B., Hassan, A.E.: The impact of code review coverage and code review participation on software quality: A case study of the qt, vtk, and itk projects. In: Proceedings of the 11th Working Conference on Mining Software Repositories, pp. 192–201. ACM (2014)

316. McMahon, P.: Extending agile methods: A distributed project and organizational improvement perspective. In: Systems and Software Technology Conference (2005)

317. Melão, N., Pidd, M.: A conceptual framework for understanding business processes and business process modelling. Information systems journal **10**(2), 105–129 (2000)

318. Mellado, R.P., Montini, D.Á., Dias, L.A.V., da Cunha, A.M., et al.: Software product measurement and analysis in a continuous integration environment. In: 2010 Seventh International Conference on Information Technology: New Generations, pp. 1177–1182. IEEE (2010)

319. Mendes, E., Lokan, C., Harrison, R., Triggs, C.: A replicated comparison of cross-company and within-company effort estimation models using the isbsg database. In: 11th IEEE International Software Metrics Symposium (METRICS'05), pp. 10 pp.–36 (2005). DOI 10.1109/METRICS.2005.4

320. Menzies, T., Butcher, A., Cok, D., Marcus, A., Layman, L., Shull, F., Turhan, B., Zimmermann, T.: Local versus global lessons for defect prediction and effort estimation. IEEE Transactions on software engineering **39**(6), 822–834 (2013)

321. Meyer, B.: The ugly, the hype and the good: an assessment of the agile approach. In: Agile!, pp. 149–154. Springer (2014)

322. Mi, Q., Keung, J., Xiao, Y., Mensah, S., Gao, Y.: Improving code readability classification using convolutional neural networks. Information and Software Technology **104**, 60–71 (2018)

323. Micallef, M., Porter, C., Borg, A.: Do exploratory testers need formal training? an investigation using hci techniques. In: 2016 IEEE Ninth International Conference on Software Testing, Verification and Validation Workshops (ICSTW), pp. 305–314. IEEE (2016)

324. Mihindukulasooriya, N., Rizzo, G., Troncy, R., Corcho, O., García-Castro, R.: A two-fold quality assurance approach for dynamic knowledge bases: The 3cixty use case. In: (KNOW@ LOD/CoDeS)@ ESWC (2016)

325. Miles, M.B., Huberman, A.M.: Qualitative data analysis: An expanded sourcebook. sage (1994)

326. Miller, A.: A hundred days of continuous integration. In: Agile 2008 conference, pp. 289–293. IEEE (2008)

327. Moha, N., Gueheneuc, Y.G., Duchien, A.F., et al.: Decor: A method for the specification and detection of code and design smells. IEEE Transactions on Software Engineering (TSE) **36**(1), 20–36 (2010)

328. Moitra, D.: Managing change for software process improvement initiatives: a practical experience-based approach. Software Process: Improvement and Practice **4**(4), 199–207 (1998)

329. Mueen, A., Keogh, E., Zhu, Q., Cash, S., Westover, B.: Exact discovery of time series motifs. In: Proceedings of the 2009 SIAM international conference on data mining, pp. 473–484. SIAM (2009)

330. Mujtaba, S., Feldt, R., Petersen, K.: Waste and lead time reduction in a software product customization process with value stream maps. In: 2010 21st australian software engineering conference, pp. 139–148. IEEE (2010)

331. Müller, M., Sazama, F., Debou, C., Dudzic, P., Abowd, P.: Survey – State of Practice "Agile in Automotive". Tech. rep., KUGLER MAAG CIE GmbH (2014). URL http://www.kuglermaag. com/improvement-concepts/agile-in-automotive/state-of-practice.html

332. Munappy, A., Bosch, J., Olsson, H.H., Arpteg, A., Brinne, B.: Data management challenges for deep learning. In: 2019 45th Euromicro Conference on Software Engineering and Advanced Applications (SEAA), pp. 140–147. IEEE (2019)

333. Munappy, A.R., Mattos, D.I., Bosch, J., Olsson, H.H., Dakkak, A.: From ad-hoc data analytics to dataops. In: Proceedings of the International Conference on Software and System Processes, pp. 165–174 (2020)

334. Needleman, S.B., Wunsch, C.D.: A general method applicable to the search for similarities in the amino acid sequence of two proteins. Journal of molecular biology **48**(3), 443–453 (1970)

335. Nentwich, C., Emmerich, W., Finkelstein, A., Ellmer, E.: Flexible Consistency Checking. ACM Transactions on Software Engineering and Methodology (TOSEM) **12**(1), 28–63 (2003). DOI 10.1145/839268.839271

336. Niessink, F., van Vliet, H.: Measurements should generate value, rather than data. In: 6th International Software Metrics Symposium, pp. 31–38 (2000)

337. Niessink, F., van Vliet, H.: Measurement program success factors revisited. Information and Software Technology **43**(10), 617–628 (2001). TY - JOUR

338. Nilsson, A., Bosch, J., Berger, C.: The civit model in a nutshell: Visualizing testing activities to support continuous integration. In: Continuous software engineering, pp. 97–106. Springer (2014)

339. Niven, P.R.: Balanced scorecard step-by-step: maximizing performance and maintaining results. John Wiley & Sons (2002)

340. Novak, J., Krajnc, A., Åjontar, R.: Taxonomy of static code analysis tools. In: MIPRO, 2010 Proceedings of the 33rd International Convention, pp. 418–422. IEEE (2010)

341. Ochodek, M., Staron, M., Bargowski, D., Meding, W., Hebig, R.: Using machine learning to design a flexible loc counter. In: Machine Learning Techniques for Software Quality Evaluation (MaLTeSQuE), IEEE Workshop on, pp. 14–20. IEEE (2017)

342. Offen, R.J., Jeffery, R.: Establishing software measurement programs. Software, IEEE **14**(2), 45–53 (1997)

343. Olsson, H.H., Alahyari, H., Bosch, J.: Climbing the "stairway to heaven"–a mulitiple-case study exploring barriers in the transition from agile development towards continuous deployment of software. In: Software Engineering and Advanced Applications (SEAA), 2012 38th EUROMICRO Conference on, pp. 392–399. IEEE (2012)

344. Olsson, H.H., Bosch, J.: From opinions to data-driven software r&d: A multi-case study on how to close the 'open loop' problem. In: 2014 40th EUROMICRO Conference on Software Engineering and Advanced Applications, pp. 9–16. IEEE (2014)

345. Olsson, H.H., Bosch, J.: The hypex model: from opinions to data-driven software development. In: Continuous software engineering, pp. 155–164. Springer (2014)

346. Olsson, H.H., Bosch, J.: Towards continuous customer validation: A conceptual model for combining qualitative customer feedback with quantitative customer observation. In: International Conference of Software Business, pp. 154–166. Springer (2015)

347. Olszewska, M., Heidenberg, J., Weijola, M., Mikkonen, K., Porres, I.: Quantitatively measuring a large-scale agile transformation. Journal of Systems and Software **117**, 258 – 273 (2016). URL http://www.sciencedirect.com/science/article/pii/S016412121600087X

348. Organization, I.S., Commission, I.E.: Software and systems engineering, software measurement process. Tech. rep., ISO/IEC (2007)

349. Paasivaara, M., Lassenius, C.: Challenges and success factors for large-scale agile transformations: A research proposal and a pilot study. In: Proceedings of the Scientific Workshop Proceedings of XP2016, pp. 1–5 (2016)

350. Paetsch, F., Eberlein, A., Maurer, F.: Requirements engineering and agile software development. In: WET ICE 2003. Proceedings. Twelfth IEEE International Workshops on Enabling Technologies: Infrastructure for Collaborative Enterprises, 2003., pp. 308–313. IEEE (2003)

351. Paige, R., Brooke, P., Ostroff, J.: Metamodel-Based Model Conformance and Multi-view Consistency Checking. ACM Transactions on Software Engineering and Methodology (TOSEM) **16**(3), 11 (2007). DOI 10.1145/1243987.1243989

352. Pantazos, K., Shollo, A., Staron, M., Meding, W.: Presenting software metrics indicators-a case study. In: Proceedings of IWSM/Mensura conference (2010)

353. Patil, D.: Building data science teams. " O'Reilly Media, Inc." (2011)

354. Peach, R.W.: The ISO 9000 handbook. Irwin Professional Publishing (1995)

355. Pernståhl, J., Magazinius, A., Gorschek, T.: A study investigating challenges in the interface between product development and manufacturing in the development of software-intensive automotive systems. International Journal of Software Engineering and Knowledge Engineering **22**(07), 965–1004 (2012)

356. Persson, M., Torngren, M., Qamar, A., Westman, J., Biehl, M., Tripakis, S., Vangheluwe, H., Denil, J.: A Characterization of Integrated Multi-View Modeling in the Context of Embedded and Cyber-Physical Systems. In: Embedded Software (EMSOFT), 2013 Proceedings of the International Conference on, pp. 1–10. IEEE (2013). DOI 10.1109/emsoft.2013.6658588

357. Pesola, J.P., Tanner, H., Eskeli, J., Parviainen, P., Bendas, D.: Integrating early v&v support to a gse tool integration platform. In: 2011 IEEE Sixth International Conference on Global Software Engineering Workshop, pp. 95–101. IEEE (2011)

358. Petersen, K.: A palette of lean indicators to detect waste in software maintenance: A case study. In: Agile processes in software engineering and extreme programming, pp. 108–122. Springer (2012)

359. Petersen, K., Feldt, R., Mujtaba, S., Mattsson, M.: Systematic mapping studies in software engineering. In: 12th International Conference on Evaluation and Assessment in Software Engineering. sn (2008)

360. Petersen, K., Wohlin, C.: A comparison of issues and advantages in agile and incremental development between state of the art and an industrial case. Journal of Systems and Software **82**(9), 1479–1490 (2009). DOI 10.1016/j.jss.2009.03.036

361. Pfahl, D., Yin, H., Mäntylä, M.V., Münch, J.: How is exploratory testing used? a state-of-the-practice survey. In: Proceedings of the 8th ACM/IEEE international symposium on empirical software engineering and measurement, pp. 1–10 (2014)

362. Pichler, J., Ramler, R.: How to test the intangible properties of graphical user interfaces? In: 2008 1st International Conference on Software Testing, Verification, and Validation, pp. 494–497. IEEE (2008)

363. Raappana, P., Saukkoriipi, S., Tervonen, I., Mäntylä, M.V.: The effect of team exploratory testing–experience report from f-secure. In: 2016 IEEE Ninth International Conference on Software Testing, Verification and Validation Workshops (ICSTW), pp. 295–304. IEEE (2016)

364. Radatz, J., Geraci, A., Katki, F.: Ieee standard glossary of software engineering terminology. IEEE Std **610121990**(121990), 3 (1990)

365. Radjenović, D., Heričko, M., Torkar, R., Živkovič, A.: Software fault prediction metrics: A systematic literature review. Information and Software Technology **55**(8), 1397–1418 (2013)

366. Raj, A., Bosch, J., Olsson, H.H., Wang, T.J.: Modelling data pipelines. In: 2020 46th Euromicro Conference on Software Engineering and Advanced Applications (SEAA), pp. 13–20. IEEE (2020)

367. Ramasubbu, N., Cataldo, M., Balan, R.K., Herbsleb, J.D.: Configuring global software teams: a multi-company analysis of project productivity, quality, and profits. In: Proceedings of the 33rd International Conference on Software Engineering, pp. 261–270. ACM (2011)

368. Ramesh, B., Cao, L., Baskerville, R.: Agile requirements engineering practices and challenges: an empirical study. Information Systems Journal **20**(5), 449–480 (2010)

369. Rana, R., Staron, M., Berger, C., Hansson, J., Nilsson, M., Törner, F., Meding, W., Höglund, C.: Selecting software reliability growth models and improving their predictive accuracy using historical projects data. Journal of Systems and Software **98**, 59–78 (2014)

370. Rashmi, N., Suma, V.: Defect detection efficiency of the combined approach. In: ICT and Critical Infrastructure: Proceedings of the 48th Annual Convention of Computer Society of India-Vol II, pp. 485–490. Springer (2014)

371. Rasmusson, J.: Long build trouble shooting guide. In: Conference on Extreme Programming and Agile Methods, pp. 13–21. Springer (2004)
372. Reis, J., Mota, A.: Aiding exploratory testing with pruned gui models. Information Processing Letters **133**, 49–55 (2018)
373. Ries, E.: The lean startup: How today's entrepreneurs use continuous innovation to create radically successful businesses. Crown Business Publishing (2011)
374. Rissanen, O., Münch, J.: Continuous experimentation in the b2b domain: a case study. In: 2015 IEEE/ACM 2nd International Workshop on Rapid Continuous Software Engineering, pp. 12–18. IEEE (2015)
375. Roberts, M.: Enterprise continuous integration using binary dependencies. In: International Conference on Extreme Programming and Agile Processes in Software Engineering, pp. 194–201. Springer (2004)
376. Robson, C., McCartan, K.: Real world research. John Wiley & Sons (2016)
377. Rodden, K., Hutchinson, H., Fu, X.: Measuring the user experience on a large scale: user-centered metrics for web applications. In: Proceedings of the SIGCHI conference on human factors in computing systems, pp. 2395–2398 (2010)
378. Rodríguez, P., Haghighatkhah, A., Lwakatare, L.E., Teppola, S., Suomalainen, T., Eskeli, J., Karvonen, T., Kuvaja, P., Verner, J.M., Oivo, M.: Continuous deployment of software intensive products and services: A systematic mapping study. Journal of Systems and Software **123**, 263–291 (2017)
379. Rogers, R.O.: Cruisecontrol. net: Continuous integration for. net. In: International Conference on Extreme Programming and Agile Processes in Software Engineering, pp. 114–122. Springer (2003)
380. Rogers, R.O.: Scaling continuous integration. In: International conference on extreme programming and agile processes in software engineering, pp. 68–76. Springer (2004)
381. Ruhe, G.: Software engineering decision support–a new paradigm for learning software organizations. In: Advances in Learning Software Organizations, pp. 104–113. Springer (2003)
382. Ruhe, G., Saliu, M.O.: The art and science of software release planning. Software, IEEE **22**(6), 47–53 (2005)
383. Rumpe, B.: Agile modeling with the uml. In: M. Wirsing, A. Knapp, S. Balsamo (eds.) Radical Innovations of Software and Systems Engineering in the Future, pp. 297–309. Springer Berlin Heidelberg, Berlin, Heidelberg (2004)
384. Runeson, P., Höst, M.: Guidelines for conducting and reporting case study research in software engineering. Empirical software engineering **14**(2), 131–164 (2009)
385. Runeson, P., Host, M., Rainer, A., Regnell, B.: Case study research in software engineering: Guidelines and examples. John Wiley & Sons (2012)
386. Runeson, P., Host, M., Rainer, A., Regnell, B.: Case study research in software engineering: Guidelines and examples. John Wiley & Sons (2012)
387. Salo, O., Abrahamsson, P.: Agile methods in european embedded software development organisations: a survey on the actual use and usefulness of extreme programming and scrum. IET software **2**(1), 58–64 (2008)
388. Sandberg, A., Pareto, L., Arts, T.: Agile collaborative research: Action principles for industry-academia collaboration. Software, IEEE **28**(4), 74–83 (2011)
389. Savolainen, J., Kuusela, J., Vilavaara, A.: Transition to agile development-rediscovery of important requirements engineering practices. In: 2010 18th IEEE International Requirements Engineering Conference, pp. 289–294. IEEE (2010)
390. Schaefer, C.J., Do, H.: Model-based exploratory testing: a controlled experiment. In: 2014 IEEE Seventh International Conference on Software Testing, Verification and Validation Workshops, pp. 284–293. IEEE (2014)
391. Schermann, G., Cito, J., Leitner, P., Zdun, U., Gall, H.C.: We're doing it live: A multi-method empirical study on continuous experimentation. Information and Software Technology **99**, 41–57 (2018)
392. Schmidt, D.C.: Model-driven engineering. IEEE Computer **39**(2), 25 (2006)

393. Schuh, P.: Integrating agile development in the real world. Charles River Media Hingham (2005)

394. Sculley, D., Holt, G., Golovin, D., Davydov, E., Phillips, T., Ebner, D., Chaudhary, V., Young, M., Crespo, J.F., Dennison, D.: Hidden technical debt in machine learning systems. Advances in neural information processing systems **28**, 2503–2511 (2015)

395. Seaman, C., Guo, Y., Zazworka, N., Shull, F., Izurieta, C., Cai, Y., Vetrò, A.: Using technical debt data in decision making: Potential decision approaches. In: 2012 Third International Workshop on Managing Technical Debt (MTD), pp. 45–48. IEEE (2012)

396. Sedano, T., Ralph, P., PÃĭraire, C.: The product backlog. In: 2019 IEEE/ACM 41st International Conference on Software Engineering (ICSE), pp. 200–211 (2019). DOI 10.1109/ICSE.2019.00036

397. Sehmi, A., Jones, N., Wang, S., Loudon, G.: Knowledge-based systems for neuroelectric signal processing. IEE Proceedings-Science, Measurement and Technology **141**(3), 215–23 (2003)

398. Senin, P., Lin, J., Wang, X., Oates, T., Gandhi, S., Boedihardjo, A.P., Chen, C., Frankenstein, S., Lerner, M.: Grammarviz 2.0: a tool for grammar-based pattern discovery in time series. In: Joint European Conference on Machine Learning and Knowledge Discovery in Databases, pp. 468–472. Springer (2014)

399. Shadish, W.R., Cook, T.D., Campbell, D.T., et al.: Experimental and quasi-experimental designs for generalized causal inference/William R. Shedish, Thomas D. Cook, Donald T. Campbell. Boston: Houghton Mifflin, (2002)

400. Shah, A., Kerzhner, A., Schaefer, D., Paredis, C.: Multi-view Modeling to Support Embedded Systems Engineering in SysML. In: Graph transformations and model-driven engineering, pp. 580–601. Springer (2010). DOI 10.1007/978-3-642-17322-6_25

401. Shah, S.M.A., Gencel, C., Alvi, U.S., Petersen, K.: Towards a hybrid testing process unifying exploratory testing and scripted testing. Journal of software: Evolution and Process **26**(2), 220–250 (2014)

402. Shah, S.M.A., Torchiano, M., Vetrò, A., Morisio, M.: Exploratory testing as a source of technical debt. IT Professional **16**(3), 44–51 (2013)

403. Shahnewaz, S., Ruhe, G.: Relrea-an analytical approch for evaluating release readiness. In: SEKE (2014)

404. Shalloway, A., Beaver, G., Trott, J.R.: Lean-agile software development: achieving enterprise agility. Pearson Education (2009)

405. Shaukat, R., Shahoor, A., Urooj, A.: Probing into code analysis tools: A comparison of c# supporting static code analyzers. In: Applied Sciences and Technology (IBCAST), 2018 15th International Bhurban Conference on, pp. 455–464. IEEE (2018)

406. Shen, M., Yang, W., Rong, G., Shao, D.: Applying agile methods to embedded software development: A systematic review. In: Proceedings of the International Workshop on Software Engineering for Embedded Systems, pp. 30–36. IEEE (2012). DOI 10.1109/SEES.2012.6225488

407. Shoaib, L., Nadeem, A., Akbar, A.: An empirical evaluation of the influence of human personality on exploratory software testing. In: 2009 IEEE 13th International Multitopic Conference, pp. 1–6. IEEE (2009)

408. Shull, F., Singer, J., Sjøberg, D.I.K. (eds.): Guide to Advanced Empirical Software Engineering. Springer London, London (2008). DOI 10.1007/978-1-84800-044-5. URL http://www.springerlink.com/index/10.1007/978-1-84800-044-5

409. Silhavy, P., Silhavy, R., Prokopova, Z.: Categorical variable segmentation model for software development effort estimation. IEEE Access **7**, 9618–9626 (2019). DOI 10.1109/ACCESS.2019.2891878

410. Silhavy, R., Silhavy, P., Prokopova, Z.: Improving algorithmic optimisation method by spectral clustering. In: Computer Science On-line Conference, pp. 1–10. Springer (2017)

411. Silhavy, R., Silhavy, P., Prokopová, Z.: Evaluating subset selection methods for use case points estimation. Information and Software Technology **97**, 1–9 (2018)

412. Singh, D., Sekar, V.R., Stolee, K.T., Johnson, B.: Evaluating how static analysis tools can reduce code review effort. In: Visual Languages and Human-Centric Computing (VL/HCC), 2017 IEEE Symposium on, pp. 101–105. IEEE (2017)

413. Sinnema, M., Deelstra, S., Nijhuis, J., Bosch, J.: Covamof: A framework for modeling variability in software product families. In: International Conference on Software Product Lines, pp. 197–213. Springer (2004)

414. Smit, M., Gergel, B., Hoover, H.J., Stroulia, E.: Maintainability and source code conventions: An analysis of open source projects. University of Alberta, Department of Computing Science, Tech. Rep. TR11-06 (2011)

415. Sommerville, I.: Software engineering. 6th. Ed., Harlow, UK.: Addison-Wesley (2001)

416. Sommerville, I.: Software Engineering, 10th edn. Pearson (2015)

417. Sorrell, S., et al.: Digitalisation of goods: a systematic review of the determinants and magnitude of the impacts on energy consumption. Environmental Research Letters **15**(4), 043001 (2020)

418. Ståhl, D., Bosch, J.: Experienced benefits of continuous integration in industry software product development: A case study. In: The 12th iasted international conference on software engineering,(innsbruck, austria, 2013), pp. 736–743 (2013)

419. Ståhl, D., Bosch, J.: Continuous integration flows. In: Continuous software engineering, pp. 107–115. Springer (2014)

420. Ståhl, D., Bosch, J.: Modeling continuous integration practice differences in industry software development. Journal of Systems and Software **87**, 48–59 (2014)

421. Ståhl, D., Bosch, J.: Industry application of continuous integration modeling: a multiple-case study. In: 2016 IEEE/ACM 38th International Conference on Software Engineering Companion (ICSE-C), pp. 270–279. IEEE (2016)

422. Ståhl, D., Bosch, J.: Cinders: The continuous integration and delivery architecture framework. Information and Software Technology **83**, 76–93 (2017)

423. Ståhl, D., Hallén, K., Bosch, J.: Achieving traceability in large scale continuous integration and delivery deployment, usage and validation of the eiffel framework. Empirical Software Engineering **22**(3), 967–995 (2017)

424. Stahl, D., Martensson, T., Bosch, J.: Continuous practices and devops: beyond the buzz, what does it all mean? In: 2017 43rd Euromicro Conference on Software Engineering and Advanced Applications (SEAA), pp. 440–448. IEEE (2017)

425. Staron, M.: Critical role of measures in decision processes: Managerial and technical measures in the context of large software development organizations. Information and Software Technology **54**(8), 887–899 (2012)

426. Staron, M.: Software complexity metrics in general and in the context of ISO 26262 software verification requirements. In: Scandinavian Conference on Systems Safety. http://gup.ub.gu.se/records/fulltext/233026/233026.pdf (2016)

427. Staron, M.: Action Research in Software Engineering. Springer (2020)

428. Staron, M., Hansson, J., Feldt, R., Henriksson, A., Meding, W., Nilsson, S., Hoglund, C.: Measuring and visualizing code stability–a case study at three companies. In: Software Measurement and the 2013 Eighth International Conference on Software Process and Product Measurement (IWSM-MENSURA), 2013 Joint Conference of the 23rd International Workshop on, pp. 191–200. IEEE (2013)

429. Staron, M., Meding, W.: Predicting short-term defect inflow in large software projects–an initial evaluation. 11th International Conference on Evaluation and Assessment in Software Engineering, EASE (2007)

430. Staron, M., Meding, W.: Predicting weekly defect inflow in large software projects based on project planning and test status. Information and Software Technology p. (available online) (2007)

431. Staron, M., Meding, W.: Ensuring reliability of information provided by measurement systems. In: Proceedings of the International Conferences on Software Process and Product Measurement. Springer Berlin / Heidelberg (2009)

432. Staron, M., Meding, W.: Factors determining long-term success of a measurement program: an industrial case study. e-Informatica Software Engineering Journal pp. 7–23 (2011)

433. Staron, M., Meding, W.: Software Development Measurement Programs: Development, Management and Evolution. Springer (2018)
434. Staron, M., Meding, W., Caiman, M.: Improving completeness of measurement systems for monitoring software development workflows. In: Software Quality. Increasing Value in Software and Systems Development, pp. 230–243. Springer (2013)
435. Staron, M., Meding, W., Hansson, J., Höglund, C., Niesel, K., Bergmann, V.: Dashboards for continuous monitoring of quality for software product under development. System Qualities and Software Architecture (SQSA) (2013)
436. Staron, M., Meding, W., Karlsson, G., Nilsson, C.: Developing measurement systems: an industrial case study. Journal of Software Maintenance and Evolution: Research and Practice 23(2), 89–107 (2011)
437. Staron, M., Meding, W., Nilsson, C.: A framework for developing measurement systems and its industrial evaluation. Information and Software Technology 51(4), 721–737 (2008)
438. Staron, M., Meding, W., Palm, K.: Release readiness indicator for mature agile and lean software development projects. In: Agile Processes in Software Engineering and Extreme Programming, pp. 93–107. Springer (2012)
439. Staron, M., Meding, W., Söderqvist, B.: A method for forecasting defect backlog in large streamline software development projects and its industrial evaluation. Information and Software Technology 52(10), 1069–1079 (2010)
440. Staron, M., Ochodek, M., Meding, W., Söder, O., Rosenberg, E.: Machine learning to support code reviews in continuous integration. In: Artificial Intelligence Methods For Software Engineering, pp. 141–167. World Scientific (2021)
441. Steghöfer, J.P., Knauss, E., Horkoff, J., Wohlrab, R.: Challenges of scaled agile for safety-critical systems. In: X. Franch, T. Männistö, S. Martínez-Fernández (eds.) Product-Focused Software Process Improvement, pp. 350–366. Springer International Publishing, Cham (2019)
442. Stolberg, S.: Enabling agile testing through continuous integration. In: 2009 agile conference, pp. 369–374 (2009)
443. Sturdevant, K.F.: Cruisin'and chillin': Testing the java-based distributed ground data system" chill" with cruisecontrol system" chill" with cruisecontrol. In: 2007 IEEE Aerospace Conference, pp. 1–8. IEEE (2007)
444. Subramanyam, R., Krishnan, M.S.: Empirical analysis of ck metrics for object-oriented design complexity: Implications for software defects. Software Engineering, IEEE Transactions on 29(4), 297–310 (2003)
445. Sunindyo, W.D., Moser, T., Winkler, D., Biffl, S.: Foundations for event-based process analysis in heterogeneous software engineering environments. In: 2010 36th EUROMICRO Conference on Software Engineering and Advanced Applications, pp. 313–322. IEEE (2010)
446. Suryadevara, J., Tiwari, S.: Adopting MBSE in Construction Equipment Industry: An Experience Report. In: 25th Asia-Pacific Software Engineering Conference APSEC (2018). DOI 10.1109/apsec.2018.00066
447. Susman, G., Evered, R.: An Assessment of the Scientific Merits of Action Research. Journal of Administrative Science Quarterly 23(4), 582–603 (1978)
448. Susman, G.I.: Action research: a sociotechnical systems perspective. Beyond method: Strategies for social research pp. 95–113 (1983)
449. Susman, G.I., Evered, R.D.: An assessment of the scientific merits of action research. Administrative science quarterly pp. 582–603 (1978)
450. Sutherland, J., Frohman, R.: Hitting the wall: What to do when high performing scrum teams overwhelm operations and infrastructure. In: 2011 44th Hawaii International Conference on System Sciences, pp. 1–6. IEEE (2011)
451. Sviridova, T., Stakhova, D., Marikutsa, U.: Exploratory testing: Management solution. In: 2013 12th International Conference on the Experience of Designing and Application of CAD Systems in Microelectronics (CADSM), pp. 361–361. IEEE (2013)
452. Tamburri, D.A., Kruchten, P., Lago, P., van Vliet, H.: What is social debt in software engineering? In: 2013 6th International Workshop on Cooperative and Human Aspects of Software Engineering (CHASE), pp. 93–96. IEEE (2013)

453. Tang, D., Agarwal, A., O'Brien, D., Meyer, M.: Overlapping experiment infrastructure: More, better, faster experimentation. In: Proceedings of the 16th ACM SIGKDD international conference on Knowledge discovery and data mining, pp. 17–26 (2010)
454. Tingling, P., Saeed, A.: Extreme programming in action: a longitudinal case study. In: International Conference on Human-Computer Interaction, pp. 242–251. Springer (2007)
455. Tom, E., Aurum, A., Vidgen, R.: An exploration of technical debt. Journal of Systems and Software 86(6), 1498–1516 (2013)
456. Torunski, E., Shafiq, M.O., Whitehead, A.: Code style analytics for the automatic setting of formatting rules in ides: A solution to the tabs vs. spaces debate. In: Digital Information Management (ICDIM), 2017 Twelfth International Conference on, pp. 6–14. IEEE (2017)
457. Tosun, A., Turhan, B., Bener, A.: Practical considerations in deploying ai for defect prediction: a case study within the turkish telecommunication industry. In: Proceedings of the 5th International Conference on Predictor Models in Software Engineering, pp. 1–9 (2009)
458. Trist, E.: The evolution of socio-technical systems. Occasional paper 2, 1981 (1981)
459. Tsai, W., Heisler, K., Volovik, D., Zualkernan, I.: A critical look at the relationship between ai and software engineering. In: [Proceedings] 1988 IEEE Workshop on Languages for Automation@ m_Symbiotic and Intelligent Robotics, pp. 2–18. IEEE (1988)
460. Tuomikoski, J., Tervonen, I.: Absorbing software testing into the scrum method. In: International Conference on Product-Focused Software Process Improvement, pp. 199–215. Springer (2009)
461. Uludag, Ö., Kleehaus, M., Caprano, C., Matthes, F.: Identifying and structuring challenges in large-scale agile development based on a structured literature review. In: 2018 IEEE 22nd International Enterprise Distributed Object Computing Conference (EDOC), pp. 191–197. IEEE (2018)
462. Umarji, M., Emurian, H.: Acceptance issues in metrics program implementation. In: H. Emurian (ed.) 11th IEEE International Symposium Software Metrics, pp. 10–17 (2005)
463. Unterkalmsteiner, M., Gorschek, T., Islam, A., Cheng, C.K., Permadi, R.B., Feldt, R.: A conceptual framework for spi evaluation. Journal of Software: Evolution and Process 26(2), 251–279 (2014)
464. Unterkalmsteiner, M., Gorschek, T., Islam, A.M., Cheng, C.K., Permadi, R.B., Feldt, R.: Evaluation and measurement of software process improvement—a systematic literature review. Software Engineering, IEEE Transactions on 38(2), 398–424 (2012)
465. Van Der Linden, F., Bosch, J., Kamsties, E., Känsälä, K., Obbink, H.: Software product family evaluation. In: International Conference on Software Product Lines, pp. 110–129. Springer (2004)
466. Van Der Storm, T.: Continuous release and upgrade of component-based software. In: Proceedings of the 12th international workshop on Software configuration management, pp. 43–57 (2005)
467. Van Der Storm, T.: The sisyphus continuous integration system. In: 11th European Conference on Software Maintenance and Reengineering (CSMR'07), pp. 335–336. IEEE (2007)
468. Van Der Storm, T.: Backtracking incremental continuous integration. In: 2008 12th European Conference on Software Maintenance and Reengineering, pp. 233–242. IEEE (2008)
469. Van Nostrand, R.C.: Design of experiments using the taguchi approach: 16 steps to product and process improvement (2002)
470. Vidgen, R., Wang, X.: Coevolving systems and the organization of agile software development. Information Systems Research 20(3), 355–376 (2009)
471. van Waardenburg, G., van Vliet, H.: When agile meets the enterprise. Information and Software Technology 55(12), 2154–2171 (2013). DOI 10.1016/j.infsof.2013.07.012. URL http://www.sciencedirect.com/science/article/pii/S0950584913001584
472. Walsham, G.: Interpretive case studies in is research: nature and method. European Journal of information systems 4(2), 74–81 (1995)
473. Watanabe, W.M., Fortes, R.P., Dias, A.L.: Using acceptance tests to validate accessibility requirements in ria. In: Proceedings of the International Cross-Disciplinary Conference on Web Accessibility, pp. 1–10 (2012)

474. Weippl, E.R.: Security in data warehouses. IGI Global, Data Ware-housing Design and Advanced Engineering Applications (2010)
475. Westerman, G., Tannou, M., Bonnet, D., Ferraris, P., McAfee, A.: The digital advantage: How digital leaders outperform their peers in every industry. MITSloan Management and Capgemini Consulting, MA **2**, 2–23 (2012)
476. Weyuker, E.J.: Evaluating software complexity measures. Software Engineering, IEEE Transactions on **14**(9), 1357–1365 (1988)
477. Whittaker, J.A.: Exploratory software testing: tips, tricks, tours, and techniques to guide test design. Pearson Education (2009)
478. Wieringa, R., Daneva, M.: Six strategies for generalizing software engineering theories. Science of computer programming **101**, 136–152 (2015)
479. Wiklund, K., Sundmark, D., Eldh, S., Lundqvist, K.: Impediments in agile software development: An empirical investigation. In: International Conference on Product Focused Software Process Improvement, pp. 35–49. Springer (2013)
480. Williams, L., Cockburn, A.: Agile software development: it's about feedback and change. IEEE computer **36**(6), 39–43 (2003)
481. Wisell, D., Stenvard, P., Hansebacke, A., Keskitalo, N.: Considerations when designing and using virtual instruments as building blocks in flexible measurement system solutions. In: P. Stenvard (ed.) IEEE Instrumentation and Measurement Technology Conference, pp. 1–5 (2007)
482. Wohlin, C., Aurum, A., Angelis, L., Phillips, L., Dittrich, Y., Gorschek, T., Grahn, H., Henningsson, K., Kagstrom, S., Low, G., et al.: The success factors powering industry-academia collaboration. IEEE software **29**(2), 67–73 (2012)
483. Wohlin, C., Runeson, P., Host, M., Ohlsson, M.C., Regnell, B., WesslÃÍn, A.: Experimentation in Software Engineering: An Introduction. Kluwer Academic Publisher, Boston MA (2000)
484. Wohlrab, R., Knauss, E., Pelliccione, P.: Why and how to balance alignment and diversity of requirements engineering practices in automotive. Journal of Systems and Software **162**, 110516 (2020). DOI https://doi.org/10.1016/j.jss.2019.110516. URL https://www.sciencedirect.com/science/article/pii/S0164121219302900
485. Wohlrab, R., Pelliccione, P., Knauss, E., Larsson, M.: Boundary objects and their use in agile systems engineering. J. Softw. Evol. Process. **31**(5) (2019)
486. Wood, W., Tam, L., Witt, M.G.: Changing circumstances, disrupting habits. Journal of personality and social psychology **88**(6), 918 (2005)
487. Woskowski, C.: Applying industrial-strength testing techniques to critical care medical equipment. In: International Conference on Computer Safety, Reliability, and Security, pp. 62–73. Springer (2012)
488. Xenos, M., Christodoulakis, D.: Measuring perceived software quality. Information and software technology **39**(6), 417–424 (1997)
489. Yaman, S.G., Fagerholm, F., Munezero, M., Münch, J., Aaltola, M., Palmu, C., Männistö, T.: Transitioning towards continuous experimentation in a large software product and service development organisation–a case study. In: International Conference on Product-Focused Software Process Improvement, pp. 344–359. Springer (2016)
490. Yaman, S.G., Munezero, M., Münch, J., Fagerholm, F., Syd, O., Aaltola, M., Palmu, C., Männistö, T.: Introducing continuous experimentation in large software-intensive product and service organisations. Journal of Systems and Software **133**, 195–211 (2017)
491. Yin, R.K.: Case study research design and methods third edition. Applied social research methods series **5** (2003)
492. Yin, R.K.: Case study research and applications: Design and methods. Sage publications (2017)
493. Yli-Huumo, J., Maglyas, A., Smolander, K.: How do software development teams manage technical debt?–an empirical study. Journal of Systems and Software **120**, 195–218 (2016)
494. Yuan, D., Park, S., Zhou, Y.: Characterizing logging practices in open-source software. In: 2012 34th International Conference on Software Engineering (ICSE), pp. 102–112. IEEE (2012)

495. Yuksel, H.M., Tuzun, E., Gelirli, E., Biyikli, E., Baykal, B.: Using continuous integration and automated test techniques for a robust c4isr system. In: 2009 24th International Symposium on Computer and Information Sciences, pp. 743–748. IEEE (2009)
496. Zaborovsky, A.N., Danilov, D.O., Leonov, G.V., Mescheriakov, R.V.: Software and hardware for measurements systems. In: D.O. Danilov (ed.) The IEEE-Siberian Conference on Electron Devices and Materials, pp. 53–57. IEEE (2007)
497. Zazworka, N., Spínola, R.O., Vetro', A., Shull, F., Seaman, C.: A case study on effectively identifying technical debt. In: Proceedings of the 17th International Conference on Evaluation and Assessment in Software Engineering, pp. 42–47 (2013)

Printed in the United States
by Baker & Taylor Publisher Services